John Locke and Modern Life

This book recovers a sense of John Locke's central role in the making of the modern world. It demonstrates that his vision of modern life was constructed on a philosophy of human freedom that is the intellectual nerve connecting the various strands of his thought. By revealing the depth and originality of Locke's critique of the metaphysical assumptions and authoritative institutions of pre-modern life, this book rejects the notion of Locke as an intellectual anachronism. Indeed, the radical core of Locke's modern project was the "democratization of mind," according to which he challenged practically every previous mode of philosophical analysis by making the autonomous individual the sole determinant of truth. It was on the basis of this new philosophical dispensation that Locke crafted a modern vision not only of government but also of the churches, the family, education, and the conduct of international relations.

Lee Ward is Alpha Sigma Nu Distinguished Associate Professor of Political Science in Campion College at the University of Regina. He previously taught in the Department of Political Science at Kenyon College and was the Bradley Postdoctoral Fellow in the Program in Constitutional Government at Harvard University. His research and teaching interests are the history of political philosophy and early-modern and American political thought. He is the author of *The Politics of Liberty in England and Revolutionary America* and has written articles on John Locke, Aristotle, Plato, Montesquieu, and Algernon Sidney. His work has appeared in the *American Political Science Review*, the *Canadian Journal of Political Science*, *Publius*, the *Journal of Moral Philosophy*, the *American Journal of Political Science*, *Ratio Juris*, *International Philosophical Quarterly*, and *Interpretation*. He also coedited with Dr. Ann Ward *The Ashgate Research Companion to Federalism*.

John Locke and Modern Life

LEE WARD

Alpha Sigma Nu Distinguished Associate Professor
Department of Political Studies
Campion College at the University of Regina

CAMBRIDGE UNIVERSITY PRESS
Cambridge, New York, Melbourne, Madrid, Cape Town, Singapore,
São Paulo, Delhi, Dubai, Tokyo, Mexico City

Cambridge University Press
32 Avenue of the Americas, New York, NY 10013-2473, USA

www.cambridge.org
Information on this title: www.cambridge.org/9780521192804

First published 2010

Printed in the United States of America

A catalog record for this publication is available from the British Library.

Library of Congress Cataloging in Publication data
Ward, Lee, 1970–
   John Locke and modern life / Lee Ward.
      p.   cm.
   Includes bibliographical references and index.
   ISBN 978-0-521-19280-4 (hardback)
   1. Locke, John, 1632–1704.   I. Title.
   B1297.W27 2010
   192–dc22   2010020079

ISBN 978-0-521-19280-4 Hardback

For Mary Charlotte

Contents

Acknowledgments

For the time that it took to bring this book from conception to fruition, I have had the honor and privilege to be a part of Campion College at the University of Regina. I am grateful to my students and to my colleagues at Campion College and in the Department of Political Science at the University of Regina for providing a vibrant intellectual community over the last six years.

I am especially indebted to Deans Samira McCarthy and Frank Obrigewitsch S.J. and President Ben Fiore S.J. of Campion College for their support over the years, as well as to the University of Regina President's SSHRCC Fund Research Grant that allowed me to spend time at the Bodleian Library in Oxford during the summer of 2006. I would also like to express my gratitude to Kris Schmaltz, my research assistant in the wonderfully productive and enjoyable summer of 2008, who helped in the preparation of the manuscript for review.

My deep thanks also go to Lew Bateman at Cambridge University Press for his wisdom and continued support for my research and to his editorial assistant Anne Lovering Rounds for her expert and always timely advice.

Earlier versions of some of the ideas and arguments in Chapters 2, 3, 4, 6, and 7 can be found in "Locke on Punishment, Property, and Moral Knowledge" *Journal of Moral Philosophy*, 6, 2 (April 2009): 218–244 published by Brill Publishing; "John Locke on Toleration and Inclusion" *Ratio Juris: An International Journal of Jurisprudence and Philosophy of Law*, 21, 4 (December 2008): 518–541 published by Blackwell Publishing; "Locke on the Moral Basis of International Relations" *American Journal of Political Science*, 50, 3 (July 2006): 691–705 published by Blackwell Publishing; "Locke on Executive Power and Liberal Constitutionalism" *Canadian Journal of Political Science*, 38, 3 (September 2005): 719–744 published by

Cambridge University Press; and in "The Natural Rights Family: Locke on Women, Nature, and the Problem of Patriarchy," in *Nature, Woman, and the Art of Politics*, Eduardo Velasquez, ed. (Lanham: Rowman & Littlefield Publishers 2000), pp. 149–179. My thanks go to the editors, publishers, and reviewers of these journals and the collected volume.

Without the love and support of my wife, friend, and colleague Ann, this book would simply not have been possible. And to my daughter Mary, may she accept and always cherish this gift as a testament of my unending love.

Regina, December 2009
Lee Ward

Introduction

This study is an effort to demonstrate John Locke's central place and important role in the development of the collection of philosophical, social, political, and theological ideas broadly defined as modernity. As an intellectual phenomenon, modernity is characterized both by what is not, that is in contradistinction to the pre-modern period, and by its constitutive aspect as the body of beliefs, principles, and attitudes toward human life that have dominated western civilization since the seventeenth century arguably through to our own time. The central question then animating this book is to what extent, if any, did Locke's thought contribute to the creation of the world we know.

Admittedly, this is a task that presents several daunting interpretive challenges. First, there is by no means consensus among Locke scholars that he even has any place among the ranks of seminal thinkers of modernity. Most notably, John Dunn established an influential line of interpretation nearly forty years ago when he insisted that he "simply cannot conceive of constructing an analysis of any issue in contemporary political theory around the affirmation or negation of anything Locke says about political matters."[1] For Dunn, as for many commentators who followed in his wake, Locke was not an apostle of modernity, but rather a somewhat forlorn figure marooned between a disintegrating Christian natural law tradition

---

[1] John Dunn, *The Political Thought of John Locke* (Cambridge: Cambridge University Press, 1969), p. x. While Dunn subsequently softened this claim somewhat, he has repeated the basic thrust of this judgment as recently as 2003. See John Dunn, "What Is Living and What Is Dead in the Political Theory of John Locke?" in *Interpreting Political Responsibility: Essays 1981–89* (Princeton: Princeton University Press, 1990) and "Measuring Locke's Shadow," in *Two Treatises and a Letter Concerning Toleration*, Ian Shapiro, ed. (New Haven: Yale University Press, 2003), pp. 257–285, esp. 271–272.

on the one hand and the emerging wave of secular modernity, the central antitheological tenets of which he could never subscribe to, on the other.[2] A more recent iteration of this interpretation can be seen in Jonathan Israel's magisterial works on Enlightenment philosophy. In Israel's view, Locke was an "essentially conservative" thinker whose body of work on a variety of subjects ranging from religious toleration, gender equality, and constitutional government represents a rejection of the democratic principles of radical modernity championed by Spinoza and others, who are the true heroic founders of modernity.[3] According to Dunn and Israel, any attempt to locate Locke among the central intellectual figures of modernity is simply an example of historical and philosophical naïveté.

On the other end of the interpretive spectrum, a very different set of difficulties arises from the ideologically charged nature of Locke scholarship since the 1960s. Over the years, Locke has often been wrenched from Dunn and Israel's dustbin of history by a different group of scholars who have made him serve as mentor or foil for the current preoccupations in contemporary political theory. Libertarian, communitarian, socialist, feminist, and postcolonial theorists, as well as the legion of combatants in the interpretive wars over the ideological meaning of the American Founding, have all to varying degrees made Locke a central figure in their analysis in recent decades. Whether cast as hero or villain, there has long been the suspicion that the spirit and substance of Locke's authentic political and philosophical teaching has too often been sacrificed to the theoretical requirements posed by contemporary concerns that Locke did not share. That is to say, if contemporary political theorists did not have Locke to serve as the touchstone for our anxieties about liberalism, they would have had to invent him. Or perhaps, Dunn might observe, they frequently have.

The third, and in some respects most daunting, challenge facing any attempt to demonstrate Locke's seminal role in the creation of modernity arises from the complexity and broad scope of Locke's body of work. Locke

---

[2] Dunn, "Measuring Locke's Shadow," 271, 278. Waldron shares Dunn's assumption about the centrality of Locke's theological commitments to his political theory, and thus agrees that Locke approached political and moral questions from a perspective very different from secular modernity. However, unlike Dunn, Waldron also sees much that is radical about Locke's commitment to equality (Jeremy Waldron, *God, Locke, and Equality: Christian Foundations in Locke's Political Thought* [Cambridge: Cambridge University Press, 2002]).

[3] See Jonathan Israel, *Radical Enlightenment: Philosophy and the Making of Modernity 1650–1750* (Oxford: Oxford University Press, 2001), pp. 259–269 and *Enlightenment Contested: Philosophy, Modernity, and the Emancipation of Man 1670–1752* (Oxford: Oxford University Press, 2006), pp. 57–58.

was a prolific writer whose published works reflected a prodigious variety of philosophic interests including epistemology, natural science, moral philosophy, educational theory, political theory, and theology. This range of interests has even led some distinguished commentators to question whether Locke's thought reflects a single unified and coherent philosophy, as opposed to a series of disjointed or contradictory intellectual commitments.[4] Moreover, many scholars who have strived to illuminate Locke's influence on the formation of modernity have understandably tended to focus their analysis on one or a few aspects of Locke's thought. In recent years, this research has produced many important specialized studies into a given dimension of Locke's modern project such as his individualistic philosophy,[5] his innovative educational theory,[6] his rational theology and teaching on toleration,[7] or the democratic foundations of his political theory.[8] However, when dealing with a concept as capacious as modernity and a thinker as wide ranging as Locke, it is perhaps inevitable that this approach will leave the answer to the larger question of Locke's role in modernity somewhat incomplete.

While recognizing the interpretive challenges outlined, it is nonetheless the contention of this study that Locke is a seminal thinker in the making of modernity. I aim to demonstrate that his vision of modern life

---

4 See, for example, Peter Laslett's assessment in the "Introductory Essay" to John Locke, *Two Treatises of Government* (Cambridge: Cambridge University Press, 1988), pp. 82–86 and P. J. Crittenden, "Thoughts about Locke's Thoughts about Education" *Journal of the Philosophy of Education*, 15, 2 (1981), p. 157.

5 For example, Charles Taylor, *Sources of the Self: The Making of the Modern Identity* (Cambridge, MA: Harvard University Press, 1989), pp. 159–176; Michael Zuckert, *Natural Rights and the New Republicanism* (Princeton: Princeton University Press, 1994), chs. 8–9; and Thomas Pangle, *The Spirit of Modern Republicanism: The Moral Vision of the American Founders and the Philosophy of Locke* (Chicago: University of Chicago Press, 1988).

6 See Peter A. Schouls, *Reasoned Freedom: Locke and Enlightenment* (Ithaca: Cornell University Press, 1992) and Nathan Tarcov, *Locke's Education for Liberty* (Chicago: University of Chicago Press, 1984).

7 For Locke's rational theology, see Nicholas Wolterstorff, *John Locke and the Ethics of Belief* (Cambridge: Cambridge University Press, 1996) and Greg Forster, *John Locke's Politics of Moral Consensus* (Cambridge: Cambridge University Press, 2005); and for his argument for toleration, see John Marshall, *John Locke: Resistance, Religion, and Responsibility* (Cambridge: Cambridge University Press, 1994) and Richard Vernon, *The Career of Toleration: John Locke, Jonas Proast and after* (Montreal: McGill-Queen's University Press, 1997).

8 See Richard Ashcraft, *Revolutionary Politics and Locke's Two Treatises of Government* (Princeton: Princeton University Press, 1986) and Ian Shapiro, "John Locke's Democratic Theory," in *Two Treatises and a Letter Concerning Toleration*, Ian Shapiro, ed. (New Haven: Yale University Press, 2003), pp. 309–340, esp. 309–311.

was constructed on the foundation of a unified and coherent philosophy of human freedom that provides the intellectual nerve connecting the various strands of Locke's mature writings. The core principles in Locke's philosophy of freedom derive from his assessment of the intellectual properties and rational capacities of the individual human mind. This was what we will call the "democratization of mind" that marked Locke's most significant contribution to modernity. The democratization of mind represents Locke's confidence that the essence of human freedom lay in the individual's ability to acquire knowledge and construct meaningful identities from the intellectual materials made available to mind through sensation and reflection. Locke's vision of modernity challenged practically every previous mode of philosophical analysis by making the autonomous individual freed from the weight of tradition, custom, and conventional inequality, the sole determinant of truth. The democratization of mind supplied Locke with the basis for refashioning a new, distinctly modern definition of philosophy deeply impacted by the empirical scientific method, which rejected what Locke took to be the misguided metaphysical pretensions characterizing philosophy in both its traditional scholastic form and the system-building aspirations of modern scientific naturalism *à la* Spinoza. The profoundly democratic character of this reorientation of philosophy toward the individual as a primary unit of analysis derived from Locke's conclusion that the epistemic capacities grounding human freedom and the acquisition of knowledge about the most important moral, ethical, and theological matters were distributed in an emphatically egalitarian manner across humankind. For Locke, modernity is inseparable from the discovery of this new mental world of human understanding, a hitherto scarcely observed terrain of interiority and subjectivity from which a new conception of freedom in the phenomenal realm would ultimately emerge.

The depth of Locke's commitment to the modern project, that is to say to the replacement of the vast intellectual inheritance of pre-modernity with a radically new dispensation, can be measured by the range and scope of his philosophical inquiry. To understand Locke's contribution to modernity simply in terms of his political philosophy is, however, to limit his impact considerably. For Locke, modernity involved, and indeed required, the critical examination of practically every authoritative institution in modern life including not only government, but also crucially the churches, the family, educational methods, and the conduct of international relations. The variety of Locke's philosophical interests was not then simply adventitious or driven by the exigencies of his immediate historical context. Rather the range of Locke's thought and writings reflected what he took to be the most important theoretical and practical imperatives confronting philosophy in the early-modern period. The *ancien régime* at the core of traditional European culture in Locke's age rested on certain venerable assumptions about the naturalness and intrinsic goodness of the hierarchical relationship between God and humanity, men and women, kings and subjects, fathers and children, as well as a set of deeply entrenched beliefs about the sacred character of ecclesiastical and civil power.[9] In pre-modernity, the individual as such was unintelligible as a meaningful political or social agent independent of one's proper place in the organic structure of society mirroring the cosmic order. In order to deracinate the complex web of hierarchical and traditional relations that characterized pre-modern life, Locke examined and reformulated authoritative institutions and rules that governed these relations under the searing light of reason and the principle of human freedom.

A major part of the conceptual difficulty facing any effort to understand Locke's contribution to modernity lies in the complex philosophical implications flowing out of the democratization of mind. Thus it is important from the outset to clarify one of the central interpretive techniques that will be employed for analyzing Locke in the present study. With the democratization of mind, Locke proposed new principles of intelligibility to replace the traditional paradigms of knowledge. These two principles are broadly analogous to rationalism and empiricism. The rational model will be identified as the *eidetic* approach, according to which Locke examined the institutions in modern life on the basis of their intellectual properties as ideas. As complex ideas, these institutions and practices derive one vital element of their intelligibility from the internal mechanics of human understanding. Central to Locke's idea of human freedom is the capacity to intellectualize phenomena in terms of ideas. However, Locke's version of idealism based on the logical agreement of composite ideas differs profoundly from the classical conception of the forms in that Locke rejected the cognitive connection between the human subject and an extrinsic intellectual, moral, or spiritual end, or *telos*. This connection was, of course, integral to the pre-modern confidence in natural and cosmic order. For Locke, the intelligibility inhering in any idea, whether it is government, the church, or individual rights, derives from the constructive capacities of human reason and not from an intrinsic connection to external reality. Thus human beings are

---

[9] Although Israel incorrectly excludes Locke from the ranks of the enlighteners, he does provide a solid account of the attitudes, theories, and beliefs that characterized pre-modern life (see Israel, *Radical Enlightenment*, vi).

capable of acquiring a true idea of government, the church, or individual rights because, in principle, the intellectual materials from which we can deduce a coherent, noncontradictory definition of these institutions and concepts are available to our minds as ideas.

However, the second principle of intelligibility for Locke relates to how things actually come to be in the world. In this regard, Locke also employs what we will call a *genetic* approach to philosophical analysis, which is characterized by empirical observation in a natural historical method. For Locke, the deepest source of complexity confronting political philosophy is the need to combine the eidetic and genetic modes of analysis, the being and becoming, as it were. For instance, comparing the idea of government or the church with the way in which governments and churches have come to be and developed in history may (and Locke believes typically do) display a radical disjunction between the true meaning of the word we use to identify an idea and the observable properties of the actual thing itself. The genetic dimension in Locke's philosophy has likely been the cause of giving it an appearance of conservatism to Israel, Dunn, and others. However, it is vital to recognize that Locke's inclusion of biological, sociological, economic, and political constraints on the actualization of ideas as factors for philosophical consideration is neither simply an unfortunate compromise with reality, nor does it signify a natural default position of conservatism in Locke's thought. Rather the progressive character of Locke's commitment to modernity lay precisely in his effort to combine observation about what is and has been with a philosophically rigorous effort to provide a normative demonstration of what by right should be. Thus in the complex interplay of distinct modes of reasoning, Locke's eidetic accounts of the state of nature, constitutional government, or the purely voluntary church stand as a measure of the legitimacy of actual churches, governments or individual rights claims in the world.

At this point it is important to indicate a few major elements of the methodology employed in this study. First, the focus is exclusively on Locke's mature works, by which is meant the body of Locke's writings published or completed between 1689 and his death in 1704, including the *Two Treatises of Government*, the *Essay Concerning Human Understanding*, the *Letter Concerning Toleration*, the *Reasonableness of Christianity*, and *Some Thoughts Concerning Education*, as well as the many subsequent editions and seemingly endless polemical controversies that followed the publication of the *Essay*, the *Letter*, and the *Reasonableness*. This study is not an analysis of the development of Locke's thinking on topics spanning his earliest to his latest writings. While such projects can be highly illuminating with respect to Locke's intellectual career, this is not the focus of the present study.[10] Our aim rather is to demonstrate the unified and coherent philosophy linking the diverse topics considered in Locke's mature writings. Indeed, one of the chief ambitions of this study is to move beyond a specialized examination of a single aspect of Locke's thought and rather try to elucidate in a comprehensive and integrative way the full range of Locke's vision of modernity as he presented it in his mature works. For this reason, the object of our analysis is Locke's contribution to the formation of modern life broadly conceived rather than Locke's philosophy or political theory strictly speaking. When Locke contemplated the range of institutions and authoritative principles in his time that required transformation, he did not operate under the same disciplinary constraints academics typically do today. He boldly and irreverently cast his gaze upon matters of philosophy, religion, science, education, and politics that extended beyond political theory as normally practiced in our time. In order to appreciate Locke's vision of modernity, it is necessary then to follow his tracks into the manifold social relations that were altered profoundly in the transition from pre-modern to modern life. Indeed, one of the signal characteristics of Locke's modern project was his willingness to challenge authoritative conceptions of institutions like monarchy, the churches, the family, and education that had remained fundamentally unchanged for centuries.

A second important methodological point has to do with the connection between our analysis of Locke's texts and the overarching purpose of the present study. Why is it important to identify Locke's role in the creation of modernity? Or to put it differently, why does it matter *pace* Dunn and Israel to read Locke back into modernity and enlightenment philosophy? On the immediate level, the answer is self-evident. An inaccurate account of a complex phenomenon such as the origin of modernity or of a prominent thinker such as Locke is problematic in itself. It can lead to a misunderstanding of formative influences on later thinkers and philosophical movements and thus produce a ripple effect impacting our reading of the history of political thought more broadly. To the extent that studying intellectual history or the major figures of political philosophy remains a valuable exercise for contemporary scholars, the onus is on serious scholarship to be accurate and faithful to the sense and spirit of its subject. On a deeper level, however, there is more at stake than simply our degree of understanding one

---

[10] See, for instance, the remarkable account of the complex development of Locke's thought on toleration in Marshall, *John Locke*, chs. 1–4.

particular thinker. Despite the great variety of opinions and interpretations among Locke scholars on a host of aspects of his thought, one conclusion reached by friend and foe alike is that Locke has, for better or
worse, become the canonical figure of classical liberalism in the English-
speaking world. This explains Locke's centrality to continuing debates over
the American Founding, as well as his frequent appearances in the past
clad in the garb of the Cold Warrior stoutly exemplifying or caricaturing
the bourgeois culture of liberalism militant. However, since the collapse of
Soviet communism and the resulting dramatic contraction of the ideological political spectrum in the West, Locke has, if anything, become an even
more salient presence among practitioners of contemporary political theory
reduced to having little left to do but highlight ever more refined strands
of differentiation within the broad orbit of liberalism – that is, to say ever
more and more about less and less. If since the end of the Cold War we are
all liberals, then the suspicion is that in some sense we are all Lockeans
now. But needless to say, ideological consolidation hardly eliminates the
sources of controversy and debate; indeed, divisions within liberalism previously suppressed by the threat of viable ideological alternatives promise
to assume new significance in liberalism triumphant.

It is in this sense that Locke's role in the creation of modernity bears
directly on the methodology of this study. Our treatments of Locke's examination of the most important institutions of his time will include reflection
upon issues with palpable contemporary resonance. Whether it be the basis
of individual rights claims vis-à-vis the government and community, the
tension between executive power and rule of law, the reform of education,
greater equality of men and women, the value of religious pluralism, or the
ethics of humanitarian intervention in international relations, we will see
in Locke's thought issues and concerns familiar to us. However, it is not
my intention either to inject Locke into contemporary debates that were
not his concern or to read modernity back into Locke by exaggerating the
importance of trace amounts of contemporary issues unearthed with difficulty from Locke's texts. Rather our analysis means to show that Locke's
influence on modernity was so pervasive that many, although certainly not
all, matters that were of philosophic import to him continue to matter to
us today. Moreover, the evidence to support this claim derives exclusively
and directly from the texts of Locke's mature writings. In order to keep our
analysis consistent with authentic Lockean concerns, this study will avoid
elaborate theoretical reconstructions of Locke's philosophical principles
designed to make Locke fit by analogy with the theoretical requirements of

current debates.[11] While such reconstructions can be very insightful treatments of contemporary issues, it is my aim to remain as closely wedded to the texture, tone, and substance of Locke's thought as possible. For our purposes, the burden of proof for demonstrating Locke's importance in the making of modernity must lie exclusively in Locke's texts and the practical issues and theoretical concerns that animated him.

Ever mindful of the dangers and seductions of historical naïveté and ideological self-congratulations, the present study hopes to demonstrate that Locke's vision of modernity bore a considerable resemblance to most liberal societies today. Locke would see much in our world familiar to his thoughts, if not to the immediate reality of his time. There is thus in this study an implicit promise that contemporary liberals may understand ourselves more fully by reflecting on one of the most influential philosophical architects of the modern world. However, it is by virtue of this very process of self-reflection that contemporary students of liberalism should be made aware of the several important issues, especially regarding theology, toleration, political equality, and the basis of moral knowledge, about which Locke reached philosophical conclusions and devised political prescriptions with which many of our contemporaries may be uncomfortable and even profoundly disagree. The historical Locke who helped preside over the birth of modernity is capable of both exciting and disappointing the modern political imagination he did so much to create.

The design of this book is intended to integrate the major elements of Locke's mature works initially in the general framework of his philosophy of freedom, and then to consider Locke's critical examination of the key institutions of modern life. As such, Chapters 1 and 2 begin with a focus on the intellectual foundations of Locke's philosophy of freedom. Chapter 1 elaborates the democratization of mind, which supplies the conceptual apparatus for understanding the epistemological principles underlying the various aspects of Locke's modern project. This chapter demonstrates the fundamental importance involved in appreciating the crucial role Locke's epistemological principles played in his political theory by locating the

---

[11] There are a number of important contemporary issues in liberal societies, such as environmentalism, multiculturalism, and the biotech revolution, that simply were not matters of direct concern for Locke and thus would not be accessible to evaluation through Locke's principles except by means of theoretical reconstruction. These modern, or perhaps post-modern, issues will not be addressed in the present volume. For an example of how a "theoretical reconstruction" approach to Locke can make a good contribution to issues in contemporary democratic theory, see Alex Tuckness, *Locke and the Legislative Point of View* (Princeton: Princeton University Press, 2002).

Essay Concerning Human Understanding in its proper intellectual and historical context. Locke set his individualistic theory of knowledge against the prevailing metaphysical tendencies dominating early-modern philosophy in both its traditional scholastic and more recent modern materialist form. The fundamental theoretical goal of Locke's epistemology was to radically transform the definition of the proper scope and procedures of philosophical activity. As such, Locke's rejection of the doctrine of innate ideas and its replacement with an egalitarian conception of ideas as the products solely of sensation and reflection by the human mind challenged the regnant paradigms of knowledge acquisition.

To Locke's mind, neither mechanistic philosophy nor dogmatic innatism could account for the demonstrable freedom inhering in human understanding. Rather human liberty derived from the self-directed mental activity of rational individuals supplied relatively equally with the natural capacities and intellectual materials necessary to exercise judgment in relative freedom from the influence of ephemeral desires or prescribed mental habits. On this basis, we will examine Locke's claim that moral knowledge – the kind of knowledge he believed was most important for human life – is capable of demonstrative certainty, and will argue that after considering Locke's treatment of the ambiguous status of human knowledge about key moral concepts such as soul and the existence of God, it becomes apparent that the democratization of mind involved Locke's conclusion that there is a variety of modes of moral reasoning available to human understanding. In Locke's new philosophical rubric, these various modes of moral reasoning, including both knowledge and probability, culminate in both a theistic and a secular formulation of the grounds of morality. It is this multifarious conception of the modes of individual moral judgment that Locke employs throughout his major works in critical examination of the most authoritative institutions of modern life.

Chapter 2 continues the task of exploring the eidetic foundations of Locke's political philosophy by turning to perhaps the most celebrated theoretical postulation in his entire corpus, namely the state of nature. The pre-civil state of nature presented in the *Second Treatise of Government* serves as both Locke's explanation for the origin of political society, as well as the testing ground for his conclusions about the rational individual's capacity to form moral judgments independently of authoritative political, social, and religious institutions. Our analysis will focus on the profoundly individualistic implications Locke derived from his theory of the natural punishment right, according to which every individual in the state of nature, being free and equal, is thus morally authorized to execute the law of nature. Locke's natural punishment right signified a radical departure from every other philosophic theory regarding punishment and individual judgment in early-modern thought. By positing individuals as the central unit of political and social analysis, Locke not only rejected traditional doctrines of natural sociability and organic society, but also established the normative grounds for the new understanding of the relation between the individual and community and the community's relation to government that would be one of the defining features of modernity. In this respect, particular attention will be paid to the centrality of Locke's theory of property for understanding his assessment of the cognitive capacity of individuals to make rational judgments about the natural law.

For Locke, the human capacity to acquire property through labor has both political and epistemic significance. On the one hand, the individual's natural right to acquire and protect property, broadly understood to include "life, liberty and estate," provides a substantive conception of the proper end and limits of civil government. Additionally, however, Locke's theory of property was intended to reformulate the philosophic understanding of what it means to be a rights-bearing individual capable of conceiving of oneself as a self-owning being with property in one's rights. Locke transforms the idea of property, traditionally one of the key grounds for natural and civil inequality, into a basis for an understanding of moral relations rooted in equality and accessible to the human mind through a kind of moral reasoning leading to sensitive knowledge about the rights of other individuals whose claims of right are, in principle, equal to one's own. From the rights of individuals in the state of nature, Locke deduced the conceptual and normative building blocks for the reformed institutions of modern life.

In Chapter 3, this study begins to consider Locke's examination of the authoritative institutions of modern life by turning to his treatment of constitutional government. The central feature in his account of government is the effort to combine eidetic analysis of what the idea of government is meant to signify with a genetic account of how most governments have actually come into being in history. Locke concludes that the fundamental problem of authoritarian governments that have typified human experience hitherto can be explained by two major intellectual errors. The first is the historical failure to properly distinguish the various functions of government, especially to clearly define and separate the concepts of executive and legislative power. Second, Locke identifies the inability for political societies in the past to understand the primary distinction between statute law and constitutional law. In his treatment of the natural history of monarchy and the extralegal practice of prerogative, Locke challenged the regnant

doctrine of sovereignty and sought to establish a new definition of constitutionalism for the modern world based on the individualist premises of
the state of nature. Locke's great contribution to the development of modern constitutionalism was his articulation of a theory of constituent power
rooted in the natural rights of individuals. It was this idea of constituent
power that allowed Locke to develop innovative principles of consent and
separation of powers that made possible a new understanding of the relation between constitution and law, and more fundamentally enabled him
to fashion a revolutionary conception of popular sovereignty that transformed contract theory. Locke introduced into modern political theory the
principle that a constitution is a body of foundational law reflecting the
most authoritative consent of the community, a kind of law that stands
above, and ultimately is authorized to regulate, the lawmaking institutions
of government. In this way, Locke foreshadowed and informed the later
development of liberal constitutionalism with the introduction of written
constitutions, judicially enforceable charters of rights, popular ratification,
and general suffrage. In his reflections on the profound inadequacies of
the pre-modern conception of government, Locke provided the theoretical
materials out of which later liberal thinkers and societies would construct
the idea of constitutional government as we have come to know it today.

By any measure, the patriarchal family was one of the most deeply
entrenched inegalitarian institutions in traditional European society.
Chapter 4 considers Locke's reflections on the family and tries to demonstrate not only the depth of his opposition to patriarchy, but more fundamentally Locke's attempt to redefine the family as an institution based on
natural rights. The chapter is designed in the form of a dialogue between
Locke's argument for the family and the body of feminist scholarship that
has powerfully probed and challenged Locke's credentials as an egalitarian
philosopher in recent years. It will be shown that Locke's opposition to
traditional gender inequality in the family closely resembles contemporary
feminism's major theoretical concerns about the family and the status of
women in society. Locke conceded that the subjection of women in the family has been a central feature of practically all previous political thought
and in the genetic development of nearly all historical societies; however, the principles of natural freedom and equality underlying his eidetic
account of the family suggested that this condition could and should be
overcome. With his theoretical defense of women's property rights and the
voluntary and consensual basis of conjugal society, Locke systematically
undermined traditional arguments for the natural subjection of women to
men. Locke presupposes that the family is a human institution and thus,

like civil government, it is capable of improvement. He was particularly sensitive to what he took to be the deep psychological and sociological connection between the patriarchal family and authoritarian politics. The natural rights family based on legal and cultural recognition of the individual rights of women emerged for Locke as the standard of legitimacy by which to judge the validity and morality of conventional practices governing this most formative institution, which impacts the life of practically every human being. Locke was not naive about the prospects for radically and immediately establishing a cultural predisposition toward egalitarian models of the family. He was well aware of the obstacles to progress posed by deeply engrained prejudices about gender, as well as the burdens placed on childrearing by economic scarcity and the primitive state of technology in his time. However, Locke challenged prevailing assumptions about the normative character of the subjection of women with his own insistence that as rational individuals, women share equal natural rights with men. It was for this reason that Locke assigned reform of the traditional family and encouragement of greater sexual equality a central role in the long-term modernization of society.

One of the most pressing theoretical concerns in the latter stages of Locke's philosophic career was the problem produced by the profoundly inadequate approach to education in early-modern Europe. Locke maintained that the humanist tradition of education inherited from the Renaissance, with its sterile pedagogic system of memorization, formal logic, and the teaching of ancient languages, had to be replaced by a new educational model that would prepare individuals for their lives as citizens in a liberal society open to the new discoveries in philosophy and modern natural science. In Chapter 5, we examine Locke's argument for the systematic reform of modern education. At the heart of Locke's reform proposals was the underlying connection between the epistemology of the *Essay* and the philosophic basis of his major educational treatises *Some Thoughts Concerning Education* and the *Conduct of the Understanding*. The democratic implications of Locke's empiricist epistemology and "way of ideas" deeply informed his theory of education. The central goal of Lockean education was the promotion of rational autonomy for individuals capable of meaningful social existence and critical thinking about the institutions of modern life.

However, the most innovative aspect of his educational proposals had to do with his assessment of the best pedagogical methods to achieve this goal. In early childhood education he advocated socialization rather than the inculcation of knowledge, as well as a model of developmental learning based on the idea of making learning a form of play. This reliance on technique and method rather than subject matter even extended to higher education with regard to which Locke stressed the importance of learning analytical skills and proper mental habits. Throughout his educational writings, Locke's egalitarian commitments were constant. He emphasized that the relatively equal distribution of rational faculties across humankind made proper pedagogical methods rather than natural intellectual gifts, the key to educational success. Moreover, while the immediate focus of his educational reforms related to private tutorial for the sons of well-to-do gentlemen, an important subtheme of his educational theory was Locke's enthusiasm for extending the basic principles of his educational methods to girls as well as the children of the poor. In clear anticipation of the vital role mass public education would play in the development of modern society, Locke concluded that providing educational opportunity on a societal scale could become in the future a legitimate policy objective of government arguably for the first time in history.

Religion was perhaps the central organizing principle in early-modern Europe because it was the churches that infused an element of the sacred into the relations between rulers and ruled, men and women, parents and children, and clerics and their flock: relations that in their totality composed the complex social structure of the *ancien régime*. It was also, however, on matters of religion that modern political theory first grappled with the problems posed by legal discrimination and unequal treatment of minorities. Thus in Chapter 6, we will examine Locke's crucial contribution to the modern idea of the church and the principle of toleration. In one sense, Locke's treatment of religion and theology signifies more clearly than any other aspect of his thought the distance between Locke's world and our own. Locke's primary theoretical concern in the *Letters Concerning Toleration* was to counter theological and prudential arguments for state-enforced religious uniformity, no longer a major concern in most contemporary liberal societies. Moreover, his assumptions about the permanent salience of soteriological concerns and the intrinsic relation between theology and morality strike a discordant note with the much more secular direction liberalism has taken over the past century. However, this chapter will argue that Locke's reflections on religion and the church made an important contribution to the development of the modern idea of freedom. By redefining churches as voluntary associations and conceptualizing individual conscience in terms of rights, Locke injected individualist principles into an institution that had historically been one of the key bastions of orthodoxy. His rigorous examination of the epistemic grounds of belief and his articulation of the possibilities for rational theology contributed to an argument for the positive value of religious pluralism as an integral feature of a free society in which the churches represent the moral authority of civil society institutions capable of limiting state power. It was from this identification of the churches with fundamental human freedom that Locke progressed toward a broader principle of civil liberties, including freedom of speech and thought, that would in time provide a basis for a legal conception of freedom applicable independently of theological criteria. It will be argued that even Locke's infamous limitations on the principle of toleration regarding atheists and Roman Catholics have to be reconsidered in the context of his commitment to the moral foundations of civil freedom and a vision of political society marked by moderation.

This study concludes with a consideration of Locke's reflections on international relations. At first blush, international relations theory may not appear to be an aspect of modernity to which Locke even made much of a contribution. Certainly international relations were not a primary focus of his work, and foreign affairs is treated less systematically by Locke than several other modern thinkers such as Machiavelli, Grotius, and Kant. However, this chapter will try to demonstrate that Locke's significance as a seminal thinker in the making of modernity included important reflections on the implications for international relations produced by liberal individualist philosophy. In a series of crucial passages in the *Second Treatise*, Locke indicated his dramatic departure from what he took to be the intellectually discredited just war and law of nations theory then regnant in early-modern Europe. Indeed, it is striking the extent to which Locke's account of the rights of individuals in the state of nature and the capacities of communities vis-à-vis governments employed, while radically modifying, the logical and semantic categories supplied by traditional moral and legal debates about just and unjust war. Locke recognized that the most urgent tests of the efficacy of moral reasoning and the limits of natural justice frequently arise in the context of conquest, war, and international aggression. This recognition was accompanied, however, by Locke's clear sense that modernity required new ways to approach international relations. Thus, this chapter shifts interpretation of Locke's account of international relations away from the discourse of sovereignty and natural law familiar to his contemporaries, and instead refocuses our analysis toward a different, and distinctively Lockean, discourse involving the concepts of self-government and international society. Locke's vision of the moral basis of international relations bears clear resonance with contemporary theories of international society for he approached foreign relations on the basis of an idea of the international state of nature, which balanced interrelated, overlapping, and even competing moral claims about sovereignty and natural law in a general framework of international norms governing the relations of self-governing societies. It is in the context of Locke's idea of international society that we will consider the important question of his connection to colonialism, and how Locke contributes to contemporary debates about sovereignty, the use of force, and the ethics of humanitarian intervention.

The majestic scope and range of Locke's political philosophy penetrated and transformed western civilization's thinking, beliefs, and attitudes toward practically every aspect of modern life. From his central philosophical discovery about the mental world of the sovereign individual and his or her capacity to grasp knowledge and truth, Locke deduced a political teaching that contributed enormously to the modernization of the idea of individual rights, constitutionalism, the family, education, the churches, and international relations. It is to a fuller examination of this process of philosophical discovery and institutional modernization that we now turn.

I

The Democratization of Mind

It may seem odd to begin a study of Locke's modern politics by turning to his most philosophic work, the *Essay Concerning Human Understanding*. Indeed, it was once quite common among Locke scholars to express serious doubts as to whether the *Essay* and Locke's political writings such as the *Two Treatises* are even compatible with the latter advancing a political theory based on natural law, natural rights, and property, and the former propounding an empiricist epistemology with little to say about rights and displaying a skeptical attitude toward any normative claims derived from nature.[1] While Locke's epistemological and political writings certainly reflect different kinds of books with discrete particular aims, it is important to understand their fundamental connection. At their deepest level, all of Locke's mature writings, whether political, philosophical, moral, or theological, reflect his consuming preoccupation with examining and defending human freedom in its various aspects.

The aspect of human freedom Locke illuminated and developed in the *Essay* involved his treatment of the intellectual foundations of modernity. This philosophic account of intellectual freedom was a feature of a novel conception of the rational faculties, which we will term the *democratization*

---

[1] See for example Peter Laslett's influential assessment in the "Introductory Essay" to John Locke, *Two Treatises of Government* (Cambridge: Cambridge University Press, 1988), pp. 82–86 (for Locke's *Two Treatises* hereafter in notes and text, treatise and section). For recent studies that ably demonstrate various aspects of the important connection between the *Essay* and the *Two Treatises*, see Ruth Grant, *John Locke's Liberalism* (Chicago: University of Chicago Press, 1987); Peter Josephson, *The Great Art of Government: Locke on Consent* (Lawrence, KS: University Press of Kansas, 2002); Jeremy Waldron, *God, Locke and Equality* (Cambridge: Cambridge University Press, 2002); and Michael Zuckert, *Natural Rights and the New Republicanism* (Princeton, NJ: Princeton University Press, 1994), ch. 9.

of mind. It was in the context of his articulation of a new philosophy of mind that Locke addressed such politically salient questions as: What does it mean to be a free moral agent and how does an individual mind come to know anything in particular, much less the general form and substance of a natural law governing human relations? The democratization of mind represented Locke's effort to remove or reduce the many conceptual and linguistic impediments to human understanding, impediments that he believed have profound implications for the study of politics, morality, and theology. Locke also, however, meant to clarify the epistemological basis of, and illuminate the range of possibilities among, the various modes of reason available to human understanding. The democratization of mind thus involved both a critical and a constructive aspect.

In terms of its critical dimension, the philosophical purpose of the *Essay* must be understood in the context of Locke's assault on the venerable tradition of speculative philosophy. Locke's empiricist epistemology and his famous "way of ideas" were designed to resist what he took to be the metaphysical ambitions pervading early-modern philosophy. The danger speculative philosophy posed for human freedom lay in the tendency to reduce the great complexity of phenomena and the diversity of human modes of reasoning to a single set of metaphysical principles governing natural, moral, and political philosophy. For Locke, this problem took several different forms, but whether it was the teleological premises of scholasticism, Cartesian dualism, or the scientific naturalism of Spinoza and Hobbes, the basic assumption underlying modern philosophy in its various forms and most authoritative expressions were identical; namely the tendency to conceive of the goal of philosophy as the construction of comprehensive accounts of being. One aim, then, of Locke's effort to craft a new and more compact definition of philosophy operating on the basis of a "Historical, Plain Method" was to dismantle the vast theoretical apparatus of speculative philosophy, and thereby provide a measure of autonomy for both natural science based on empirical analysis and moral and political philosophy derived from an account of the epistemological foundation of human freedom in the internal structure and operation of mind. In this sense, the distinctly Lockean form of modernity presupposed a dramatic shift in the philosophic paradigm that had dominated speculation about politics, morality, and religion in Europe for centuries.

The constructive aspect of Locke's democratization of mind involved establishing a new philosophic dispensation on the basis of the relative equality of human cognitive capacities. On one level, this required replacing the traditional philosophical conceptions of substance, innate ideas, essences, and the natural hierarchy of beings and ends with a new focus on the fundamentally egalitarian premises of his empiricist epistemology. Locke advanced the proposition that the perceptions, beliefs, and judgments of the self-conscious individual are both the building blocks of knowledge and the sole basis for meaningful reflection upon the many issues of politics, morality, and religion that do not admit of certain knowledge. As such, for Locke the role of philosophy properly understood is neither to be the comprehensive master science of ultimate reality nor a mere adjunct to the empirical sciences. On the political level, this modest conception of philosophy would have a liberating effect on political life by allowing new possibilities for the study and understanding of moral and political concepts to emerge in relative freedom from the burden of dubious, and inherently contestable, metaphysical presuppositions. In the democratizing thrust of Locke's epistemology, we recognize the seeds of an intellectual and social culture that would encourage a critical stance toward all authoritative institutional claims to knowledge or truth, by subjecting them to systematic examination by individuals all naturally and, at least in principle, equally capable of discernment and reflection upon their own mental activity.

The fundamentally democratic orientation of Locke's account of human understanding based on interiority and the structural properties of mind does not, however, reflect any philosophic naiveté about the limitless possibilities of either natural science or moral philosophy. While always holding out the prospect that moral knowledge can achieve demonstrative certainty and that traditional political and social institutions can be reformulated and designed on the basis of rational principles, Locke was not reticent about the enormous conceptual and epistemological difficulties confronting any philosophical attempt to do so. Likewise, while Locke was optimistic about the great discoveries of nature made possible by the new empirical sciences, he expressed serious doubts as to whether the natural sciences could ever achieve certainty even about the nature of substance, not to mention the more ambitious goal of providing the intellectual foundation for a new modern scientific metaphysic to replace the old speculative philosophy of the Schools. In order to clarify the limits and possibilities of human freedom, especially in its modern political expression, Locke called upon philosophy to redefine the terms of its own activity.

THE INTELLECTUAL CONTEXT OF THE ESSAY

Before we can appreciate the democratizing impact of Locke's philosophy of ideas, it is important to clarify the intellectual context of the *Essay*.

The central feature of intellectual life in seventeenth-century Europe was the conflict between the established philosophy of the "Schools" and the newly emergent scientific philosophy most fully systematized by Descartes, Bacon, Spinoza, and Hobbes. As both a classically trained scholar and a practitioner of the new science, Locke was intimately familiar with both the old and new philosophy. While there were obvious differences between the Schools and their modern philosophic critics such as René Descartes, Benedict Spinoza, and Thomas Hobbes, they also shared fundamental assumptions about the scope and authority of philosophy as the pursuit of certainty and truth. The old and new philosophy presented alternative accounts of nature and reality; however, they fundamentally agreed that the proper goal of philosophy is to construct comprehensive metaphysical systems from which a doctrine of ethics, morality, and natural science would logically flow. It was Locke's distrust of the metaphysical tendencies of early-modern philosophy, and his concern about the implications for human freedom derived from both classical and scientific naturalism, that would perhaps more powerfully inform his aim and method in the *Essay* than any other consideration.

The dominant philosophic tradition among the educated class in Locke's time was scholasticism. This inheritance of Aristotelian philosophy modified by the central tenets of medieval Christianity still held considerable sway over the intellectual life of seventeenth-century Europe. Scholastic texts and methodology pervaded university curricula throughout the period, and Locke's exposure to and training in scholastic philosophy as a student and scholar at Oxford connected him to the formative intellectual experience of practically every educated European of the day. In England, this included groups as diverse as the Cambridge Platonists, leading Anglican divines, and the many classically trained university philosophers who imbibed scholastic metaphysical doctrines from the very wellspring of their education.[2] The scholastic system of metaphysics wedding ethics, logic, theology, and natural science in a complex, seamless web of unified being was simply the most authoritative and publicly respectable voice of philosophy in Locke's world.

The main features of scholastic philosophy derived from its classical inheritance. As followers of the Aristotelian tradition of metaphysics, early-modern scholastics grounded their philosophy on the methodology of

---

[2] Samuel C. Rickless, "Locke's Polemic against Nativism," in *The Cambridge Companion to Locke's "Essay Concerning Human Understanding,"* Lex Newman, ed. (Cambridge: Cambridge University Press, 2007), p. 33.

Aristotle's four causes, his formal logic based on syllogistic reason and a complex system of elaborate definitions and categories. They also adapted the Aristotelian notion of substance, which operated as both the first and most fundamental logical category, as well as a composite of form and matter.[3] From this venerable philosophic tradition, which held that substance is the foundational principle for certain knowledge of the world, scholasticism derived the influential doctrines of substantial form and immutable essences. According to these doctrines, substantial form is what makes a thing able to subsist independently of anything else: The substance of a thing is its nature. The real and immutable essence of a thing is thus the substantial form providing the natural end or *telos* informing the causal basis of a thing's powers and qualities.[4] In scholastic philosophy, the removal of something's essential quality effectively destroys its substantial form.

The logical complement to the scholastic doctrine of substance was the philosophical commitment to the existence of certain innate speculative and practical principles imprinted by God on the human mind. These innate ideas operated on two levels. First, on the level of epistemology, scholasticism assumed that all knowledge of natural and supernatural phenomena available to human understanding is based on fundamental axioms of speculative reason. These axioms or maxims are theoretical principles, such as the causal principle that nothing comes from nothing and the law of noncontradiction establishing that a thing cannot be and not be at the same time. These are basic theoretical principles of cognition that neither require nor are capable of proof. On the normative level, innate practical principles were presumed to include natural knowledge of an individual's moral and religious duties, without which it was assumed humans would be unable to achieve even a modicum of certainty about God's law, and thus societies would be condemned to stark moral relativism and civil disorder. While there were varieties within scholasticism, with some adopting a naïve or "occurent" form of innatism based on immediate and active apprehension of certain principles, and others advancing a more sophisticated or "dispositional" version of innatism that stressed the natural existence of faculties with the potential to grasp these principles, scholastic innatism as such rested on broad agreement that the building blocks of knowledge are gifts

---

[3] Edwin McCann, "Locke on Substance" in *The Cambridge Companion to Locke's "Essay Concerning Human Understanding,"* Lex Newman, ed. (Cambridge: Cambridge University Press, 2007), p. 157.
[4] McCann, "Locke on Substance," pp. 163, 188.

of divine providence reflecting the essentially syllogistic character of human reason.[5]

In contrast to the venerable scholastic tradition of philosophy, the new scientific philosophy emerging in the seventeenth century represented a still somewhat insurgent shadow curriculum in the universities of Locke's time. He was, of course, intimately familiar with the main texts and thinkers of the new science, which can be subdivided into Baconian experimental science, Cartesian philosophy, and the mechanistic metaphysic of Hobbes and Spinoza. The unifying thread linking the various strains of the new philosophy was that they all assumed a common front against the authority of scholastic metaphysics.

The experimental science championed by Francis Bacon in the early part of the seventeenth century, with its emphasis on empirical observation and testable hypotheses, was a powerful challenge to scholastic doctrines of substance and axiomatic natural philosophy. Baconian natural science typically eschewed metaphysical pretensions by placing much more importance on experiment than theory as a means to give a correct account of the natural world. Locke's professional and personal interest in the work of scientists such as Robert Boyle and Richard Lower, then working in Oxford, made him an enthusiastic devotee and practitioner of the new experimental science.[6] His admission as a member of the Royal Society, created to encourage experimental science soon after its establishment in 1662, signified both Locke's close connection to the new science and its growing respectability in the emerging intellectual counterculture of the period. Most significantly, the "corpuscularian" hypothesis developed by Boyle, which proposed that the internal constitution of a thing is a product of its atomic structure, had a considerable influence on Locke's assessment of the grave defects in the scholastic doctrine of substantial form.[7] Corpuscularianism offered Locke a very different account of nature based on the idea of body as minute particles of matter the basic properties of which are, at least in the present state of technology, largely unobservable.

While Baconian experimental science was arguably only just beginning to achieve intellectual respectability in Locke's lifetime, the most important alternative to scholasticism in the broader new scientific movement was

---

5   For a good account of the difference between "occurent" and "dispositional" innatism, see Rickless, "Locke's Polemic against Nativism," p. 37.
6   For Locke's endorsement of Baconian experimental science, see Peter Myers, *Our Only Star and Compass: Locke and the Struggle for Political Rationality* (Lanham, MD: Rowman & Littlefield, 1998), pp. 67, 76–7, and 85.
7   McCann, "Locke on Substance," p. 190.

the philosophy of René Descartes. Cartesianism arrived on the scene in England from the continent at mid-century and had an enormous impact on educated Englishmen of the period.[8] It was much more theoretically ambitious than the experimental science of Bacon and arguably offered the first comprehensive alternative account of both nature and the supernatural to capture the imagination of a generation educated by the Schools. Descartes rejected scholastic formal logic and replaced it with an epistemology inspired by the mathematical mode of reasoning based on "clear and distinct" ideas. The goal was to achieve scientific certainty and truth by means of rigorously examined ideas.

Insofar as Cartesianism sought a mechanistic explanation for natural phenomena, it broke decisively from the Schools and thus bore a certain kinship with Baconian experimental science.[9] However, in its conception of ideas and its metaphysical scope, Cartesianism also departed considerably from the philosophy of Bacon and his Oxford adherents. Descartes maintained that there are three kinds of ideas – adventitious, constructed, and innate – innate ideas being the most crucial because the truth of what a thing is is innate.[10] The proposition that there are innate ideas neither constructed by the mind nor prompted by sense impressions provided not only a formal link to the systematic philosophy of the Schools; it also supplied the theoretical foundation for a doctrine of substance and real essences bearing striking similarities with scholasticism. For Descartes as for the scholastics, core innate ideas are foundational principles of knowledge. On the basis of the innate idea that the thinking self is not a corporeal or material thing, Descartes deduced the immateriality of soul.[11] On the basis of the proposition that knowledge of substance provides evidence that mind is substance whose essence is to think, Descartes grounded his influential mind/body

---

[8] For Descartes' profound impression on the early Locke, see G. A. J. Rogers, "The Intellectual Setting and Aims of the Essay," in *The Cambridge Companion to Locke's "Essay Concerning Human Understanding"* Lex Newman, ed. (Cambridge: Cambridge University Press, 2007), p. 12. For the traditional view that Locke's *Essay*, especially the attack on innate ideas in Book I, was directed primarily against Descartes and the Cartesians, see Richard I. Aaron, *John Locke, 2nd Ed.* (Oxford: Oxford University Press, 1955), pp. 88–94.

[9] John Cottingham, "Cartesian Dualism: Theology, Metaphysics, and Science," in *The Cambridge Companion to Descartes*, John Cottingham, ed. (Cambridge: Cambridge University Press, 1992), pp. 238–239.

[10] See Rickless, "Locke's Polemic against Nativism," p. 35, and René Descartes, *The Philosophical Writings of Descartes*, John Cottingham, Robert Stoothoff, and Dugald Murdoch, eds. and trans. (Cambridge: Cambridge University Press, 1984), Volume II, p. 26 and Volume III, p. 183.

[11] Descartes, *Philosophical Writings*, Volume II, p. 132.

dualism: both the notion of extended substance (body) and thinking substance (mind) can be "clear and distinct" ideas. Thus, Descartes assumed that the intellectual means to knowledge of the essence of substances progressed from the foundational premise of the certainty of the thinking self toward a scientific demonstration of the existence of God. The Cartesian combination of innate ideas and the notion of clear and distinct ideas as the criterion for truth culminated in sweeping metaphysical claims that rivaled the theoretical ambition of the Schools.

The materialist, mechanistic philosophy of Thomas Hobbes and Benedict Spinoza represented the third key element of the seventeenth-century new science. As the preeminent English philosopher of Locke's formative years, Hobbes' scathing attack on the Schools and Descartes made him one of the leading voices in the anti-innatist wing of the new mechanistic philosophy.[12] The main features of Hobbes' "first philosophy" constituted a direct assault on the idea of metaphysics as traditionally understood. He offered a mechanistic conception of natural phenomena explained exclusively as the result of the motion and impact of material particles. Hobbes thus rejected any consideration of nonmechanical principles of causation, such as scholastic substantial forms or Cartesian innate ideas.[13] For Hobbes, the exclusion of nonmechanical principles in nature meant the inconceivability of any notion of incorporeal substance including, most notably, the prevailing philosophical conception of God. Hobbes insisted that to the extent that we can say anything about God, we must say God is a body because, contra Descartes, every thinking thing must be corporeal. He joined the Italian philosopher Gassendi in criticizing Descartes' proposition that mind is thinking substance by offering the objection that experience of dreamless sleep proves that it cannot be the essence of mind to always think.[14] For

---

[12] Despite Locke's rather implausible claim in 1698 that he was "not so well read in Hobbes or Spinoza," his perhaps somewhat ironic condemnation of "those justly decried names" suggests more than a passing familiarity with the work and theories of these two leading lights of seventeenth-century scientific naturalism. See John Locke, *Works*, Volume IV (London: Tegg, 1823), p. 477 and Laslett's commentary on p. 74 of the *Two Treatises*.

[13] See Thomas Hobbes, *Leviathan* (Indianapolis, IN: Hackett, 1994), ch. 1, sec. 4–5, p. 7; ch. 2, sec. 1–2, pp. 7–8. For helpful discussions about Hobbes' mechanistic account of body and motion, see Gary B. Herbert, *Thomas Hobbes: The Unity of Scientific and Moral Wisdom* (Vancouver: University of British Columbia Press, 1979), pp. 40–62; Douglas Jesseph, "Hobbes and the Method of Natural Science," in *The Cambridge Companion to Hobbes*, Tom Sorrell, ed. (Cambridge: Cambridge University Press, 1996), p. 86 ; A. P. Martinich, *Hobbes* (New York: Routledge, 2005), pp. 24–32; and Thomas A. Spragens, *The Politics of Motion: The World of Thomas Hobbes* (Lexington, KS: University Press of Kansas, 1973), pp. 77–92.

[14] Rickless, "Locke's Polemic against Nativism," p. 35.

Hobbes, in a universe characterized solely by bodies in motion, essences are simply "accidents" with indeterminate causes rather than real things signifying moral purposes inhering in nature.

Hobbes' natural philosophy shared the Baconian focus on matter but, like Cartesianism, it also exhibited greater theoretical ambition than experimental science. Hobbes argued that the study of nature rests on a philosophy of causality and necessity: In the material world, every cause is necessary and sufficient for the effect. If everything that happens in nature is necessary, then any perceived anomaly in the putative "laws of nature" is merely evidence of human ignorance of its causes.[15] Hobbes famously contrasted the necessarily hypothetical constructions of the natural science of motion with the certainty derived from geometry. He asserted that the mathematical mode of reasoning employed by geometry makes it the only "real science" because its operative terms are constructs of the human mind that are capable of careful definition and explication, and whose causes are in principle completely intelligible because they derive from a human source.[16] Conversely, Hobbes relegated natural science to the realm of opinions and hypothesis, according to which we can only try to explain natural phenomena by speculating about most probable causes for the action in question. Hobbes' materialism differs from Baconian natural science inasmuch as it is deduced from mechanistic first principles and downplays the role of experiment, but it departs even more significantly from the innatism of Descartes and the Schools with Hobbes' insistence that natural science cannot determine the true causal definition of things.[17] By replacing traditional metaphysics with physical science, Hobbes was not only exposed to the charge of atheism for reducing God to body, but also faced hostility from critics who were deeply suspicious of his conception of the relation between natural necessity on the one hand and morality on the other. With a moral order deduced from natural human passions, especially self-preservation, and supported not by nature but by human artifice in "the commonwealth," it seemed, not unreasonably to many, that in Hobbes' philosophy morality and necessity were for all intents and purposes indistinguishable.

15 Yves Charles Zarka, "First Philosophy and the Foundations of Knowledge," in *The Cambridge Companion to Hobbes*, Tom Sorrel, ed. (Cambridge: Cambridge University Press, 1996), pp. 70–71, 73

16 Hobbes calls geometry "the only science it hath pleased God hitherto to bestow on mankind" (*Leviathan*, ch. 4., sec 12, p. 19; also ch. 5, sec. 7, p. 24). See also, Jesseph, "Hobbes and the Method of Natural Science," pp. 87–88.

17 Jesseph, "Hobbes and the Method of Natural Science," p. 102.

The scientific naturalism of Spinoza extended the materialist philosophical premises of Hobbes far beyond the Englishman's mechanistic account
of nature. While Spinoza followed Hobbes and Descartes in adopting the
mathematical mode of reasoning as the basis of the new scientific philosophy, he radically transformed the traditional conception of substance by
assimilating it to the eternal order of nature co-extensive with the eternal
existence of God. As such, Spinoza addressed the concept of freedom in
terms of a scientific knowledge of substance including metaphysics, epistemology, and theology. By positing God as "substance consisting of infinite
attributes," so that there is no substance besides God, Spinoza reduced
the parts of substance, including both human and nonhuman nature, to
the status of "modes" or attributes of God.[18] It was on the basis of this
all-encompassing conception of substance that Spinoza could claim with
assurance that all sciences are directed to "one end and aim," namely
the knowledge of substance.[19] Thus, in principle, political science and
natural science seek an identical goal. It is hardly surprising then that
Spinoza's political teaching is essentially a deduction from his analysis of
substance.

One central focus of Spinozist metaphysics was his effort to efface the
traditional distinction between human and nonhuman nature. The human
being must be understood immersed in the eternal order of nature, a mode
of substance whose primary motivations can be deduced from the general
laws of substance. As Spinoza related: "I shall consider human actions and
desires in exactly the same manner, as though I were concerned with lines,
planes, and solids."[20] Spinoza followed Hobbes' lead in assigning primary
significance to the desire for self-preservation as the great spur to human
action. However, while Hobbes' first philosophy of motion maintained some
element of the distinction between human and nonhuman nature, with the
human as the one being in nature manifesting a kind of motion different
from the internal structure of other kinds of motion, Spinoza presented
nature as eternal order prior to and independent of human action, and thus
made the intelligibility of nature the precondition for human understanding. Ideas, or human impressions of nature, can only be adequate or clear
when they express the nature of a mode in its reality. However, Spinoza
insists that the internal structure of a mode is deducible from the general

---

[18]   Benedict Spinoza, *Ethics Including the Improvement of the Understanding* (Amherst,
       NY: Prometheus Books, 1989), pp. 39, 60.
[19]   Spinoza, *Ethics*, p. 5.
[20]   Spinoza, *Ethics*, p. 128.

structure of substance, and therefore modes can be known as they really are rather than as they simply appear to human beings.[21] Philosophy in this view is the master science devoted to understanding the structure of substance, and as such, study of political and moral matters is inseparable from the scientific analysis of the visible expressions of the infinite articulations in the structure of substance. In contrast to the absolutist political implications that Hobbes deduced from a scientific, nonteleological understanding of material nature, Spinoza famously grounded the naturalness and superiority of democracy on its capacity to express the heterogeneity of diverse human types and to place under the control of reason the collected power of the individuals in the state of nature.[22] However, despite their important differences about the nature of sovereignty, both Hobbes and Spinoza shared the fundamental assumption of the new materialist philosophy that moral, political, and physical sciences were intelligible as deductions from certain first principles.

The old and new philosophy comprising the intellectual context of Locke's *Essay* thus was marked by both substantive differences and important underlying commonalities. Despite advancing contrary positions about body and soul, innate ideas and the doctrine of substance, each of the major philosophical Schools of the seventeenth-century milieu, with the exception of Baconian experimentalism, offered sophisticated theoretical accounts of reality. The dominant philosophic camps of the period each represented ambitious efforts to account for reality and truth, and they did so with speculative *éclat* quite distinct from the more mundane and academically marginalized Baconian natural science. While the new scientific criticisms leveled against regnant scholasticism moved some distance toward puncturing the metaphysical pretensions of the Schools, prior to Locke the process of establishing modern scientific philosophy was itself beset by grand system building tendencies within the new philosophy. The *Essay* was thus first introduced into an intellectual world in which philosophy was still largely understood as the attempt to produce a comprehensive account of the whole.

[21] Stanley Rosen, "Benedict Spinoza," in *History of Political Philosophy, 3rd ed.*, Leo Strauss and Joseph Cropsey, eds. (Chicago: University of Chicago Press, 1987), p. 461.
[22] Benedict Spinoza, *A Theologico-Political Treatise and A Political Treatise* (Mineola, NY: Dover Publications, 2004), pp. 205–207. For good treatments of Spinoza's account of democracy and his differences from Hobbes, see Etienne Balibar, *Spinoza and Politics*, Peter Snowdon, trans. (New York: Verso, 1998), pp. 31–36, and Steven B. Smith, *Spinoza, Liberalism, and the Question of Jewish Identity* (New Haven, CT: Yale University Press, 1997), pp. 122–137.

THE ATTACK ON INNATE IDEAS

The opening statement of authorial intent in the "Epistle" to the *Essay* is a curious blend of modesty and self-conscious innovation. Locke identifies this work as both the "Ground clearing" exercise of a humble intellectual "underlabourer" with a "Historical, Plain Method," and yet at the same time as a stinging rebuke to followers of "antick Fashion" in the established philosophic Schools.[23] Locke herein prepares his reader for a new conception of philosophy, one that modestly eschews the metaphysical projects then practically synonymous with philosophy, but which nonetheless promises a rigorous critique of many of the most cherished doctrines of the Schools and their opponents. By presenting his philosophic activity as an essentially remedial project, Locke positioned the *Essay* as a potential counterweight to the innatist philosophy of the scholastics and Cartesians, on the one hand, and more subtly to correct the materialist philosophy of Hobbes and Spinoza, on the other. As the preface can only suggest, and the main body of the work is designed to demonstrate, Locke's Baconian humble "Historical, Plain Method" in the *Essay* thus represented nothing less than a bold effort to alter the direction of modern philosophy.

The opening two books of the *Essay* established the foundation of Locke's famous "way of ideas." In Book I he launches a frontal assault on the doctrine of innate ideas central to scholastic and Cartesian philosophy. Book II follows with Locke's presentation of the argument that ideas acquired by sensation or reflection are the only sources of knowledge available to human understanding. In the process, Locke revolutionized the concept of ideas propounded by Descartes, and generally eschewed by Baconian natural science, by detaching the cognitive meaning of ideas from the foundational innate principles traditionally thought to anchor these ideas in reality. Locke's philosophy of ideas points away from assumptions about essentialized nature or substance toward the subjective reality of the individual human mind that perceives and constructs these ideas.

The first book of the *Essay* firmly plants Locke in the anti-innatist wing of the new philosophy. In keeping with Hobbes, and in contrast to Descartes and the Schools, Locke categorically rejects the notion that certain ideas are of a "Character stamped upon the Mind of Man" by God (1.2.1.48). Locke's immediate target is the innatist assumption that God is the source of innate speculative principles that serve as the certain

---

[23]   John Locke, *An Essay Concerning Human Understanding.* Peter Nidditch, ed. (Oxford: Oxford University Press, 1975), p. 10 and Book 1, chapter 1, section 2, page 44 (hereafter in text and notes simply bk, ch, sec, and page).

epistemological foundation for practical principles of action. It is Locke's contention that both naïve and sophisticated forms of innatism converge in the conviction that the source of truth in speculative and moral philosophy is intertwined in innate ideas. Locke's "ground clearing" exercise thus seems to require, in its most direct form, establishing at least the possibility of some other plausible explanation for the original source of knowledge. His two-pronged strategy for making the case against innatism involves first demonstrating that innatism is not the only causal explanation for widespread acceptance of some principles, and then proving that the logical self-evidence of supposed innate ideas makes it redundant for them to have been imprinted by God.[24] Relative rational autonomy and natural equality of intellectual faculties will replace innate ideas as the core elements in Lockean epistemology.

Locke clarifies the philosophic point at issue in the debate by challenging innatists to show that the principles they identify as innate are principles to which no human can fail to assent. He develops this stringent standard of proof in these terms: "this argument of universal consent, which is made use of, to prove innate Principles, seems to me a demonstration that there are none such, because there are none to which all mankind give an universal assent" (1.2.4.49). Notably, Locke does not deny that there are several logical principles that have the appearance of being innate because they are so widely acknowledged. However, the standard of proof Locke sets for demonstrating innateness is designed to show that there is no sense in which even basic logical principles can be said to be universally accepted. For instance, even the law of noncontradiction cannot be said to be universally recognized because not only do "Children and Ideots" have no idea of this principle, but also a "great part of illiterate People, and Savages, pass many years of their rational Age, without ever thinking on this" (1.2.12.53). Locke never suggests that noncontradiction is invalid as an intellectual principle, even a foundational one, but rather his focus is to undermine the idea of innateness *tout court*. He admits that some propositions are self-evident and thus can be known early in life and with great certainty. His main claim, however, is that even very basic logical principles such as noncontradiction cannot be acquired independently of experience: "The senses at first let in particular ideas, and furnish the yet empty cabinet" (1.2.15.55). Fundamental speculative axioms cannot be understood by a being that has not had prior experience with simple ideas, and thus the cognitive building blocks of human understanding are not

---

[24] Rickless, "Locke's Polemic against Nativism," 43.

theoretical principles but rather the simple ideas upon which even the most fundamental axioms are constructed.

Thus, Locke replaces innateness with self-evidence as the operative principle to account for widespread, but hardly universal, acceptance of basic speculative principles. Self-evident propositions involve more mental activity than innate ones because they are dependent not only on ideas but also crucially on language to express those ideas such that an individual can be brought to grasp self-evident principles only when "the consideration of the Nature of the Things contained in the words would not suffer him to think otherwise" (1.2.21.59). The principle of equality may be self-evident, but Locke insists one must have an idea of seven before one can understand that three plus four equals seven (1.2.16.55). Locke dilutes the practical significance of claims to innateness even further by asserting the astonishing variety of simple ideas that are self-evident. For instance, "Red is not yellow" is a proposition as certain to the mind as any of the speculative first principles of the Schools. Either there are no innate ideas, as Locke claims, or there are so many innate ideas as to be practically indistinguishable from sense perception. In either case, Locke stresses the epistemological claims of the Schools and the Cartesians do not hold up.

The underlying thrust of Locke's argument is that the fundamental human experience of knowledge is affected more by the way we learn than by the logical content of various axioms. For instance, one can understand the law of noncontradiction without ever having heard it formulated. The democratic implications of this emphasis on experience extend to a critique of the entire system of logic constructed by the Schools on the basis of innate ideas. Locke contrasts the intuitive certainty derived from the experience and natural faculties of rational human beings with the abstruse syllogistic reasoning of the educated elites whose foundational axioms "not one of Ten thousand" people understand as syllogism (4.17.4.676). Locke's claim that at its root, human reasoning is experiential and discursive rather than syllogistic undermines the innatist foundation of the entire metaphysical system elaborated in the Schools. The innate ideas and a vast array of syllogistic proofs and axioms upon which the scholastic intellectual world is built simply do not reflect the way human beings know even the most basic speculative principles.

With respect to innate practical principles, Locke launches an even more direct assault on the notion of universal assent, because he claims practical principles are even less certain or self-evident than speculative principles. He cites the principles of justice and the idea of God as two crucial practical principles that exhibit no empirical evidence of universal assent. The stunning array of brutal customs in the world past and present, as well as evidence that in many parts of the world the idea of God is unknown, demonstrate, according to Locke, that there is no basis for claiming the existence of innate practical principles (1.3.9.70; 1.4.7–8.87–8). Even the practice of justice among a gang of robbers, who respect the proprietary rights of each other while gleefully violating the rights of everyone else, only proves that the idea of justice is a learned rule of convenience rather than an innate moral principle (1.3.2.66). By the terms of Locke's stringent standard of proof, any breach of a supposed innate moral principle means that it is not innate. In this respect, the ubiquity of cruel customs in the world is decisive: "The breaking of a Rule, say you, is no Argument, that it is unknown. I grant it: But the *generally allowed breach of it anywhere*, I say, *is a Proof, that it is not innate*."[25] By its own internal logic, the doctrine of innate ideas does not admit of degrees: An idea cannot be kind of innate or innate in some people and not others.

According to Locke, the fundamental difference between practical and speculative principles is that, with regard to morality, there is much less of even an appearance of innateness. Unlike basic speculative principles to which Locke ungrudgingly ascribes logical self-evidence, he claims that "there cannot any one moral rule be proposed, whereof a Man may not justly demand a Reason" (1.3.4.68). While his admission of the greater opacity in moral, as opposed to speculative, first principles advances Locke's attack on innatism, it also seriously complicates his case for the existence of a law of nature comprehensible to human reason "without the help of positive revelation" (1.3.13.75). The natural moral law of which "we being ignorant of may attain to knowledge of by the use and due application of our Natural Faculties" is described in terms rather different from Locke's account of speculative first principles (1.3.13.75). In Book I he does not explicitly describe moral principles in terms of self-evidence derived from experience and reflection, but rather emphasizes the complex mental effort involved in determining moral rules that may potentially be far from self-evident. Thus, one of the major issues Locke leaves unresolved in the course of his attack on innatism has to do with the extent to which moral principles may be said to be self-evident.

The political implications of this question are obvious. If moral principles are self-evident, then how are we meant to understand the purpose and scope of government? Depending on the ease with which these practical principles may be understood, could we not see government and civil

---

[25] 1.3.12.73 (italics in original).

law as supererogatory? Conversely, if Locke believes no moral truths are self-evident, then what guarantee is there that even individuals who exercise their natural faculties properly will discover their moral duties?[26] Can Locke prove his later argument that morality is as capable of demonstration as mathematics without first demonstrating that the foundational moral principles are as capable of logical self-evidence as the principle of equality in math?

The attack on innatism is an important preliminary stage in the process of "ground clearing" central to Locke's project in the *Essay*. His deep suspicion of the moral and intellectual effects of innatism on politics and philosophy pervades this account. Underlying the innatist's excessively theoretical explanation of the first principles of knowledge acquisition, Locke detects an unhealthy intellectual laziness in which the assumption of innate ideas spares the mind the "pains of search" for truth through discursive reason (1.4.24.101). Locke also expresses his suspicion about the inegalitarian tendencies flowing from this theoretical bent. He charges that dogmatic philosophy in the innatist mold privileges the educated elites who propound these axioms: "And it was no small advantage to those who affected to be Masters and Teachers, to make the Principles of Principles, that Principles must not be questioned" (1.4.24.101). The authoritarian potentialities of innatism rest on what Locke takes to be the dangerous effects of positing certain truths that must not be questioned, and thus ascribing awesome power over the intellectual life of a people to a class of philosophical guardians entrusted with propounding these truths and decrying their challengers as extreme relativists or even atheists. Innatism not only stifles genuine scientific progress by presupposing metaphysical explanations for the very phenomena most in need of critical and empirical examination, but it also radicalizes political and moral debate for to challenge the innatist account of knowledge is, in the eyes of its many and powerful adherents, to cast doubt upon the providence of God and the moral meaning of nature itself. That is to say, criticism of the doctrine of innate ideas may be presumed to be the product of malicious will rather than any inherent obscurity in the principles themselves.

LOCKE'S WAY OF IDEAS

Locke follows the attack on innate ideas with his presentation of the "way of ideas," his alternative account of the source of human knowledge. While

---

[26] Rickless, "Locke's Polemic against Nativism," 62–3.

Locke's emphasis on ideas signifies a formal connection with Descartes and a departure from Hobbes and the empiricist Bacon, both of whom rarely employed the rhetoric of "ideas," the foundation of Locke's argument is directly contrary to Cartesian innatism. The way of ideas is then the positive or constructive aspect of Locke's epistemology flowing from his assault on innatism. The bedrock principle is that the human mind is originally devoid of any ideas whatsoever. Locke calls the mind prior to the introduction of ideas "White Paper" or an "empty Cabinet" ready to receive and construct ideas (1.3.22.81; 2.1.2.104; 1.2.15.55). The central epistemological question is then, how is the mind furnished with ideas?

The only source of ideas is experience in the form of either sensation produced by external sensible objects or reflection upon the internal operation of one's own mind. Locke insists that these two sources are the "Fountains of Knowledge, from whence all the ideas we have, or can naturally have, do spring" (2.1.2.104). In contrast to the inherent elitism of innatism, Locke grounds the way of ideas not in theory or deductive logic, but rather in the democratic foundation of "Everyone's own Observation and Experience" (2.1.2.104). While Locke admits that reflection, as distinct from sensation, allows for inegalitarian conclusions inasmuch as children take time to develop this capacity and even many adults may never adequately do so, he maintains the broader egalitarian thrust of his argument by emphasizing that every mind acquires ideas the same way and, in principle, all rational beings can be trained to improve their faculties of reflection (2.1.8.107). Locke joins with Hobbes and Gassendi in rejecting Descartes' identification of the essence of soul as thinking, but he does so less to challenge directly Cartesian dualism than for the more narrowly epistemological concern to prove that sensation and reflection are the only sources of ideas (2.1.16–7.113–4). Locke recognizes that if the mind is still thinking during a dreamless sleep, then there is a massive conceptual opening for another source of ideas, especially innate ideas, apart from sensation and reflection.

The three kinds of ideas produced by sensation and reflection are simple ideas, complex ideas composed of multiple simple ideas, and mixed modes. Simple ideas are formed by "qualities that affect our senses" (2.2.1.119). The qualities in bodies may be primary such as bulk, figure, number, or motion; secondary qualities that reflect the power of insensible objects to produce in us ideas such as color, sound, taste and smell; and finally qualities that are powers that make a body operate on our senses such as the sun's power to turn wax white (2.8.23.141). Simple ideas are the real building blocks of knowledge for Locke. The egalitarian implications of this emphasis on simple ideas operate on two levels. First, Locke insists that the difference between primary and secondary qualities of bodies derives from the "ideas produced by them in the Mind" (2.8.22.140). They do not reflect any ontological priority or hierarchy of qualities in nature, but rather illustrate the epistemological structure of mind. Second, Locke claims that all the simple ideas that are combined by the mind to form a complex idea are "perfectly distinct" in themselves (2.2.1.119). This means that the whiteness, roundness, and coldness that characterize the idea of a snowball are each distinct and independent ideas, and thus no one single quality more fully embodies the being of a snowball than any other (2.8.8.134). This ideational atomism not only reflects Locke's indebtedness to corpuscularianism, but also perhaps parallels his conception of the atomistic individualism of mind. In the democratizing effects of Locke's epistemology, just as qualities and simple ideas operate on mind free of any ontological priority, so too presumably do the instruments of cognition, individual human beings, engage the world independently of any politically or morally significant natural hierarchy among themselves.

Complex ideas are thus merely simple ideas combined by mind. With complex ideas, however, mind is not simply a passive receptor of sense impressions. Complex ideas signify the constructive activity of mind and reflect a fundamental intellectual freedom to transcend mere sensory impression through mental activity (2.12.1.163). Locke identifies three kinds of mental activity or "Faculties of Mind" involved in simple and complex ideas. The most fundamental is perception, which supplies the basic resource of human understanding. A child raised in a dark box will have no idea of the colors scarlet or yellow because she has no sensory perception of them in her experience (2.1.6.107). Locke even suggests that a human being completely deprived of all senses would be in cognitive terms little better than the lowest degree of animals "such as a cockle or an oyster" (2.9.14.149). A more advanced form of mental activity is what Locke terms retention or "contemplation." This involves the capacity to keep or recall an idea in mind after sense impression has worn off. Locke's radically egalitarian reinterpretation of contemplation is striking. Contemplation was a term with venerable philosophical significance and held by classical philosophers to be the product of education and training, or even a dedicated philosophic way of life opposed to, and transcending, the active life.[27] Locke, however, reduces contemplation to the status of a mental activity available to any

---

[27] For the classical conception of contemplation and the philosophic life, see Aristotle, *Nicomachean Ethics*, Martin Oswald, trans. (New York: MacMillan, 1962), 1177a12–1179a32 and Plato, *Republic*, Allan Bloom, trans. (New York: Basic Books, 1991), 505a–511d.

being capable of perceiving and memorizing ideas. Even animals can have memory (2.10.2.150; 2.11.5.157). For Locke, the most advanced forms of mental activity are discernment and abstraction rather than contemplation. Discernment involves comparing ideas and distinguishing them from each other. Abstraction occurs when ideas taken from particular beings become general representatives of all the same kind (2.11.9.159). Animals have a little discernment, according to Locke, but have no power to abstract general names of types of things. If perception is the floor of mental activity, abstraction may be said to be its zenith.

Simple and complex ideas reflect the range properties of human intellect. Both possess some connection to natural "archetypes" or patterns perceptible or discernible in nature (2.30.1.372). However, Locke is clear that they also illustrate considerable differences in the way the human mind understands nature. Locke's choice of "Beauty, Gratitude, A Man, an Army, [and] the Universe"(2.12.1.164) as prime examples of complex ideas, as opposed to simple ideas such as white, cold, hot, and sharp, demonstrates that for Locke, the difference between simple and complex ideas is not merely a matter of counting the number of constituent ideas in each general idea. Complex ideas are often relational and subject to interpretation and dispute. The cognitive status of nature can also differ with respect to complex and simple ideas, with simple more closely reflecting the natural archetype than complex. Complex ideas involve construction or even imposition on nature. It is the enhanced mental activity involved in the formation of complex ideas that accentuates the intermediate character of ideas per se. For Locke, what we can know about nature from our ideas is that as products of the human mind, ideas are capable of being better or worse, more or less accurate copies of what exists in nature.

Mixed modes are the most abstract form of complex idea because they exist at the furthest remove from nature. Whereas nonmodal ideas, simple or complex, depend on a natural archetype, modes are solely products of the human mind's capacity to discern relations and separate ideas by abstraction. Modes are free from dependence on nature and are thus not to be "looked upon to be characteristical marks of any real Beings that have a steady existence" (2.22.1.288). Geometric forms such as a triangle or moral terms such as gratitude and homicide do not, Locke claims, depend on the existence of anything in nature conforming to or even resembling these ideas (2.12.4.165). Freed from the heuristic properties of natural archetypes, mixed modes are purely of human invention. The freedom implied in mixed modes relates both to the mind's capacity to hold together the unity of a complex idea without a natural pattern, as well as the intellectual freedom to ascribe moral meaning to actions without ever experiencing or seeing such actions committed. However, the connection between mixed modes and simple ideas, while attenuated, is still foundational. Modes are constructed by mind on the basis of material supplied by distinct simple ideas (2.22.3.289). More importantly, Locke relates that mixed modes are the kinds of complex ideas that "are the greatest part of the words made use of in Divinity, Ethics, Law, Politics and several other Sciences" (2.22.12.294). The way of ideas, then, aspires not only to explain how we can know anything, but also what we can know and the degrees of certainty possible through ideas.

The primary distinction between what can and cannot be known emerges in Locke's discussion of substance. Insofar as the truth of ideas relates to their conformity with an archetype in nature, both simple and modal ideas possess plausible claims to truth. Locke argues that simple ideas are true because their validity depends on the power of things on our mind, independent of any determination of the reality of the thing itself. Similarly modes have no reality apart from the "minds of Men," and therefore Locke insists that by definition they cannot be imperfect or inaccurate reflections of natural archetypes. For instance, the idea of a triangle "cannot but be adequate" because it is not a copy of a real "archetype" in nature (2.30.4.373; 2.31.3.377). The real issue for the limits of knowledge thus has to do with the complex ideas of substances. Here Locke claims we can have no clear idea of substances. In contrast to the Spinozist conception of substance as the foundational principle of intelligibility, Locke demotes the meaning of substance to being the vague term people use to describe the unknown thing that holds corporeal bodies together (2.23.2, 4. 296–7). Our ignorance of the real nature of substance is due to the mind having no idea what unites corpuscles into form and no sense of the infinite variety of potential relations and powers in any, even apparently the most simple, substance (2.23.25–6. 309–10). This presumption of ignorance partly derives from Locke's commitment to a corpuscular account of nature according to which we have "but very obscure and confused ideas of . . . minute bodies." The "perfectest" idea of a particular substance of which we are capable is based on collecting "most of those simple ideas, which do exist in it." However, Locke insists that there is no way to know all the possible powers possessed by a substance (2.29.16.370; 2.23.7.299). As such, it is impossible to speak of essential properties in any particular substance. For example, Locke identifies the power of drawing iron as simply "one of" the observable powers in a loadstone (2.23.7.299). Of the "infinite other Properties" (2.31.10.382) unobserved in this or any other substance, we know nothing.

The implications of this ignorance of substance for Locke's way of ideas are enormous. To start, the elusive properties of substance mean that, contrary to Hobbesian and Spinozist materialism, there is no epistemological basis for rejecting the notion of immaterial substance. The boundaries of human knowledge are, on the one hand, the substratum of physical nature in which "there is not a Plant or Animal that does not confound the most inlarged understanding," and, on the other hand, the immaterial superstratum of angels and such in which, for all we know, there may be "more Species of Intelligent Creatures above us" than material beings below (3.6.9.444; 3.6.12.447). More importantly, Locke maintains that our intrinsic ignorance of substance means that human understanding is constitutionally incapable of proving or disproving the immortality of soul. Of this crucial theological and, by extension, political doctrine, Locke concludes, "it becomes the Modesty of Philosophy, not to pronounce magisterially, where we want that evidence that can produce knowledge"(4.3.6.541–2). The corpuscularian hypothesis can neither completely explain mental activity internal to mind, nor can it support or refute metaphysical speculation about soul. Locke is thus fully aware of the limits placed on natural philosophy by the perceiver-dependent basis of our understanding of substance.

At its most primary level, Locke's account of substance is an attack on the notion of essences central to scholastic and Cartesian metaphysics. The problem of essentialism is related to innatism in the sense that both doctrines assume greater possibilities for certainty about many things than the faculties of understanding allow. Scholasticism and Cartesianism are guilty in Locke's view of collapsing substance and mixed modes, that is to say moralizing substance by ascribing ontological priority to essences that either have no significance, being qualities that are all equally perceptions of mind, or that are in principle unknowable.[28] In Locke's radically particularistic ontology, "All things that exist" are "particulars" (3.3.1.409), and as such the proper philosophic stance toward being is to resist the temptation to deduce general sorts or species from presumed essential qualities. By rejecting the possibility of a purely intellectual route to knowledge of the essence of substances, Locke dismisses the basis of Descartes' mind/body dualism as well as the grounds for much of his claims to scientific certainty about substance.[29] The fundamental problem shared by scholastics and Cartesians, Locke claims, is their failure to recognize the problem of

---

[28] Nicholas Jolley, "The Reception of Descartes' Philosophy" in *The Cambridge Companion to Descartes*. John Cottingham, ed. (Cambridge: Cambridge University Press, 1992), pp. 416–17.

[29] Rogers, "The Intellectual Setting and Aim of the *Essay*," 14.

language whereby one word can be used to mark a multitude of particular existences. In principle, language is one of the great vehicles for advancing human knowledge; however, the problem of dogmatic philosophy is the logical fallacy of assuming that any general name can reflect the essence of a particular thing. According to Locke, it is the inherent arbitrariness of words as human constructs that requires any truly philosophic perspective to involve distinguishing the "nominal essence" – the name we give to a sort of thing displaying certain observable characteristics – and the "real essence" or its internal constitution, which is given the limited cognitive capacities of human beings as irreducibly mysterious as the internal machinery of the Clocktower at Strasbourg to the uneducated peasant in the field (3.6.3.440). Of course, the impossibility of achieving perfect identity between the nominal and real essence of substance contrasts sharply with the situation relating to mixed modes in which they are, in principle, identical inasmuch as modes are themselves entirely the constructs of mind.

Locke's assault on the idea that human beings can know the real essence of substance is intended to strike at the heart of early-modern metaphysics in its various forms. Both Cartesian and scholastic philosophies assume greater certainty about substance than is possible and thus fundamentally exaggerate the capacity of language to express the reality of material or, for that matter, immaterial substance. Whereas mixed modes can in principle be known with certainty precisely because they are constructs of mind indistinguishable from their linguistic representation, in natural science, language can facilitate improved understanding only when it is acknowledged to provide descriptions of simple ideas, rather than real essences of things, and thus can never be more than provisional accounts of observable natural phenomena. Locke's argument for the provisional, and at best probabilistic, character of natural science thus knocks out one of the chief theoretical pillars supporting the complex edifice of scholastic and Cartesian metaphysics.

On the other side of the philosophic spectrum, Locke's account of substance also, however more subtly, undermines the plausibility of Hobbes' materialist first philosophy of causality and motion. According to Locke, to reduce all of being to material body, as Hobbes typically does, is also to speak with greater certainty about substance than we can possibly know. Likewise, the Spinozist account of substance is staked to the possibility of acquiring certain knowledge about the general laws of nature, but Locke questions the coherence of any such effort to deduce metaphysical principles from natural phenomena the causes of which are largely opaque. No comprehensive natural science, much less moral and political philosophy, can derive from a source as limited as human comprehension of substance. Thus, from Locke's perspective, Hobbes and Spinoza are each in their own way as dogmatic about materialism as Descartes and the scholastics are about essences. Locke's way of ideas is then a challenge to the fundamental principles of both metaphysical and mechanistic thought considered to be central to the philosophic project as hitherto conceived.

LIBERTY AND MIND

Locke's way of ideas established the individual human mind as the basis of knowledge and the search for truth in the vast "Ocean of Being" (1.1.7.47). As we have seen, the democratizing effect of the way of ideas on philosophy operated on several levels. First, in terms of epistemology, the way of ideas was a powerful challenge to many of the authoritative assumptions underlying the metaphysical systems then in fashion, because it undermined the notion of innate ideas and substance upon which speculative philosophy was based in the seventeenth century. Moreover, the radical particularity of Locke's ontology, with its egalitarian conception of qualities, rejected any plausibility for the principle of ontological priority of qualities, essences or *telos* informing philosophical defenses of natural hierarchy. In addition, Locke's account of substance and the intermediate character of complex ideas injected a lethal dose of uncertainty and skepticism into one of the fundamental logical categories of traditional metaphysics. By narrowing the range of scientific certainty and expanding dramatically the philosophical importance of probability and fallible individual judgment with respect to some of the most significant religious, theoretical, and moral controversies, Locke introduced a fundamentally leveling principle into philosophy.[30] The way of ideas set dogmatic certainty and philosophical inquiry, as well as authoritative institutions such as the Schools and individual moral and intellectual autonomy, in the pattern of binary opposition that would characterize philosophy for much of the modern era.

However, the question of freedom in Locke's way of ideas took a particular form that developed only gradually through the several revisions Locke made to the *Essay* in the years following 1690. As some early readers of the *Essay* observed, there were crucial *lacunae* in Locke's original account of ideas.[31] These objections typically followed two general lines

---

[30] Neal Wood, *The Politics of Locke's Philosophy* (Berkeley: University of California Press, 1983), p. 126.
[31] See Peter Nidditch's "Foreword" to Locke's *An Essay Concerning Human Understanding* (Oxford : Oxford University Press, 1975), p. xx.

of argument. First, if all complex ideas are originally products of sensory experience (in other words, simple ideas), then how does Locke explain the way in which an individual mind can distance or free itself from the constant bombardment of external sensible stimuli in order to reflect on its own experience, and thereby construct the complex ideas and modes so central to Locke's epistemology? Second, if – as Locke concedes – reflection differs from sensation insofar as the former requires greater mental sophistication, how exactly does Lockean epistemology account for error? That is to say, if all thinking derives from the same source in the senses, then how does Locke explain how some individuals can reflect rigorously and grasp abstruse compound ideas, while others by his own admission "have not any very clear, or perfect ideas of the greatest part of them all their lives" (2.1.8.107)?

Locke's philosophical predecessors approached this last question in distinct ways. The classic problem in innatist philosophy was also the difficulty of accounting for erring judgment. If, in principle, all human beings do or can know the good with certainty, then why do they often do wrong? In answer to this problem, scholasticism developed the doctrine of free will based on a complex account of soul composed of articulated parts in which reason and will represent distinct faculties. While scholastics insisted that knowledge of speculative and practical first principles is lodged in every human conscience, they also maintained that it is possible for this knowledge to be obscured by vicious habits or faulty education through which erring reason directs the will away from the good and true.[32] This explains the scholastic emphasis on the centrality of moral education for decent political life. Moreover, innate principles are necessarily general in nature and thus allow considerable scope for error with respect to their application in particular situations, especially when self-interest interferes with moral duty. For scholasticism, moral responsibility reflects basic freedom to act or not to act upon the knowledge imprinted on the human soul.

For his part, Hobbes famously rejected the scholastic doctrine of free will. In the necessitarian logic of Hobbes' first philosophy of bodies in motion, freedom means nothing more than motion without external impediment. By dismissing the scholastic and Cartesian conception of soul on the materialist grounds that there is no immaterial substance, Hobbes reduced reason and will to mere instruments of the passions, most fundamentally

---

[32] See for example, Thomas Aquinas, *On Law, Morality and Politics* 2nd ed. William P. Baumgarth and Richard J. Regan, eds. (Indianapolis: Hackett Publishing, 2002), ST I, q. 79, art. 12, p. 2; ST I-II, q. 95, art. 1, p. 52.

the desire for self-preservation. It was on the basis of his claim for the ontological priority of the passions that Hobbes advanced his argument for the compatibility of liberty and necessity. Liberty amounts to necessity unobstructed by external objects, much as a river is free to run its course within its banks.[33] The scholastic account of moral responsibility was thus unintelligible within the terms of reference established by Hobbesian materialism. There is no natural basis for moral obligation in a world of existent things that are impelled by natural necessity. For Hobbes, the philosophical heavy lifting with respect to moral theory would not be done by any natural phenomena such as innate ideas or will conforming to unerring reason, but rather by conventional agreements and sovereign enforcement power in civil society.

Locke's most important contribution to the free will debate is contained in his heavily revised twenty-first chapter of Book II of the *Essay* entitled "Of Power." In this by far the lengthiest chapter in the entire work, Locke argues that both innatist metaphysics and Hobbesian materialism fundamentally misunderstand and, in different ways, overly constrain human freedom. Not surprisingly, Locke connects liberty to a simple idea, the idea of power (2.7.8.131). Power, he claims, relates to change so that a power is a capacity to make or receive change (2.21.1–2.233–34). The active power to effect change is naturally more a function of reflection than sensation. Thus for Locke, the active power of reflection is not a faculty of will, as the Schools mistakenly identify it, but rather "a power of mind to consider ideas and prefer motion or rest"(2.21.3–5.234–6).

It is on this basis that Locke dismisses the scholastic doctrine of free will as "unintelligible" (2.21.14.240). He insists that the Schools approach the question of freedom from the completely wrong angle. Part of the problem is their conception of soul in which the intellectual faculties are "spoken of as distinct agents" (2.21.20.243). The key question for Locke, which the Schools fail to address, is not whether the faculties such as will are free, "but whether a Man be free" (2.21.21.244). Liberty is a power belonging only to agents and thus is not an attribute of intellectual faculties in any immediate sense. The will cannot direct understanding, because that would mean a power acting on a power in absence of any active agency. For Locke, the act of preferring is an intellectual faculty of mind originating in the agency of substance such that, with respect to human understanding, "it is the mind that operates, and exerts these Powers; it is the Man that does the Action,

---

[33] Hobbes, *Leviathan*, 21.2.136

it is the Agent that has power" (2.21.19.243). The free will doctrine thus totally misconceives the nature of intellectual and moral agency.

From Locke's perspective, Hobbes, unlike the Schools, asks precisely the correct question "Is Man Free?" but reaches the wrong conclusion. In Hobbes' effort to prove that liberty is compatible with necessity, he proposed that all voluntary acts are free but not products of free will.³⁴ With his famous example of desperate passengers throwing their luggage overboard a struggling ship in a storm, Hobbes sought to illustrate that it is not free will but rather the human response to necessity that conditions freedom.³⁵ Individuals are free to do whatever they are not impeded from doing. In response, Locke signaled his break from Hobbes early in Book I of the *Essay* when he criticized those philosophers who deny all freedom to human beings by reducing them to "bare Machines," and thus taking away "not only innate, but all moral rules whatsoever" (1.3.14.76). Locke's ostensibly moral objection to Hobbesian mechanism derives from his argument that there may be volition where there is no liberty. In a memorable illustration of this point, Locke insists that if I am locked in a room with a dear friend I have not seen in years, I may desire to be in the room, but I cannot claim to be free (2.21.10.238).³⁶ Locke contends that voluntary is not opposed to necessity, but rather to involuntary. He concedes that there is a measure of necessity whether to think or not and to act or not, but in response to the objection that the Lockean individual appears to be trapped in the realm of sensory perception, Locke maintains that the capacity to stop or continue thought or action is within the power of a free agent. Hobbes thus exaggerates, and yet at the same time strangely limits, human freedom by placing the emphasis on external impediments. While Locke allows considerable scope to the power of mechanical explanation to account for change in the physical world, he also presents a complex picture of the internal operation of mind that casts doubt on mechanism as the only causal factor in the motion of bodies.³⁷ Locke's theory of the freedom of mind rests on a more sophisticated conception of human subjectivity than we see in Hobbes.

The heart of Locke's theory of the freedom of the human mind is his account of happiness and the suspension of desires. The happiness doctrine

---

³⁴ See Martinich, *Hobbes*, 47–53 and Vere Chappell, "Power in Locke's Essay" in *The Cambrigde Companion to Locke's "Essay Concerning Human Understanding"* Lex Newman, ed. (Cambridge: Cambridge University Press, 2007), p. 142.

³⁵ Hobbes, *Leviathan*, 21.4.137.

³⁶ Chappell, "Power in Locke's *Essay*," 142.

³⁷ For instance, Rogers observes that Locke was open to nonmechanistic accounts of motion such as Newton's theory of gravity ("Intellectual Setting," 16).

represents Locke's reworking of the Hobbesian idea of necessity. Locke admits that there is a basic lack of freedom at the root of human understanding. Individuals are free to act or not, but they are not free to not think or not prefer. While Locke rejects real essences and the doctrine of intelligible substance, there is nonetheless a conception of organic vitalism underlying his epistemology. Human faculties are necessarily activated by pleasure and pain, and it is these two conditions that constitute the materials of happiness. Complete happiness "is the utmost Pleasure we are capable of, and Misery the utmost Pain" (2.21.42.258). As living beings, we cannot but "constantly desire happiness," and are thus naturally drawn to the pleasant and seek to avoid what is painful (2.21.39.257). Locke initially frames this hedonic calculation in distinctly Hobbesian terms as a rejection of the classical idea of a natural *telos* or greatest good to which the human soul is naturally directed. In Locke's Hobbesian-inspired reinterpretation of divine providence, he identifies pleasure and pain as the innate desires, notably not ideas, implanted by God to assist self-preservation (2.7.4.130).[38] Pain has a more powerful impact on mind precisely because it is a better indicator of the dangers to preservation than pleasure is.

The operative principle in Locke's hedonic conception of happiness has both a passionate and an intellectual dimension. Locke maintains that the spur to calculations about happiness is not the rational faculty but rather a feeling of "uneasiness" that anticipates pain and accompanies the absence of a particular pleasure. It is the fundamentally future-regarding character of uneasiness that allows mind to transcend the realm of the immediate given. This is not to suggest that Locke does not admit that unease about pain and pleasure near at hand can, and usually does, trump consideration of distant goods or evils. Locke recognizes this and in the process provides a ready explanation for the problem of error, especially as it helps account for the effect or inefficacy of heaven and hell as motives for action. Indeed, what is notable in Locke's modernized conception of *eudaemonia* is its lack of specific content.[39] This is also a function of Locke's democratization of mind for it is the subjective feelings of individuals – all, in principle, equal – rather than substantive ideas of the good that seem to move the faculty of preferring. However, does that not mean that it is uneasiness, that is to say desire, rather than reason that determines the will?[40] In order

---

[38] See also Grant, *Locke's Liberalism*, 71 and Peter Schouls, *Reasoned Freedom* (Ithaca: Cornell University Press, 1992), p. 149.

[39] Thomas Pangle, *The Spirit of Modern Republicanism* (Chicago: University of Chicago Press, 1988), p. 188, 207.

[40] Schouls, *Reasoned Freedom*, 126–7.

to demonstrate that it is not desire that solely determines choice, Locke has recourse to a power of mind by which the individual avoids complete incorporation into the mechanism of sensation through a complex mental activity that involves the suspension of desires.

Whereas Locke's account of happiness seems indistinguishable from Hobbesian mechanism, it is in his theory of suspension of desire that he departs most dramatically from Hobbes' epistemology. Locke identifies the core of human freedom to be in the power of mind "to suspend the execution and satisfaction of any of its desires, and so all, one after another, is at liberty to consider the objects of them; examine then all sides, and weigh them with others. In this lies the Liberty Man has" (2.21.47.263; 2.21.67.279). It is the rational capacity to "suspend any particular desire" that prevents unease "from determining the will" (2.21.50.266). In contrast to the multifaceted soul of the Schools, Locke's rationalism avoids complete immersion in mechanism precisely by basing the suspension power on an integrated understanding of soul in which discursive reason operates through an active power of mind to exercise judgment about the plethora of ideas that bombard the senses and faculty of reflection. Locke does not, of course, reject the Hobbesian principle of self-preservation, but rather suggests that the interaction of reason and desire produces a more complex mental process than Hobbes allows.

The democratic implications of Locke's suspension theory are in one sense obvious. It reflects a new philosophical approach to freedom emphasizing interiority and thus helps lay the epistemological foundation for Locke's seminal claim that the individual is ultimately responsible for forming his or her own beliefs. In principle the suspension power reflects an egalitarian distribution of capacities and a radically subjective basis for a variety of conceptions of happiness. Individual tastes and preferences replace the classical idea of the good as the proper object of human desire: "the Philosophers of old did in vain inquire, whether *summum bonum* consisted in Riches, or Bodily Delights, or Virtue or Contemplation: And they might have as reasonably disputed whether the best relish were to be found in Apples, Plumbs or Nuts" (2.21.55.269). Suspension is an argument clearly suited to a philosophy of mind that places importance on subjective judgment and uncertain probability rather than ascribing wide range for deductive certainty.

As we have seen, Locke also offers the suspension power and the doctrine of happiness as a way to provide an epistemological account for error in understanding. While Locke insists that mind never mistakes present good and evil, he concedes that it is easy to misjudge the future consequences of present action. Even the promise of eternal happiness can be drowned out by the desire to avoid even a little pain in the present (2.21.60.273). However, this explanation for the possibility of error points beyond the obvious difficulty of establishing the rational basis for religious or moral duty by also opening up Locke's theory to questions about the epistemological status of the suspension power itself.[41] Why, in principle, does the suspension power work well for some people and not for others? Locke's response that intellectual laziness, encouraged by reliance on fashions in thinking and common opinion, obscures judgment suggests that before one is truly free to exercise the suspension power, one must first be aware of it (2.21.69.281). Human beings may have a natural desire for happiness, but we are also apparently disinclined to engage in difficult mental activity, especially when the power to suspend desires and to deliberate is not self-evident or pleasant in itself. Moreover, is the human mind ultimately not still subsumed in the given realm of pleasure and pain, that is to say, does the range of intellectual powers include the capacity to reform or alter one's ideas of the painful and the pleasant? Locke indicates that "in many cases" individuals can "correct their palates through practice" and virtues may be acquired, as are tastes, through "repetition" (2.21.69.280). The ultimate epistemological significance of the suspension power is thus inseparable from the difficulties confronting moral judgment and deliberation about competing ideas of pleasure and pain, good and bad.

THE PROBLEM OF DEMONSTRATIVE MORALITY

Suspension of desires explains the source of human freedom for Locke. However, it does not on its own account for the knowledge of moral principles without which this freedom appears in effect indistinguishable from Hobbesian mechanism. If, as Locke claims, moral knowledge is neither innate nor simply a deduction from the passions, then how does the individual acquire it? Locke raises the epistemological stakes for this issue dramatically when he advances perhaps the most striking claim in the entire *Essay*; namely, that "Morality is capable of demonstration, as well as Mathematicks" (3.11.16.516; 4.3.18.549). In order to understand Locke's argument for the certainty available in moral knowledge and its impact on the democratization of mind, we first need to consider what Locke means by knowledge.

---

[41] For example, Michael Ayers calls this aspect of Locke's theory "incoherent" (*Locke: Epistemology and Ontology* [New York: Routledge, 1993], Vol. I, p. 193).

Locke identified three kinds of knowledge: intuitive, demonstrative, and sensitive. While knowledge in general involves the mind's perception of the agreement or disagreement of ideas, each of the three kinds of knowledge possesses distinct properties. Intuition occurs when the mind perceives the agreement or disagreement between ideas immediately; for example, white is not black (4.2.1.531). Intuition is the root of all knowledge as it is upon intuitive certainty of the connection between the various ideas in a proposition that "all the Certainty and Evidence of all our knowledge" rests (4.2.1.531). Demonstration is less perfect than intuition because it relies on intermediate proofs in which "every step in reasoning produces knowledge [having] intuitive certainty" (4.2.2.532). Demonstration is thus a function of discursive reason exemplified by mathematics wherein general propositions about triangles, for instance, obviate the need to demonstrate the basic properties of each particular triangle. Finally, sensitive knowledge is more certain than probability but is not as complete as demonstration or intuition. Here too, intuition is the base of knowledge inasmuch as our knowledge that the idea we receive from an external object is in our mind is intuitive. Proof that we can know of the "existence of anything without us," Locke derives from the fact that we can discern the difference between the memory of an idea such as fire and the present sensation produced by placing one's hand over an open flame (4.2.14.537–8). The ultimate limitation of sensitive knowledge is that we can only know the idea that a thing produces in our mind; we cannot know the real essence of the thing itself.

Locke first introduced the idea that morality is capable of demonstration in Book I of the *Essay* when he proposed that the definition of justice as the keeping of contracts was self-evident (1.3.1–2.65–66). There his point was to show that the existence of self-evident principles made innate ideas redundant. In the context of Book IV, however, Locke's aim is rather different. Here he means to prove that even though intuition does not directly apply to all areas of inquiry, for example, with respect to speculation about the immortality of soul, nonetheless all the ends of morality can be served through propositions accessible to demonstration. The propositions that "Where there is no Property, there is no Injustice" and that "No Government allows absolute liberty" are as "certain as any in Euclid" (4.3.18.549). Moral ideas are like math in the sense that both involve mixed modes that, in theory, avoid the problem of intermediation between the idea and the reality of things, precisely because they are, in essence, arbitrary constructions of the human mind. Locke observes that the mathematical model is incompatible with the study of existent natural bodies. The elusive real essences of substances lead Locke to suggest that, in contrast to math or morality, "natural Philosophy is not capable of being made a Science" (4.12.10.645). Locke continues that given the limitations of our knowledge of substance, "'tis rational to conclude, that our proper imployment lies in those Enquiries, and in that sort of knowledge, which is most suited to our natural capacities, and carries in it our greatest interest," namely, eternal salvation (4.12.11.646). This is frequently interpreted to mean that Locke contrasted the inevitable mediocrity of natural science with the certainty of moral philosophy.[42] However, it may be wise to avoid jumping to this conclusion too briskly.

When we carefully consider Locke's arguments about the possibilities and limitations of natural science and moral theory respectively, it becomes apparent that Locke believed that moral knowledge is less certain and accessible, and the knowledge of natural bodies more rigorous and expansive, than it first appears in his account. To start, while Locke identifies the acquisition of moral knowledge as the Proper "Business of Mankind," he hastens to add that he "would not therefore be thought to disesteem, or dissuade the study of nature" (4.12.12.647). Morality is the proper business of human beings partly because it is a study suited to an egalitarian distribution of rational capacities, whereas unlocking the "Secrets of Nature" is suited to the "private talent of particular Men" such as the "Master Builders" of modern science like Newton, Boyle, and Sydenham (4.12.11.646, "Epistle" pp. 9–10). The elitist tendencies in the study and practice of natural science do not, of course, diminish the very positive contributions made to human flourishing by scientific advances, and Locke recounts with great aplomb the civilizational significance of the discovery of iron and quinine (4.12.11–2.646–7). Locke's sense of the great potential for advance in natural science is revealed with delightful irony in his comparison between the power of human senses and that of a microscope. At one point, Locke suggests that if only human beings had microscopes for eyes, we would approach the knowledge of substance presumably enjoyed by angels and other intelligent immaterial species (2.23.11–2.301–03).[43] The irony is that, as Locke was well aware, human beings are capable of supersensory perception through the invention of technology like the microscope, and in the

---

[42] See for example John Colman, *John Locke's Moral Philosophy* (Edinburgh: Edinburgh University Press, 1983), pp. 4–5 and Catherine Wilson, "The Moral Epistemology of Locke's Essay" in *The Cambridge Companion to Locke's "Essay Concerning Human Understanding"* (Cambridge: Cambridge University Press, 2007), p. 382.

[43] John Yolton even suggests that Locke entertained the possibility that there is an internal structure of physical bodies from which we could, in due course, build a deductive science of nature (*The Two Intellectual Worlds of John Locke* [Ithaca: Cornell University Press, 2004], p. 27).

hands of a trained professional this device can potentially tell us a great deal about the previously unobservable properties of natural substances.[44] Locke herein even subtly implies the possibility of revolutionizing atomic theory with the discovery of ever more minute subatomic particles.

Locke's presumed pessimism about natural philosophy could thus be seen less as a diminution of natural science vis-à-vis moral philosophy and more likely as a caution that the real promise of natural science not be obscured by the excessive theorizing, and the resultant diminution of the importance of experimental science typical of the scholastic, Cartesian, and Spinozist view of natural philosophy. This complexity in Locke's argument is a function of what he takes to be the multidimensional character of the problem modern philosophy has shown in working out the relation between natural and moral philosophy. The unscientific metaphysics of the Schools and the metaphysical elements of Descartes' new *scientia* stymie natural philosophy by burdening it with unempirical, and essentially theological, assumptions about the order of nature. For its part, the scientific naturalism of Spinoza and, to a lesser extent, Hobbes reduces theology and moral philosophy to being a mere subset of physical science. In both traditional metaphysics and the new science, Locke identifies totalizing tendencies in their philosophic premises that result either in natural science being absorbed into moral philosophy or moral philosophy being swallowed up by a materialistic naturalism. Human freedom is, for Locke, inextricably connected to allowing and encouraging reason to examine nature, morality, and theology on the basis of distinct forms of evidence proper to each endeavor.

In order to maintain separate spheres of knowledge pertaining to moral and natural philosophy, Locke advances the claim that the real problem in understanding the proper relation of natural and moral philosophy lies with the presumptuous metaphysician rather than the humble experimentalist. Locke stresses that there is no perfect science of bodies and thus, with regard to natural science, "Experience here must teach me, what Reason cannot" (4.3.26–29.556–60). By emphasizing the hypothetical character of natural science, Locke neither precludes better and worse judgments of bodies based on empirical observation, nor does he set an absolute predetermined limit to what conclusions experience can validate. However, Locke does

---

[44] Locke was, of course, intimately familiar with the work of the great pioneers of microscopy, Anton von Leeuwenhoek and Robert Hooke, who were acquiring much attention in scientific circles in Locke's time. For Locke's contact with Hooke and Leeuwenhoek, see Roger Woolhouse, *Locke: A Biography*, (Cambridge: Cambridge University Press, 2007), pp. 158, 164, 239.

intend to chasten certain proponents of the modern scientific perspective who believe that the conclusions of natural science can be the basis for a new metaphysical dispensation. In calling on metaphysicians to be wary of overconfidence about a complete science of bodies, Locke in no way intends to discourage experimental science. Even corpuscularianism he offers as a working hypothesis rather than a complete science (4.3.16.547). In Locke's view, natural philosophy may be an endless task, but it is certainly capable of real and tangible advances in understanding.

In addition to observing Locke's perception of the potential advances of natural science, it is also useful to recognize the important qualifications he places on the certainty of moral philosophy. In a crucial passage in chapter twelve of Book IV, Locke restates his famous claim about the demonstrativeness of moral knowledge with the major caveat, "if a right Method were taken, a great part of Morality might be made out with that clearness... of the Truth of Propositions in Mathematics" (4.12.8.643–44). Not only does certainty in morality depend on use of the "right method" for acquiring knowledge, but Locke insists that even then only a "great part," but not all of the rules of morality, can be known with mathematical certainty. The truth of the matter is that in practice, morality is not capable of the degree of certainty possible with mathematical propositions. The epistemological problem produced by language and the difficulties Locke identifies with establishing clear definitions of terms ensures that mathematical truths, unlike morality, need not be "lost in the great wood of words" (4.3.30.561; 2.28.4.351).[45] Were moral philosophy able to replace what Locke rather humorously calls the "prevailing custom" of using words with more clearly defined symbolic representation, it would in theory be possible to approach the certainty of math in a regular way. He even encourages moral philosophers to imitate natural scientists who employ drawings and sketches rather than words to record their observations (3.11.25.522–3). While Locke does not in the *Essay* lay out in detail the proper method of moral demonstration, he does succeed in drawing the reader's attention to the striking parallel between the limitations of moral and natural science. The chief lesson Lockeans can draw from the problems emerging in modern speculative philosophy is to beware overconfidence in the power of words to grasp truth not only about substance but also in moral matters. Locke thus encourages the philosophical study of ethics and morality in order to provide them

---

[45] For an interesting discussion of the problematic effect of Locke's linguistic theory on his account of civil society more generally, see Hannah Dawson, "Locke on Language in (Civil) Society," *History of Political Thought*, Vol. 26, No. 3 (Autumn) 2005, pp. 397–425.

with greater rigor, even as he tries to trim back metaphysical claims that have traditionally accompanied these studies.

The problem, then, that Locke's argument for demonstrative morality is designed to address is how to establish a modest account of philosophy and its goals that eschews metaphysical pretensions without simply reducing philosophy to being a mere adjunct of the natural sciences. Locke insists that philosophy can assist natural science by helping clarify its terms, sorting through its theoretical confusions, and making its practitioners aware of the limitations in the way in which the human mind represents the world in thought and language. However, Locke hardly displays philosophical naiveté about the capacity for natural science to provide access to issues of ultimate political, moral, and theological concern.

In order to appreciate the high stakes for political life involved in Locke's argument for demonstrative morality, it is perhaps helpful to briefly consider a key element of his natural rights teaching. In the course of his seminal account of the state of nature, Locke adduced two discrete arguments to support the moral principle of natural equality. First, he claims that there "is nothing more evident, than that Creatures of the same Species" sharing all the same faculties "should also be equal one amongst another without Subordination or Subjection" (II: 4). Second, Locke maintains that human equality is also grounded on the fact that we are "all the Workmanship of one Omnipotent, and infinitely wise Maker," who furnished us "with like Faculties," and did not establish any natural subordination among human beings (II: 6). Thus, human membership in a common species and the existence of a creator God seem to be foundational for Locke's moral and political philosophy. But are the concepts of species and the existence of God supported by Locke's account of natural science and epistemology in the *Essay*?

The idea of species was central in scholastic metaphysics as one of key logical categories for defining natural sorts or kinds of things. The assumption of scholastic moral philosophy was that the human being is a certain kind of substance with a distinct ontological status. For the Schools, we can speak with certainty about the moral properties of human beings because we are part of an intelligible natural order composed of distinct species of things.[46] In the *Essay*, Locke attacks this traditional cornerstone

---

[46] Locke's use of the term "species" in the *Second Treatise* perhaps shows the pervasiveness of scholastic categories at least in the rhetoric of his natural rights philosophy. For a good discussion of the problem of harmonizing Locke's idea of equality with the traditional notion of species, see Jeremy Waldron, *God, Locke and Equality* (Cambridge: Cambridge University Press, 2002), pp. 53–68.

of scholastic metaphysics on several fronts. First, in keeping with his general assessment of the problem of language, Locke argues that while nature may admit of observable resemblances among things, the names of species are purely conventional due to the arbitrariness of words. The deeper problem with the common idea of species has to do with the ineluctable character of real essences. The awareness of the distinction between the real and nominal essence of substances includes implicitly accepting that even observable resemblances are irreducibly provisional, and thus a realistic assessment of natural kinds must tend toward an astonishing proliferation of species: "each abstract idea with a name to it, makes a distinct species" (3.6.38.463). Locke's radically particularist ontology rejects the traditional notion of species because it undermines the conception of essences upon which natural species depends: "it is absurd to ask, whether a thing really existing, wanted anything else to it" (3.6.5.441). Moreover, as the distinction between kinds of dogs, such as a "Shock and a Hound," clearly suggests, nominal species are subject to internal modification through breeding (3.6.38.463).[47] Simply put, species are artificial categories with no relation to the real essences of natural things.

For Locke, the problem of essentializing species is particularly acute for morality with respect to efforts to define the human species. Throughout the *Essay*, Locke examines a number of definitions of the human being in order to answer the question: Who or what is a human being to whom one has moral obligations? A number of these fairly standard definitions emphasize reason as the defining characteristic of what it means to be human. For instance, Locke raises the possibility that it is the power of abstraction that most clearly distinguishes humans from the "Brutes" (2.11.11.160). He also considers the definition of human as a "corporeal rational creature" or a "Forensic term" applied to a rational being capable of obeying certain moral laws (3.11.16.516; 2.27.26.346). These various definitions share the traditional philosophical premise held since Aristotle that the species human is defined by rationality.

At no point does Locke simply accept the rationalist basis of human identity *tout court*. Indeed, he ruthlessly exposes the deeply inegalitarian potentialities of the traditional celebration of reason by claiming that given the considerable range of intellectual capacities within humanity, it can be the basis for a massive system of exclusion. He suggests that for most

---

[47] In this respect Locke's idea about the fluidity and inherent instability in the concept of species clearly foreshadows Darwin's account, although Locke does not of course identify anything like the notion of natural selection.

people, it is body shape rather than rational faculties that determines membership in the human species. For most people, a severely mentally defective human is "a dull irrational Man," but a bird that can hold a conversation is still just "a very intelligent rational Parrot" (2.27.8.333). Locke's point is not to denigrate the view of the common person vis-à-vis the educated elites. Rather he suggests that there is some sense in the common view emphasizing body shape. The thrust of Locke's account of species is to show that the philosophical attempt to define natural kinds is much more difficult than typically supposed. The many debates about the moral status of "naturals," "changelings," and fetal monstrosities are, in Locke's view, reflections of the fact that each of these beings with its own "particular constitution" belies the rigid scholastic categories of species (3.6.16–7.448–9). For Locke, from what we do know about the nature of substance, which is of course very little, we can at least say conclusively that rationality is not the whole essence of human.

Locke's treatment of species indicates that our ignorance of substance is a problem for our understanding of morality. The human being is both substance and mixed mode at the same time, and thus with regards to the internal constitution of the human we can only have limited insights.[48] To define the human simply on the basis of *logos* as it has been traditionally understood is to open moral philosophy to a dogmatic and unscientific inegalitarianism. However, to identify the human simply on the basis of external sensible resemblances is also potentially to allow for a massive system of exclusion based on the most superficial features (4.7.16.607). Locke's epistemology thus seems to discredit the whole logic of natural species precisely because there is no way to establish demonstrative certainty about the essence of the human: "None of the definitions of the word Man, which we yet have, nor descriptions of that sort of Animal, are so perfect and exact, as to satisfy a considerate inquisitive person much less to obtain a general consent" (3.6.27.455). Locke does not mean by this that moral philosophy is doomed to intellectual paralysis. As we shall see in the following chapter, Locke's natural rights teaching in the *Two Treatises* builds upon and broadens his skepticism about natural species with the clear intention of establishing a minimalist standard of inclusion in the human race as the automatic default position anchoring the basis of human equality. Locke's point, however, here in the *Essay* is that terms like species have often been used hitherto to "darken truth and unsettle People's Rights" (3.10.13.497).

---

[48] Yolton (*Locke's Two Intellectual Worlds*, 21–4) sees this duality as a distinction between a secular "self" and a moral "person."

Presumably the "considerate inquisitive person," who understands the distorting effects of the essentialist tendencies in traditional moral and natural philosophy, will recognize that politics, at its core, involves adjudicating the various claims of nature in a civil context.

While Locke's account of the problem of species points away from the quasi-biological ethics of the Aristotelian scholastics, it is not species but rather his proof of the existence of God that gets to the heart of his claim that morality is capable of demonstration.[49] Early in Book I of the *Essay*, Locke introduced an important voluntarist element into his account of morality by suggesting that "the only true ground" of morality is a God "who sees Men in the dark, [and] has in his Hand Rewards and Punishments" (1.3.6.19). Thus the moral idea of the human as a being subject to law ultimately seems to depend upon knowledge of the existence of the divine "Law Maker" (2.28.5.351). The hedonic calculations operative in Locke's suspension theory of human freedom thus hinges on two things: the existence of a God who rewards and punishes, and evidence that each individual human being, as opposed to a collective idea of the species, is accountable in the future for his or her present acts.

Locke prefaces his argument for the proof of the existence of God with a prior account of the knowledge of one's own existence. Knowledge of one's own existence, Locke claims, is intuitive as it neither needs nor is capable of proofs and yet is capable of the "highest degree of certainty" (4.9.3.619). In contrast to the radical skepticism that produced Descartes' formulation of the *res cogens*, Locke appeals to knowledge rooted in an individual's own experience. Not only do I know that "I think, I reason," but I also know with certainty that I also "feel pleasure and pain" (4.9.3.618). The first pangs of hunger assuage the existential doubts of even the most committed skeptic. Notably, Locke's account of the intuitive knowledge of one's own existence ascribes enormous cognitive significance to sensible experience for it is sensory perception rather than complex mental activity that makes us "conscious to ourselves of our own being" (4.9.3.619; 4.10.2.619–20).

Early in Book I of the *Essay*, Locke denies the existence of innate ideas about God's existence, but in Book IV he exhibits confidence that application of rational faculties can lead one to knowledge of God. This knowledge is not intuitive, strictly speaking. It is rather a demonstration arising from certain deductions on the basis of intuitive knowledge. The two central arguments proving the existence of God derive from our intuitive knowledge that nothing comes from nothing and that "incogitative

---

49 Ayers, *Locke*, Vol. II, p. 188.

matter" cannot produce a thinking being (4.10.3.620; 4.10.10.623). Locke does not explain in this account of matter the tension between his general assumption that substance is unknowable because of limited human cognitive capacities and his specific claim in this context that matter is not absolutely indeterminate, and thus matter cannot now or ever have possessed attributes unobservable to us, such as cogitative power. Locke also does not explain how this logical demonstration of God's existence and "omniscience" proves God's goodness or concern for us (4.10.12.625). Recall that it is a providential God who rewards and punishes in the Afterlife that Locke identifies as the ultimate guarantor for any theory of moral obligation. But of this God capable of demonstration, Locke can only conclude that we "cannot comprehend the Operations of that eternal infinite Mind" (4.10.19.630). Perhaps most problematically, nothing in Locke's demonstration of the existence of God indicates how human beings are meant to know the particulars of the natural moral law. Locke's assurance in Book I that we have "light enough" to know our moral duty is hardly advanced by his discussion of the existence of God in Book IV. For if moral ideas are mixed modes detached from nature but, unlike geometrical forms, depend on the existence of a being who rewards and punishes, and whose nature is elusive or beyond human comprehension (unlike presumably a triangle), then on what basis can we know that our moral ideas are suitable standards or guides of human conduct?[50] Locke thus leaves open the distinct possibility that the most important matters of religion and morality are not capable of demonstrative knowledge, but rather are matters pertaining to judgment, probability, and ultimately of faith.

Even many of those in Locke's original audience who were sympathetic to his general argument expressed surprise and disappointment that his proof of the existence of God was not followed by a substantive account of the particulars of the law of nature.[51] Instead, Locke's demonstration of God's existence in effect introduces a lengthy treatment of the grounds

---

[50] Grant, *Locke's Liberalism*, 37.

[51] See for instance the responses of William Molyneux and James Tyrrell. Locke's old friend Tyrrell complained to him after reading the first edition of the *Essay*: "it is likewise to be doubted by some whether the rewards and punishments that you mentioned can be demonstrated as established by your divine law" (repeated in Locke's letter to Tyrrell, August 4, 1690 in the Lovelace Collection ms Locke c. 24, fos. 277–78). Locke's response along the lines that there are probably millions of propositions in mathematics that have not yet been demonstrated, but may be in the future – thus too for moral propositions – would we suspect hardly have been encouraging to Tyrrell and others. For Molyneux's difficulties with Locke's demonstrative morality, see Nidditch's "Foreword" to Locke, *An Essay Concerning Human Understanding*, p. xx.

of belief short of knowledge. It turns out that "the proper business of Mankind" has to do largely with forms of mental activity that produce results far below the degree of certain knowledge. Probability is the term Locke uses to describe the rational faculty supplied by God to assist where knowledge cannot be had (4.15.3.653). Knowledge requires intuitive certainty about the connection between ideas, but "in belief not so" (4.15.3.655). Reason here examines the grounds of probable connections among ideas, but it does not achieve certainty. The practical significance of probability logically rises as the expectations about the range of things capable of knowledge narrows. As Locke admits: "our knowledge is so narrow" that it is inevitable that the "greatest part of Men, if not all," must have diverse opinions about crucial areas of morality without certain proof of truth (4.16.4.659). Probabilism thus has a similar function in Locke's account of morality as the role experimentalism plays in his treatment of substance.

The parallel between probabilism in morality and hypothesis in experimental science is, however, complicated by Locke's account of faith, which practically concludes the *Essay*. Faith is an assent to any proposition not deduced from reason, but rather "upon the credit of the proposer as coming from God," and thus has no direct analog in Locke's account of natural science (4.18.2.689). Resting as it appears on revelation, faith is distinct from both knowledge and probability. It is not, however, severed from reason. Locke even asserts that "Reason is Natural Revelation" and must be "our last Judge and Guide in everything" (4.19.4.698). Reason assists faith by helping determine both what is proper to faith, namely, what is not directly contrary to "clear intuitive knowledge," and by determining what is and is not, properly speaking, revelation (4.18.5.692). If properly understood, reason operative in faith is particularly self-conscious of its own natural limits but, unlike reason in natural science, it does not expect confirmation by observable empirical evidence.

Locke's account of probability and faith deepens the process of democratizing mind. In his assessment of the egalitarian distribution of natural intellectual faculties, all individuals are, in principle, capable of reflecting on "matters of Religion" because "God has furnished them with Faculties sufficient to direct them in the way they should take" (4.20.3.708). Locke presents his account of the epistemological grounds of faith with its various degrees of assent as an antidote to the twin problems of dogmatism and "enthusiasm;" that is to say, to elites wedded to dubious theological principles, on the one hand, and fanatics who wish to expunge all reason from religion, on the other.[52] The individual as individual, according to Locke, faces no inherent epistemological obstacle to forming judgments about religion and morality independently of authoritative institutions, and given the high stakes of soteriological concerns, the motivation to subject revelation to rational examination is self-evident. Despite the clear conceptual distinction between knowledge and belief, it would not be completely misleading to conclude that, for Locke, religion and morality are, when properly understood, philosophical activity for the masses.

In one sense, Locke's account of demonstrative morality in the *Essay* appears to be hamstrung by the problems relating to the nominal character of species and the difficulty in demonstrating the voluntarist dimension of divine support for the moral law. This difficulty is resolved at least partially if we accept that Locke conceived of demonstrative morality in two senses.[53] First, there is the weaker version of moral demonstration, according to which Locke emphasizes the certainty that is produced by the perception of agreement between ideas. If the connection between the discrete ideas forming a moral concept such as homicide or adultery can be demonstrated through logical steps by means of "intervening Proofs," then in a sense we are capable of acquiring "real knowledge" of morality, in addition to mathematics (4.2.4.532, 4.4.7.565). However, as is true of any mixed mode, this is largely a formal demonstration with no necessary connection to a real pattern or archetype in nature, and thus the normative character of the moral idea remains still somewhat murky. A second sense of moral demonstration would involve a stronger version of the argument. This would require establishing a potentially quite lengthy chain of rational deductions directly connecting the ideas contained in a moral concept to an ultimate source of obligation. This version of moral demonstration would theoretically deal with the problem of normativity by positing a God who rewards and punishes in the afterlife, but this brings us back to the difficulties raised by probability and faith that we have already encountered. Perhaps all we can really conclude is that the *Essay* does not seem to resolve the matter definitively either way, and we will need to turn to Locke's other mature writings for further clarification.

---

[52] James Tully argues persuasively that Locke's doctrine of assent was designed to deal with the problem of religious conflict in post-Reformation Europe ("Governing Conduct," in *An Approach to Political Philosophy: Locke in Contexts* [Cambridge: Cambridge University Press, 1993], p. 184).

[53] For thoughtful discussions about the ambiguity in Locke's conception of demonstrative morality, see Greg Forster, *John Locke's Politics of Moral Consensus* (Cambridge: Cambridge University Press, 2005), pp. 97–100 and Nicholas Wolterstorff, *John Locke and the Ethics of Belief* (Cambridge: Cambridge University Press, 1996), pp. 142–8.

However, Locke's epistemology perhaps offers some basis for a conception of demonstrative morality that is at once more modest than the stronger version above and yet has more normative force than the weaker formal version of demonstration. While a detailed account of the particulars of the law of nature is elusive in the *Essay*, we may find in Locke's theory of personal identity potential support for both a naturalistic and a theological account of moral obligation. Locke insists that the self must be aware of itself as a distinct being extending in secular reality to the past, present, and future in order for the punitive aspect of demonstrative morality to make any sense whatsoever. One's present self and one's future self must be the same person with an identity not dependent on being annexed to the same continuous substance, if punishment is to play any meaningful role in judgments about moral obligation (2.27.10.336; 2.27.16.340).[54] In contrast to traditional notions of immaterial soul, Locke argues that self-consciousness is an epiphenomenon of both understanding and sensation, and thus the concept of personal identity suggests possibilities for other forms of moral reasoning apart from rational demonstration; ones that could involve judgment based on empirical evidence.

At the very least, Locke maintains that the mental activity involved in considering part of the world to be oneself is a form of intellectual awareness capable of intuitive knowledge, in other words, the proof of one's own existence. This allows intuitive knowledge, not probability or faith, that two individuals are the same person if the actions of one are the most direct potential source for pleasure and pain for the other.[55] Personal identity and self-consciousness are a potentially promising epistemological foundation for Locke's theory of human freedom. On the most basic cognitive level, the thinking thing that suspends its desires in order to form judgments must be self-conscious of the connection between present action and future pleasure and pain in this life or the Afterlife. While Locke does not go so far in the *Essay* as to suggest that his treatment of self-conscious personal identity is the basis for reconstructing a new taxonomy of the human to replace the problematic account of species, self-consciousness does at least support an egalitarian conception of reason that may provide some new ground for speaking meaningfully about the "Forensic Term" defining the human person (2.27.26.346). Moreover, self-conscious personal identity promises at least the theoretical possibility of doing so without recourse to

---

[54] Gideon Yaffe, "Locke on Ideas of Identity and Diversity" in *The Cambridge Companion to Locke's "Essay Concerning Human Understanding"* Lex Newman, ed. (Cambridge: Cambridge University Press, 2007), p. 194.

[55] Yaffe usefully terms this Locke's "Susceptibility to Pain Theory" of personal identity ("Locke on Identity and Diversity," 225).

philosophically dubious doctrines of soul and grand metaphysical systems. Whether Locke succeeds in producing a philosophically rigorous account of personal identity that can support the considerable conceptual burden placed on it by the requirements of Locke's moral philosophy will be a question that we will return to in later chapters.

PHILOSOPHY AND POLITICS: DEMOCRATIZATION OF MIND

Locke's assault on the philosophical tradition of metaphysics raises a number of important questions with respect to his conception of the relation between philosophy and politics. While many recent commentators correctly refuse to follow Laslett's reading that the *Essay* and the *Treatises* are incompatible, Locke's account of moral knowledge in the *Essay* is sufficiently ambiguous to invite caution about asserting the precise nature of the relation between his epistemology and his moral theory.[56] Although much more will be said on this matter in the following chapters, it is clear on the basis of our analysis of Locke's way of ideas that there is neither an irreconcilable chasm nor a smooth, seamless connection between Locke's philosophic and political works. The disjunction between Locke's empiricist epistemology and his rights-based moral theory, which Laslett correctly highlights, not only reflects a source of tension between the *Essay* and the *Treatises*, but also, as we have seen, exposes a fundamental ambiguity within the argument of the *Essay* itself. The *Essay* raises the possibility of demonstrating moral truth while simultaneously showing the extreme difficulty of doing so. Locke's commitment to the possibility of a law of nature discernible by human reason in part flows out of the epistemology in the *Essay*, even as his ontological premises seem to make demonstrating moral truth, as opposed to validating probability or faith, practically prohibitive.

The problem of harmonizing Locke's professed ambitions for moral philosophy with his caution regarding the possibility for acquiring moral knowledge suggests that there is a connection between his philosophy and political theory, but it is not the connection we might expect. Locke's political commitment to natural rights is grounded in the process we have termed the democratization of mind, not so much as this new philosophical dispensation supplies a substantive moral doctrine, but rather primarily with respect to the critical process of dismantling expansive and, Locke argues, unfounded claims to knowledge physical, moral, and theological that characterizes the *Essay* as a whole. The "ground clearing" nature of Locke's

---

[56] For Laslett's argument for the incompatibility of Locke's epistemology and his natural jurisprudence, as well as recent studies that depart from this position, see this chapter n. 1.

philosophical activity is directed against all manner of metaphysical tendencies in philosophy and thus limns the features of a new and more modest conception of philosophy. This narrow definition of philosophy does not, however, reduce it to being a mere adjunct to the empirical sciences. The democratization of mind includes considerable ambitions for the role that Locke's philosophic method can play in developing a new, substantive conception of politics and morality. The political order flowing from these philosophical premises would encourage experimental natural science based on mechanistic hypotheses, while advancing moral philosophy rooted in the intellectual autonomy of the self-conscious individual, rather than theologically charged and philosophically controversial ideas of soul.

In the Lockean vision of philosophy framed by the parallel atomisms of corpuscularianism in natural science and of self-conscious individual identity in moral philosophy, the self shorn of the comforting doctrine of substance is a being capable of awareness of its own existence on the basis of intuitive knowledge and of a future life only conceivable on the basis of a recognition of the limits of human knowledge. It is for this reason that attempts to stress the theological foundation of Locke's rights philosophy to the absolute exclusion of a secular basis of morality are often misplaced.[57] What we can glean from Locke's epistemology is that the *sine qua non* of demonstrative morality is some notion of the self-conscious identity of a being subject to reward and punishment in the future, whether in this life or the next. Locke's epistemology demonstrates only that there is no certain way to exclude the possibility of a theological foundation for morality. It does not demonstrate that a theological foundation is the only possible ground for morality. One important, but often ignored, feature of Locke's epistemology is his willingness in the *Essay* to entertain the plausibility of both the theological and secular basis for morality.[58] The democratization of mind with its effort to narrow the definition of what constitutes knowledge and its simultaneous attempt to broaden our conception of the subjective intellectual processes involved in belief formation lays these parallel secular and theological tracks running through the heart of Locke's moral philosophy. The probabilistic thrust of Locke's democratic epistemology in the *Essay* ensures that the constant, if not always harmonious, coexistence

---

[57] See for instance Waldron 2002, pp. 81–2 and John Dunn's influential *The Political Thought of John Locke* (Cambridge: Cambridge University Press, 1969) both of which suggest that Locke's political philosophy cannot be understood in any sense as a secular teaching.

[58] Two commentators who do clearly observe this duality in Locke's argument are Grant, *Locke's Liberalism*, 38–9 and Michael Zuckert, "Locke – Religion – Equality" *Review of Politics*, Vol. 67, No. 3 (Summer) 2005: 430–1.

of rationalist moral philosophy and theology on the one hand and empirical science on the other would be an important element in Locke's vision of modernity.

Locke's account of the philosophical problem in arriving at demonstrative moral knowledge thus needs to be understood in the context of his concern about the more fundamental problem of metaphysics. Examination of the perplexities produced by the difficulty of proving moral rules with demonstrative certainty is the "proper business" of philosophy, whereas metaphysical system building is the fatal disease of philosophy old and new. The democratization of mind aims to make metaphysics as traditionally conceived unintelligible, as it frames the limits of human understanding within a range set by "substratum" or substance, on the one hand, and the supernatural or "superstratum," on the other; between the mysterious properties of the blade of grass and the incomprehensible operation of the "eternal infinite Mind" of Almighty God. Locke thus belies Weber's famous contention that modernity is essentially a process of demystification for in the complex double-movement of Locke's philosophy, both substance and supernature are simultaneously rationalized and problematized.[59] Substance is demystified by the possibilities of experimental science, even as Locke demolishes the doctrine of essences once thought to be the source of intelligibility in nature. Locke's natural theology demystifies the supernatural by subjecting miracles, prophecy, and revelation to rational scrutiny, while at the same time validating diverse beliefs about God, soul, and the Afterlife on the basis of probability and recognition of the impossibility of reaching certain demonstrative truth in these matters.

By strengthening the epistemological claims of what can be known, while simultaneously limiting the scope of knowledge as opposed to belief, Locke presents a vision of modernity that is intrinsically sectarian and pluralistic because he reduces what is distinctively modern to the product of individual subjectivity.[60] The deep ambiguity here, of course, is that self-consciousness is on one level a nonsectarian concept, a new intellectual substratum as it were, upon which various conceptions of happiness and soteriological concerns may be supported independently from authoritative statements of speculative philosophy. However, as Wolterstorff correctly observes, while Locke was deeply concerned with the cultural fragmentation in post-Reformation Europe, the political implications of his democratization of mind ensured

[59] See Nicholas Wolterstorff's good discussion about Weber's influence on contemporary critics of Locke such as Charles Taylor (*John Locke and the Ethics of Belief* [Cambridge: Cambridge University Press, 1996], pp. 233–5).
[60] Wolterstorff, *Ethics of Belief*, 231.

that fundamental philosophical and religious differences are neither excluded nor even minimized in Locke's conception of liberal society.[61] Indeed, they are transformed by being cut adrift from the metaphysical doctrines that support them, and in this sense Locke contributes to cultural fragmentation, even as he tried to regulate rather than minimize its effects. By deemphasizing metaphysics while accentuating the political relevance of moral ideas that potentially can be clearly defined and tested against the standard of demonstrative knowledge, Locke contrasts the narrow range of moral certainties with the welter of great unknowns about which one cannot speak definitively because of the limits of human cognitive capacities. The terms of demonstrative morality are thus epistemologically constrained, but it is not thereby a static concept, because Locke suggests that a great deal of what we can know about politics and morality can be deduced from the internal operation of the human mind of which Locke claims we are only just beginning to be aware. The first crucial step, then, in the democratization of mind involves redirecting philosophy from constructing metaphysical systems and refocusing it on examining the workings of the human mind.

The primary aim of the *Essay* is thus not to formulate a new moral theory but rather to establish a new definition of philosophy. The central dynamic in Locke's epistemology driven by the twin forces of nominalism and particularist ontology is therefore a reflection of two distinct facets of the democratization of mind. Locke's argument for the particularity of every existent thing understood independently of any natural *telos* or hierarchy shatters the ontological foundation of traditional metaphysics. With the nominalist conception of the self as a being with the mental power to construct and validate expressions of moral truth, Locke makes the individual human mind the central unit of philosophical analysis. The conjunction of the destruction of metaphysics and the construction of the self produces a new and more compact definition of philosophy than hitherto existed. Prior to Locke, philosophy was comprehensive and synthetic, encompassing mathematics, physics, and theology as well as logic and ethics. In the *Essay*, we perhaps see the genesis of modern analytical philosophy in Locke's reduction of the scope of philosophy to its proper, more modest "underlabourer" role of clarifying terms and concepts in service of philosophy of mind, language, ethics, and moral and political philosophy.

Locke's understanding of the corrective or, as Rogers describes it, "therapeutic" function of philosophy requires two things.[62] First, Locke follows

---

[61] Wolterstorff, *Ethics of Belief*, 4–8.
[62] Rogers, "Intellectual Setting," 30.

Descartes by focusing on determining sound methods and procedures for the operation of mind. Second, and most fundamentally, Locke's new, more modest philosophy requires, in contrast to Descartes, that both natural science and theology avoid being absorbed into philosophy. Philosophy can contribute to these studies in the manner proper to it, but it must abandon its traditional pretensions to being the master science of all knowledge. The effect of the democratization of mind on philosophy is to make it both more modest and yet, in Locke's view, more important. It is modest in the sense that Locke's philosophy greatly reduces the scope for claims of certainty in comparison to the theology of the Schools and Descartes' expansive ambitions for the new *scientia*. Locke's new idea of philosophy, however, also promises to be more foundational than prior philosophy inasmuch as the intellectual methods he describes are applicable to the beliefs of all individuals. In his attempt to provide a rational basis for belief, judgment, and faith, Locke elevated the philosophical significance of opinion, or *doxa*, to a level arguably not seen in the western tradition since the Platonic Socrates.

The impact of this new direction in modern philosophy on the political realm is obviously considerable. Freeing the philosophy of mind from the deadweight of metaphysical controversies has the indirect effect of liberating analysis of the political realm from the smothering grasp of speculative philosophy. By making philosophy conceptually more compact, Locke leaves political life both less supported by metaphysical doctrines and yet at the same time more independent as it is less enmeshed in divergent interpretations of being. In the range between substratum and superstratum, Locke carves out an epistemological zone of relative freedom for mind to operate in a realm of ideas embracing both certainty and probability. Locke insists that both the extreme skepticism in the spirit of experimental natural science and the soteriological concerns of dogmatic theology need to be distinguished from the moral and ethical requirements of political life, which necessarily involves judgments about the many matters of importance that resist deductive certainty.[63] Moral and political philosophy freed from the claims to certainty advanced by both dogmatic theology and scientific naturalism need not lead to either intellectual paralysis or the reduction of philosophy to being a mere adjunct of the empirical sciences.

Locke's claim for demonstrative morality raises the expectation that law and government can be constructed on a rational basis, even as his epistemology shows the extreme difficulty involved in this. Sectarian divisions over morality have no real parallel in mathematics. However, Locke indicates that moral ideas and substance, while always distinct, are nonetheless

---

[63]   Grant, *Locke's Liberalism*, 48–9.

connected in the broader probabilistic and fallibilistic framework that is political life. For instance, Locke's attack on the traditional notion of species prepares the way for the logic of rights to replace the ethical theory of Aristotle and the Schools by suggesting that there is much we can learn about moral ideas through empirical observation – in this case, the inadequacy of the regnant ideas about human being. As both a moral idea and a substance, it is impossible to isolate the moral idea of the human from the experience of being human. As Wilson observes, for Locke, the kind of intellectual method required to understand political phenomena is not only analytical, but also, in many respects, observational and experimental.[64] Politics, then, necessarily involves the challenge of harmonizing the moral and the material.

The kind of politics, the distinctly modern politics, which flows from the democratization of mind is the central theme of the chapters that follow. However, on the basis of our analysis of the *Essay*, we are perhaps in a good position to adumbrate a few of the key elements we will examine. Most commentators find Locke's politics to be of a decidedly realist variety. They tend to point to what they perceive to be his conservative views on religion and monarchy, his presumed class bias and apologetics for nascent bourgeois capitalism, or his supposed pessimism about the prospects for general enlightenment.[65] There is certainly something to the argument for Locke's pragmatism. Indeed, his contention that most of the major moral controversies that plague peoples and governments can be safely considered as matters admitting of only probability and contestable judgment is definitely designed to be an antidote to a certain kind of doctrinaire politics. However, even this realist call for partisans to acknowledge their "mutual ignorance" serves what was at the time the radical political agenda to encourage a spirit of humility and toleration of dissenting opinions (4.16.4.660). Admittedly, Locke's emphasis on the limits of certain knowledge reflects a kind of realism, but it is one with a progressive internal logic that is often overlooked. Rejection of metaphysics should not be confused with philosophical or political conservatism. For Locke, speculative doctrines about a fixed natural order, or even fixed rules of motion, over-determine and constrain politics insofar as political knowledge is thought

---

[64] Wilson, "Moral Epistemology," 403.

[65] See for instance Jonathan Israel, *Enlightenment Contested: Philosophy, Modernity and the Emancipation of Man 1670–1752* (Oxford: Oxford University Press, 2006), pp. 52, 60; C. B. McPherson, *The Political Theory of Possessive Individualism* (Oxford: Oxford University Press, 1962), chapter V; Wood, *Politics of Locke's Philosophy*, pp. 6–7; and Steven Forde, "What does Locke Expect us to Know?" *Review of Politics*, Vol. 68, No. 1 (2006), pp. 234.

to be simply deductions from substantive general principles of first philosophy. In his rejection of traditional dogmatic philosophy, Locke envisions a fundamentally critical stance toward political and social institutions in a progressive spirit akin to natural science. The natural rights theory of Locke's political writings is at root the product of his effort to articulate the nascent moral and political realities emerging from this new philosophical dispensation. Locke herein invests venerable juridical terms like right or *jus* with new meaning supplied by an evolving conception of the possibilities for human knowledge.

In a fundamental sense, Locke's conservative critics from the past, such as Blackstone and Hume who railed against his "abstract" and "visionary" political philosophy, were more accurate readers of Locke than many modern commentators.[66] Locke's progressive tendencies extend beyond merely exhibiting a near total lack of sentimentality toward political and moral traditions. The emphasis on logical rigor and reducing propositions to simple ideas that characterizes his epistemology translates in the context of his political, religious, and educational writings into a spirit of inquiry according to which traditional institutions and authoritative doctrines are subject to the kind of critical examination exemplified in the *Essay*. As we shall see in what follows, in Locke's mature writings, the prevailing ideas about the individual, constitutional government, the family, education, the churches, and international relations are ruthlessly reexamined in light of the new philosophical understanding of what can be known and what forms the basis of judgments about better and worse modal constructions. With the democratization of mind, Locke sought to uncover new possibilities for improved understanding of things political, as the intellectual capacities of the self-conscious individual reflecting on the external world and the internal operation of mind provide the source of this improvement. In the next chapter, we will continue our consideration of Locke's modern politics by examining his most foundational political concept and perhaps the most famous of all Lockean mixed modes: the state of nature.

66 See for example, William Blackstone's criticism of "theoretical writers" such as Locke in the *Commentaries on the Laws of England*, Volume I (London, 1791), pp. 43–8, 152, 161–2 and David Hume's condemnation of the state of nature as "a mere philosophical fiction" in *A Treatise of Human Nature* (Oxford: Clarendon Press, 1967), pp. 493–4, 501. For good accounts of Hume's critique of Locke's philosophical partisanship in the radical Whig cause, see Paul Rahe, "John Locke's Philosophical Partisanship," *Political Science Reviewer*, Vol. 20 (1991): 1–43 and H. T. Dickinson, *Liberty and Property*, (London: Weidenfeld and Nicolson, 1977), p. 137.

2

The State of Nature

Perhaps no single idea is more deeply ingrained in the psyche of liberalism than the political and moral salience of the "individual." In this respect, John Locke is often regarded as perhaps the preeminent founder of liberalism for to many it is in the account of the state of nature in Locke's *Second Treatise* that modernity was first introduced to the natural rights-bearing, pre-civil individual who made possible the liberal civic person "constituted by moral sovereignty over one's core beliefs and practices."[1]

Yet the state of nature motif also presents something of a paradox for those trying to understand the individualist premises of Locke's political theory. On the one hand, the state of nature is a decidedly abstract account of the rights of the generic individual in a pre-civil condition, and as such looks like a compendium of purely formal logical deductions from a set of distinct moral propositions. On the other hand, Locke presents this theoretical account as the philosophical basis of individual rights, such as the right to own property and the right to rebel against government, that have enormous practical significance in virtually any conceivable form of political life. It is this combination of theory and practice, abstraction and contextualization, that makes the state of nature concept at once so central to Locke's political teaching and yet so difficult to grasp.

This chapter will suggest that in order to understand the meaning of Locke's use of the state of nature concept, we need to recognize its connection as a modal construction with his epistemology in the *Essay Concerning Human Understanding*. The state of nature is only fully intelligible as a feature of the democratization of mind. In a striking parallel, just as Locke

---

[1] James Tully, *An Approach to Political Philosophy* (Cambridge: Cambridge University Press, 1993), p. 53.

made the rational and sensory faculties of the individual the epistemological basis of judgment and belief formation on the philosophical level, similarly does he posit the individual functionally reduced to the use of his or her own faculties alone as the intellectual origin of government and society. The state of nature thus plays a dual role for Locke. First, it serves as a mixed mode *par excellence*. Unlike simple or complex ideas, which depend on their conformity to a natural archetype in the substantial realm, the state of nature is a modal idea that is primarily a construction of mind. Like any mixed mode, the state of nature bears some relation to the reality behind the simple ideas from which it is constructed. This is why Locke insists that the state of nature is not a philosophical fantasy. The state of nature recurs for Locke as a concept of great valence in a variety of contexts, many of them with clear practical application. Insofar as the idea of the human being combines elements of both a moral concept and the properties of physical substance, any theoretical device employed to explain or describe the rights of such a being could hardly do without a considerable degree of conceptual flexibility. Thus in order to understand the state of nature as a political concept, Locke indicates that we must refer back to the intellectual source of this mixed mode in the properties of the human mind.

The state of nature also, however, plays a more specific role in Locke's continuous efforts to grapple with the problem of moral knowledge that was introduced but left largely unresolved in the *Essay*. As we have seen, the *Essay* tantalized the reader with the possibility of achieving demonstrative moral knowledge as certain as the truths of mathematics, but Locke conspicuously neglected to provide any such demonstration. Ruth Grant has helpfully suggested that understanding the relation between the *Essay* and the *Two Treatises* can assist us in this regard. She suggests that whereas the former work lays out the epistemological conditions necessary to acquire demonstrative knowledge, it is only in the latter political works that Locke actually offers this logical demonstration.[2] In particular, Grant argues that Locke used the state of nature concept to demonstrate the moral proposition of natural equality.

This suggestion is promising and clearly on the right track regarding the integral relation between Locke's political theory and his philosophy strictly speaking. However, as a proposition intended to firmly stake Locke's claims for the grounds of moral knowledge, the state of nature perhaps raises as

---

[2]   Ruth Grant, *John Locke's Liberalism* (Chicago: University of Chicago Press, 1987), p. 51. See also Jeremy Waldron, *God, Locke, and Equality* (Cambridge: Cambridge University Press, 2002), p. 95.

many questions as it answers. If the state of nature was meant to be Locke's substantive, as opposed to purely formal, account of demonstrative moral knowledge, then one would expect Locke's discussion of the state of nature to include a comprehensive treatment of the law of nature, which he identifies as the rational, and in principle wholly accessible, basis of moral truth. This is not, however, what Locke's state of nature theory does. Instead, Locke focuses his attention in the state of nature account on the mental processes and intellectual resources available to the individual who engages in moral judgment about the execution of the law of nature. In Locke's epistemological theory, the problem of moral knowledge is presented in only half of its complexity; that is as a matter of apprehension and intelligibility. However, in the state of nature discussion central to Locke's political theory, the difficulty of comprehending moral truth is compounded considerably by the problems of application and execution that necessarily arise with greater awareness of contextualization. Far from being a utopian fantasy or a completely detached theoretical portrait of a scene from nowhere, Locke's state of nature is a richly textured and multidimensional account drawing on human experiences everywhere.

The state of nature thus carries an enormous conceptual burden as the demonstration of the individualist premises of Locke's political theory. However, it is a load distributed fairly evenly among two main concepts: the natural right to punish and the natural right to property. The natural punishment right, or as Locke terms it "the executive power of the law of nature," is Locke's admittedly "very strange" sounding doctrine according to which the individual as individual is morally authorized to punish violators of the natural law. Perhaps the most radical innovation in Locke's entire state of nature account is his insistence that the individual is capable of performing *ex tempore*, and completely independently of authoritative political and religious institutions, extremely complex moral reasoning relating to difficult questions about reparation, restraint, deterrence, and mutual assistance. By placing this heavy cognitive burden on private judgment, Locke set his political theory on a path different from practically all of his contemporaries in seventeenth-century philosophy, none of whom extended such an important normative claim to the private judgment of individuals.

It is in this context that Locke's famous natural right of property, whereby the individual has a natural right to acquire property because he or she has property in one's "own Person," emerges not only as part of a political doctrine stipulating a select set of key individual rights, but moreover as an integral cognitive element of Locke's moral theory. Locke's treatment of property in his state of nature account raises possibilities for important forms of moral reasoning, including sensitive knowledge, which supplement in crucial ways his discussion of demonstrative morality in the *Essay*. To Locke, the individual is both a moral idea and unique kind of self-conscious substance that is both an agent of property acquisition and a kind of property at the same time. The relation between these two aspects of what it means to be human produces the logical thread uniting the various theoretical elements of Locke's state of nature. The difficulty in explaining this relationship in terms of self-conscious personal identity, not to mention Locke's repeated admission of his own recourse to theoretical innovation in his state of nature account, suggests that the state of nature is perhaps as much a test of a viable normative hypothesis as it is a demonstration of moral truth.

THE "VERY STRANGE DOCTRINE" OF
NATURAL EXECUTIVE POWER

In the *Second Treatise*, Locke introduced his state of nature account with the claim that "to understand Political Power right, and derive it from its Original, we must consider what State all Men are naturally in," that is "a State of perfect Freedom...a State also of Equality, wherein all Power and Jurisdiction is reciprocal, no one having more than another."[3] The state of nature is apolitical in a sense – there is no government or natural rulers – but Locke indicates that it "has a Law of Nature to govern it, which obliges everyone" (II: 6). This universally obligatory moral law is accessible to individuals through the natural faculty of "Reason, which...teaches all Mankind, who will but consult it, that being all equal and independent, no one ought to harm another in his Life, Health, Liberty or Possessions" (II: 6). The no-harm principle at the core of Locke's law of nature flows from basic human equality as the "Workmanship" of a common divine maker and sharers "in one Community of Nature" (II: 6). The law of nature stipulates that the individual is obligated to preserve him- or herself, and "when his own Preservation comes not in competition," the individual is bound to do "as much as he can, to *preserve the rest of Mankind*" (II: 6).

The law of nature, then, is a complex amalgam of moral requirements characterized primarily by the underlying tension between the emphatic

---

[3] John Locke, *Two Treatises of Government* (Cambridge: Cambridge University Press, [1690] 1988) Peter Laslett, ed., *Second Treatise*, section 4 (hereafter treatise and section in text and notes).

particularity of the right of self-preservation, on the one hand, and the universalism of the duty toward global preservation, on the other. The concept Locke postulates in order to bridge the chasm between the self-regarding claims of right and the humanitarian duties to the collective good is what he admits will sound a "very strange Doctrine to some Men" – the executive power of the law of nature, according to which every individual in the state of nature "has a right to punish transgressors" of the law of nature "to such a Degree as may hinder its Violation" (II: 7). The natural law principle of nonaggression includes a natural right to punish aggression in a manner proportionate to the crime and regulated by the principles of "Reparation and Restraint," for otherwise the law of nature "would be in vain," if individuals were not authorized to execute its commands on the basis of private judgment (II: 8). The law of nature permits every individual to "destroy" an aggressor not only against oneself, but also against anyone else in the state of nature, because any single act of aggression is a "tresspass against the whole species" (II: 8). Thus violation of the no-harm principle of the law of nature is permissible only in service of this very same principle in the general sense.

The political implications of this "very strange Doctrine" of natural executive power are enormous. Locke argues that the civil magistrate's right to punish criminals originates in the "common right of punishing put into his hands" by the individual members of society (II: 11, 128). Thus Locke's "very strange" doctrine not only authorizes the individual *as* individual to punish another human being even to the point of death without the sanction of religious or political institutions, but it is also the natural source of political power per se: The power of government derives from the natural power of individuals.

Locke's account of the government's right to punish deriving from the punishment right of individuals in the state of nature calls to mind another important discussion of punishment in Locke's *Letters Concerning Toleration*. In his toleration writings, Locke famously sought to counter the claim that government may legitimately employ coercive means in order to punish dissent and promote the "true religion." While the state of nature account in the *Two Treatises* does not explicitly treat the issue of moral sovereignty over beliefs in the manner that would preoccupy Locke in his toleration writings, it is nonetheless notable that in the treatment of punishment in both the *Letters* and the *Second Treatise*, the fundamental issue for Locke is the same, namely the status of individual moral authority. An aspect of Locke's argument for toleration that is often overlooked is the extent to which his clear effort in the state of nature account to narrow the legitimate use of force to punishment for aggression underlies his claims regarding the limits on coercive power in the toleration writings.[4] Punishment, according to the law of nature, relates solely to physical harm, not to belief or opinion. Admittedly, Locke's theory provides for an expansive notion of physical harm that includes theft and even willful waste of perishable goods (II: 18–19, 31). Moreover, in his toleration writings, Locke affirmed that certain opinions inimical to "human Society" may be proscribed.[5] However, even in the case of intolerable opinions, Locke is careful to link these beliefs with potential injury to the peace and order of society rather than any conception of true and false religion. There is thus a clear structural connection between Locke's natural right to punish and his effort to limit government's coercive power with respect to opinions, as opposed to actions, with harmful consequences.

Perhaps the most striking aspect of Locke's account of natural executive power is his insistence that it will sound like a "very strange Doctrine to some Men" (II: 9). The semantic range of the adjective "strange" provides several interpretive paths for this curious statement. Locke may simply mean that his natural right to punish aggressors will sound alien to his readers, although given the at least formal resemblance between Locke's theory of natural punishment and traditional English legal custom this is unlikely.[6] He may also be anticipating his own response to the practical objection that it is "unreasonable for men to be judges in their own cases" (II: 9, 13). However, on a more philosophical level, Locke invites us to consider the possibility that his "strange" argument is only fully intelligible in light of

---

[4] For more on the topic of toleration generally, see Chapter 6. Even among the excellent recent studies of Locke's theory of toleration such as Alex Tuckness, *Locke and the Legislative Point of View* (Princeton: Princeton University Press, 2002); Richard Vernon, *The Career of Toleration* (Montreal: McGill-Queen's University Press, 1997); Kirstie McClure, "Difference, Diversity, and the Limits of Toleration" *Political Theory*, 18, 3 (August 1990), 361–391; and Ingrid Creppell, "Locke on Toleration: The Transformation of Consent" *Political Theory*, 24, 2 (May 1996): 200–240, there is no systematic effort to explore the connection between Locke's idea of punishment and harm in his toleration writings and in his seminal state of nature account. An exception is Jeremy Waldron, "Locke, Toleration, and the Rationality of Persecution," in *Justifying Toleration: Conceptual and Historical Perspectives*, Susan Mendus, ed. (Cambridge: Cambridge University Press, 1988), pp. 61–86, esp. 74–76.

[5] John Locke, *A Letter Concerning Toleration* (Indianapolis: Hackett Publishing, 1983 [1689]): 49–50.

[6] See, for instance, Kirstie McClure, *Judging Rights: Lockean Politics and the Limits of Consent*, (Ithaca: Cornell University Press, 1996), pp. 150–153 and Tully, *Locke in Contexts*, 20–21, 35 for the formal resemblance between Locke's natural executive power doctrine and seventeenth-century English legal practice and the accusatory system of the twelfth-century, respectively.

its departure from other, perhaps more familiar doctrines on punishment. Locke hereby encourages us to reflect upon the ideas informing the skepticism and even hostility of those that will find his argument strange. In this respect, to whom is Locke referring?

The most direct and explicit target is, of course, the English champion of divine right monarchy, Sir Robert Filmer. He is Locke's announced adversary in the preface to the *Two Treatises* and the first of these works is replete with Locke's animadversions against Filmer. Filmer would find Locke's idea of natural executive power "very strange" to say the least because he rejected the basic premise of this doctrine – the principle of natural equality.[7] According to Filmer, government cannot be construed to be the product of consent, but rather is a manifestation of divine providence whereby Kings are anointed by God and are authorized to rule their subjects in the most absolute manner.

Despite the obvious conflict between Locke and Filmer over the principle of natural equality, Locke implies that Filmer is not the only object of his reference to "some Men" who will find his natural executive power doctrine strange. Indeed, Locke suggests that the "very strange" feature of his natural executive power argument is not only the foundational proposition of natural freedom and equality (to which Filmer and his divine-right supporters would certainly object), but also the specific provision that the *individual* is authorized to execute the law of nature. It is in direct response to the argument that "every Man hath a Right to punish the Offender, and be Executioner of the Law of Nature" that Locke confesses his teaching "will seem a very strange Doctrine to some Men" (II: 8). Locke forces us to consider why "some Men" who, unlike Filmer, would endorse natural equality and the principle of consent to government also simultaneously resist the conclusion that the individual is authorized to execute the law of nature solely on the basis of private judgment. What could explain this resistance?

NATURAL LIBERTY AND THE PROBLEM OF PUNISHMENT

Locke presents his state of nature account as a theoretical innovation, but it is an innovation of a certain kind. The idea of a state of nature from which

---

[7] Robert Filmer, *Patriarcha and Other Writings*, J. P. Somerville, ed. (Cambridge: Cambridge University Press, [1679] 1991), pp. 6–12, 131–171. For fuller discussions of Filmer's theory of patriarchal divine right monarchy, see James Daly, *Sir Robert Filmer and English Political Thought* (Toronto: University of Toronto Press, 1979); Gordon Schochet, *Patriarchalism in Political Thought* (Oxford: Oxford University Press, 1975), pp. 11–13, 121–130, 150–151 and Lee Ward, *The Politics of Liberty in England and Revolutionary America* (Cambridge: Cambridge University Press, 2004), chs. 1–3.

condition naturally free and equal individuals form government and society did not originate with Locke, nor does he claim to have invented this
concept. Indeed, prior to Locke, Thomas Hobbes and Samuel Pufendorf, to
name only two, had made the state of nature motif central to their political theory. Moreover, the "natural liberty" school of seventeenth-century
political thought was broadly understood to include other thinkers such as
Richard Hooker and Hugo Grotius who, while they did not develop a full-
fledged state of nature theory, did in no uncertain terms derive the origin
of government from the consent of naturally equal individuals. Thus in
this sense, the natural liberty school constituted a multifarious and admittedly eclectic but nonetheless united front against the divine right monarchists such as Locke's explicit nemesis in the *Two Treatises*, Robert Filmer.
Locke's novelty had to do specifically with the natural right to punish. He
suggests that it is this concept that must be understood in contrast not
only to Filmerian divine right, but also to prevailing theoretical assumptions about individual rights *within* the natural liberty tradition. A brief
survey of prominent natural liberty theorists such as Hooker, Hobbes,
Grotius, and Pufendorf reveals not only the problems these thinkers associated with the notion of a private punishment right, but also the extent to
which Locke's state of nature concept animated a radical departure from
the natural liberty school.

Richard Hooker stands in the *Second Treatise* and in the history of
political thought more generally as the most prominent English representative of the venerable Christian natural law tradition. As one commentator observes, the scholastic Hooker is "the traditional natural law source
to whom Locke most clearly directs our attention in the *Two Treatises*."[8]
Hooker agrees with Locke about the principle of natural freedom and equality, arguing that in nature there is "no reason that one man should take
upon him to be lord and judge over another."[9] Political society is a product of consent by which people band together to "ordain government…
and yield themselves subject thereunto." Locke and Hooker also concur

8   Michael Zuckert, *Natural Rights and the New Republicanism* (Princeton: Princeton
     University Press, 1994), p. 222 (cf. Locke II: 4, 5, 15, 19, 60 61, 74, 90, 94, 98, 111, 135,
     and 239). In regard to the individual right to punish, Hooker may be said to stand in for
     the venerable tradition of Christian natural law theory, including Aquinas and Suarez,
     who made arguments akin to Hooker and very different from Locke's "very strange" doc-
     trine of natural executive power. See, for example, St. Thomas Aquinas, *Political Writings*
     (Cambridge: Cambridge University Press, 2002), II.II art 63, p. 256 and Francisco Suarez,
     Selections from Three Works (Oxford: Clarendon Press, 1944), pp. 708–709, 863.
9   Richard Hooker, *Of the Laws of Ecclesiastical Polity* (Cambridge: Cambridge University
     Press, 1989 [1593]), bk. 1, sec. 10, para. 4 (hereafter book, section and paragraph).

that there is a natural law by which human beings can rationally deduce "the greatest moral duties we owe towards God or man." The chief moral duty, according to Hooker as well as Locke, is to refrain from harming any other human being, for "if I do harm, I must look to suffer; there being no reason that others should show greater measure of love to me, than they have by me showed unto them."[10] With respect to the fundamental ideas of natural equality and the consensual origins of government, Locke and "the Judicious Hooker" appear to speak with one voice.

However, while Hooker affirms a natural law justification for individual self-defense whereby "where force and injury was offered, they might be defenders of themselves," he rejects Locke's notion that individuals are hereby authorized to punish violators of the natural law: "No man might in reason take upon him to determine his own right."[11] In distinguishing the logic of punishment from self-defense, Hooker stresses that punishment is the sole purview of government inasmuch as the power of government inheres in the social nature of community and does not derive from any purported natural right of individuals. The supreme political authority derives its power "from a whole entire multitude" and as such government represents a moral reality in which the whole exceeds the sum of its individual parts: "The good which is proper unto each man belongeth to the common good of all as part of the whole's perfection." For Hooker, the common good rests on a teleological assumption about the "perfection" to which all things, including political society, naturally incline.[12] Thus when Hooker and Locke claim that civil government is the product of consent, they mean by this rather different things.

In Hooker's conception of the spiritual and temporal content of the "whole's perfection," consent relates primarily to the free choice about a people's form of government – rule by "many, few, or one." However, the actual source of political power, regardless of regime type, is divine authorization of human institutions. Regarding the relation of subjects to sovereigns, Hooker concludes that subjects must "stand meekly to acknowledge them for God's lieutenants."[13] The teleological assumptions underlying Hooker's conception of the communal "whole" not only enjoins passive obedience, but also supports a policy of religious uniformity. He declares:

[10]   Hooker 1.10.4, 1.8.11, 1.8.7.
[11]   Hooker 1.10.4; cf. Locke II: 92.
[12]   Hooker 8.3.4, 1.5.1–2, 8.3.4.
[13]   Hooker 8.3.1–2. It is important to observe that Hooker's endorsement of monarchy does not preclude royal government limited by law, as he believed to be the case in England (1.10.8; 8.6.11).

"A gross error it is to think that regal power ought to serve for the good of the body and not of the soul, for men's temporal peace and not their eternal safety; as if God had ordained Kings for no other end and purpose but only to fat up men like hogs and to see that they have their mash." Thus political rulers "have authority and power to command even in matters of Christian religion."[14] Hooker enjoins the civil authority to use its coercive power to punish dissenters against the established church: "Will any man deny that the Church doth need the rod of corporal punishment to keep her children in obedience." By appealing to "the Civil Magistrate for coercion of those that will not be otherwise reformed," Hooker insists that civil supremacy should not be seen as a diminution of religious authority; rather "secular power doth strengthen it."[15] Hooker's natural law teaching encourages civil power to be the temporal sword of the church.

Hobbes and his followers would also find Locke's doctrine of natural executive power "strange" and objectionable, but for different reasons than Hooker. As the preeminent English political philosopher in the generation prior to Locke, it is not surprising that Hobbes' thought had a considerable impact on the development of Locke's state of nature concept. For all intents and purposes, Hobbes practically invented the idea of a pre-civil state of nature in which naturally equal individuals must lay down their natural liberty in order to form government. However, while Hobbes ascribes to the individual in the state of nature an absolute right of self-defense, or "a right to everything," he does not countenance Locke's notion of a natural right to punish.[16] For Hobbes, there is an enormous distinction between a right to punish and any other kind of private judgment. Public authority is woven into the very fabric of Hobbes' idea of punishment, which he defines as "an evil inflicted by public authority on him that hath done or omitted that which is judged by the same authority to be a transgression of the law." The pervasive positivism in Hobbes' conception of punishment ensures that, in contrast to Locke, individuals authorize sovereign power only in the sense of laying down their natural right more or less completely and promising

---

[14] Hooker 8.3.5, 8.2.1, 8.3.5. Insofar as civil government is partially of human origin whereas the church is wholly divine, in important respects Hooker actually places the state at the service of the church. See Robert Faulkner, *Richard Hooker and the Politics of a Christian England* (Berkeley: University of California Press, 1981), chs. 10–11; Peter Josephson, *The Great Art of Government*, 241; and John Marshall, *John Locke: Resistance, Religion, and Responsibility* (Cambridge: Cambridge University Press, 1994), p. 211.

[15] Hooker 8.3.5.

[16] Thomas Hobbes, *Leviathan* (Indianapolis: Hackett Publishing, 1994 [1651]), ch. 13, sec. 8, p. 78 (hereafter ch, sec, and page.)

to assist the sovereign. He insists that sovereign power is not a delegated authority deriving from individuals. Significantly, Hobbes anticipated and roundly rejected an argument similar to Locke's: "It is manifest that the right which the commonwealth...hath to punish is *not* grounded on any concession or gift of the subjects."[17] But why did Hobbes so emphatically reject the idea of an individual natural punishing power, and in effect nip Locke's "very strange Doctrine" of natural executive power in the bud?

Hobbes' rejection of the philosophical premise of Locke's natural executive power is obviously connected to his concern to establish the rational and moral grounds for absolute sovereignty. To Hobbes the natural state of war is the logical corollary of the inefficacy of any substantive natural moral law. The contract forming political society is a product of consent, but this act of consent is not the efficient cause of sovereign power. Rather the sovereign derives his or her authority by virtue of being the single uncontracted agent watching over society while retaining his or her natural freedom entire.[18] Hobbes feared that any notion of the individual as an executor of an unwritten law would place the individual as a moral agent in some sense above the government, in a position to judge or even punish sovereign actions and thus threaten to return all to the terrible state of nature.

The reach of Hobbes' absolute sovereign extends as far into spiritual matters as does Hooker's. However, in contrast to Hooker, Hobbes abandons teleological considerations and views political control over religion purely in terms of security.[19] Religion for Hobbes is little more than state-sponsored propaganda: "Fear of power invisible, feigned by the mind, or imagined from tales publically allowed, Religion; not allowed, Superstition." Legal positivism so thoroughly shapes Hobbes' view of religion that he even defines "divine law" as that "which is declared to be so by the law of the commonwealth." Thus Hobbes agrees with Hooker that civil power can be used to punish "dissenters about the liberty of religion," especially if this dissent causes political agitation.[20] While they reflect radically different philosophical premises, Hobbes and Hooker's rejection of the private punishment right concludes in surprisingly similar accounts of state power with respect to enforcement of religious uniformity.

---

[17] Hobbes 28.1.203–04 (emphasis added).

[18] Hobbes also, of course, rejects any notion of a right of revolution or constitutional limits on sovereign power on the same grounds (18.6–7.173–4, 28.12.205).

[19] Robert Kraynak, "John Locke: From Absolutism to Toleration" *American Political Science Review*, 74, 1 (March 1980), 53–69, p. 57.

[20] Hobbes 6.36.31, 26.40.188, 18.16.116.

Some scholars maintain that Locke's Dutch predecessor Hugo Grotius advanced the concept of a natural right to punish more or less "identical to Locke's 'very strange doctrine'."[21] There is certainly more than a passing resemblance between Grotius and Locke on this matter. For example, Grotius claims that the first duty of the law of nature is self-preservation, and thus the use of force or "private war" is justified by the natural law to repel injuries.[22] Moreover, Grotius shares with Locke the equality of this right to use force that "may be exacted by anyone at all according to the law of nature." He even insists that, in contrast to Hobbes, the individual right to use force is not entirely subsumed by civil authority.[23] Thus Grotius clearly incorporates some notion of individual private judgment about the use of force into his natural law theory.

Despite the formal similarities between Locke and Grotius on natural punishment, the substantive differences are more fundamental. First, the right Grotius identifies is much more narrowly construed than the punishment right Locke extends beyond direct victims of aggression to include third parties.[24] Properly speaking, Grotius identifies a self-defense right, not a natural right of punishment. This is shown by the many qualifications he places on this right, including his insistence that it may be restricted to "wise" men of sound judgment and his unLockean conclusion that it is "most suitable that punishment be inflicted by one who is superior."[25] In the now familiar pattern of seventeenth-century natural jurisprudence, even if some notion of self-defense can be understood as a function of natural equality, punishment for Grotius, as for Hobbes and Hooker, presupposes civil subjection.

Most importantly, however, Grotius does not locate this self-defense right in a fully developed state of nature account, and as such he does not

---

[21] See Richard Tuck, *Natural Rights Theories*, 171 and Wolfgang von Leyden, "Locke's Strange Doctrine of Punishment," in *John Locke: Symposium Wolfenbuttel*, Reinhard Brandt, ed. (Berlin: Walter de Ruyter, 1981), pp. 113–127, esp. 114. For other accounts that share my skepticism regarding the claims for Grotius' originality with respect to the individual natural punishing power, see Tully, *Locke in Contexts*, 20; Perez Zagorin, "Hobbes without Grotius" *History of Political Thought*, 21, 1 (Spring 2000), 16–40, especially 37–38; and Zuckert, *Natural Rights*, 230–234. For a nuanced treatment of the relation of Grotius and Hobbes that carefully illuminates their commonalities and differences, see Martin Harvey, "Grotius and Hobbes" *British Journal of the History of Philosophy*, 14, 1 (February 2006), 27–50.

[22] Hugo Grotius, *The Rights of War and Peace, Three Volumes* [1625] (Indianapolis: Liberty Fund, 2005), vol. 1, ch. 2, sec. 1 and 1.3.1 (hereafter volume, chapter and section).

[23] Grotius 2.20.7; 1.3.2; 2.20.8,9

[24] Locke II: 6, 11. See John Simmons, *Lockean Theory of Rights* (Princeton: Princeton University Press, 1992), p. 133.

[25] Grotius 2.20.8; 2.20.3.

derive the source of government from the pre-civil rights of individuals in the manner of Locke.[26] For Grotius, the source of political power is compact signifying the agreement of subjection supported by natural law.[27] This idea of compact not only includes an inherent "law of non-resistance," but also involves the possibility of contractual absolutism should a community consent to such a form of government.[28] In contrast to Locke's theory of natural law and delegated powers, Grotius' voluntarism gives compact much greater normative salience, and therefore it is not surprising that Grotius allowed the sovereign to use coercive power in the regulation of religious worship. This is a sovereign right Grotius never even pretends to find in any commensurable natural right of individuals rooted in self-defense.[29] Thus, in crucial respects relating to the contractual basis of political power and the potential extent of government control over religion, Grotius is much closer to Hobbes than to Locke.

For his part, German theorist Samuel Pufendorf developed a state of nature concept deeply indebted to Hobbes but nonetheless possessing a more historical and empirical quality than we see in the great English absolutist. In one crucial respect, Pufendorf's account of the natural condition in his magisterial *De Jure Naturae et Gentium* (1672) bears more than a formal resemblance to Locke's state of nature, for like Locke, Pufendorf resists Hobbes' conclusion that the state of nature is coequal to a state of war. Pufendorf allows much greater sociability in his state of nature than Hobbes countenances in his. All individuals in the state of nature are equal and, Pufendorf insists, have an equal right to "preserve their body and life."[30] However, Pufendorf agrees with Locke that the individual in

---

[26] Even Tuck admits that Grotius "did not have precisely the concept of the 'state of nature'," so crucial for Hobbes and Locke (Grotius, *Rights of War and Peace*, "Introduction," p. xix). But see also Harvey, "Grotius and Hobbes," 32–33.

[27] Grotius 1.4.7.

[28] Grotius 1.3.8; 1.4.7.

[29] See Tuck's discussion of Grotius' *Pieta Ordinum* written in the context of the Remonstrant Controversy in Holland (Richard Tuck, "Grotius," in *Cambridge History of Political Thought* [Cambridge: Cambridge University Press], 1991: 509–514).

[30] Samuel Pufendorf, *De Jure Naturae et Gentium*, C. H. and W. A. Oldfather, trans. (Oxford: Clarendon Press, 1934), book 2, ch. 2, sec. 8, pp. 170–172 (hereafter in notes Pufendorf, DJNG, bk, ch, sec, and pages). For general treatments of Pufendorf's political philosophy, see Leonard Kreiger, *The Politics of Discretion: Pufendorf and the Acceptance of Natural Law* (Chicago: University of Chicago Press, 1965); Craig Carr and Michael Seidler, "Pufendorf, Sociality and the Modern State" *History of Political Thought*, 13, 3 (Autumn 1996), 352–378; Alfred Dufour, "Pufendorf," in *Cambridge History of Political Thought, 1450–1700*, J. H. Burns and Mark Goldie, eds. (Cambridge: Cambridge University Press, 1991), pp. 561–588; and Lee Ward, *The Politics of Liberty*, pp.105–113.

the state of nature is still subject to a moral law, or "to the rule of natural laws and right reason."[31] It is the natural human capacity to comprehend moral laws in the natural condition that grounds Pufendorf's claims for a quasi-natural sociability as "even those who live in a state of nature can, and should, and frequently do, lead a mutually social life."[32] For Pufendorf, individuals and social groupings in the state of nature may, and typically do, find that it serves to better secure their lives by forming compacts that establish sovereign governments with coercive power to enforce laws, but in contrast to Hobbes, the possibility of human sociability does not depend on the establishment of sovereign power.

By virtue of their common view that the natural law contains an important normative component or moral duty to which the individual in the state of nature is subject, Locke and Pufendorf are in basic agreement on a fundamental issue of natural jurisprudence. However, where they disagree profoundly is, not surprisingly, on the matter of a natural punishment right. Here Pufendorf sides with Hobbes and shares the latter's presumption that punishment logically requires a relationship of superiority and subordination that only emerges with the formation of government. For Pufendorf, the supreme sovereign assumes a "moral quality" containing the right to punish that no individual has as a private person.[33] The individual natural right of self-preservation includes a right of self-defense, but this does not imply the moral quality inhering in Locke's right to punish. The distinction between the right of public power and the right of private individuals is crucial for Pufendorf as "moral bodies" produced by compact "can possess some right, consequent upon their union, which was not formerly inherent in any of the individual members," and thus the "head of a moral body" possesses a "faculty of restraining each member by punishments, which faculty, however, was not before that time in individuals."[34] Insofar as the "right to exact punishment differs from that of self-preservation," then punishment is excluded from the moral purview of individuals in the state of nature. Not surprisingly, Pufendorf's account of the sovereign right to punish produces authoritarian political implications that are more akin to Hobbes and Grotius than they are to Locke. He flatly rejects a natural right of revolution and insists that sovereign right includes "the obligation of non-resistance" on the part of subjects.[35] Moreover, he dismisses any natural basis for religious

---

[31]   Pufendorf, DJNG, 2.2.3.158–59.
[32]   Pufendorf, DJNG, 2.2.5.166.
[33]   Pufendorf, DJNG, 7.6.1.1055.
[34]   Pufendorf, DJNG, 8.3.1.1159; 8.3.2.1161.
[35]   Pufendorf, DJNG, 7.8.1.1103.

toleration by stipulating that only those religious communities with specific contractual guarantees have a claim for toleration.[36] Natural liberty does not imply or necessitate a broad range of civil liberties.

This brief survey of seventeenth-century natural liberty theory puts us in a better position to appreciate why Locke expected that the natural executive power doctrine at the heart of his state of nature theory would sound "very strange" to many of his contemporaries. By positing a natural right to interpret the law of nature and to punish violators of the moral law, Locke's individualist premises extend far beyond the conceptual reach of the right of self-defense common at the time. Explaining and defending the radical individualist implications of this doctrine would constitute one of the primary goals of his state of nature theory.

THE INDIVIDUALIST IMPLICATIONS OF NATURAL PUNISHMENT

Having examined Locke's natural executive power doctrine in the context of its relation to the prior natural law tradition, we must now consider the political implications of Locke's natural executive power theory. Natural executive power is practically woven into the fabric of Locke's account of the creation of civil society wherein those who "hath quitted this natural Power" of punishing violators of the law of nature and have "resign'd it up into the hands of the Community…and have a common establish'd Law and Judicature to appeal to, with authority to decide Controversies between them, and punish Offenders, are in Civil Society one with another" (II: 87). All those who have no such common law and judge, Locke claims, "are still in the state of Nature" (II: 87).[37] Thus civil society begins and the state of nature ends when a group of individuals agree to establish a common legislature and judicature invested with the natural executive power of the individuals in society.

It is on the basis of this proposition that Locke advances the general theoretical claim that "all Men are naturally in" the state of nature until "by their own Consents they make themselves Members of some Politick Society" (II: 15).[38] If, however, the creation of civil society involves the

---

[36] Samuel Pufendorf, *Of the Nature and Qualification of Religion in Reference to Civil Society* (Indianapolis: Liberty Fund, 2002), sec. 49, pp. 104–107.

[37] Locke cites ancient peoples in the process of political founding, native peoples in contemporary times, and rulers of independent states as testimony to the actual existence or latent possibility of the state of nature (II: 9, 14, 103; see also Locke, "Third Letter Concerning Toleration," *Works*, Vol. 6 [London: Tegg, 1823], p. 225).

[38] Ostensibly Locke draws this conclusion from a passage in Hooker, but whereas Hooker presents the condition without government in order to demonstrate its inherent inability

surrender of individual natural executive power, then we must consider how Locke can maintain that the law of nature is a moral standard existing independently of any given political society by which every individual and "all the rest of Mankind are one Community" (II: 128). That is to say, given the absorption of natural executive power into civil government, how do the rights and obligations of the law of nature belong "to men as men, and not as Members of Society" (II: 14)?

The philosophic naturalism underlying Locke's normative claim for individual judgment of the law of nature emerges emphatically in his crucial treatments of the biblical story of Cain and the political status of aliens. In the middle of his account of the state of nature, Locke cites the example of Cain in *Genesis* as biblical support for his natural executive power doctrine. He states that Cain assumed the existence of something like natural executive power when he told God that "Everyone that findeth me, shall slay me" as punishment for the murder of Abel (II: 11). Locke infers from Cain's reaction to his exposure by God that "the Great Law of Nature, Who so sheddeth Man's Blood, by Man shall his Blood be shed" is a truth plainly "writ in the Hearts of all Mankind" (II: 11). However, Locke radically alters the biblical account in order to make it conform to his theoretical premises.[39] Locke conflates two scriptural passages with very different, even opposite meanings, and reverses their chronological order. He practically equates the divine command to Noah at *Genesis* 9.6 "Who so sheddeth Man's Blood" with the law of nature, and then refers to Cain's reaction at *Genesis* 4.14 "Everyone that findeth me shall slay me" as proof of the universal recognition of a natural punishing power in individuals. By citing ex post facto proof for an antecedent proposition, Locke leaves the false impression that *Genesis* 4.14 sanctions the natural right to punish. However, God's famous response to Cain ("Whosoever slayeth Cain, vengeance shall be taken upon him sevenfold"), which Locke conveniently omits, is a direct rejection of this natural right. Far from endorsing Locke's "very strange" doctrine of natural executive power, God in *Genesis* chapter 4 explicitly denies the punishment power to human beings, and even promises vengeance against anyone who presumes to exercise this right.

> to provide for a life "as our nature doth desire, a Life, fit for the dignity of Man (Hooker 1.10.1)," Locke suggests in this argument something rather different, namely that there is no necessary continuum of human sociability providing for the temporal and spiritual ends implied in Hooker's conception of civil society.
>
> 39 This general line of argument is suggested in Michael Zuckert, *Launching Liberalism* (Lawrence: University Press of Kansas, 2002), pp. 93–95 and Cox, *Locke on War and Peace*, 56–57 (but cf. Martin Seliger, *The Liberal Politics of John Locke* [London: Praeger, 1968], p. 57 and Dunn, *Politics of Locke*, 168–169).

God's response to Cain suggests that natural reason may indicate to the mind of the first homicide (a dubious exemplar of natural reason) something akin to the natural executive power, but divine will does not.[40] Thus Locke's account is seriously misleading inasmuch as the legal code given to Noah in *Genesis* 9 (and later confirmed for Moses) may partly support the findings of Locke's (and Cain's) natural reason, but the Bible indicates that the authority for human beings to punish others with death derives solely from divine permission.[41] Scripture is clear that express divine grant was the only thing lacking in the lawless period prior to Noah, therefore the punishment right cannot be natural in Locke's sense, but rather a product of divine positive law. The authentic biblical teaching on punishment is thus much closer to Hooker's natural law theory, which emphasizes the divine ordination of political power, than it is to Locke's philosophic naturalism.[42] With the use of carefully redacted scriptural passages, Locke leaves the reader with the suspicion that he seeks to draft the venerable authority of the Bible into the service of his state of nature account in order to replace the traditional Christian natural law emphasis on divine providence and human createdness with a new natural rights teaching that asserts human rational autonomy and owes more to the democratization of mind than the authentic biblical teaching. In order to make *Genesis* appear compatible with the epistemological premises of his state of nature, Locke refashions the interpretation of Scripture in a manner that must have appeared "very strange" to many.

The second major example of natural executive power in Locke's state of nature account relates to the "Right any Prince or State [has] to put to death, or punish an Alien, for any Crime he commits in their Country" (II: 9). Locke claims that the "promulgated Will of the Legislature" reaches "not a Stranger" for the civil laws of the host nation "speak not to him, nor if they did, is he bound to hearken to them" (II: 9). Locke concludes that the only way a host government may punish an alien is by virtue of the right to punish "every Man naturally may have over another" (II: 9). In keeping with the logic of the argument for the surrender of natural executive power being the efficient cause of civil government, Locke appears to be granting the state a sweeping right to punish individuals based on a contractual

---

[40] Josephson, *Great Art of Government*, 79.

[41] Grotius noted that the immunity of Cain indicates that the individual right to punish was introduced only at the time of Noah (1.2.5). In this respect, Grotius more closely follows Scripture than Locke and thus highlights the greater philosophical naturalism of the latter.

[42] Hooker 1.10.4; 8.3.1.

authority over citizens and a natural one over aliens. For all intents and purposes, the state seems to reserve practically plenary power over anyone residing within its jurisdiction.

However, later in the *Second Treatise*, Locke qualifies this account of the civil power to punish in significant ways. First, he admits that aliens may be understood to offer tacit consent to the host government such that by "enjoying the privileges and protection of it...they are bound, even to submit to its administration, as far forth as any denison" (II: 122).[43] Locke is quick to add, however, that the "homage due" from a foreigner to a host nation does not make a "man a member of that Society" (II: 122). Thus Locke's argument here signifies as much a call on governments to provide noncitizens access to the judicial system as it is an exhortation for aliens to respect the laws of the host nation that are consistent with the law of nature.

The suggestion that an alien is subject to civil law of the host nation without being a full member of that society indicates that for Locke, such an individual is in certain respects still in a state of nature vis-à-vis the host government. The theoretical implications of such a condition are certainly, at least potentially, subversive of civil power because given Locke's claim that there is no qualitative moral difference between the state's right to punish and that of the individual in the state of nature, then logically the alien must reserve some share of the executive power of the law of nature with respect to the host government. Just as the host government may punish an alien on the basis of the natural law command to preserve humankind, so too on the same grounds may an alien legitimately come to the aid of oppressed members of the host society such as persecuted religious minorities or systematically impoverished groups.[44] Any contest between a magistrate authorized to employ the "force of the community" and an individual alien may be a hopelessly lopsided affair, but Locke's theoretical point is that the standard for legitimacy of punishment is reason, not sheer strength or institutional prestige. He argues that "the Municipal Laws of Countries" are "only so far right, as they are founded on the law of Nature," which supplies an "Eternal Rule to all Men, Legislators as well as others" (II: 12, 135). Remarkably, Locke's natural law teaching suggests that an alien has

---

43   For the tension in Locke's two accounts of the political obligation of aliens, see John Simmons, *The Edge of Anarchy* (Princeton: Princeton University Press, 1993), p. 21.

44   In this sense, Locke's natural law theory may be said to foreshadow the moral and political claims of the nongovernmental organizations and international human rights groups of today. See James Tully, "Introduction" *A Letter Concerning Toleration* (Indianapolis: Hackett Publishing, 1983), p. 10.

the natural right to scrutinize, interpret, and even resist the civil laws of a host nation if they contradict the law of nature.

Locke's treatment of aliens uncovers the underlying structural connection between the individual natural executive power and other characteristically political contexts such as those described in his influential account of the right of revolution whereby in any conflict between a community and abusive government, the government dissolves and "every man is judge for himself" about the law of nature (II: 241). In contrast to the legal positivism of Hobbes, for whom "the law of nature and the civil law contain each other, and are of equal extent," Locke posits the law of nature as a standard of right that is theoretically contradistinguished from civil law and accessible to the rational individual whether citizen or foreigner.[45] The notion of individual moral agency underlying both Locke's account of the status of aliens and his theory of the dissolution of government suggests that the breach of trust involved in revolution is, at least in principle, universalizable in the sense that every individual may view any government, including one's own, in some sense, from a naturalistic, as opposed to a purely civil, perspective.

In order to get a sense of the connection between Locke's right of revolution and his individualist philosophical premises, one needs only to contrast Locke's view on the subject with that of many of his predecessors and contemporaries in the history of political thought. Resistance theories were a common feature of constitutional thought in the period and ranged from the political theology of the Huguenot thinkers in sixteenth-century France to the contractualism of Grotius and Pufendorf. However, Locke's right of revolution is unique on two counts. First, resistance theory among influential Huguenot thinkers such as Francois Hotman and the author of the celebrated *Vindicae contra Tyrranos* Phillipe de Mornay was rooted in the moral judgment of a community acting in its corporate capacity, or at least special officers charged to act in the name of the community.[46] However, for Locke, the moral judgment involved in the "Appeal to Heaven" that results

---

[45] Hobbes 26.8.174.

[46] For discussions about various aspects of Huguenot resistance theory, see Robert Kingdon, "Calvinism and Resistance Theory, 1550–1580," in *Cambridge History of Political Thought, 1450–1700*, J. H. Burns and Mark Goldie, eds. (Cambridge: Cambridge University Press, 1991), pp. 194–218; Quentin Skinner, *The Foundations of Modern Political Thought*, Vol. 2 (Cambridge: Cambridge University Press, 1978), pp. 194–224; Harro Hopfl and Martyn Thompson, "The History of Contract as a Motif in Political Thought" *American Historical Review*, 84, 4 (October 1979), 929–934; Julian Franklin, *Constitutionalism and Resistance in the Sixteenth Century* (New York: Pegasus, 1968); and Ward, *The Politics of Liberty*, pp. 49–57.

from a government violating the trust of the community is profoundly individualistic: "Every Man is Judge for himself, as in all other cases; so in this, whether another has put himself into a State of War with him" (II: 241; also 176, 242). Each member of the community must, and is morally authorized to, decide one's own loyalties in such a condition. However, Locke's precise construction of the operation of the right of revolution can be confusing in this regard. In the event of a "Dissolution of Society," in which the social bonds of a community as well as its government have been destroyed, typically through foreign invasion, Locke insists that the natural executive power given by each individual to the government devolves back to the individual, "and so everyone return[s] to the state he was in before, with a liberty to shift for himself, and provide for his own Safety" (II: 211). The dissolution of society thus reveals the potentially seamless logical and conceptual connection between the state of nature and civil society that exists on one level of Locke's analysis.

However, with what Locke terms the "Dissolution of Government," the situation is more complicated. The dissolution of government occurs when a government or a part of it (normally the executive power) violates public trust and sets itself in opposition to the permanent interests of the community. In this case, the society remains intact and in effect rebels against its government. Here Locke insists "the Power that every individual gave the Society, when he entered into it, can never revert to the Individuals again, as long as the Society lasts, but will always remain in the Community" (II: 243). The formal resemblance between this argument and the more communitarian and conservative resistance theories such as the Huguenot variety has led some scholars to underestimate the radical thrust of Locke's teaching on revolution.[47] By arguing that the dissolution of government does not result in a return to the state of nature, Locke does not mean to suggest that the society formed by a compact that preceded the creation of government acts during a rebellion in its corporate capacity. Rather his point is that in such circumstances, the "People" understood as a critical mass of the individuals in society may act as the legislative body and set up a new government (II: 243). Society persists, even as government dissolves, because the moral obligations *among* the individual members of society remain intact, and thus they remain one community. However, the moral referent for judgment about not only the actions of government, but also

---

[47]   See, for instance, Ronald Becker, "The Ideological Commitment of Locke: Freemen and Servants in the *Two Treatises of Government*" *History of Political Thought*, 8, 4 (1992): 631–656, esp. 638–641. For the classic statement of Locke as a revolutionary democrat, to which Becker sets his reading in contrast, see Richard Ashcraft, *Revolutionary Politics & Locke's Two Treatises* (Princeton: Princeton University Press, 1986).

of social relations within society devolves to the natural executive power of individuals, who are obviously no longer morally bound by civil legislation when the legitimacy of the civil power is precisely what is at issue. The Lockean notion of revolution is certainly a form of mass political participation, but it is an activity that derives its moral authority from an irreducibly individualistic core principle.

The second, and related, sense in which Locke's right of revolution and the more traditional right of resistance differ is with respect to the crucial question about the practical point of justification. For contractualists like Grotius and Pufendorf, a community is morally justified to resist its rulers if the government violates the terms of the contract or compact upon which the legitimacy of its rule depends. Resistance then, as traditionally conceived, really amounts to armed legal adjudication, or perhaps better to say, military execution of a quasi-legal judgment. But as we saw earlier in this chapter, continental contractualist thinkers such as Grotius and Pufendorf were nowhere near endorsing a right of revolution – indeed they typically affirmed a moral obligation of nonresistance for subjects.[48] For Locke, however, individual moral judgment about the law of nature takes an explicitly extra-legal form. He does not describe the basis of political legitimacy in terms of contract, but rather through the more amorphous concepts of consent and trust. As such, Locke's idea of resistance sheds the largely restorative justification typical among his contemporaries, and produces rather a concurrent dissolution process in which the community, or more properly speaking the individuals in society, may choose to restore the government on its former basis or even to set up an entirely "new Legislative" power (II: 223, 243). Contract, for Locke, cannot define or limit the justification or ultimate result of resistance to government.

Locke is, of course, careful to insist that his right of revolution is not a recipe for anarchy. He suggests that there is a natural conservatism among the people in any organized society, who will be predisposed toward order and security. Rebellion is unlikely to gain much popular traction in the event of anything less that a "long train of Abuses" (II: 225) by government, which convinces the people of the existence of a deliberate and settled design to deprive them of their rights. Indeed, Locke claims that a public philosophy acknowledging the natural right of revolution is in fact the "best fence against rebellion" precisely because a vigilant public will moderate the abusive proclivities of government (II: 226).[49] The barely

---

[48] See, for example, Grotius 2.20.3,8 and 1.4.7 and Pufendorf, DJNG 7.8.1.1103.

[49] See Nathan Tarcov, "Locke's *Second Treatise* and the 'Best Fence against Rebellion'" *Review of Politics*, 43 (April 1981), 198–217.

concealed radical underpinning of Locke's putatively conservative argument is the more fundamental reorientation of the individual's relation to government that his right of revolution presupposes. Locke's state of nature account grounds an idea of government in which what is civil and what is natural are distinct but also conceptually conjoined in a larger political principle. The *raison d'etre* of contractualism in the Grotian, Pufendorfian, and for that matter Hobbesian mold was to establish a clearly delineated boundary between civil society and anything even remotely resembling a state of nature. For Locke, however, the individual moral right to execute the law of nature inevitably impinges on the normative claims of government. Nature is always a latent and, in contrast to Hobbes, morally justifiable or at least ethically neutral possibility in Locke's conception of civil society. Even if Locke maintains that in practice a right of revolution is not equivalent to anarchy, he is quite aware that theory will inform practice by encouraging not only moderation on the part of government, but also, or even especially, by encouraging a skeptical attitude toward government on the part of the people.

This attitude of popular skepticism is indicative of the experimental mode of analysis and judgments about probability that marked the wide range of propositions Locke's epistemology set off as falling short of certain knowledge. The democratic basis of the right of revolution lies not only in it being a matter of judgment involving every individual in society. It is also a function of the dual nature of government. Government is both a mixed mode created by human contrivance through the complex idea of consent and at the same time an extremely complex and compound substance containing innumerable possible relations and powers among individuals, and thus can be judged only provisionally on the basis of observation and probability. In other words, Locke's epistemology of political revolution flows directly out of his account of individual moral reasoning in the state of nature.

THE PROBLEM OF MORAL KNOWLEDGE REDUX

The individualist implications of the natural executive power doctrine establishes an inescapable connection between Locke's state of nature theory and the problem of moral knowledge raised in the *Essay Concerning Human Understanding*. In the course of his effort to articulate in the *Essay* a new democratic conception of human intellectual faculties, Locke understandably approached the issue of moral knowledge from the perspective of an epistemological question. However, in the state of nature account foundational for his political teaching, Locke is forced to address the issue of moral knowledge with a different set of criteria arising from the problems raised by various contextual conditions. In the state of nature account, it is no longer simply an epistemological question as to whether the human mind is in principle capable of demonstrating moral knowledge with as much certainty as the truths of mathematics. Now the questions are: How can the individual know the natural law in a variety of situations involving multiple, and competing, moral claims and ethical concerns? What contextual factors encourage or occlude understanding of moral truth? And to what extent are natural human passions an obstacle to clear reasoning? In other words, the possibility of acquiring moral knowledge becomes a much more emphatically political or social problem in the state of nature account than it appears in Locke's philosophy per se.

Locke's claim that the natural executive power not only constitutes the source of government's punishment power but also the right of individuals and communities to resist government clearly signifies an important departure from earlier versions of the natural liberty doctrine. However, Locke's conception of natural executive power holds problematic implications for his broader state of nature account, problems anticipated by his predecessors. First, there is the logical problem of explicating why human beings would ever leave this state of perfect freedom and equality, in which autonomous individuals are governed by and authorized to execute the rational law of nature, and rather submit themselves to civil authority. That is to say, how can Locke account for the existence of any actual government in the world? Conversely, the second problem relates to what Locke admits are the "Inconveniences" of the natural condition "which must certainly be great, where men may be judges in their own case" (II: 13). He admits that "self-love will make men partial to themselves" and encourage such hasty and malicious punishments that the state of nature is "very unsafe, very unsecure," and is so much like a state of war that human beings are "quickly driven into Society" (II: 13, 123, 127). How then can the law of nature be said to ground morality in anything but in a negative, Hobbesian sense?

The problems Locke identified in the state of nature are inextricably connected to the natural power to punish, which places a heavy cognitive burden on the private judgment of individuals who are expected to resist the impulses of excessive self-love and perform *ex tempore* highly complex moral reasoning relating to difficult questions about reparation, restraint, deterrence, and mutual assistance. The problem of the law of nature in the state of nature appears to be both a matter of enforcement *and* understanding. Locke partially admits the force of the objection based on self-love and implicitly recognizes that the egalitarian distribution of natural rights threatens the stability of the state of nature and leads many to reach Hooker's conclusion that "God hath appointed government to restrain the violence and partiality of Men."[50] However, the difficulties associated with enforcement of the law of nature point to the even more fundamental epistemological problems Locke associates with the law of nature. Does he have any confidence that individuals can know the law of nature and act on it in a reliable way? The evidence in the *Second Treatise* suggests that Locke is highly skeptical about autointerpretation of the law of nature. Although the law of nature should be "as intelligible and plain to a rational Creature...as the positive Laws of Commonwealths; nay possibly plainer," Locke concedes that the "greater part" of humanity are "no strict Observers of Equity and Justice" due both to their self-interest and to the "want of Study" of the natural law (II: 12, 123–4). For his part, Locke hardly helps matters when he cautions that it is "besides my present purpose, to enter here into the particulars of the law of nature, or its measures of punishment" (II: 12).

If the "present purpose" of the politically charged *Second Treatise* was not to detail the features of the natural law, then perhaps we must return to the more philosophic *Essay Concerning Human Understanding* in which he considers the epistemological grounds of the natural law in depth. As we have seen previously, the democratization of mind underlying Locke's epistemology abandoned innate practical principles but replaced them as the foundation of moral knowledge with self-evident propositions comprehensible through discursive reason operating in an egalitarian distribution of intellectual faculties. It was on this basis that Locke famously promised to provide a demonstration that "moral knowledge is as capable of real Certainty, as Mathematicks."[51] However, the epistemological ground of moral knowledge differs from mathematics insofar as the former depends on the human capacity to know God's relation to His "Workmanship," especially God's providential role as the lawgiver who rewards and punishes.[52] Civil laws can only judge human actions, but for natural law to be effective it requires the support of a God "who sees men in the dark and has in his Hand Rewards and Punishments."[53] Thus, Locke's demonstrative

---

[50]   Locke II: 13. Cf. Hooker 1.10.4.
[51]   John Locke, *Essay Concerning Human Understanding*, Peter Nidditch, ed. (Oxford: Oxford University Press, 1975 [1690]), bk. 4, ch. 4, sec. 7; 4.3.18 (hereafter E bk., ch., sec.).
[52]   E 4.3.18; also I: 53–4, II: 6.
[53]   E 1.3.12, 6.

morality appears to depend on certain proof of the existence of a providential lawgiver God who can punish or reward the immortal soul.

Strikingly, Locke scholars of practically every interpretive hue agree that he failed to produce such a fully convincing demonstration of these matters in the *Essay*.[54] The epistemological limitations on moral knowledge that Locke discovers include our inability to "comprehend the operations of that eternal Infinite Mind, who made and governs all things," as well as the incapacity of unassisted human reason to establish the immortality of the soul; a proposition that, Locke argues, must be taken "purely as a matter of Faith; with which Reason, has directly nothing to do."[55] The *Essay*, and its democratization of mind, then appears to provide no greater confidence regarding the substantive application of the natural law than does the *Second Treatise*.

However, this impression is misleading. In one sense, even Locke's failure to produce a demonstrative moral science supports the radical implications of his state of nature account by undermining the epistemological and experiential claims of the scholastic philosophy that underlies Hooker's natural law, which relies on the proposition of speculative and practical first principles the knowledge of which are lodged in the conscience. For Hooker, the moral knowledge necessary for "man's salvation" is "so familiar and plain, that truth from falsehood, and good from evil is most easily discerned in them" by virtue of basic principles of right "sufficient for any man's conscience to build the duty of obedience upon." Moreover, even in "more doubtful cases," Hooker assures that "God hath appointed" not only government, but also special ministers who "might be a light to direct others."[56]

Locke's account of the epistemological challenges confronting any rigorous natural law theory stands in stark contrast to Hooker's scholastic metaphysics. That "real certainty" about morality cannot be deduced from the conscience is, Locke claims, witnessed by the stunning array of brutal and irrational practices and customs that have stained history with cruelty and

---

54 See for example, Hans Aarsleff, "The State of Nature and the Nature of Man in Locke," in *John Locke: Problems and Perspectives* (Cambridge: Cambridge University Press, 1969), pp. 99–136, p. 106; Creppell, "Locke on Toleration," 213; Dunn, *Politics of Locke*, 194; Steven Forde, "Natural Law, Theology, and Morality in Locke" *American Journal of Political Science*, 45, 2 (April 2001), 396–409, p. 397; Ruth Grant, *John Locke's Liberalism* (Chicago: University of Chicago Press, 1987), pp. 26, 48; Thomas Pangle, *Spirit of Modern Republicanism* (Chicago: University of Chicago Press, 1988), pp. 198–201; and Tully, *Locke in Contexts*, 312.

55 E 4.10.19, 4.18.7.

56 E Pref. 3.2, 6.3.

inhumanity. So far are moral truths from being easily accessible through the conscience that Locke suggests that the very idea of God and the law of nature are not universal.[57] Locke's remedy to this problem, whereby human faculties lack the capacity for certainty on matters of moral goodness, is his conception of probabilism.[58] Locke claims that even though "true knowledge" is "short and scanty" and "so narrow," human reason can deduce some proofs to a degree of probability by which the natural faculty of judgment can "supply defect to our knowledge and guide us to where that fails." Despite the many causes of error such as partisan prejudice, lack of leisure for study and deeply ingrained customs, Locke maintains that by nature the individual as individual can attain probable judgments about morality that approach certainty and provide "light enough" to conduct our actions according to the law of nature.[59] The implications of his rejection of innate ideas and endorsement of probabilism for Locke's theory of punishment are considerable.

Notably, Locke's skepticism about the individual's capacity to deduce certain knowledge about religious truth places severe limits not on the moral sovereignty of the individual, but rather on the legitimate use of force by government. The logical structure of his natural executive power doctrine thus provides one of the moral and epistemic grounds for the principle of toleration. It is in this sense that the liberal civic person "constituted by moral sovereignty over one's core beliefs and practices" emerges as an important theme in Locke's state of nature account. Insofar as the individual cannot know religious truth with absolute certainty, the power to punish belief cannot be delegated to government from the right of individuals. On the basis of Locke's epistemology in the *Essay*, no political or religious authority can claim infallible moral knowledge of the good because no individual can.[60] Of course, this does not mean that Locke's natural executive power doctrine requires absolute toleration. He affirms that certain practices and even opinions may be proscribed because they are incompatible with contestable judgments about the public good.[61] However, the justification for this intolerance is some notion of physical harm and civil order rather than claims to superior judgment about religious truth. Locke allows that the

---

[57] E 1.3.13, 1.3.9; 1.2.27, 1.4.19, 1.3.24.
[58] See the good discussions about Locke's probabilism in Michael Ayers, *Locke: Epistemology & Ontology*, Vol. I (London: Routledge, 1993), pp. 113–124 and Tully, *Locke in Contexts*, 312–313.
[59] E 4.14.1, 4.15.4; 4.20, 1.1.5.
[60] Aarsleff, "The State of Nature," 107.
[61] Locke, *Letter on Toleration*, 42, 49–51. See also Vernon, *Career of Toleration*, 50.

magistrate may make a plausible claim to superior knowledge about what constitutes harm, but he insists that the magistrate cannot assume the right to determine what is and is not properly a matter of religious belief. The practical judgments of probability, whether by civil magistrates or individuals in the state of nature, simply lack the intrinsic authority to compel conscience and enforce religious uniformity.

The new conception of epistemology in the *Essay* thus sheds considerable light on the problem of moral knowledge in Locke's state of nature. Locke admits that some measure of conflict is inevitable in the state of nature where "Men may be Judges in their own Case" (II: 13, 90). Self-regarding passions obscure the individual's judgment of the natural law and thus insure that autointerpretation of the law of nature in the state of nature falls far short of a guarantee of peace and security (II: 16). Indeed, Locke's extension of the highly permissive standard for the legitimate use of individual force to third parties practically ensures widespread conflict, and even lawful despotism as a quasi-substitute for capital punishment.[62] The establishment of settled laws with known impartial judges and a common power to apply this law is the obvious "remedy" to the "inconveniences" of the natural condition (II: 124–27). For Locke, rigorous examination of human rational faculties simply does not support teleological assumptions about the naturalness of political life.

In one sense, then, Locke's account of the problem of moral knowledge aligns him much closer with Hobbes than with Hooker. However, it is in the course of clarifying the difference between the state of nature and the state of war that Locke makes his most pointed reference to Hobbes and his followers as "some men" who "have confounded" these two conditions (II: 19). In contrast to Hobbes, Locke suggests that the primary difference between these two conditions is not the presence or absence of a common civil power, but rather the use of force with or without "Right" (II: 19). Whereas Hobbes saw any use of force in the state of nature as rightful and any individual use of force in civil society not authorized by the sovereign as illegitimate, Locke reconceptualized the framework of legitimate and illegitimate use of force such that both may occur in the state of nature and in civil society. For example, the natural executive power allowing the individual to punish an aggressor persists in civil society if the individual does not have recourse to the protection of law (II: 17–20). Moreover, Locke

---

[62] Simmons, *Lockean Theory of Rights*, 87–88; Coby, "Is Locke a Hobbesian?" 10–11; Paul Rahe, *Republics Ancient and Modern, Vol II* (Chapel Hill: University of North Carolina Press 1992), p. 270 and Zuckert, *Natural Rights*, 237.

identifies practically any use of force by an absolute monarch unrestrained by civil law – the *sine qua non* of Hobbesian sovereignty – as the exemplar of the use of force without right, and thus the individual and community are authorized by the law of nature to resist and in effect punish an absolute ruler (II: 235, 239).

Locke thus denies that nature is coterminus with war and that government necessarily excludes the use of force without right. In so doing, he replaces Hobbes' stark dichotomy of nature/war versus civil society/peace with a more complex structure of interrelated moral conditions based on different criteria of legitimacy whereby the state of nature and the state of war are defined as relational terms such that an individual can be in both conditions at the same time with respect to different parties.[63] Locke considers nature and war in relation to a multidimensional set of moral coordinates for determining the use of legitimate and illegitimate force. He bases his framework on the overlapping distinctions between reason and lack of reason, on the one hand, and between a condition without a common judge in which individual force is employed and a condition in which there is a common judge to employ the collective force of the community, on the other. The thrust of Locke's normative argument in the state of nature mixed mode is thus not directed primarily at demonstrating that the condition without government is necessarily one either of peace or war.[64] Rather his aim is to provide the measure of legitimacy for various moral relations within or outside of civil society. In Locke's fluid schema of moral relations, the conceptual slippage among these relations reflects the interconnected logical premises underlying a variety of conditions. An individual may be in a state of war with an aggressor but in a state of nature with the rest of humanity (II: 17). Likewise, a group of individuals may be in a state of nature among themselves but at war with an absolute government (II: 211, 225).[65] By Locke's reasoning, Hobbes' stark bifurcation

---

[63] Richard Ashcraft, *Revolutionary Politics and Locke's Two Treatises of Government* (Princeton: Princeton University Press, 1986), p. 319 and John Scott, "The Sovereignless State and Locke's Language of Obligation" *American Political Science Review*, 94, 3 (September 2000), 554.

[64] Grant, *Locke's Liberalism*, 71. But see McClure, *Judging Rights*, 154–155, who argues that the natural executive power is compatible with natural harmony, at least prior to the introduction of money.

[65] Locke's position on absolute government is complicated. At one point, he indicates that absolute monarchy is "no form of government at all" (II: 90) because it rests on arbitrary will rather than standing law and admits of no impartial judges. However, Locke clarifies that the very thing that makes absolute regimes so terrible is the putative sovereign's capacity to use his status "increased with power" to tyrannize individuals in society with armed "force… 100 000 times stronger" than an individual in the pure state of

of nature and government is unable to recognize the moral complexity of either nature or legitimate government because natural reason provides individuals with greater access to principles of right than Hobbes supposed. Amazingly, Locke suggests that Hobbes has not seriously thought through the problem of war.

The "inconveniences" of Locke's state of nature are neither the building blocks of Hobbes' Leviathan nor the vestibule to Hooker's Christian polity. Locke's reflections on the limits and possibilities of moral knowledge in the *Essay* and the *Second Treatise* undercut the philosophical foundations of both the traditional natural law and Hobbesian natural rights. However, despite his emphatic rejection of Hobbes' moral reductionism and Hooker's natural teleology, we still do not know the basis of moral knowledge in Locke's law of nature or what intellectual and sensory materials are available to human reason in the state of nature. For this we must consider the last key element in Locke's state of nature: his theory of property.

PROPERTY AND SELF-OWNERSHIP

Locke's admission that the ability to know and act on the principles of the law of nature is problematic in the state of nature raises several questions: What grounds and supplies even a measure of probability for knowledge of the natural law? Moreover, how can the other-regarding dimension of the law of nature have any substantive content if self-preservation is as much of an irreducible feature of human psychology and the moral economy of the passions as the problems in the state of nature suggest? In the natural right of property Locke discovers a basis of morality with great import for both his epistemology and his politics.

The discussion of property in Chapter 5 of the *Second Treatise* concludes Locke's treatment of the state of nature proper and provides the capstone for his argument about the origins of political life. Famously, Locke observes that both "natural reason" and "revelation" indicate that human beings "have a right to their Preservation," which can only be effective if they have a concurrent right to the material goods necessary for self-preservation (II: 25).[66] The addition of labor to natural objects gives the property

war (II: 93). Locke quite explicitly infers from this common sense observation about the collective dimension of tyranny that absolute monarchy, despite its illegitimacy, is a recognizable form of rule like "other Governments of the World" (II: 93).

[66] Unlike many of his contemporaries such as James Tyrrell and Samuel Pufendorf, Locke did not infer from this a natural "theft" right in cases of extreme necessity. Rather, he took a different course and drew from the right of self-preservation a much fuller theory of labor than any of his contemporaries. For the differences on this issue between Locke

right its exclusive and individualist character: "labour put a distinction between them and the common, That added something more than Nature, the common Mother of all, had done; and so they became his private right" (II: 28). Locke grounds the natural property right in the proposition that "every Man has a Property in his own Person. This no body has a Right to but himself. The Labour of his Body, and the work of his Hands, we may say, are properly his" (II: 27, 44). Society may, and Locke affirms it lawfully does, regulate private property rights, but in the most fundamental sense, political society does not create them.

The epistemological dimension of Locke's teaching on property is thus pivotal. As we have seen, Locke insisted that we can know with a high degree of probability complex moral relations or "mixed modes" that we construct from simple ideas, even as the real essence of substances remains permanently elusive.[67] Significantly, Locke's paradigmatic example of a moral idea that can be demonstrated with a degree of certainty is, not surprisingly, the right of property. With an oblique reference to Hobbes, Locke argues that "Where there is no Property, there is no Justice, is a Proposition as certain as any demonstration in Euclid."[68] However, whereas Hobbes saw this moral axiom as proof that there is no justice in nature, Locke reconfigured the meaning of the state of nature as a mixed mode so that in his reconstruction of the idea of nature and property, there is a natural property right flowing from a form of property in the state of nature that every individual has in his or her "own Person" (II: 27). For Locke, the idea of property is a mixed mode that, like all modes, has its root in simple ideas readily available to sense perception – in this case, to bodily needs logically deduced from the fundamental proposition of self-ownership. For Hobbes and practically the entire natural liberty tradition prior to Locke, property as a natural phenomenon was purely a matter of substance, not of moral relations. Property only assumed a moral status in civil society. However, for Locke, the human "Person" has property in his or her actions because they are the products of rational choice – the primary property is the self, the creator of moral right in the physical world.[69] Locke's account of property in the state of nature thus presupposes the concept of personal identity we first encountered in the *Essay*. For Locke, the epistemological connection

---

on the one hand and Tyrrell and Pufendorf on the other, see Ward, *Politics of Liberty*, 130–132.

[67] E 2.23.3–6, 3.6.9–10.

[68] Compare Locke E 4.3.18 with Hobbes 13.13.78. Locke clearly contrasts the epistemological basis of his state of nature with that of Hobbes who famously asserted a natural right to everything including "to one another's body" (14.4.80).

[69] Zuckert, *Natural Rights*, 275–287 and McClure, *Judging Rights*, 143.

between natural physical needs, which can be deduced from experience, and the right to acquire property by the extension of the conscious self in moral relations with others is simply more "visible and certain" than other conceivable claims of right.[70]

Locke's emphasis on the natural basis of the property right marks an important conceptual break from virtually the entire natural liberty tradition of seventeenth-century philosophy. In this respect, the natural property right is a crucial element of Locke's attempt to deal with the problem of moral knowledge. The rights of the appropriating self that are rooted in the universal human experience of material need and contact with physical nature ground a moral teaching that Locke concludes is more accessible to rational examination than the knowledge of God's "Workmanship," and is much less prone to sectarian controversy.[71] The converse of Locke's epistemological skepticism about innate ideas is a relative optimism about the intellectual resources available to the rational faculties through simple ideas produced by sense perception and elementary reflection on basic physical needs. In this way, Locke's theory of property provides an added dimension to his treatment of demonstrative morality in the *Essay*. Just as demonstration is not the only kind of knowledge, so too is demonstration not the only form of moral reasoning. Sensitive knowledge is the least certain kind of knowledge, less certain than intuitive and demonstrative, but it is also crucially the most accessible to human understanding because it has its roots in evidence supplied by sensible experience "of particular external objects" that produce perception (E 4.2.14.537–8). The obvious limitation on sensitive knowledge is that we can only know the idea that a thing produces in our minds and not the real essence of the thing itself. However, as a form of moral reasoning, this limitation is not decisive. Locke insists that sensitive experience can produce knowledge about the integrity of the self and by extension allow for the identification with other selves that can provide some basis for moral judgments. Moreover, the structure of this form of moral reasoning has its cognitive foundation in very simple ideas derived from physical sensation.

These simple ideas rooted in "Natural Wants" such as "Hunger, Thirst, Heat, [and] Cold" are the proper "Materials of our Knowledge," and provide a firmer basis for morality than "fantastical...Acquired Habits" such as the "itch after Honour, Power, [and] Riches."[72] Simple ideas of pleasure

---

[70] E 4.15.3.
[71] Forde, "Natural Theology," 396, 403.
[72] E 2.2.2, 21.45. See the valuable discussion in Peter Myers, *Our Only Star and Compass: Locke and the Struggle for Political Rationality* (Lanham: Rowman & Littlefield, 1998), p. 110.

and pain supply an epistemological and empirical ground for a notion of harm rooted in demonstrable physicality that has obvious implications for Locke's constitutional theory of limited government, as well as his philosophy more generally.[73] It is this ability to construct and abstract a conception of harm from simple ideas of pleasure and pain that renders scholastic debates about species redundant. The universal experience of human physicality and the natural intellectual capacity to understand a conception of harm derived from our physical nature combine to produce natural law principles of morality accessible to any individual "who will but consult" her or his somatic reality.

Thus for Locke, the problem of moral knowledge that explains the difficulty in applying the law of nature in the world is the human tendency to view moral principles either with Hooker in terms of natural rational faculties informed by a comprehensive teleology or as purely legal products of human will à la Hobbes, rather than referring complex moral ideas back to the simple ideas of which they are comprised. Locke's concept of self-ownership supplies the natural basis for the moral conclusions Hobbes thought untenable in the state of nature. Hobbes' state of nature is so far from including anything like Locke's idea of self-ownership that he denies any natural right to property and even allows a natural right to "one another's body."[74] In contrast, Locke claims that the individual is capable by nature of deducing the reciprocal character of rights and duties by reflecting on one's own status as a rights-bearer: I can reason from my self-ownership that others are self-owners too.

This is not to suggest that Locke's theory of self-ownership renders civil society supererogatory. He assumes that the moral knowledge available to individuals in the state of nature is generally inadequate to ensure peace in that condition. For Locke, the transition from the state of nature to civil society is perhaps best understood as a consequence of the inherent fallibility of human faculties that can only imperfectly adjust to the unreasonable demands of self-love, on the one hand, and to inadequate sensory knowledge, on the other. Locke suggests that the "inconveniences" of the state of nature are also tied to the material conditions of the state of nature, which becomes conspicuously less harmonious with the introduction of money and the expanded holdings it allows (II: 48, 51).[75] For our

---

[73] This is not, of course, to suggest that Locke's conception of harm is not itself contestable. For example, see McClure, "Limits of Toleration," 378–381.

[74] Hobbes, Leviathan, 14.4.80.

[75] For good treatments of the problems produced in Locke's state of nature by the use of money and expanded holdings, see McClure, *Judging Rights*, ch. 4 and Tully, *Locke in Contexts*, 27–29, 35–36.

purposes, however, the key is that Locke emphatically concluded that the moral knowledge deduced from a conception of self-ownership is a reliable basis for determining the terms of individual agency and the proper limits of political obligation.

The antiabsolutist thrust of Locke's argument contrasts sharply with Hobbesian and, to a lesser extent, Grotian and Pufendorian contractualism. For Locke, the security of property not only shapes the purpose, but also establishes the limits of legitimate government. He affirms that the natural right of reparation, unlike the restraint right, is not absorbed completely within the competence of government. The government may not remit reparation for an injured party who Locke claims has "a Right to demand in his own Name" just compensation for damages presumably through laws of equity, chancery and civil courts (II: 11). Moreover, Locke's argument that the "Power to lay and levy Taxes on the People" relies on "the Consent of the Majority" makes some form of representative assembly a vital element of legitimate government (II: 140). While Locke insists that property rights are subject to reasonable regulation by public authority, the relative security of property provides an important measure of legitimate government action.[76] According to Locke's reasoning, Hobbes' formulation of the sovereign's absolute control over property is the model of arbitrary government *par excellence*.

Whereas the core of Locke's critique of Hobbes is his objection to the latter's diminution of the intellectual provision for natural justice, Locke's break from the traditional natural law rests on the notion that we are in a crucial sense less provided for by nature than Hooker assumed. Locke's account of natural scarcity, especially his assertion that unassisted nature is worth "little more than nothing" (II: 43), counters what he takes to be the exaggerated notion of natural beneficence underlying scholastic natural law theory.[77] Hooker's natural teleology placed physical needs far below moral

---

[76] While Tully (James Tully, *A Discourse on Property: Locke and his Adversaries* [Cambridge: Cambridge University Press, 1980]) and Kramer (Matthew Kramer, *John Locke and the Origins of Private Property* [Cambridge: Cambridge University Press, 1997], pp. 240–254) are correct to identify an important collectivist dimension in Locke's treatment of property, the private root of the property right in personal self-ownership makes any interpretation of Locke as a thoroughgoing communitarian hard to sustain.

[77] Myers, *Our Only Star*, 117–120. For Locke, of course, it is human labor and the introduction of money by human convention that allows the overcoming of natural scarcity as witnessed, he suggests, by the relative prosperity of agricultural and monetarized England compared with the crushing poverty of precolonial America (II: 41, 37, 48, 46; cf. C. B. MacPherson, *The Political Theory of Possessive Individualism* [Oxford: Oxford University Press, 1962], pp. 199–220 and McClure, *Judging Rights*, 210).

and spiritual truth in the ascending scale of values directing political life – government must mean more than simply supplying the "hogs" with their "mash."[78] For Locke, the "strong desire of self-preservation" (I: 86) is the only justification human beings require in order to acquire property: We do not need any higher moral purpose or end.[79] Just as the scholastics mistakenly postulated innate speculative and practical ideas, Locke charges that so too do they erroneously assume that material provision for human needs can be derogated to authoritative expressions of moral and spiritual goods. According to Locke, both "mash" and comprehensive moral knowledge are harder to come by than Hooker believed.

This is not, of course, to suggest that epistemological skepticism was the sole, or even primary, basis for Locke's support of toleration. Rather we mean to suggest that Locke's theory of property and natural executive power reveals both a positive and negative dimension of his toleration argument. The negative aspect involves the epistemological limitations on knowledge of the means to salvation. However, for Locke, these limits do not undermine the moral sovereignty of the individual but rather serve on the political level primarily to restrict the claims of government to exercise legitimate coercive power in service of this goal. The positive aspect of Locke's argument is contained in his theory of property, which not only provides the epistemological basis for his idea of self-ownership and the conception of harm flowing from this premise, but also allows for the incorporation of these fundamental moral insights into the civil realm through the logical structure of a theory of delegated powers deriving from individuals. Thus it is the conjunction of the negative and positive, or skeptical and constitutive aspects of Locke's epistemological argument for moral knowledge that gives his theory of property its distinctive political and theological implications.

While his reconsideration of the epistemological grounds of morality relates only tangentially to the theological questions surrounding the doctrine of personal salvation, the primary political effect of Locke's argument is to narrow the scope of legitimate political power and consequently to remove matters of religious faith largely beyond the purview of government. As such, far from being unrelated or only marginally related to matters of religion and politics, the state of nature and its individualist and possessive premises are central to Locke's tolerationist commitments.

---

[78] Hooker 8.3.5.
[79] Harvey Mansfield, "On the Political Character of Property in Locke," in *Powers, Possessions and Freedoms: Essays in Honour of C.B. MacPherson* (Toronto: University of Toronto Press 1979), pp. 23–38, esp. 29.

Property permeates Locke's narrow definition of government in the *Letter Concerning Toleration*, which he argues is instituted by individuals solely "for the procuring, preserving and advancing of their own Civil Interests" by which he means "Life, Liberty, Health...and the Possession of outward things, such as Money, Lands, Houses, Furniture, and the Like."[80] This account of government in turn produces a radical reinterpretation of the meaning of a Church as "a voluntary Society of Men, joining themselves of their own accord, in order to the publick worship of God, in such a manner as they judge acceptable to him, and effectual to the Salvation of their Souls."[81] By decisively severing the nature and goals of religion from that of government, and validating both by a conception of harm with a presumably solid epistemological foundation in sensory perception of simple ideas, Locke's theory of property aims both to limit the power of government and to expand the moral claim of the sovereign individual to exercise private judgment on the most fundamental matters of conscience.

The self-owning individual executor of the law of nature in Locke's state of nature account is at once both familiar to us as the embodiment of the moral and political individualism associated with modern liberalism and yet also a more complex social being than the "atomistic individual" or "unencumbered self" we often encounter among liberalism's contemporary critics.[82] Lockean epistemology and its assessments of the limits and possibilities of moral knowledge support a conception of shared moral goods not only compatible with, but in a crucial sense deriving from, individual natural rights. While the natural right to punish and the idea of the self contained in Locke's theory of property have a self-regarding core, Locke argues that these individual rights must, at least in a general sense, be understood in light of a fundamental social dynamic.

According to Locke's state of nature theory, individual judgment about the moral requirement of the law of nature lies at the root of civil government. However, Locke not only maintains that concern for individual rights animates civil society, he also confirms that the moral sovereignty of the individual necessarily includes the possibility of extended moral sympathies based on the epistemologically apprehensible recognition of basic human equality and rational autonomy. The uneasy combination of

---

[80] Locke, *Letter Concerning Toleration*, 26.
[81] *Ibid.*, p. 28.
[82] See, for example, Charles Taylor, "Atomism," in C. Taylor, *Philosophy and the Human Sciences: Philosophical Papers, Vol. II* (Cambridge: Cambridge University Press, 1985), pp. 185–210 and Michael Sandel, *Democracy's Discontent: America in Search of a Public Philosophy* (Cambridge: Belknap Press, 1996).

empiricist epistemology in the *Essay* and universalist rights philosophy in the *Second Treatise* may signify the extent to which Locke is willing to pay a hedonic price for social goods. To the extent that the state of nature is part of a logical demonstration of Locke's claims for the possibility of understanding moral truth, this account also supports the goal of moral philosophy as Locke presents it in the *Essay*. However, as the difficulties presented by the state of nature seem to suggest, Locke was well aware that this demonstration is only partially completed in the state of nature. The problem for acquiring moral knowledge embedded in his discussion of the natural right to punish and the normative dimension of self-ownership flowing from the natural right of property point beyond the state of nature to the political possibilities logically deduced from the natural condition. Government thus is a complex moral idea perpetually suggested to the human mind by the situation produced in its absence. The political mani-festation of the democratization of mind in the constitution of government is, we realize, never far from the surface in the state of nature.

3

Constitutional Government

The state of nature points beyond itself to the establishment of civil government. Indeed, government is the ever-present latent possibility coursing through Locke's account of the state of nature. However, while the state of nature clearly ascribes to the individual the status of primary unit of political analysis, the moral principles flowing from natural freedom and equality provide no obvious explanation as to how government comes into being or how it should be constituted. The only theoretical prerequisite that Locke's state of nature places on the origin of government is that it presupposes the centrality of the idea of consent: Naturally free and equal beings who logically have no natural rulers can only be governed rightfully by individuals or institutions to whom they have consented to be ruled.

In order to understand more fully the relationship between the state of nature and civil government in Locke's political theory, we need to begin by locating the phenomenon of government in the context of Locke's way of ideas. Government is, by virtue of its eidetic character, a prime example of a Lockean mixed mode for it is an idea that can exist as an intelligible idea independently from the material and logical reality of the state of nature. The intellectual materials of government pre-exist its actual establishment; indeed, the logical coherence of Locke's state of nature theory depends on the possibility that some individuals can in principle conceive of civil government on the same basis that we can understand moral ideas like adultery or homicide without ever having seen a government or of living under civil rule. Thus, the complex moral reality of the pre-civil state of nature poses no insuperable intellectual or epistemological obstacle to the creation of government. However, the individualist premise of Locke's state of nature requires rejecting the classical teleology, which presupposed the idea of natural human sociability. Lockean individuals may be well suited for society and likely flourish in a structured civil order, but in contrast to Aristotle and his many followers in the schools and pulpits of early-modern Europe, Locke's state of nature account signifies a total repudiation of the notion that the political community enjoys an ontological priority over the individual. As the creators of government from a condition notable by its absence, individuals are both logically and existentially its masters.

But if government is a mixed mode composed of a number of other ideas, themselves deeply complex, where in Locke's state of nature theory do we find the constituent ideas that combine to produce our notion of government? From our examination of the state of nature in the previous chapter, it is apparent that there are at least two complex ideas central to both the state of nature and Locke's idea of government: punishment and property. Neither idea alone, or even together, simply amounts to government and society like a mathematical equation. Rather the state of nature is the seed-bed of government through a more complex and circuitous means. The theoretical coherence of Locke's state of nature, as well as its expository value for describing the formation of government, crucially depends on the dual propositions that the individual in a pre-civil condition can understand oneself as a distinct self-owning, rights-bearing person and that this self-conscious individual can understand oneself as authorized to execute the law of nature. Punishment and property are then the cognitive and conceptual building blocks of government, and in this sense, the state of nature and civil government are inextricably connected in the central moral dynamic of Lockean liberal politics.

Locke's account of the origins and characteristics of government is thus derivative from, and necessarily dependent on, his state of nature theory. However, the distinct eidetic and genetic dimensions of Locke's approach to political philosophy assumes greater significance in his treatment of government than in either his state of nature theory or the philosophical considerations of his epistemology. In the eidetic account, in which Locke focuses on the formal properties of government, the central organizing principle is the equality of natural rights-bearing individuals. In this respect, Locke's constitutional theory flows directly from his moral philosophy: If we are to conceive of a government consistent with this theoretical and normative starting point, then it would need to have certain properties. Government thus must be the product of meaningful consent, directed to securing rights, placing limits on natural liberty, providing institutional expression for a pre-existing social reality, and having certain limits placed on its own power to avoid endangering its people. Government, for Locke, is an idea constructed to remedy the natural "inconveniences" of the state

of nature, while remaining a recognizable embodiment of the moral principles of freedom and equality. In this sense, Locke's account of the formation of government takes on the character of a logical demonstration.

However, Locke's genetic account, which focuses on observations about
how a thing actually comes to be, ventures onto the very different ground
of natural history. As we shall see in what follows, in the course of discuss-
ing the historical origins of government, Locke revises his initial treatment
of the state of nature considerably by adding anthropological and sociological analysis that sheds new light not only on his formal account of the properties of government, but also even toward a different, and in some respects
fuller, development of the state of nature. As a mixed mode, the idea of government can, in principle, be known completely because it is not dependent
on an archetype in nature. However, as Locke's account of the historical
origins of government illustrates, government is also an idea inseparable
from the cognitive and physical reality of human beings and thus necessarily possesses some of the opacity he typically associates with substances. It
is hardly surprising then that Locke entirely abandons the classical ideal of
the best regime as the goal of political philosophy. Indeed, he scarcely even
considers the classical regime typology that had dominated western political
thought for two millennia. Rather the fluid relational character of Locke's
state of nature encourages an experimental and pragmatic approach to the
analysis of government. Lockean political science thus bears considerable
intellectual kinship with his natural philosophy.

In this chapter, we will examine Locke's theory of constitutional government. We will follow the lead set by Locke's "way of ideas" and try to
illuminate the nature of government by decomposing this complex idea
and reconstructing its constituent parts. Prior to Locke, the "constitution"
of government meant primarily the arrangement of political offices and
institutions in a given regime. However, Locke's philosophical commitment to a novel epistemology and a systematic approach to the construction of ideas contributed enormously to a new perspective on the study
of government. The distinct ideas or, more properly, powers of which the
complex idea of government is composed are, Locke claims, the ideas of
legislative and executive power. Each of these powers emerged in the state
of nature account in a different aspect. Legislative power was, of course,
most marked by its absence. Natural laws without the support of civil
institutions proved to be deeply problematic both with respect to issues
of apprehension and especially application. Thus on one level, the *raison
d'etre* of civil government is quite simple: to create "a common establish'd
Law and Judicature to appeal to, with Authority to decide Controversies"

among individuals.[1] With respect to executive power, the exact opposite is true; there is an abundance, or more accurately an overabundance, of executive power in the state of nature. Locke's argument for the primacy of the natural executive power inhering in individuals leaves little doubt that he viewed the idea of executive power as naturally stronger and more deeply rooted in human experience than the idea of legislation. It is the natural imbalance between the relative clarity and force of the two constituent ideas that together form the intellectual core of government, which requires the nearly complete surrender of natural executive power as a precondition for the formation of civil government. While government is a combination of legislative and executive power, Locke insists that legislative power is more artificial, and hence more of a human contrivance, than executive power.

If the melding of the ideas of legislative and executive power forms the theoretical peak of Locke's account of civil government, then his natural historical account of the origin of government can be said to create an additional layer of complexity to an already very complex idea. As we shall strive to demonstrate hereafter, Locke believed that the inherited idea of civil government was problematic in several senses. First, historically the complex idea of government has typically proven to be too complex for many past societies to grasp. Rather than melding legislative and executive power, the historical experience of government initially involved the assimilation of the complex idea of government into the simpler, constituent idea of executive power. For much of human history, government was basically just executive power as embodied in unregulated monarchy; a natural tendency Locke identifies in the proponents of absolutism in his own time. Thus one aim of Locke's treatment of constitutional government is to clearly distinguish legislative and executive power, which he does in a manner that foreshadows the later development of separation of powers theory by Montesquieu, Hume, and Madison. Legislative power and a theory of legislative supremacy is the truly modern discovery Locke seeks to enunciate in his constitutional theory. However, Locke's account of civil government goes beyond simply distinguishing legislative and executive power. At its most fundamental level, Locke seeks to redefine what is meant by constitutionalism. The complex idea of government requires a new idea of constitution, rooted in the individualist premise of the state of nature,

---

[1] John Locke, *Two Treatises of Government*, Peter Laslett, ed. (Cambridge: Cambridge University Press, 1988), Second Treatise, sec. 87 (hereafter in notes and text Treatise and section).

which establishes the constituent power of society as the active principle governing even the institutions of government. The most significant theoretical achievement of Locke's reflections on government is his conception of a legal power to control the legislative power itself. It is to Locke more than any previous political thinker that the western tradition owes a debt for recognizing most clearly that there was something deeply problematic about the way for centuries it had approached the whole question of constitutional government.

LOCKE'S CONSTITUTIONAL PROBLEMATIC

Today we typically associate constitutionalism with many or most of the following characteristics: a fundamental law expressed in a written constitution drafted by a special convention or assembly, ratified by the people and amendable only by an extraordinary supralegislative process, which prescribes the rule of general standing laws produced by representative institutions operating on the basis of some form of separation of powers and limited by a charter recognizing judicially enforceable basic rights reserved by individuals. In sum, liberal constitutionalism is practically inseparable from the principle that any legitimate political order must be governed by a fundamental law governing and regulating the persons and institutions that make and execute the law.

By this standard, Locke is often seen as a problematic, or at least deeply ambiguous, theoretical forbearer of modern liberal constitutionalism. Although he is generally recognized as a seminal thinker in the development of the liberal idea of rights, many commentators challenge Locke's liberal constitutionalist credentials on the grounds that not only did he understand the rule of law as identical to the rule of the lawmaking body, but he also endorsed the extralegal power of executive prerogative that allows the executive "to act according to discretion, for the publick good, without the prescription of the Law, and sometimes even against it" (II: 160). This fundamental tension between legislative supremacy and executive prerogative is frequently seen as the theoretical core of Locke's constitutional problematic. As one observer notes: "One of the great challenges to a reading of Locke's work as essentially democratic and liberal is his explicit teaching of the prerogative of the executive."[2] Far from being one of the founders of liberal constitutionalism, in the judgment of many Locke uncomfortably

---

[2] Peter Josephson, *The Great Art of Government: Locke's Use of Consent* (Lawrence: University Press of Kansas, 2002), p. 231.

straddled a major conceptual divide with one foot in modern legalism and the other firmly planted in the prerogatives of England's pre-modern monarchical heritage.

In the effort to account for the legitimation crisis of Lockean constitutionalism marked by the conflicting claims of omnipotent legislatures and executive majesty, commentators have typically produced two contrary interpretations of Locke's teaching on executive power: a "broad" and "narrow" interpretation. In the *broad* view of executive power, prerogative is interpreted to signify Locke's endorsement of extraconstitutional power as a requirement of effective or enlightened political leadership. In his assessment of political contingency, harsh natural necessity, and the need to direct popular consent to the rational directives of the law of nature – so the argument goes – Locke registered his criticism of the harmful legalism encouraged by the notion of legislation as the sole regulative principle of common political life.[3] For their part, proponents of the *narrow* interpretation of Lockean executive power minimize the significance of prerogative by arguing that he intended the executive to be purely ministerial in relation to the supreme legislature, and thus even prerogative must be seen in terms of a merely temporary measure which is subject to the validation or reversal by the legislature once it is convened.[4] While the *broad* and *narrow* interpretations of executive power are in one sense radically divergent, viewing it as either an extraordinary authority to set aside law at discretion or an entirely subordinate function bound tightly to the service of all-powerful legislatures, they are similar in another, perhaps more fundamental, sense inasmuch as both strands of interpretation rest on the premise that Locke conceived of law and constitution as coextensive. For some, Locke's identification of constitutional government with legislative supremacy means that executive discretion to discard or even violate law must make prerogative

---

[3] See, for example, Larry Arnhart, "The 'God-Like Prince': John Locke, Executive Prerogative, and the American Presidency" *Presidential Studies Quarterly*, 9, 2 (Spring 1979): 122–125; Clement Fatovic, "Constitutionalism and Contingency: Locke's Theory of Prerogative" *History of Political Thought*, 25, 2 (Summer 2004): 278–284; Josephson, *Great Art*, pp. 240–241; Pasquale Pasquino, "Locke on King's Prerogative" *Political Theory*, 26, 2 (April 1998): 198–201; and Martin Seliger, *The Liberal Politics of John Locke* (London: Allen & Unwin, 1968), pp. 367–372.

[4] See, for example, Richard Ashcraft, *Locke's Two Treatises of Government* (London: Allen & Unwin, 1987), pp. 187–190; Alex Tuckness, *Locke and the Legislative Point of View* (Princeton: Princeton University Press, 2002), pp. 118, 121–126; J. M. Vile, *Constitutionalism and the Separation of Powers*, 2nd ed. (Indianapolis: Liberty Fund, 1998), p. 72; Jeremy Waldron, *The Dignity of Legislation* (Oxford: Oxford University Press, 1999), p. 66; and David Weaver, "Leadership, Locke and the Federalist" *American Journal of Political Science*, 41, 2 (April 1997): 426–428, 431–434.

an essentially extraconstitutional power. For others, it is precisely Locke's concern to maintain legislative supremacy over the executive that reduces prerogative to a largely ministerial function. In either view of Locke's executive power, the constitution is what the legislature says it is.

This chapter proposes that Locke is much more of a liberal constitutionalist than the typical interpretive framework would allow, and indeed that the fundamental assumption underlying the current debate about Locke and executive power, namely that he conceived of law and constitution as coextensive, is mistaken. Whereas the focus of the debate generally relates to the perceived tension between natural and civil law (whether or not Locke grants the executive natural law authorization to transgress civil law), the connected and in some respects equally important question of what Locke meant by the term *constitution* has received much less attention.[5] We shall see that the theoretical core of Locke's executive power teaching is neither prerogative nor legislative supremacy, but rather his conception of a principle of constitutional legitimacy that is distinct from and superior to normal legislation. In Locke's formulation, executive prerogative is a potentially enormous extralegal power, but it is not in the most crucial sense extraconstitutional. Rather Locke understood "just" prerogative as a constitutionally authorized discretionary power delegated by the people to be exercised on trust within the parameters of legitimacy defined by the fundamental laws and structures of a given constitutional order. Once we recognize Locke's subordination of the formal principle of legislative supremacy to the substantive principle of constitutionality, it is possible to understand both the broad and narrow reading of executive power as consistent with the normative and legal framework embedding executive power in the multiform institutions originating in the constituent power of the individuals in society.

By examining Locke's treatment of executive power from its conceptual root in his foundational state of nature account through to his analysis of the civil executive and the relation between prerogative and the constitution, it can be shown that Locke's theory of executive power is framed by many of the core principles of constitutionalism familiar to modern liberals. This is true in two senses. First, Locke contends that the fundamental rules constituting the legislature established by the people are in most cases unalterable by the legislature. Second, Locke employed the concept of the

---

[5] But see Robert Faulkner, "The First Liberal Democrat: Locke's Popular Government" *Review of Politics*, 61, 3 (Fall 2001): 11–12 and Harvey Mansfield, *Taming the Prince: The Ambivalence of Modern Executive Power* (New York: Free Press, 1989), pp. 187–188.

separation of powers in a way that allows the nonlegislative elements of the constitution legal standing not dependent on the authority of the legislature. Locke's theory *permits*, although it does not *require*, the people to entrench constitutionally the executive's power. For example, in his account of supreme executive power, Locke suggests that an executive acting in his or her executive capacity may have not only a legally prescribed but also a constitutionally protected role in the government.

However, Locke's constitutional theory was also fundamentally incomplete, even on its own terms, inasmuch as he did not formulate or recognize clear constitutional limits on the substance of what government does, as opposed to how it is constituted. The omission from Locke's argument of an explicit statement of substantive constitutional limits on government action is not due to his supposed commitment either to prerogative or legislative supremacy, but rather to his inability or unwillingness to complete his constitutional theory with a systematic account of the structural mechanics of constitutional framing and his surprising reticence about the legitimating principle of general suffrage. Locke was a harbinger of a more democratic and distinctively liberal form of constitutionalism than he explicitly endorsed. However, there is nothing in the logic of Locke's argument that rules out the possibility of written constitutions, charters of rights, and clear statements of the constitutionally protected set of nonlegislative executive and judicial powers; indeed, his concept of delegated powers and constituent authority is a theoretical precondition for liberal constitutionalism as we understand it. Locke's great achievement then was to adumbrate these important elements in the development of nascent liberal constitutionalism and to bequeath a rich body of constitutional thought to his intellectual heirs in the eighteenth- and nineteenth-century Age of Revolution and Reform, and even to our own time.

THE NATURAL HISTORY OF EXECUTIVE POWER

In order to understand the complex dimensions of Lockean constitutionalism we need to reconsider briefly Locke's reflections on the origin and development of political power per se. For Locke, "Political, or Civil Society" (II: 89) must be understood largely by reference to two pre-political conditions reflecting distinct aspects of human experience: the state of nature and pre-political society. In contrast to his state of nature account proper, which centered primarily on logical deductions from first moral principles, Locke's full treatment of the origins of government also involved a considerable dependence on the use of the natural historical method of observation and empirical analysis that he associated most directly with natural philosophy in the *Essay Concerning Human Understanding*. It turns out that for Locke, government is a complex idea that contains multifarious properties and is amenable to various modes of examination.

As an analytical postulation that defines the concept of natural rights and supplies the measure of legitimacy for any political institution, the state of nature is the theoretical core of Locke's political philosophy. It is also, however, as a theoretical proposition an inauspicious seedbed for constitutional government because it is a condition characterized primarily by the absence of civil law.[6] The state of nature is a "State of perfect Freedom" and "also of Equality" (II: 4) wherein there is no natural principle of rule or authoritative institutions. Although consent is the only legitimate basis for political rule, Locke maintains that there is a natural moral rule governing the state of nature which is based on "Reason, which is that Law, [and] teaches all Mankind, who will but consult it, that being all equal and independent, no one ought to harm another" (II: 6). In addition to the no-harm command, the law of nature also enjoins: "Everyone as he is bound to preserve himself... so by like reason when his own Preservation comes not in competition, ought he, as much as he can, to preserve the rest of Mankind" (II: 6). The central moral reality of the state of nature is "the Power to Execute" (II: 7) the law of nature by which the individual is authorized to punish aggressors who violate the no-harm principle of the natural law. Thus, the transgression of the no-harm command of the natural law in particular cases is justified only in service of this same principle in the general sense, for otherwise, Locke concludes, the law of nature would "be in vain" if no one in "the State of Nature, had a Power to Execute that Law" (II: 7).

There are three main features of Locke's discussion of executive power in the state of nature that have a direct bearing on his constitutional theory. First, he indicates that the execution of the unwritten natural law does not imply a form of rule; punishment does not contradict the principle of natural equality, and thus any understanding of government must be rooted in consent. Second, the natural executive power of the law of nature is by definition a wholly discretionary power whereby the individual is authorized to punish another human being without the sanction of any political or religious institution (II: 87). The rational individual is authorized to act purely on the basis of auto-interpretation of the natural law. Third, Locke

---

[6] John Scott, "The Sovereignless State and Locke's Language of Obligation" *American Political Science Review*, 94, 3 (September 2000): 554–555 and John Simmons, *The Edge of Anarchy* (Princeton: Princeton University Press, 1993), p. 20.

identifies in this natural power of individuals the primal root of civil executive power inasmuch as from the individual natural right to punish violators of the natural law "which right of punishing is in everybody" comes
the legitimate power of the civil magistrate "who hath the common right
of punishing put into his hands" (II: 11). The source of political power is
the natural executive power of individuals.[7] As we have seen, this natural executive power is both the source of government and, for Locke, the
source of the serious "Inconveniences" in the state of nature such as hasty,
irrational, and self-serving punishments that make society both desirable
and in a sense necessary (II: 13, 21, 123–7). The constitutional significance
of Locke's state of nature account lies then, at least partly, in the fact that
not only is executive power the innate political phenomenon, but in its
original form in the state of nature executive power is also conceptually
coeval with prerogative.

The second important element in Locke's natural history of executive
power, which extends his analysis beyond the state of nature, is his account
of pre-political society or the condition of human sociability prior to, or
independent of, the formal creation of civil society and government. It is in
this genetic account of the origin of society that Locke adds a crucial historical and sociological element to the mainly eidetic features of his state of
nature theory, and as such, executive power and prerogative play a central
role not only in the largely analytical device of the state of nature, but also in
Locke's more anthropological account of patriarchal and monarchical rule
in pre-political society. Locke indicates that the pre-political condition contains a degree of social organization and hierarchy but lacks the authoritative
legislative institutions characterizing civil government: The rule of fathers
and the first kings, he claims, was "nearly all prerogative" (II: 162). The pre-
political form of rule is essentially nonlegal and based in filial deference to
paternal discretion. Even though grown children, like all individuals in the
pre-political condition, retained their natural executive power, they would
routinely submit to the father's authority "and joyn with him" in punishing wrongdoers because "the Custom of obeying him, in their Childhood,
made it easier to submit to him, rather than to any other" (II: 105). Paternal
prerogative emerges then as a primal sociological condition that can direct
the natural executive power of the individuals in a relatively tight network of
blood relations, and thus in historical terms may serve to stabilize somewhat
the inconveniences inherent in the state of nature.

---

[7] James Tully, *An Approach to Political Philosophy: Locke in Contexts* (Cambridge:
      Cambridge University Press, 1993), p. 15, 21.

It was the trusting passivity encouraged by patriarchalism, Locke claims, that accustomed people in the pre-political condition to one-man rule over the extended social unit. In the simpler ways of pre-political society prior to the great economic expansion allowed by the introduction of a monetary system, individuals had few possessions to protect and hence had "no need of many laws" to decide disputes that arose among them. The purpose of rule set by "the equality of a poor way of living" was tied almost exclusively to the needs of communal defense "against Foreign Force" (II: 107). Thus pre-political peoples "used their natural freedom" to select as leader "the wisest and bravest man to conduct them in Wars" (II: 105, 107).

There are two striking features of Locke's account of monarchy in pre-political society. First, while the early kings were not limited by law, Locke argues that the terms of their rule were narrowly construed to being "little more than Generals of their Armies" who may have enjoyed sweeping prerogative over matters of war, but "at home and in times of peace, they exercised very little Dominion" (II: 108). Locke implies that so strictly confined was the power of these captains to issues of war that early monarchy and patriarchal rule over families were probably mutually compatible and overlapping kinds of rule in the informal web of pre-political authority. Locke's second point, however, is that both patriarchal and early monarchical rule must be understood as essentially consensual. The considerable discretionary power of patriarchs and chieftains was "tacitly submitted to" by the inhabitants of pre-political society who demonstrated their implied consent by both their compliance and the bare fact of nonresistance (II: 110). In pre-political society, Locke identifies a measure of social organization and the principle of command, but not civil government in the full sense because generals and *paterfamilias* do not have the authority to make laws carrying the power of life and death that regulate the actions of an entire community in the manifold aspects of life (I: 129, II: 3). Locke explicitly contrasts these simple forms of social existence with the formal bonds of civil society that depend on "the consent of Individuals, to joyn and make one Society" with a "common establish'd Law and Judicature" (II: 106, 87). The prevalence of prerogative in patriarchal and early monarchical rule is thus a function of the political minimalism in the pre-civil condition, one defined essentially by the absence of a shared legislative power. By the standards of legitimacy applicable to civil government, the almost uniformly discretionary rule in pre-political society, that "Government without Laws" (II: 219), is for all intents and purposes no government at all.

The theoretical import of Locke's account of pre-political society as it relates to his teaching on civil government is that it establishes the basis both

for his crucial conceptual distinction between executive power and prerogative and a foreshadowing of separation of powers theory that would became
central to later liberal thought. While executive power and prerogative are
practically coterminus in the state of nature, Locke deduces from the historical experience of patriarchy and early monarchy a developing political
awareness as individuals in pre-political society become conscious of the need
to set "express limits" on the discretion of rulers and to devise "Methods of
restraining any Exorbitances" of prerogative through "balancing the power
of Government, by placing several parts of it in different hands" (II: 112,
107; 162–6). In contrast to the historical tendency of early monarchy in
which the rule of one reduces inexorably to unlimited prerogative, Locke
maintains that the intellectual root of civil government derives from the
recognition that individuals and their property "could never be safe" until
"every single person became subject, equally with other the Meanest Men,
to those Laws, which he himself, as part of the Legislative had established"
(II: 94). Locke indicates that the idea of civil government is born in the
repudiation of unlimited prerogative, and thus the establishment of civil
government necessarily involves both the disentangling of executive power
and prerogative, and the articulation of natural political power, which in
its original form is wholly executive, into discrete legislative and executive
functions with a distinct institutional expression. Civil government presupposes a radical transformation in the nature of executive power.

The natural history of executive power stands then as an important
element in Locke's reconstruction of the theoretical development of the
complex idea of government. The history of government and society is not
always a happy tale, but Locke indicates that a clear understanding of the
practical development of the pre-civil condition is a salutary exercise that
further deepens our sense of the already considerable complexity inherent
in the formal properties of any social organization composed by natural
rights bearing individuals. He does so, however, by means of the "plain,
historical method" quite distinct from the logical demonstrations familiar
to us from his state of nature account in the opening chapters of the *Second
Treatise*. Observation and empirical analysis confirms what the state of
nature could only postulate; namely, that executive power enjoys a natural
primacy in human experience and cognition. It is this intellectual primacy
that threatens perpetually to obscure society's understanding of both the
moral foundation and the proper structures and practical goals of civil government. History, Locke suggests, teaches us that we need to plumb the
depths of moral and political theory ever more deeply, if we are to have any
real hope of truly grounding right political practice.

THE CONSTITUTION OF GOVERNMENT

Locke's theoretical account of the creation of civil government involves a complex and multilayered process. It requires first of all complete unanimity among a people to form civil society in an act including the "consent of every individual" (II: 96). The form of consent in this process differs markedly from the tacit consent characterizing pre-political society primarily because deliberate and "express consent" is the necessary precondition for any individual to become a full member of society and to register conscious authorization of the transfer of his or her natural executive power to the community (II: 119, 121).[8] The creation of civil government, however, involves not societal unanimity, but rather communal majority rule insofar as society authorizes the majority to act for "the whole" in the construction of government (II: 96–99). As a both practical and moral principle, the express delegation of natural authority and the structuring of communal will represent the very core of the process of making government. The converse of this distinct process of forming civil society and government is the possibility of its "dissolution," a theoretical postulation applying to civil life that is inconceivable for either the state of nature or pre-civil society precisely because these conditions lack the formal consensual bonds of social union underlying civil government. The central decision reserved exclusively for the majority in society is where to locate the "Legislative Power," for the common "Umpire" supplied by a legislature is both the "soul" of the political society and the one institution most clearly demarcating civil government from the pre-political condition (II: 132, 87, 212).

We must be careful not to interpret Locke's conception of the creation of society and government as two completely different processes. Despite the difference between the universalist basis of society and the majoritarian ground of government, they are best understood as conceptually distinct but interdependent processes of social unification and delegation of power.[9] Locke presents civil society as both a contractual relation produced by an explicit and express form of consent, and at the same time as the sole moral and jural entity that is capable of creating civil government. Pre-political

---

[8] Obviously Locke's *genetic* account of the historical rise of government through the restraints on prerogative is in some tension with his *eidetic* argument about the establishment of civil government in a discrete act of express societal consent. For interpretations of Locke's constitutionalism that give rather more normative weight to his historical argument than do I, see Josephson, *Great Art*, pp. 183–203 and Jeremy Waldron, "John Locke: Social Contract versus Political Anthropology" *Review of Politics*, 51, 2 (Winter 1989): 3–28.

[9] J. D. Mabbott, *John Locke* (London: MacMillan, 1973), p. 155.

social existence differs from "civil society" properly speaking because only the latter condition contains the element of express consent generating the immanent possibility of civil government. Unlike pre-political society, Lockean civil society is in a sense a form of government, the original form of all government, majority-rule democracy.[10] However, the majoritarian foundation of civil government does not necessitate the formation of a democratic regime. Locke indicates that democracy is only one of the three pure, and of infinite number of compound, forms of government available to societal choice (II: 132). The majority in society may locate the legislative power in a variety of structures and persons including hereditary offices. The majoritarian activity of constituting government may even have deeply countermajoritarian political implications.[11] Lockean civil society is the workshop of constitutional government: Society makes government.

In arguing that societal choice regarding the location of the "Power of making Laws" determines the form of government, Locke firmly establishes the efficient cause of government in the consent of the majority in society. However, the key to understanding the meaning of Locke's account of the creation of civil government is to recognize his crucial distinction between "the *Constitution* and *Laws* of the Government;" that is between two separate forms of activity – constituting and legislating – and the particular kinds of enactment that emerge from these distinct processes (II: 226). When Locke identifies the "Constitution of the Legislative" as the "first and fundamental Act of Society (II: 212)," he is referring to the active principle of constituent power, which involves the consent of the majority of society and is, as we have seen, entirely distinct from the activity of civil legislation that may, and perhaps most likely will, be performed by representative institutions that are not necessarily democratic in character.

Locke's use of the term "constitution" is one of the most striking features in his account of the origin of civil government. He routinely employs some form or cognate of *constitution* to designate the primal act of legislation by which "the Legislative constituted by Society" (II: 214) comes into being. This "First and Fundamental Positive Law" is unique, however, in the realm of legislative possibilities precisely because the actions of society that produce the legislature are logically and existentially prior to the instantiation of civil legislative power (II: 134). Locke indicates that the legislature is capable of acting only by virtue of a fundamental law providing

10   Nathan Tarcov, "Locke's *Second Treatise* and the 'Best Fence against Rebellion'" *Review of Politics*, 43, 2 (April 1981): 205.
11   Willmoore Kendall, *John Locke and the Doctrine of Majority-Rule* (Urbana: University of Illinois Press, 1941), p. 124.

and delimiting prior societal authorization to specific persons and institutions. The act of constituting government does not, however, necessitate the complete surrender of the regulative power of the community because not only may the community resume its constituent authority upon the dissolution of government (II: 243), but society may also delegate its authority to government as a strictly temporary power "if the Legislative Power be at first given by the Majority to one or more Persons only for their Lives, or any limited time" (II: 132).[12] Locke suggests that civil legislative power is so intrinsically a creature of the community that it may have a shelf life predetermined by society in the original act of constituting government.

The conceptual distinction between constituting and legislating pervades Locke's use of the terms "Constitution" (II: 153, 168, 226), "Positive Constitution" (II: 50), "Constituted Commonwealth" (II: 143, 149, 152–3, 205), as well as related terms such as "Forms of Government" (II: 198) or "Frame of Government" (II: 107, 156, 159, 192, 230).[13] In each of these instances, Locke is referring to the constitutional root of the legislative branch, to the formal structures and rules establishing a system of laws connecting enactments, institutions and authorized persons in a matrix of legitimate authority that is distinct from both pre-political society and the species of positive law generated by ordinary legislatures. In his use of the term "Constitution" to designate the extraordinary law created by civil society to govern the government, Locke appears to have envisioned something like the liberal principle of constitutional supremacy over ordinary legislative power.

Locke's openness to a wide variety of legitimate governments, including mixed popular and monarchical forms, reflects a clear theoretical bias toward the importance of constitutional foundations in consent. However, Locke is concerned not only to demonstrate the importance of consent, but also to show that a logically consistent theory of consent to some extent limits the choice of government available to the people. For example, Locke allows two logical alternative accounts for the process of constitutional framing. On the one hand, there is the readily identifiable process of

---

[12] As Scheuerman observes, Locke proposed a "Fundamental Constitution" for colonial Carolina that was not only unalterable by the legislature, but also established a time limit for any piece of legislation (see William Scheuerman, "Liberal Democracy and the Empire of Speed" *Polity*, 34, 1 [Fall 2001]: 56 and John Locke, "The Fundamental Constitutions of Carolina," *Political Essays*, Mark Goldie, ed. [Cambridge: Cambridge University Press, 1997], pp. 175–176, 181).

[13] See good discussions in Faulkner, "First Liberal Democrat," 11–12 and Mansfield, *Taming*, 187–188.

constitutional formation in which the constituent power of society generates a legislature that then by its own authority creates other constitutional actors such as the executive. In this *direct delegation* model of consent, the "first and fundamental positive Law" (II: 134) that creates the legislature represents the sum total of the community's direct participation in the act of constitutional framing. In this account, the legislature created by society originally acts like a constituent assembly that formulates and implements a constitutional plan for the community. The direct delegation model suggests a view of government that takes the constitution and law as being more or less coextensive, at least insofar as the constitution is what the legislature says it is, and the executive is, at least formally, subordinate as a delegated power of the legislature. Although Locke insists that every legislature is subject to certain natural law limits consistent with the proper end of government (II: 135–42), constitutionally speaking, the legislative power in this view is dominant because the community has little alternative but to recognize it as such.

Locke's theory of consent also, however, allows for a more refined and graduated process of constitutional framing that emphasizes the broad range and scope of societal constituent power rather than the omnicompetence of the legislature. In this *articulated delegation* model of consent, the "first and fundamental" act by which society creates the legislature is the necessary but by no means sole expression of societal choice. The act of constituting civil government can extend beyond simply the creation of a legislature toward the more comprehensive activity of complex constitutional design for the entire "Frame of Government" (II: 159). In this model of consent, the people may delegate their authority in a manner unmediated by the legislature so as to authorize a variety of institutions performing a multitude of political functions stipulating discernible limits and specific goals.[14] It is in terms of this articulated model of delegated powers that Locke offers his most important reflections on the civil executive and the nature of constitutionalism by presenting a conception of constitutional government in which *both* the legislative and executive power may be understood as having independent sources of legitimacy rooted in constituent authority and ultimately accountable to the community. But how does Locke explain the theoretical basis for the articulated delegation of power from the community to government? For this we must turn to Locke's considerations of the properties and role of executive power in civil society, especially as it relates to the principle of legislation.

[14] See Tuckness, *Legislative Point of View*, 128, 132–133, 140.

THE CIVIL EXECUTIVE

Locke's complex treatment of consent in both its direct and articulated form of delegated power not only has a direct bearing on his theory of the separation of the executive and legislative powers, but also establishes the general rubric of legitimacy by which we can deduce the particular characteristics of Lockean constitutionalism. As we recall, Locke indicates that one of the crucial distinctions between civil government and pre-political society is the act of "balancing...the Power of Government by placing parts of it in different hands" that characterizes all "well order'd Commonwealths" (II: 107, 143). He argues that insofar as the primal root of the powers of government is the natural power of individuals in the state of nature, the creation of civil government necessitates a bifurcated transmission of this natural authority. The natural right to do "whatever" is necessary for self-preservation and the preservation of the "rest of Mankind," Locke claims, is surrendered in part to the legislature to be "regulated by Laws" so far as self-preservation and the good of society "shall require" (II: 129). Typically society places this legislative power in "collective Bodies of Men, call them Senate, Parliament, or what you please," so that "no man in civil society" will be exempt from the law (II: 94). However, discretionary natural executive power the individual must "wholly" surrender in order "to assist the Executive Power of the Society, as the Laws thereof shall require" (II: 130). Civil executive power then is necessarily less discretionary than the natural executive power enjoyed by individuals prior to the separation of the legislative and executive functions.[15] The act of constituting civil government appears to be the moral and logical antipode of prerogative, the example of collective deliberation, common intentions, and regularized social cooperation *par excellence*. In this sense, both the conceptual and historical movement from the state of nature to civil government seems to be defined chiefly by the diminution, and even disappearance, of discretionary power and prerogative.

Yet Locke affirms that executive power and even prerogative retain their salience in his constitutional teaching, although both are transformed dramatically from their pre-political expression. Legislative and executive power both are delegated powers, but Locke argues that they are distinguishable by their respective functions and ends. In terms of their formal construction, the executive is emphatically subordinate to legislative power. As such, the legislature is supreme because while the government subsists,

---

[15] Arnhart, "God-like Prince," 124.

what gives laws and direction to the other elements of government must be superior (II: 150). Executive subordination to the legislature is axiomatic inasmuch as it is essentially a derivative function that logically can only execute laws previously enacted by the legislative power. Whereas the legislature has a right to direct "the Force of the Commonwealth," Locke describes the executive power as little more than "the Image, Phantom, or Representative of the Commonwealth... [which] has no Will, no Power, but that of the Law" (II: 143, 151). Perhaps the most telling piece of evidence demonstrating the formal subordination of executive power is that in Locke's list of the limits on legislative power, such as the prohibition on arbitrary decrees and the confiscation of property without due process (II: 135–41), there is no mention of the legislature violating the rights of the executive. Civil executive power is simply not by its nature an intrinsic check on legislative power.

Locke does, however, suggest two significant qualifications on executive subordination. The first relates to what he identifies as "Federative Power," which involves the direction of society with respect to foreign relations and is, Locke claims, "always almost" united with executive power (II: 145–6). Locke's insistence on the near fusion of executive and federative power reserves some, and potentially a great deal of, discretionary power to the executive given that foreign relations are "much less capable" of being directed by antecedent positive law than domestic affairs, although Locke eschews identifying this discretion with prerogative, preferring to call it "Prudence" (II: 147). The second and, constitutionally speaking, more fundamental qualification on executive subordination is Locke's account of supreme executive power. In a thinly veiled allusion to the English constitutional practice of royal assent, Locke argues that the executive may also have "a share in the Legislative" (II: 151). This practice suggests that a constitutionally authorized person may serve multiple political functions. If the executive does not share the legislative power, then she or he is "visibly subordinate and accountable to it" and may be replaced, removed, or punished by the legislature for "mall-administration against the laws" (II: 151, 153). But Locke indicates that if the executive does possess some share of legislative power, this person may in a "tolerable sense" be called "Supream" (II: 151) inasmuch as all inferior magistrates derive their authority from him or her and since by virtue of the veto power this executive may be said to command all and receive commands from none.

The significance of Locke's treatment of supreme executive power is twofold. First, it indicates that while Locke views the executive function as naturally subordinate to the legislative, this does not necessarily mean that the executive must be institutionally subordinate to the legislature. The constitutional arrangement of power may delegate legislative authority to distinct persons or bodies. Locke's theory of consent suggests that the very essence of constitutional government is to alter and compound the natural functions of government in a mix of persons and institutions: Constitutionalism means that nature must give way to human artifice. The second important feature of this discussion is Locke's insistence that the source of supreme executive power is not the fusion of legislative and executive power, but rather the independence of the executive (II: 153).[16] His allusion to England's hereditary monarchy suggests that he believed the most important component of supreme executive power is precisely its independence from the legislative assembly. But from where then does Locke derive the source of supreme executive power, if not from the legislative?

As we have seen, Locke's theory of consent offers two possibilities for the origin of supreme executive power. According to the direct delegation model, the legislature may create an independent executive as part of the original process of constitutional formation. This is a theoretical possibility, but Locke reveals that it is rather implausible in practice. Given his assessment of the self-regarding character of political officeholders (not to mention human beings more generally), it is no more likely that a legislature would respect the independence of an executive who is its creature than a supreme executive would voluntarily defer to legislative authority. Locke slyly opines that the altruistic self-limitation exercised by such an executive "one may conclude will be but very little" (II: 152).[17] Another indication that the supreme executive is likely not a creation of the legislature is that Locke explicitly states that the legislative power can create subordinate magistrates (II: 152), but he makes no mention of any legislative competence to create a supreme executive or refer

---

[16] Thus Locke would find cabinet government problematic inasmuch as a cabinet dependent on legislative majorities would not satisfy his criteria for supreme executive power (Vile, *Separation*, 73, but cf. Faulkner, "First Liberal Democrat," 6). Faulkner argues that Locke viewed supreme executive power as indicative of "special cases" of mistaken political orders (p. 26); however, this argument perhaps diminishes too much the significance for his general reflections on constitutionalism of Locke's treatment of executive independence regarding the veto, apportionment, and convoking the legislature.

[17] It is striking the extent to which Locke's discussion of supreme executive power foreshadows the kind of institutional physics underlying Madison's separation of powers theory in the American context in which he famously argued "Ambition must be made to counteract ambition" (see James Madison et al., *The Federalist Papers*, Clinton Rossiter, ed. (New York: New American Library, 1961), #51, p. 322). For both Locke and Madison, the crucial element in the separation of powers is not making the branches interdependent but rather giving them an independent source of authority in the constitution.

to any legislative reservation of plenary power with respect to such an executive.

The more plausible account of the origins of supreme executive power lies in the articulated delegation model of consent whereby society delegates partial shares of the legislative power to distinct persons or bodies as part of the process creating the "Original Constitution" (II: 153–4). The natural law, which forbids the legislature from transferring any of its own authority from where the community first placed it by the "positive voluntary Grant" of society (II: 141), effectively precludes the possibility that the legislature could legitimately parcel out its own authority to anything other than a merely subordinate body.[18] Conversely, Locke's theoretical grounding for the naturalness of legislative supremacy means that the supreme executive is constitutionally prohibited from exercising full legislative power, and thus keeping in part with the traditional argument for legislative supremacy, Locke affirms that prerogative can never assume the character of law solely on the basis of executive authority. In his account of executive power, Locke not only eschews the translegal categories in the traditional discourse of sovereignty, he further clarifies the salience of law by maintaining that, in contrast to Hobbes, for instance, executive judgment is not coterminus with law. Hobbes saw executive and legislative power as practically identical expressions of sovereignty precisely because he maintained that the sovereign is the one uncontracted agent in the commonwealth and thus his or her authority is natural – deriving from unmediated natural right – and cannot be construed as delegated from the people.[19] For Locke, on the other hand, the proposition of the conventionality of civil executive and

---

[18] In contrast to Pasquino ("Prerogative," 202) who argues that Locke's executive is stronger than the classical Roman dictator because the former does not derive authority to act with discretion from a prior legislative grant, I maintain that Locke fundamentally limits civil executive power by insisting that the legislature can never transfer its full authority to another body or actor – a Lockean legislature can never create a dictator with full executive *and* legislative power, because such a grant is incompatible with the fiduciary character of the original delegation of power from society to government. For a very Lockean response to the classical problem of legal dictatorship, see Thomas Jefferson's criticisms of the Virginia legislators during the Revolutionary War (Thomas Jefferson, *Notes on the State of Virginia* [New York: Palgrave, 2002], pp. 165–168).

[19] At II: 159 Locke seems to offer a Hobbesian argument for prerogative when he claims that the executive "has by the common Law of Nature, a right to make use of" natural executive power. However, this does not mean that Locke specifically derives civil prerogative from the natural right to execute the law of nature. Quite the contrary, it demonstrates the mix of natural and legal power in the civil executive, which distinguishes it from the wholly natural power both of individuals in the state of nature and of Hobbes' sovereign. Cf. Thomas Hobbes, *Leviathan* (Indianapolis: Hackett, 1994), pp. 172–178, 204.

legislative power flows from the basic premise of delegated powers deriving in a mediated way from the natural power of individuals (II: 11, 129–31). Lockean political power has both a natural root and a legal fiduciary character, and thus even the royal veto with which Locke associates the supreme executive is not a power inherent in executive authority, but rather must be understood as a latent possibility permitted, if not required, in the act of constitutional framing produced by societal choice.

In his treatment of the civil executive, we recognize that the ideas of constitution and legislation are not only very different for Locke, but their relation is essentially the archetype for his teaching on constitutional supremacy and subordination. Even the theoretical possibility of supreme executive power reflects Locke's idea of the delegation of authority to a multitude of institutions constitutionally separated from each other and having discernible limits and goals set by the constituent power of the community. One such delegated authority uniquely in the executive is prerogative.

PREROGATIVE AND THE CONSTITUTION

The issue of prerogative pervades Locke's entire discussion of the civil executive and serves more clearly than any other element of his constitutional theory to illuminate the fundamental distinction between constitution and law. For Locke, the prerogative power "to act according to discretion, for the publick good, without the prescription of law, and sometimes even against it" (II: 160, 164) is implied in the very notion of a supreme executive with a share of the legislative power. Locke claims that the existence of an executive to some extent independent of the legislative is a feature of all "well-framed Governments" and generally indicative of intelligent constitutional design (II: 159). The heart of the debate among commentators is whether Locke conceived of prerogative narrowly as essentially a ministerial function performed by the executive on an ad hoc basis until the legislature can be convened to validate or nullify the measure, or if Locke intended prerogative to be understood broadly as a discretionary power admitting few, if any, substantive institutional or legal checks on the executive. However, arguably neither alternative accurately reflects Locke's conception of prerogative. In order to solidify this claim, it is crucial to consider who or what, in Locke's view, authorizes prerogative and whether it is compatible with the rule of law and constitutional government.

Prerogative almost by definition involves extralegal authority because it is an exercise of executive judgment not directly determined by general standing laws. However, Locke indicates that it also must be understood in terms of a trust invested in the executive by the community in which the trustee is assigned a function or goal to perform and given some discretion as to how this goal is reached (II: 158, 164).[20] For example, the executive is allowed some "latitude" to act for the public good in situations where either the law is no guide or when the legislative body is not in session (II: 160). In these situations societal trust permits executive discretion in order to fulfill the intentions of law such as in the case of the executive convening the legislature at unusual times in order to meet "the Exigencies of the Publick" (II: 154). On the basis of the fiduciary relationship between governors and the governed, Locke not only allows the executive to mitigate legal sanctions or pardon offenders, but even to break the law him- or herself in dire emergencies, for example, by pulling down "an innocent Man's House to stop the Fire" threatening to envelop an entire district (II: 159). Both the pardon and emergency power conform to the narrow interpretation of prerogative according to which Locke endorses executive discretion to apply judgment to particular cases that are not fully accounted for in the generality of law, but are subject to the approval or disapprobation of the legislature once it "can conveniently be Assembled to provide for it" (II: 159).[21] Prerogative in this sense is an extralegal power justifiable only insofar as it furthers the preservationist intention of law, which is to protect the "rights of all members of Society" (II: 222).

In contrast to Locke's broad conception of prerogative in the state of nature or pre-civil society, the civil executive exercises prerogative in a context of legality embedded in the framework of laws comprising constitutional legitimacy.[22] For example, Locke suggests that executive discretion

---

[20] Ross Harrison, *Hobbes, Locke and Confusion's Masterpiece* (Cambridge: Cambridge University Press, 2003), p. 212.

[21] See Weaver, "Leadership," 426, 428 and Waldron, *Legislation*, 66. We may also, however, interpret Locke's defense of the pardon power more broadly as an encouragement to the executive to move, however qualifiedly, to protect the basic rights of religious dissenters against legislative encroachment by mitigating "the severity" of discriminatory laws (cf. Richard Ashcraft, *Revolutionary Politics and Locke's Two Treatises of Government* [Princeton: Princeton University Press, 1986], p. 111 and Mark Goldie, "John Locke and Anglican Royalism," in *John Locke: Critical Assessments, Volume 1*, Richard Ashcraft, ed. [New York: Routledge, 1991], p. 165).

[22] Locke's claim that the "wisest and best Princes" may have had "some Title to Arbitrary Power" (II: 166) has led some to draw the conclusion that he believed prerogative is, theoretically at least, an arbitrary power illimitable by law (see Simmons, *Anarchy*, 55; Arnhart, "God-like Prince," 125; and Josephson, *Great Art*, 231–232). However, in this passage, Locke's allusion is to a "Title" more honorific and empirical than normative, and reflects the admittedly dangerous tendency of the people to defer almost implicitly to wide-ranging and even absolute power in the hands of just rulers who use this power uniformly to do good. Locke's further claim that prerogative involves an "Arbitrary Power

must not be construed to undermine the constitutional role of "indifferent and upright," "known authoris'd Judges" to "decide Controversies" about "the rights of the subject" on the basis of standing laws (II: 131, 136). Indeed, Locke cites undue executive interference with the judiciary as one of the hallmarks of tyranny (II: 20, 208). Another very basic but crucial element of the legal basis of prerogative is Locke's insistence that the constitution determines who is permitted to exercise discretion.[23] Locke insists that no one can "by his own Authority, avoid the force of Law" (II: 94), and therefore prerogative cannot legitimize "Usurpation," which he defines as the exercise of constitutionally delegated and perfectly legitimate authority by unauthorized persons or bodies (II: 198). The legitimacy of prerogative presupposes its exercise by authorized agents designated by law. Locke is clear, however, that the principle of legality framing prerogative need not be restricted to normal legislation and can, in fact, reside in the fundamental law "which had its establishment originally from the people" (II: 198). He even goes so far as to suggest that "in all lawful Governments" the specific powers delegated to particular structures and persons are prescribed by "the First Framers of the Government" (II: 156). The outer limit of executive prerogative is the dimensions of constitutional authority.

The constitutional basis of prerogative belies the vision of a sweeping natural force often presented in the *broad* interpretation of Lockean executive power. However, Locke's treatment of prerogative articulates a conception of executive power that also extends in range and vitality well beyond the purely ministerial role maintained by the *narrow* interpretation. Far from being simply a power entirely subject to *ex post facto* approval or disapprobation by the legislative body, Locke's most instructive examples of prerogative involve the executive's considerable capacity to regulate the manner in which the legislature fulfills its representative function. The first relates to the executive power to convoke and dissolve the legislature. Locke argues that it is neither necessary "nor so much as convenient" (II: 153) that the legislative body be in perpetual session given his fear of the legislators assuming an interest distinct from society by not being subject to its own laws. Locke suggests that in order to overcome this natural disability facing any legislature, there are several possibilities to regulate its assembly and

---

in some things left in the Prince's hands to do good" (II: 210) must be qualified in light of his complete rejection of any "Absolute Arbitrary Power, or Governing without settled standing Laws" (II: 137) such that prerogative involves a power directed both by law and by discernible and salutary ends.

[23] John Dunn, *The Political Thought of John Locke* (Cambridge: Cambridge University Press, 1969), p. 51.

dissolution. The legislature may by an "Act of their Supreme Power" recon-
vene when "their own Adjournment appoints" or whenever "they please" if
"no other way [is] prescribed to convoke them" (II: 153). With both of these
possibilities, the legislature is manifestly supreme and there is no substantive discretionary role for the executive.

However, Locke also indicates a third alternative in which the legislature
may be required by the "Original Constitution" to assemble and dissolve
"either at certain appointed Seasons, or else when they are summon'd to it"
(II: 154). If the terms of the assembly or the specific periods for new elections are set by the original constitution, Locke concludes that the executive power to call and dissolve the legislature is primarily a ministerial and
subordinate function, although in this case subordinate to the "Original
Constitution" rather than the legislature. If, however, the timing for new
assemblies and elections is not set by the constitution or positive law, then
the choice is typically left to the discretion or "Prudence" of the executive
(II: 154). Despite Locke's perhaps overly earnest assurances that it is not his
"business here to inquire" whether it is better to convene the legislature at
"settled periods" or by a "Liberty left to the Prince," he does not demur
from offering that executive discretion is the "best remedy" to the necessary defect in foreknowledge of the "First Framers of the Government"
who could not presumably have predicted with prophetic wisdom all the
correct or necessary times for new assemblies and elections (II: 156).[24] With
this discussion, Locke subtly suggests not only that the executive can play
a key role in the operation of legislative powers, but more importantly that
control over elections and convoking the assembly may be a constitutionally protected power of the executive that society would be well advised
to place beyond the purview of ordinary legislation and legislative interference. While Locke's theory only *permits* rather than *requires* that the
people constitutionally entrench the executive's power, he offers an implicit
endorsement of the principle of enlightened constitutional design by "First
Framers" who are farsighted enough to recognize the limits of their own
foresight and to delegate to the executive constitutional authority to exercise
discretion with regard to the mechanics of convening and electing assemblies.[25] The obvious corollary of this argument for executive discretion as a

---

[24] Locke is also open to the possibility of a "mixture of both" (II: 159) executive discretion
and constitutionally appointed times for convening the legislature in a format not unlike
that set out in Article II, section 3 of the United States Constitution. Cf. Josephson, *Great
Art*, 226–227.

[25] Locke shows concern both for the danger of executives abusing discretion to extend
assemblies inordinately, such as the eighteen-year Cavalier Parliament in Restoration
England, and also anticipating the problems of parliaments extending their own tenure by

product of constitutional design is Locke's clear implication that this kind of power is not inherent in the executive function but must be understood as governed by an overriding constitutional authority. In this instance, Lockean executive discretion has a most deliberative origin.

The second, and in the constitutional sense more important, example of prerogative Locke supplies relates to the vexing issue of apportionment. Locke argues that one of the major problems facing constitutional government is the oligarchic tendency for the system of representation to become inequitable over time. While "things of this world are in so constant a Flux, that nothing remains in the same State," Locke complains that the "gross absurdities" of custom (not to mention the narrow self-interest of legislators) typically ensure that representation in the legislature "becomes very unequal and disproportionate to reason as it was first establish'd" (II: 157). In contrast to hereditary elements of the government, time is the peculiar enemy of rational popular representation. Showing remarkable anticipation in the seventeenth century of the reform movement of the nineteenth, Locke attacks the phenomenon of the "rotten borough" wherein a district with "scarce so much Housing as a Sheep-coat; or more Inhabitants than a Shepherd is to be found sends as many Representatives to the Grand Assembly of Law-makers, as a whole County numerous in People and powerful in riches" (II: 157). Locke claims that all sensible people agree that this problem "needs a remedy," but it has proven "hard to find one" due to the assumption that "the Constitution of the Legislative" is the original act of society antecedent to positive law, and thus "no inferior power can alter it" without dissolving the entire system of government (II: 157). By this logic, the doctrine of legislative supremacy is, perhaps paradoxically, the single greatest obstacle to electoral reform.

The inability of his contemporaries to conceive of a constitutional means to redress malapportionment is indicative of the mindset Locke believes needs to be overcome if they are to grasp correctly the relation between constitution and law. In apparent contradiction to the doctrine of legislative supremacy, Locke argues that an executive "who has the power of Convoking the Legislative" may exercise prerogative to regulate "not by old custom, but true reason, the number of Members, in all places, that

a simple act of legislation as happened in 1716 in England with the repeal of the Triennial Act, which established elections every three years, and its replacement by the Septennial Act that established seven-year terms. For a good treatment of Locke's understanding of the temporal, and especially futural, character of legislation, as well as the executive's role in ameliorating the defects in predicting future exigencies, see Scheuerman, "Empire of Speed," 51–52, 55–56.

have a right to be distinctly represented" (II: 158). He insists, however, that the erection of a "fair and equal Representative" does not give the executive any superiority over the legislature or mean that the legislature has been altered from the original condition "depending wholly on the People" (II: 157). Locke argues that prerogative in this case does not signify executive supremacy because it is a discretionary power authorized by the people in the "Original Frame of Government" (II: 158), which initially entrusted the power of convoking the legislature to the executive.

The discussion of reapportionment confirms the underlying complexity in Locke's theory of consent inasmuch as the executive's authority to act contrary to the will of the people expressed through their representatives reflects a form of consent to constitutional government that is more fundamental than the authority of legislative institutions.[26] The implicit populism in Locke's treatment of prerogative and apportionment, by which the executive is authorized to reform representation on the basis of changes in a district's population and economic contribution "to the publick" (II: 158), suggests the democratic foundation of civil executive power that supplies a measure of legitimacy that overrides conventional legal usage.

If the executive alters or disables the legislature in a fundamental way, then this is a classic example of tyranny, and the necessary consequence is the dissolution of government (II: 214–8). However, Locke contends that reapportionment does not alter the legislature so much as restore "the old and true one" on the basis of the "True Foundations" prescribed by the original consent of the community (II: 158).[27] It is by reference to this original consent rather than a legislature based on distorted representation that Locke predicts the executive who modernizes apportionment is an "Establisher of the Government…[and] cannot miss the Consent and Approbation of the community" (II: 158). In this instance, prerogative is a considerable extralegal power extending far beyond the strict purview of legislative oversight.[28] However, Locke also determines that this executive discretion presupposes the existence of constitutional structures and norms more fundamental than the law produced by the legislative body the executive is reforming.

---

[26]   Josephson, *Great Art*, 233.

[27]   Faulkner ("First Liberal Democrat," 32) and Seliger (*Liberal Politics*, 343–349) argue that, contrary to Locke's protestations, reapportionment by prerogative does alter the legislature, and thus in effect dissolves the government. However, they base this argument on the premise that Locke does not clearly distinguish legislative and constitutional authority, an argument that I maintain is precisely the mistaken assumption that Locke seeks to correct among his contemporaries.

[28]   This is in contrast to Weaver, "Leadership," 431.

Locke's idea of prerogative is thus a capacious concept ranging from *ex tempore* emergency powers to fundamental electoral and institutional reform. It is neither simply a narrowly construed ministerial function, nor a potentially limitless extraconstitutional power. The treatment of prerogative illuminates Locke's understanding of the proper limits of normal legislative power, but it also demonstrates his concern to formulate this important executive power as an authority intrinsically contextualized within a constitutional order that limits and defines its legitimate exercise. By defining prerogative within a range of legitimate government action framed by constitutional authority, Locke indicates that not every public act assumes the general character of law.[29] However, he also retains an important element of the principle of legislative supremacy when he reserves some authoritative public acts such as taxation solely to the representative assembly effectively excluding them from executive discretion (II: 140). The public good, according to Locke, must inform "just" prerogative, but civil executive power must also never be completely detached from the underlying mediation of constitutional authority.

Locke's attitude towards prerogative, then, is complex. On the one hand, it is a vital element of good government that should be provided for in the original act of constitutional framing. Wise rulers, he claims, "cannot have too much prerogative" (II: 164). Moreover, the opportunity to exercise this power will be frequent given that the people will demand extralegal action in dire situations or at least are "very seldom, or never scrupulous" about transgressions of the law, if the action is not manifestly against the public good (II: 161, 164).[30] On the other hand, Locke also identifies serious dangers in prerogative most notably the tendency for precedents established by good rulers to be exploited by bad or self-serving ones (II: 166). His core concern is that the overturning of laws and overly expansive interpretations of delegated powers can create the impression that prerogative is inherent in the executive function rather than a constitutionally authorized power. An example of the potentially pernicious effect of exalted executive power is the traditional English "sacred person" doctrine by which "the Person of the Prince by the Law is Sacred," and thus is "free from all Question or Violence" (II: 205). Although Locke sees some value in a measure of executive immunity from legislative harassment in the proper exercise of his or her duty, he is adamant that sovereign immunity must be interpreted

---

[29] Seliger, *Liberal Politics*, 364–367 and Michael Zuckert, *Launching Liberalism: On Lockean Political Philosophy* (Lawrence: University Press of Kansas, 2002), p. 305.

[30] See Arnhart, "God-like Prince," 122–124 and Fatovic, "Constitutionalism and Contingency," 288–290.

very narrowly. It is more a legal fiction than a theological fact that must never extend to ministers of the crown and only pertains to the sovereign's performance of constitutionally authorized actions (II: 206). Any supreme executive, even an English monarch, who exceeds constitutional authority "ceases in that to be a Magistrate, and may be opposed, as any other Man" (II: 202). Locke maintains that the extension of prerogative beyond constitutionally delegated limits may be checked by "express laws" or even active resistance (II: 162–3, 202).

Thus in some respects, Locke's constitutionalism retains clear sympathy with the traditional English parliamentary argument for legislative control over the executive.[31] The effect of the frequent use and abuse of prerogative on the political psychology of a people may, Locke fears, be to inure the citizens and leaders to the importance of law and risk a gradual reversion to the trusting passivity and political primitivism so vividly presented in his natural historical account of pre-civil society. As such, it is perhaps no coincidence that Locke first directly and explicitly introduced his theory of the right of revolution in the *Second Treatise* in the context of his treatment of prerogative. Locke indicates that the kind of abuses of power that justify a revolutionary response may involve either the executive or legislative power violating the natural rights of the people (II: 221). However, he assumes that the usual culprit will be an executive employing his or her prerogative to alter the legislature or to disable it from playing its representative function in the way society originally intended (II: 214–19). Notably the final arbiter in disputes over prerogative is not the legislature but rather the community, or more properly the individuals in society, who will "Easily decide" the question on the basis of whether the people "feel" the palpable design of oppression (II: 161, 225). Thus the logical and moral corollary of the extralegal prerogative power of the executive is Locke's vision of a highly strung political culture grounded on popular vigilance and a good deal more "scrupulous" about the legality of government action than has been the custom traditionally.

[31] Legislative supremacy had been a central theme of English constitutional thought, at least since the quarrels between king and parliament in the early-seventeenth century that culminated in the Civil Wars of the 1640s. Supporters of the parliamentary cause such as Philip Hunton and Henry Parker crafted sophisticated theories of legislative supremacy during the civil war era that were well known to the later generation of Whigs, including Locke. For discussions of parliamentary theory and Hunton and Parker in particular, see Michael Mendle, *Henry Parker and the English Civil War* (Cambridge: Cambridge University Press, 1995); Lee Ward, *The Politics of Liberty in England and Revolutionary America* (Cambridge: Cambridge University Press, 2004), ch. 2; and Michael Zuckert, *Natural Rights and the New Republicanism* (Princeton: Princeton University Press, 1994), pp. 49–76.

In the dissolution of government resulting from abuse of power, the separation of executive power and prerogative that marked the creation of civil society to some extent collapses with the reversion of natural executive power to the individuals in society. More radical from the constitutional perspective is Locke's defense of the logic of anticipatory resistance, whereby the people have a natural right not only to resist tyranny but also "to prevent it" from arising (II: 220). While Locke maintains that the supreme power of the community must remain largely dormant until the legislature and government are dissolved (II: 149), he also insists that the people will decide when the government is dissolved (II: 224–8). The final and only truly extraconstitutional prerogative in Locke's theory lies in the revolutionary judgment of the community.

As we saw in the previous chapter, Locke's theory of the dissolution of government fundamentally flows out of the individualist principles of his state of nature account. When government violates its fiduciary relationship with the community, society reverts to a quasi-state of nature in which every individual in the community is "Judge for himself, as in all other cases; so in this, whether another has put himself into a State of War with him" (II: 241). As an issue for moral philosophy, Locke considers revolution to be a matter of free personal choice exercised under certain (hopefully) unique conditions. With respect to his constitutional theory, Locke's teaching on the right of revolution ultimately has no less radical implications. By reinterpreting the traditionally communal concept of resistance in the more individualist terms of dissolution of government, Locke was clearly driven on one level by his dissatisfaction with the inability of the English notion of a balanced constitution to prevent executive abuses of power in late-seventeenth-century England. History demonstrated all too clearly that the familiar doctrines of parliamentary sovereignty and legislative supremacy simply had failed, in his view, to provide the rigorous conceptual and legal restraints on executive power that were required to ensure limited government.

On a more theoretical level, the dissolution of government theory also signified Locke's effort to look beyond the specific problems of the English Constitution toward remedying what he took to be the basic flaw in practically all notions of constitutionalism existing hitherto. He sought to reorient the analysis of general principles of political legitimacy away from determining the properties and characteristics of particular forms of regime such as the classical regime types based on the rule of one, the few, and the many. Rather Locke's approach to constitutional government redirected the primary theoretical concern toward establishing the normative grounds of the dissolution of any and every government. For Locke, the traditional determinant of the boundaries for types of governments – namely who rules – is no longer simply the means of differentiation among regimes. In Locke's constitutionalism, the fundamental question, "Who rules?" practically always requires two answers, the one constitutionally variable and the other the naturally uniform rule of the people. For Locke, every constitutional government presupposes as an integral feature of its very legitimacy the moral justification of its own demise.

LOCKE AND LIBERAL CONSTITUTIONALISM

This chapter has suggested that Locke's executive power teaching rested on a notion of constitutional government adumbrating many of the central tenets of modern liberal constitutionalism. His civil executive is neither the bearer of unstoppable primal force nor simply the pliant instrument of an omnipotent legislature. Locke's argument for executive power reveals important liberal constitutionalist elements in his thought including the notion of fundamental rules establishing the legislature and the idea of nonlegislative actors with a constitutionally protected role in the government. In prerogative Locke identifies an important extralegal power, but it is one manifestly modulated within a context of fundamental constitutional structures and laws. In contrast to the common view that Locke held constitution and law as coextensive, we have seen that he not only distinguished *constitution* (societal consent in a constituent process) from *law* (the product of a representative legislative process), but he moreover sought to ground a theory of legitimate government on this very distinction. While Locke does not explicitly formulate substantive constitutional limits on government action, there is nothing in his argument that in principle contradicts the possibility of written constitutions, charters of fundamental rights, or the establishment of constitutionally authorized executive and judicial power. Indeed, Locke's concept of delegated powers and constituent authority is the theoretical precondition for the enactment of these characteristic elements of liberal constitutionalism.

However, Locke's constitutional theory is in a crucial sense incomplete, even on its own terms. His argument for constituent power is at once a beacon of originality and yet a source of deep opacity. Locke tantalizes us with the awesome spectacle of an entire people assembling to organize their government on the basis of consent (II: 95–9), but he provides no systematic treatment of the mechanics of constitutional formation. While his emphasis on broad societal consent seems to preclude recourse to a Rousseauian semi-mythical sole Legislator whose primal law stands above normal legislation, we are left to wonder how precisely Locke's social contract produces authoritative institutions. Who or what body drafts the constitution delimiting legislative and executive power? Are special constitutional conventions required or will an ordinary legislature suffice? How do people register their assent to a frame of government? Elections? Plebiscites? Is a general franchise required for constitutional ratification and reform or will a restricted suffrage suffice to bind the nation?[32] Locke's failure to account for the process by which civil government comes into being in all but the most general and abstract terms is arguably, as commentators past and present have observed, "a damaging lacuna" in his constitutional theory.[33]

Locke's neglect to complete his theoretical postulation of constitutionalism as a fundamental law that governs the lawmaking body with a systematic account of the practical mechanisms by which such a fundamental law can come into being is in one sense understandable. Both as a matter of theory and practice, there was simply no significant precedent in English or European constitutional history for a comprehensive constitutional proposal ratified by the free expression of broad popular consent.[34] Locke was

---

[32] There has been considerable debate about Locke's attitude toward the franchise with some emphasizing the elitist character of the Lockean idea of representation (for example, C. B. MacPherson, *The Political Theory of Possessive Individualism* [Oxford: Clarendon Press, 1962], pp. 221–238 and Ellen Meiskins Wood, "Locke against Democracy: Consent, Representation and Suffrage" *Two Treatises*" *History of Political Thought*, 13, 4 [Winter 1992]: 657–689) and others interpreting Locke more as a populist committed to an expanded suffrage or at least holding principles compatible with a democratic franchise (for example, Ian Shapiro, "John Locke's Democratic Theory," in *The Two Treatises of Government and a Letter Concerning Toleration*, Ian Shapiro, ed. [New Haven: Yale University Press, 2003], pp. 309–340, esp. 327–331; Faulkner, "First Liberal Democrat," 13–14; and Ashcraft, *Revolutionary Politics*, 228–285). While my aim is not to weigh the relative merits of these arguments, I do think it is important to recognize the considerable tension between Locke's idea of representative government, which did not include any substantive and systematic argument for universal suffrage, and the greater egalitarianism of contemporary ideas of democratic legitimacy (cf. Scheuerman, "Empire of Speed," 43, n. 3).

[33] John Dunn, "Consent in the Political Theory of John Locke" *The Historical Journal*, 10, 2 (1967), 166 (cf. Richard Ashcraft, *Locke's Two Treatises of Government* [London: Allen & Unwin, 1987], p. 151). For historically influential critiques of the abstract character of Locke's social contract theory, see, for example, David Hume, "Of the Original Contract," in *Essays Moral, Political and Literary*, Eugene Miller, ed. (Indianapolis: Liberty Fund, 1985), pp. 469–476 and William Blackstone, *Commentaries on the Laws of England*, Vol. 1 (London, 1791), p. 162, 213.

[34] Although the Levellers in civil war era England proposed something like a written constitution resting on general suffrage, this proposal was never implemented, and the argument for popular consent expressed through a politicized military was neither influential nor congenial to Locke (see Julian Franklin, *John Locke and the Theory of Sovereignty*

venturing into uncharted territory. Perhaps we can only surmise from the context of the *Second Treatise* in Exclusion and Glorious Revolution-era England that Locke initially believed the historical English Parliament, in a somewhat modified form, could be the proper mechanism for effecting major constitutional revision. There is some evidence in Locke's correspondences of the time that he believed Parliament could serve temporarily as a constituent assembly "to find remedies and set up a constitution that may be lasting for the security of civil rights and the liberty and property of all the subjects of the nation."[35] If the Convention Parliament of 1689, which put William III on the throne, could overcome the shortsighted and partisan "piecemeal" approach he saw as typical of normal legislatures, Locke believed it could produce measures that would at the very least ensure regular elections, provide for an independent judiciary, fix civil control over the military, and guarantee the civil rights of religious dissenters.[36] The key, for our purposes, is that Locke wanted the Convention to provide these measures on the basis of an authority greater than that of normal legislation, to give "laws to kings, yes to the whole parliament, and set bounds to it" by an expression of popular consent so "great, aweful, and august that none may be able to quarrel [with] it."[37] Locke wanted nothing less than to establish a zone of constitutional law and fundamental rights relatively immune from legislative encroachments.

The palpable disappointment Locke felt about the English experience of constitutional reform in 1689 perhaps reflected the deepening of his own understanding of both the populist and institutional implications of his constitutional theory. While he always publicly defended the halting

[Cambridge: Cambridge University Press, 1978], 125–126). The first constitution in history drafted by a special convention and popularly ratified by broad suffrage independent of royal assent was the product of Locke's American Whig heirs in revolutionary Massachusetts in 1780 (see Ward, *Politics of Liberty*, 422–425).

35   Locke quoted in Ashcraft, *Revolutionary Politics*, 592.

36   Ashcraft, *Revolutionary Politics*, 592. Contrary to the suggestion that the English Constitution was Locke's ideal (for example, J. W. Gough, *John Locke's Political Philosophy* [Oxford: Clarendon Press, 1950], p. 102 and Dunn, *Political Thought*, 52–53), I maintain that the radical thrust of his delegated powers argument included a forceful critique of what he identified as the "Acknowledg'd Faults" and "Original Defects" (II: 223) in the English Constitution such as malapportionment, ill-defined prerogative, the political role of the bishops, the Crown's role as head of the established church, and the legislative persecution of religious dissenters (II: 158, 162–163, 239; see also John Locke, "Letter from a Person of Quality" *Works*, 10 [London: W. Sharpe & Sons, 1823] 200–212).

37   This statement by Locke's radical Whig colleague John Wildman (quoted in Franklin, *Sovereignty*, 117) captures, I believe, the spirit of Locke's expectations for English constitutional reform in early 1689.

Glorious Revolution settlement against its divine-right monarchist and Tory opponents, Locke nonetheless castigated the Convention Parliament in his private correspondences for letting slip an opportunity to mend the "great faults" in England's "frame of government" by acting more like a "parliament" or legislative body than a constitutional assembly.[38] He perhaps came to realize that a legislature historically based on a narrow suffrage was seriously limited in its capacity to initiate the kind of dramatic reform he advocated or even to make laws exempt from alteration, repeal, or amendment solely by its own authority: Parliaments as traditionally understood do not make constitutions as Locke conceived of them.

Although it would take nearly a century for the acceptance of the principle of general suffrage to transform and in effect operationalize his idea of constituent power, Locke was a harbinger for a version of constitutionalism more liberal and democratic than he was capable of fully enunciating or prepared to endorse in an explicit and emphatic way. In the great liberal revolutions of the eighteenth century and the democratic reform movements that followed, the Anglo-American and European political traditions would extend Locke's constitutional principles in radical directions with ideas such as special constitutional assemblies and popular ratification with broad franchise as the means to establish fundamental legal instruments unqualifiedly superior to normal legislation that can in principle guarantee individual rights against undue government interference. Despite the limits in Locke's account of constitutional formation, his innovative ideas about consent and delegated powers arguably adumbrated the modern doctrine of the separation of powers and written constitutions establishing fundamental rights. Locke provided the theoretical materials out of which modernity would construct a revolutionary new idea of constitutional government based on popular sovereignty. In this sense, the genesis of liberal constitutionalism is inconceivable without Locke.

---

[38] See James Farr and Clayton Roberts, "John Locke on the Glorious Revolution: A Rediscovered Document" *The Historical Journal*, 28, 2 (June 1985): 385–398 and Locke quoted in Franklin, *Sovereignty*, 121.

4

The Natural Rights Family

Discerning the political significance of the family has always been a major concern in the history of political thought. At least since Plato and Lycurgus, it has been well understood that any radical change in political structures and institutions will also require dramatic alteration in society's conception of the family.[1] However, typically pre-modern political theory viewed the family in a conservative light as an institution reflecting generational continuity and primal or subpolitical forms of attachment that point beyond themselves to their greater significance as constitutive elements of political society. For instance, in the organic conception of politics articulated by Aristotle and his followers over the centuries, political theory was charged with the task of properly defining the economic and educative role of the family in the web of natural associations that compose the *polis*. Relations within the family were held to be midlevel theoretical concerns, secondary to the goal of establishing the correct purpose of the family in the context of this larger, and ontologically prior, social reality.

With Locke, however, in early modernity, understanding the family's role in political theory assumed new significance and indeed acquired a palpable sense of urgency. The animating spirit of Locke's epistemology, his "democratization of mind," proposed new principles of intelligibility to replace the traditional paradigms of knowledge. With its foundation in the basic equality of all humans as rational beings and a focus on understanding complex ideas and institutions by breaking them down into constituent parts, Locke's entire approach to political theory signaled a radical break from the past intellectual tradition. If the pre-modern conception of

---

[1] See Plato, *Republic*, Allan Bloom, trans. (New York: Basic Books, 1968), Book V and Plutarch, "The Life of Lycurgus," in *The Lives of Noble Grecians and Romans*, John Dryden, trans. (New York: Everyman, 1952).

practically every aspect of human life, including the family, derived from faulty assumptions about nature, then what did Locke propose to replace the traditional conception of the family?

The family presented a problem for Locke's political theory on at least three different levels. First, on the philosophical level, his commitment to the abstract principle of equality was profoundly challenged by the traditional conception of the family. Both in the history of political thought and in terms of centuries of empirical evidence, the family had rarely been perceived as an egalitarian institution. Quite the contrary, typically the relations of parents and children, husbands and wives, and masters and servants were identified as invariably hierarchical relations existing in the social stratum underlying the civic realm defined by full membership in the political community. Pre-modern political theory presupposed a definition of the family that was antithetical to the individualist principles central to Locke's political philosophy. For example, to many in Locke's time, the extension of the idea of natural freedom to children's relation to parents, or assuming equality in a wife's relation to her husband, appeared to strain the credibility of consent theory to absurd lengths. Practically the entire philosophy of human nature upon which the tradition was built rejected an individualistic conception of the family.

The family also presented a problem for one of the central features of Locke's own political theory, namely the state of nature. Strikingly, the family was not an important theme in Locke's seminal account of the state of nature in the opening chapters of the *Second Treatise*. This discussion elaborated the rights of individuals *as* individuals understood independently of any social or political institution including the family. However, as we have seen, the family intrudes crucially in Locke's later reflections on the origins of constitutional government. Indeed, the genetic account of the emergence of government, in which the family plays a central role with male heads of families assuming a pre-civil form of rule, effectively revised Locke's theoretical account of the state of nature. The quasi-political status of the "first Fathers" not only reveals Locke's concerns about the authoritarian tendencies in political psychology, but also raises serious difficulties for his formal account of the natural condition from which all principles of political legitimacy supposedly derive. Are male heads of families in the pre-civil state of nature the true "individuals" who consent to form governments, and in effect subsume the political obligation of their dependents by the paternal act of consent? Does the historical role of the family in the actual formation of governments and societies bring into question the practical significance of the egalitarian principles of Locke's state of nature?

Finally, the task of determining the political meaning of the family was to some extent thrust upon Locke by his immediate political and intellectual context in seventeenth-century England. The most influential challenge to natural liberty theory in the period was the argument for divine right monarchy championed by Locke's primary antagonist in the *Two Treatises*, Sir Robert Filmer. The supporters of monarchical power in the constitutional battles between king and parliament during the Exclusion Crisis of 1679–1681 vigorously appealed to the philosophical authority of Filmer to defend the monarch's prerogatives – and the patriarchal family was absolutely central to Filmer's divine right theory. In his classic work *Patriarcha*, Filmer argued that all rightful rulers derive their claim to authority from God's grant of power to Adam in *Genesis*. As the "first father" of humanity, Adam ruled over all who sprang from his generative source, and he ruled them absolutely, with no legal or moral limits on his power.[2] For Filmer, the model for the unity and absoluteness of political rule is the patriarch's rule over his wife and children: As fathers rule their families absolutely, so too do all kings rule their subjects as a kind of father of the nation. With this potent cocktail of scripture and the ubiquity of the patriarchal family as his main support, Filmer constructed a political theology rooted in the notion of human creatureliness that extended the chains of subjection from children to fathers, to kings, and ultimately to God. However, patriarchalism was more than just a political theory, or even political theology, conveniently trotted out by partisans in a particular political controversy. Patriarchalism was a comprehensive worldview penetrating practically every aspect of social existence in early-modern Europe. In Locke's England, for instance, Bishop Overall's Convocation of 1606 made patriarchy and a highly politicized interpretation of the Fifth Commandment the official doctrine of the Anglican Church.[3] Filmer's divine right argument was thus really only an extreme version of an ideology with broad cultural acceptance. Thus, on

---

[2] Robert Filmer, *Patriarcha and other Writings*, Johann Somerville, ed. (Cambridge: Cambridge University Press, 1991), pp. 6–7, 10–11, 15–18. For Filmer's divine right theory, see also James Daly, *Sir Robert Filmer and English Political Thought* (Toronto: University of Toronto Press, 1979) and Lee Ward, *The Politics of Liberty in England and Revolutionary America* (Cambridge: Cambridge University Press, 2004), chs. 1–3. For a contrary view that disputes the importance of patriarchalism in Filmer's argument for divine right monarchy, see Rachel Weil, "The Family in the Exclusion Crisis: Locke versus Filmer Revisited," in *A Nation Transformed: England after the Restoration*, Alan Houston and Steven Pincus, eds. (Cambridge: Cambridge University Press, 2001), pp. 100–124, esp 101, 103, 109, 111, 121, 124.

[3] For the classic treatment of patriarchalism and its pervasive impact in early-modern England, see Gordon Schochet, *Patriarchalism in Political Thought* (Oxford: Oxford University Press, 1975), pp. 92–95.

one level, Locke had no choice but to deal with the family because the patriarchal family was central to the argument of the opponents to limited government.

The *ancien régime* in early-modern England had then at its core a conception of the family in which the ideas of authoritarianism, political absolutism, sexism, and religious intolerance formed a nexus in a deeply entrenched institution. Yet whereas Locke's constitutional theory had revolutionary implications that were experienced politically almost immediately, the patriarchal family remained to various degrees a feature of modern society for centuries after Locke. Among the issues that raise questions about the relevance of Locke's teaching for today, perhaps there is no respect in which this is more germane than with regards to Locke's view of the family. This chapter and the next address this issue by examining Locke's theory as it applied first to sexual equality and then, in the following chapter, to education. Here we will argue that the family was far from a subtheoretical or marginal concern for Locke. Rather the attack on patriarchy was a constitutive element of his larger political philosophy. His reflections on the family culminate in what we will term "the natural rights family"; that is to a reformed conception of the family deeply impacted by Locke's individualist principles. The radical thrust of his argument lay in his effort to illuminate the complex idea of the family and then to reconstruct familial relations in a way that reflected natural equality. Both the *eidetic* and *genetic* approaches characteristic of Locke's political philosophy play a major role in this reconstruction of modernity's idea of the family; a vital institution Locke insists has been badly misunderstood in the past.

Not surprisingly much of the most penetrating recent commentary on Locke's treatment of the family has typically come from feminist scholars who have also in many respects issued a powerful challenge to Locke's egalitarian credentials. Feminist scholarship has incisively asked the questions most often previously left unspoken, namely, if Locke systematically excluded one half of the human race from his basic conception of natural freedom and equality, and moreover failed to apply his standards of legitimate rule to the family – perhaps the most formative kind of human association – then in what sense can he plausibly be identified as a founder of modernity? This chapter will argue that Locke does deserve recognition as a philosophical originator of the world familiar to us today; however, Locke's argument with respect to the family is exceedingly complex and takes an at-times frustratingly circuitous path through his political writings. Feminist scholarship has unearthed many of the key concepts and ambiguities in Locke's teaching on the family, thus we will begin by following this lead and strive to engage in dialogue with feminist commentators who have challenged Locke's philosophical consistency so powerfully. Only in this way can we really test whether Locke's political philosophy, and modern liberalism more generally, truly transcended the patriarchal assumptions it claims to oppose.

LOCKE AND MODERN FEMINISM

In recent times, the thought of John Locke has been the subject of intense debate involving feminist commentators concerned with the position of women in liberal theory. This is perfectly understandable inasmuch as both liberalism and much of modern feminism rest on a foundation of individualism.[4] Indeed, Locke's argument that freedom and equality are natural for beings whose "common Nature, Faculties and Powers, are by Nature equal, and ought to partake in the same common Rights and Privileges" rings through much of the modern debate about women's position in the family and political society.[5] As modern feminism has amply demonstrated, both as a theoretical and practical matter, the equality of women must be an issue for natural rights politics.

The current debate over the status of women in Lockean natural rights theory has pitted critics of Locke's argument concerning women against those who defend his natural rights argument as a clear, if partial, advance for sexual equality in the family and in political society. The contemporary critique of Locke is varied and has focused on many diverse elements of his thought, but there are four common themes that recur throughout the literature. The first is concern that Locke's abstract understanding of natural freedom and equality conceals a deeper patriarchal argument for the natural inequality of men and women. It has been argued that Locke's conception of the family rests on a kind of natural male rule based on men's supposed superiority in strength and ability and on women's presumed natural disadvantage in reproduction.[6] Another line of criticism holds that Locke's theory of property rights in the family constitutes a rejection of

---

[4] Carole Pateman, *The Disorder of Women* (Stanford: Stanford University Press, 1989), p. 118.

[5] John Locke, *Two Treatises of Government*, Peter Laslett, ed. (Cambridge: Cambridge University Press, 1965), *Treatise* I, sec. 67 and *Treatise* II, sec. 4. (Hereafter in notes and text *Treatise* and section.)

[6] Lorenne Clark, "Women and Locke: Who Owns the Apples in the Garden of Eden?" in *The Sexism of Social and Political Theory*, Lorenne Clark and Lynda Lange, eds. (Toronto: University of Toronto Press, 1979), pp. 16, 19, 25, 36; Diana Coole, *Women in Political Theory* (Boulder: Lynne Reinner, 1979), p. 64; and Pateman, *Disorder*, 121.

women's capacity to acquire property on equal terms with men, and thus Locke denies that women possess the degree of rationality required to participate in the forming of civil society, and even that he systematically excludes women from his conception of political society because he intends to provide the theoretical justification of the absolute right of males to pass their property to their legitimate male heir.[7] A third criticism is that Locke maintains the constant subordination of women through the terms of the marriage contract, but does so under a thinly veiled "gloss of consent."[8] A fourth element of the argument among Locke's feminist critics is that his theoretical distinction between conjugal and political society encourages a dichotomization of human life into a public, political sphere and a private, familial sphere, which perpetuates the subjection of women in the private sphere of family life.[9] These four major streams of criticism all involve an argument that in one sense or another Locke's political teaching includes a violation of his own individualist principles when they are applied to women.

It may be unfair to generalize on the basis of all too brief a summary of what is an extremely complex criticism, but perhaps we can draw one principal conclusion from the major themes of Locke's feminist critics: They see his critique of patriarchy as, at best, a timid and incomplete attempt to extend the principles of natural freedom and equality to women and, in the worst case, a dismal sham systematically subordinating women in the family while extending his newly articulated freedom exclusively to men. What is common to all of these critics is the argument that though Locke sought to challenge patriarchy as a model and moral support for absolute monarchy in the seventeenth century, he did so consciously seeking to avoid destabilizing the rule of husbands over wives in the family.[10] In this way, Locke's critique of patriarchy is clearly inadequate and thus demands a critique of liberalism inasmuch as patriarchy, at least insofar as it provides a rationale for the inequality of women, is a "constitutive part of the theory and practice of liberalism."[11]

[7] Teresa Brennan and Carole Pateman, "'Mere Auxiliaries to the Commonwealth': Women and the Origins of Liberalism" *Political Studies*, 27, 2 (1979): 183–220, esp. 193–195; Clark, "Women in Locke," 16, 32; Coole, *Political Theory*, 70, 73.

[8] Brennan and Pateman, "Mere Auxiliaries," 183–184, 191–193.

[9] Jean B. Elshtain, *Public Man, Private Woman* (Princeton: Princeton University Press, 1981), pp. 122, 127; Susan Moller Okin, *Justice, Gender and the Family* (New York: Basic Books, 1989), p. 111; and Pateman, *Disorder*, 120.

[10] Coole, *Political Theory*, 68; Carole Pateman, *The Sexual Contract* (Stanford: Stanford University Press, 1988), pp. 3, 22.

[11] Pateman, *Disorder*, 123.

Locke's defenders argue that his critique of English patriarchalism constitutes a partial, though significant, assertion of a natural ground for the equal rights of women in the family and in political society. This defense of Locke's argument concerning women rests on two main aspects of his thought. The first element of this defense points to the salutary consequences for women of a natural rights argument rooted in individual freedom and equality. It is argued that, though Locke retains some patriarchal assumptions regarding natural male superiority in the family and in political life, his individualist principles contain a logic of equality that can be extended through all familial relations and be applied consistently to many of the questions surrounding women's participation in politics and education. In being true to Lockean individualist principles, liberals "would be forced to bring their views on women into line with their theory of human nature."[12] In this view, despite what Locke may have said or failed to say about women and the family in the course of fierce seventeenth-century polemics, feminism has benefited from the progressive dynamic of his egalitarian political theory.

Another strand of the contemporary defense of Locke's natural rights argument as it relates to women emphasizes the possibilities for greater equality and individual freedom embedded in his theoretical distinction between the private and public realms of activities. According to this argument, Locke's view of society is comprised of a "multitude of interacting and partially integrated spheres," which promotes a greater degree of equality for women in each sphere by preventing the form of authority in one sphere from seeping into another.[13] Though many commentators have observed great caution in Locke's writings, perhaps due to his sensitivity to the prevailing prejudices of his time, even many of his defenders suggest that Locke failed to fully follow through on the implications of his natural rights argument as it pertains to the status of women.[14] Locke's general

---

[12] See Melissa Butler, "Early Liberal Roots of Feminism: John Locke and His Attack on Patriarchy" *American Political Science Review*, 72, 1 (March 1978): 135–150; Ruth Grant, "John Locke on Women and the Family," in *Two Treatises of Government and a Letter Concerning Toleration*, Ian Shapiro, ed. (New Haven: Yale University Press, 2003), pp. 286–308; and Jeremy Waldron, "Locke, Adam, and Eve," in *Feminist Interpretations of John Locke*, Nancy J. Hirschmann and Kirstie M. McClure, eds. (University Park: Pennsylvania State University Press, 2007), pp. 247–267, esp. 243–245.

[13] Mary Walsh, "Locke and Feminism on Private and Public Realms of Activities," *Review of Politics* 57 (Spring 1995): 251–277, esp. 252.

[14] For good discussions of Locke's famous caution, see Butler, "Early Liberal Roots," 147; Richard Cox, *Locke on War and Peace* (Oxford: Oxford University Press, 1960), pp. 1–44; Elshtain, *Public Man*, 121–122; Thomas Pangle, *The Spirit of Modern Republicanism* (Chicago: University of Chicago Press, 1988), pp. 132–138; Leo Strauss, *Natural Right*

theory, in this view, established a more promising conceptual framework for sexual equality than his specific arguments would suggest.

This chapter reexamines Locke's political teaching in light of this contemporary debate in order to determine whether Locke's claims to a new understanding of human freedom and equality can be seen as encouraging real sexual equality. It will be shown that there is much greater harmony between Locke's specific arguments concerning women and his more general natural rights theory than has been supposed by both his critics and his defenders. That is to say that reforming the family on the basis of egalitarian principles was not peripheral to Locke's theoretical ambitions for liberal politics, but rather was central to it and indeed led him to a radical reconceptualization of both the family and politics. When the different strands of his argument are connected in a conceptual whole, we can recognize Locke's self-conscious awareness that natural rights principles must pervade practically every aspect of the family and politics. Particularly in Locke's reformed version of the family, the natural rights family, we can see that his attack on patriarchy produced a radical, if often implicit, critique of the established conceptions of conjugal society, the historical origins of patriarchy, the distinct but interrelated spheres of the family and civil society, women's property rights, and the importance of educational reform. Locke's destruction of the patriarchal family as a model for government ushered in the creation of a new understanding of the family and politics, one consistent with the natural freedom and equality of women. In reflecting upon Locke's critique of patriarchy, the modern reader will appreciate the importance of this reformulation of the conception of women and the family for the origin of modern politics.

CONJUGAL SOCIETY AND THE PROBLEM OF NATURE

The state of nature is, of course, the theoretical grounding of Lockean individualism and the foundation for his conception of human nature. However, Locke's account of the state of nature in chapters 2 and 3 of the *Second Treatise* offers no direct discussion of the family. As several feminist commentators have observed, this begs the question: How do Lockean individuals first come into being in the genetic sense? And how do

and History (Chicago: University of Chicago Press, 1953), pp. 206–208, 220, 246; and Michael Zuckert, "Fools and Knaves: Reflections on Locke's Theory of Philosophical Discourse" *Review of Politics*, 36, 2 (1974): 544–564 and "Of Wary Physicians and Weary Readers: The Debate on Locke's Way of Writing" *Independent Journal of Philosophy*, 2 (1977): 55–66.

his assumptions about the structure of the family impact Locke's theory of natural freedom and equality?

It seems fitting therefore to begin our reflections on the family by examining Locke's later treatment in chapter 7 of the *Second Treatise* of what he terms "Conjugal Society." Locke begins this discussion with a quasi-biblical appeal: "God having made man such a Creature, that, in his own Judgement, it was not good for him to be alone, put him under strong Obligations of Necessity, Convenience and Inclination to drive him into Society" (II: 77). Whereas the creation of Eve in *Genesis* 2: 18–22 marked an expression of divine providence, in Locke's reformulation of the first society of man and woman, the individual is "driven" by necessity and inclination to form a larger unit. The first society, Locke continues, was between "Man and Wife," which led to an expanding web of relations, including parents and children and later that of "Master and Servant" (II: 77). Soon, however, Locke drops the scriptural rhetoric entirely when he reveals that "Conjugal Society is made by a voluntary Compact between Man and Woman" consisting in "such a Communion and Right in one another's Bodies, as is necessary to its chief End, Procreation" (II: 78). The family must ensure "mutual support, and Assistance" of the parents, but also what is "necessary to their common Offspring, who have a Right to be nourished and maintained by them" (II: 78). When we recall that in *Genesis* – which was the authoritative source for Filmer – there is no talk of voluntary compacts or children having rights, then the reader begins to sense that Locke's new formulation of marriage will differ greatly from traditional notions.

Locke's account of the origins and structure of the family follows from his observations of the natural world. Like the animals, the union of the human male and female is intended not simply for "Procreation, but the continuation of the Species," and as such it "ought to last, even after Procreation, so long as is necessary to the nourishment and support of the young Ones" (II: 79). But Locke argues that human biology differs from that of the animals "because the female is capable of conceiving, and de facto is commonly with Child again, and Brings forth too a new Birth long before the former is out of a dependency for support on his Parents help" (II: 80). The unique circumstances of extended infancy and female fecundity explain "why the Male and Female in Mankind are tied to a longer conjunction than other creatures" (II: 80). As a result, the human male "who is bound to take care of those he hath begot," is under greater "Obligation" than the males of most other species (II: 80). The union of male and female is made "more lasting" than that of other animals so that "their Industry might be encouraged, and their Interests better united, to make Provision, and lay up Goods for their common Issue" (II: 80). Locke's naturalistic account of the family concludes with a return to semireligious language as "the Wisdom of the great Creatour," who, to facilitate the biological needs of humanity, has "given to Man foresight and an Ability to lay up for the future" (II: 80).

In contrast to the patriarchalist claims that scripture teaches the subjection of women and children to fathers (and especially Filmer's claim that all political rulers rule in the name of the first father, Adam), Locke argues for a naturalistic understanding of the origin of the family derived from the particular needs of human biology. This naturalistic argument deemphasizes the notion that parents, especially fathers, derive any natural authority over their children from being their source. Rather humans, like the other animals, are bound to sustain their children until "they are able to shift and provide for themselves" (II: 79). Yet Locke's account shows the human family is distinguished from the animals in several ways. First, it originates in a voluntary compact between a man and a woman. The voluntary basis of human conjugal society is an expression of natural freedom. Second, only human offspring have a "Right" to be maintained (II: 78). The logic of rights does not seem to operate in the nonhuman world. It is for this reason Locke argues that the conjugal union "ought to last" long enough to support the young until maturity. Of this general rule, "the Inferiour Creatures steadily obey," but Locke is strangely silent about the natural support for human obedience to this rule (II: 80). Instead, he argues that humans have been given "foresight" and an ability to accumulate property for future use. Whereas animals are restricted to the supply of "present necessity," the human family reflects our unique sense of futurity (II: 80). As we know from Locke's crucial chapter on property, it is the insecurity that results from our desire to secure future pleasure and to avoid future pain, which is the spur to human labor and industry.[15] The human self is conscious both of its needs and of its inherent neediness, and it is this futural orientation that most distinguishes humans from other creatures.

This naturalistic philosophic account of the origins of the family stands in some tension with what Locke argued previously in the more polemical *First Treatise*. It was there, in the midst of his attack on Filmer's argument for paternal right acquired through being the primary source of generation, that Locke argued that the simple "Act of begetting" imports no right to paternal dominion (I: 50). This was at least partially based on his observation that: "What Father of a Thousand, when he begets a Child, thinks

---

[15] See Locke II: ch. 5.

farther then the satisfying his present Appetite?" (I: 54). While the idea
of the family may presuppose foresight as an important intellectual component of its formal properties, the act of begetting requires no such foresight. Locke concedes that children are not produced in a manner involving
reason and foresight, but rather by "strong desires of Copulation" (I: 54).
The foresight required to preserve the young is not simply derived from
the desire to copulate. In fact, the only natural mechanism to continue the
species operates "without the intention, and often against the Consent and
Will of the begetter" (I: 54). How then are we to understand foresight as the
ground of the human family?

Locke's distinction between conjugal society, which requires foresight,
and copulation, which implies none, raises a serious problem regarding
consent. It is a central Lockean tenet that all human association derives its
legitimacy and even its very existence from the consent of the contracting
parties. Yet his argument that most parents do not consent to having children, and even those who "design and wish to beget them" have no actual
control over whether and when conception will occur, raises the question
of why parents are morally obligated to care for their children (I: 54).[16]
Underlying this discussion of the family is the possibility of a potential
existential tragedy, in that humans are naturally free beings produced by
a process that violates the principle of consent supposedly animating all
legitimate obligation. Individuals consent to marriage, government, and
even language, but they can neither truly consent to begetting nor consent to be begotten.[17] Though the voluntary union of man and woman
should morally, if not necessarily biologically, precede the relation of parent
and child, children are not the product of foresight, but rather of a strong
desire. While this situation may partly explain the patriarchalist tendency
to see the universal facts of human birth as a sign of our natural subjection,
Locke implies that it is this desire rather than the "Act of begetting" that is
the true natural beginning point for understanding the family.[18] To understand the way in which Locke perceived that this potential tragedy could
be overcome in a reformulated idea of the family, we must delve deeper into
Locke's account of human desires.

---

[16] David Foster, "Taming the Father: John Locke's Critique of Patriarchal Fatherhood"
    Review of Politics, 56, 3 (Fall 1994): 641–670, esp. 659; and Ingrid Makus, *Women,
    Politics and Reproduction* (Toronto: University of Toronto Press, 1996), p. 67.
[17] For consent to language, see John Locke, *Essay Concerning Human Understanding*,
    Peter H. Nidditch, ed. (Oxford: Oxford University Press, 1975), bk. 3, ch. 2, sec. 8 (here-
    after in text and notes ECHU bk, ch, and sec).
[18] Foster, "Taming," 659.

The principal human desires involve a primary desire for self-preservation and a secondary desire to perpetuate oneself through one's children. As Locke explains:

> The first and strongest desire God planted in Men, and Wrought into the Very Principles of their Nature being that of Self-preservation, that is the Foundation of a right to the Creatures, for the particular support and use of each individual Person himself. But next to this, God planted in Men a strong desire also of propagating their Kind, and continuing themselves in their Posterity. (I: 88)

The first desire grounds the right to property while the second, subordinate desire points to family life.[19] The significance of this account of the desires is twofold. First, Locke stresses that the right to property is rooted in the universal desire for self-preservation, and thus children, being born weak and helpless, have a right to be "nourished and maintained by their Parents" (I: 89). Second, the hierarchy of human desires differs from that of animals for whom "the Preservation of their Young, as the strongest Principle in them overrules the Constitutions of their particular Natures" (I: 56). The primacy of the particular, individualistic desires results from human rationality. With clear echoes of his democratized epistemology in the *Essay*, Locke argues that God directs all humankind by their "Senses and Reason," as he does "the inferior Animals by their Sense and Instinct" (I: 86). The human lack of reliable instinct makes explaining concern for children a complex matter. Whereas animals "steadily obey" the rules of conjugal society necessary to preserve their young, humans, while possessing an "Intellectual Nature," are uniquely unprovided with instinct (II: 80, I: 30).[20] The human family is an institution that, among all the creatures, is both the most required and yet perhaps also the least provided for in nature.

The absence of a regular and stable instinct to govern family life presents Locke with two major problems. First, he has to explain how caring for the young is compatible with the self-preservation of the parents. This is why the concern for property pervades Locke's discussion of the family. Conjugal society must encourage "their Industry...and lay up Goods for their common Issue" (II: 78, 80). If the goal of the family is seen as accumulating property, then the family will be consistent with the preservation of all its members. Locke's second problem is the insecurity of the male's attachment to his children. When Locke argues that concern for propagation derives

---

19 Foster, "Taming," 646.
20 Nathan Tarcov, *Locke's Education for Liberty* (Chicago: University of Chicago Press, 1984), p. 67–69.

from concern for self-preservation, he implies that this parental concern is activated only by the actual presence of one's offspring.[21] A mother who carries a child is more likely to effect such an attachment than a father who may not see his child or be certain that a child is his, and thus capable of continuing his self through his "Posterity."[22] Recall that it was particularly in respect to men that Locke asked, "What Father in a Thousand, when he begets a Child, thinks farther then the satisfying his present Appetite?" (I: 54). Thus, Locke's account of conjugal society emerges as less of an observation of natural behavior than a prescription of what ought to be a stable union that both secures the parent's attachment to their children and activates foresight to help secure the family needs.

Locke's discussion of conjugal society and the principal desires underlying it makes the family appear as another of what Locke identifies as a "complex idea."[23] The human family requires the synthesizing of many ideas and desires because it is not the product of unthinking instinct. The family is a rational response to natural necessity, but as a human contrivance and product of reason, it is capable of better or worse formulation. By reconsidering the family in light of the goal of childrearing rather than by reference to the origin of authority, Locke attempts to place the family on more rational grounds than traditionally held. In a direct assault on Filmerian patriarchy, Locke argues that to ascribe the origin of political power to the family is to misunderstand the purpose of both institutions. The great potential for tragedy and subjection, made manifest in patriarchy, may be overcome when we see the family as a human construction not simply determined by unfree biological necessity. Perhaps the true "foresight" underlying the family is that of the philosopher who formulates a conception of it consistent with our natural freedom and equality. The reformed family may, by harmonizing the two strongest human desires, come to be an integral, constituent element of modernity.

A NATURAL BASIS OF INEQUALITY?

The feminist critique of Locke's argument for natural freedom and the voluntary, contractual basis of the family holds that it does not redress the traditional subjection of women.[24] How does Locke account for the

---

[21]   See Foster, "Taming," 647 and Tarcov, *Education*, 68.
[22]   Pangle, *Spirit*, 68.
[23]   ECHU 3.3.1–7, 3.10.22–3, and 2.9.11, 15. See also the extended treatment of the political significance of Locke's "way of ideas" in Chapter 1.
[24]   Brennan and Pateman, "Mere Auxiliaries," 183; Coole, *Political Theory*, 64–65.

historical subjection of women? This issue first emerges for Locke in the *First Treatise*. In the course of attacking Filmer's argument that scripture supports a husband's rule over his wife, Locke addresses the key scriptural passage regarding the curse of Eve at *Genesis* 3:16. Locke argues that any subjection implied in this passage may extend only to Eve or at least imports "no more but that subjection they [wives] should ordinarily be in to their Husbands" (I: 47). However, he suggests that the curse may actually signify no more than an act of "Providence," a kind of prediction that a woman "should be subject to her husband, as we see that generally the Laws of Mankind and the Customs of Nations have ordered it so" (I: 47). But far from simply accepting patriarchal assumptions, Locke moves quickly to limit the effect of this traditional subjection by arguing that "there is no more Law to oblige a Woman to such a subjection, if the circumstances either of her Condition or Contract with her Husband should exempt her from it" (I: 47). Moreover, Locke stresses that husbandly power may be variable, limited by contract, does not include the political power over life and death, and in no sense extends to a woman's children or "all that should come of her" (I: 47–49).[25] However, wary readers are most struck by Locke's concession that, despite all his proposed limitations on husbandly power, there is "I grant, a Foundation in Nature for it" (I: 47).

How are we to understand this "Foundation in Nature"? Is it something demanding our moral respect and obedience?[26] The first indication of Locke's attitude toward this natural foundation for female subjection may be seen in the broader context of his scriptural analysis. The discussion of the curse of Eve is preceded by Locke's general treatment of the issue of biblical interpretation. Here Locke argued that God, "when he vouchsafes to speak to Men, I do not think, he speaks differently from them, in crossing the Rules of Language in use amongst them" (I: 46). Thus, the meaning of scripture is unambiguous. But when speaking of Eve in particular, Locke claims that "*Thy desire shall be to thy Husband*, is too doubtful an expression, of whose signification Interpreters are not agreed, to build so confidently on, and in a Matter of such moment, and so great and general Concernment" (I: 49). The position of women in the family thus becomes a crucial part of Locke's reinterpretation of scripture, for if the biblical account of the subjection of wives is "too doubtful an expression" to build on confidently, then Locke's "Foundation in Nature" does not rest on biblical authority.

---

[25] Tarcov, *Education*, 59.
[26] See Pangle, *Spirit*, 173 and Waldron, "Locke, Adam, and Eve," 250–254.

Alternatively Locke suggests that the foundation for the traditional subjection of wives may be found in "the Laws of Mankind and Customs of
Nations" (I: 47). In this view, God's providence is virtually equated with the
general agreement among civil societies. However, this formulation of the
"Foundation in Nature" raises two obvious problems. The first is Locke's
ambivalence toward looking to providence as a guide for human action: "If
anyone will say that what happens in Providence to be preserved, God is
careful to preserve as a thing therefore to be esteemed by Men as necessary
or useful, 'tis a peculiar Propriety of Speech, which every one will not think
fit to imitate" (I: 147). He implies that equating the biblical curse on women
with providence amounts to an admission that this subjection carries no
paradigmatic or obligatory status. The second problem arises from Locke's
general criticism of making "the Example of what hath been done, be the
Rule of what ought to be" (I: 57). By such reasoning, Locke argues, one
could not only justify subordinating wives, but also cannibalism, adultery,
incest, and every form of child abuse imaginable (I: 57–59). The laws and
customs of nations often lack a foundation in reason, which is humanity's
"only Star and compass," and thus cannot be said to establish a foundation
in nature for anything in familial relations (I: 58).

The context of this discussion, namely the curse of Eve, suggests that the
foundation of sexual inequality involves the female role in reproduction.
This has led some commentators to argue that Locke simply accepts the
female reproductive capacity as a natural disadvantage codified in law.[27]
But if Locke equates a wife's subjection with the "disadvantage" of childbirth, this is far from a simple subjection. He argues that there is no more
law to oblige a woman to this subjection than "there is, that she should
bring forth Children in Sorrow and Pain, if there could be found a remedy for it" (I: 47). Locke's individualist principles suggest that just as a
woman may improve the terms of conjugal society by contract, she may
also blamelessly employ any device to reduce the pain of childbirth. Both
the mutability of the marital contract and the potential for medical treatment overcoming birth pains suggests that there is, for Locke, considerable
malleability in human affairs that can allow for improvement in the position of women in the family and society. It is significant that only three
women are named in this crucial section, Eve and the two English queens,
Mary and Elizabeth. Locke cites the last two as examples to show the

---

[27] See, for example, Clark, "Women and Locke," 17; Coole, *Political Theory*, 64; Elshtain,
      Public Man, 125.

absurdity of the patriarchalist argument for the subjection of wives: "And will anyone say…that either of our Queens Mary or Elizabeth had they married any of their Subjects, had been by this Text put into a Political Subjection to him?" (I: 47). The contrast between Eve, denizen of the pre-political Garden of Eden, and Mary and Elizabeth, both rulers of civil societies, suggests that the "Foundation in Nature" for wifely subjection may be changeable depending on the degree of rationality and sophistication of the institutions and laws of civil government. In a rational society, the traditional subjection of women may be anachronistic.

Another clue regarding the meaning of the "Foundation in Nature" for the subjection of women emerges much later in the *Second Treatise* when Locke indicates that in a disagreement between husband and wife "the last Determination, i.e., the Rule, should be placed somewhere, it naturally falls to the Man's share, as the abler and stronger" (II: 82). Now the "Foundation in Nature" seems to embrace what Lorenne Clark calls a "natural male superiority in virtue."[28] Perhaps it is simply the inoperability of the principle of majority rule in the relation of only two contractors. Locke characteristically limits this exclusive male rule as "reaching but to the things of their common Interest and Property, [it] leaves the Wife in full and free possession of what by Contract is her peculiar Right" (II: 82). Thus the husband's control over family property does not extend to the wife's particular property protected by contract, nor does it assign the wife to some particular role or way of life.[29] Likely the common concern over which the husband presides involves only authority over the children.[30] Nonetheless, Locke's argument that male rule in the family is natural remains problematic for his egalitarian principles.

On this point Locke's feminist critics have been particularly incisive. A key element of this critique is that the natural inequality implied in the rule of husbands as "abler and stronger" violates Locke's fundamental political principles by creating a de facto inequality beneath a "gloss of consent," for even if Locke rests a husband's rule not on nature but on contract, he always assumes that married women will subject themselves.[31] This observation forces us to consider: What is the status of a natural rule in an institution that is not simply natural? Is the natural subordination of women operable in all cases of conjugal society, both in nature and civil society?

---

[28] Clark, "Women and Locke," 19.
[29] Coole, *Political Theory*, 66.
[30] "Schochet, *Patriarchalism*," 249–250.
[31] Brennan and Pateman, "Mere Auxiliaries," 183–184, 191–193.

Can the "Foundation in Nature" for the subjection of wives be overcome by human contrivance?

THE HISTORICAL ORIGINS OF PATRIARCHY

In order to understand the problematic status of married women in Locke's account of conjugal society, we need once again to reach back into his treatment of the historical origins of government. In this foray into natural history, Locke distinguishes his rationalist conception of conjugal society from the traditional notions that have governed human society by arguing that "in the first Ages of the World...the Father of the Family" was "Prince of it" (II: 74). This authority originally involved two distinct powers. First, the father alone in the family was permitted "that executive Power of the Law of Nature" that involves the right to punish other individuals in order to "preserve the innocent and restrain offenders" who would use force without right against any other individual (II: 74,7–13,18). Second, paternal power extended to the settling of disputes and "controversies" over his children's property (II: 75,107,108). Thus Locke concedes that paternal power emerged as a primitive model for government rooted in the need for a recognized agent in the punishment of criminals and in the judging of property disputes.

Is Locke's historical account of paternal power not a large concession to the patriarchalist argument?[32] In one sense, it clearly is given that Locke affirms the existence of predictable, quasi-natural tendencies toward patriarchy. From the perspective of genetic analysis, the family has, Locke admits, come into being through much of human history in a form that is unmistakably patriarchal. However, Locke qualifies this claim in several ways. First, he reduces the naturalism of patriarchy by insisting that the principle of consent can account for even the most patriarchal familial arrangement. The consent of women to marriage and the consent of children to paternal rule maintain the principle of natural freedom even in an imperfect model of authority.[33] Second, while Locke admits that the patriarchal family is historical, he does not concede that it is right. He explicitly linked the emergence of one-man political rule to the patriarchal family: "We shall generally find them under the Government and Administration of one man. I am also apt to believe, that where a Family was numerous to subsist by it

---

[32] Several commentators suggest that it clearly is. See, for example, Brennan and Pateman, "Mere Auxiliaries," 194; Coole, *Political Theory*, 69; Foster, "Taming," 651; and Pateman, *Sexual Contract*, 92–93.

[33] See Foster, "Taming," 652 and Tarcov, *Education*, 75.

self...the Government commonly began in the Father" (II: 105). The link between the patriarchal family and monarchy reveals that the structure of the family – the first and most formative social relation – can be a source of habitual, unthinking submission in which women and adult children (or all subjects save the king) endanger their natural freedom. The establishment of legitimate government based on principles consistent with freedom and equality would seem to require, in Locke's view, a reformation of traditional attitudes towards the family.

Even if patriarchy was the original form of the family, this example is not authoritative now: "An argument from what has been, to what should of right be, has no great force" (II: 103). The family is a complex idea that requires reason and experience, rather than simple instinct, to determine the structure consonant with freedom and equality. In the "innocence of the first Ages" patriarchy emerged, like monarchy, as a "simple" idea, one "most obvious to men" (II: 94, 107). Locke even suggests that patriarchy suited that "poor but Virtuous Age," when there were few people and few possessions (II: 110,105). He also, however, indicates that this "Golden Age" had a seamier side, as some fathers lost their authority due to "Negligence, Cruelty, or any other defect of Mind" (II: 111,105).[34] Far from simply offering a concession to patriarchalism, Locke suggests that the patriarchal family inevitably led to faultily constructed governments that required people of greater experience to "examine more carefully the Original and Rights of Government, and to find out ways to restrain the Exorbitances, and prevent the Abuses of that Power" (II: 111).[35] Thus the problem of patriarchy on the familial level parallels the problem of pre-political executive power on the constitutional level, as with both conditions human beings, lacking instinct or a natural political end, must often use experience to lead them to a goal not immediately apprehensible to reason as such.

This account of the historical origins of patriarchy becomes even more problematic, however, when we turn to a curious passage in the heart of Locke's treatment of paternal power. In the course of his argument against Filmer's claim for absolute paternal dominion, Locke makes a revealing argument:

And what will become of this *Paternal Power* in that part of the world where one Woman hath more than one Husband at a time? Or in those parts of America where when Husband and Wife part, which happens frequently, the Children are all left to the Mother, follow her, and are wholly under her Care and Provision? (II: 65)

---

34 Foster, "Taming," 652.
35 Tarcov, *Education*, 75.

Here Locke suggests that there are parts of the world in which polyandry is accepted practice.[36] More importantly, we see that in some "parts of America," there is a conception of the family that appears to violate Locke's argument against the "uncertain mixture, or easie and frequent Solutions of Conjugal Society" (II: 80). The problem in the "wastes" of America then is not patriarchy but rather that there is no reliable paternal presence at all. The full significance of this statement comes to light only when we remember that "In the beginning all the World was America, and more so than it is now" (II: 49).

Locke's conception of conjugal society is a highly conventional body because there is deficient natural support for the family, especially for the nomadic male who may never see his own child. Perhaps the mother may recognize the survival of her children as an expression of her desire to perpetuate herself through them, but as we recall from Locke's discussion of the principal human desires, it would seem that parental concern for children is elicited only by the actual presence of one's offspring (I: 54–56, 88).[37] The frequent parting of husband and wife in America is a further reminder that Locke did not see in nature a reliable guarantee of a father's concern for his offspring.[38] Perhaps this is why Locke implied the possibility of matriarchy when he spoke of a "Family, wherein the Master or Mistress of it had some sort of Rule proper to a Family" (II: 77). When we consider Locke's account of the historical origins of patriarchy in light of his consideration of the infrequency of a lasting and reliable conjugal society in America, patriarchy assumes a new significance for Locke as a later stage of development in human relations – a severely flawed but in some sense understandable response to the natural necessity to preserve offspring. The patriarchal family is thus in its primal form a voluntary compact in which a woman submits to the authority of a husband by allowing him secure access to her body (which reinforces the vital corollary of paternal legitimacy) and in return gains a regular helper in securing the preservation of herself and her children. The male desire to copulate, as distinct from the desire to perpetuate himself through his offspring, becomes the grounding

---

[36] Walsh, "Locke and Feminism," 265.

[37] Tarcov, *Education*, 68.

[38] Pangle, *Spirit*, 236. In this respect, Pfeffer is incorrect to conclude that Locke did not see the lack of stable conjugal units in America as a condition that compromised the vital educative and preservative function of the family (Jacqueline Pfeffer, "The Family in Locke's Political Thought" *Polity*, 33, 4 (Summer 2001): 593–618, esp. 599–600). Rather in this passage Locke's point is that the patriarchal family is an albeit deeply flawed improvement over the natural condition per se.

of spousal relations, and the particularizing of this desire through the regular cohabitation with a voluntary partner becomes the foundation for stable conjugal society.

Though the patriarchal family is clearly a deeply flawed improvement over the extreme penury of the natural state, Locke is willing to concede that "Without such nursing Fathers tender and carefull of the publick weale, all Governments would have sunk under the Weakness and Infirmities of their Infancy" (II: 110). The "Foundation in Nature" that explains the traditional subjection of wives seems to be rooted in a woman's voluntary subjection to a man to help secure her offspring. Locke suggests that this subordination is the product of a faulty familial arrangement that emerged in the poverty of the "first Ages," and is ultimately an inadequate attempt to overcome natural necessity and preserve the species.[39] The real question is whether Locke rests content with this patriarchal familial arrangement.

In light of Locke's account of the historical origins of patriarchy, it is understandable to inquire whether Locke's theoretical distinction between the state of nature and political society confirms or confutes the findings of historical practice. If we follow the suggestion of some feminist commentators and read the patriarchal family back into Locke's state of nature, we perceive differently his claim that civil government is the "proper remedy for the Inconveniences of the State of Nature, which must certainly be Great, where Men may be Judges in their own Case" (II: 13).[40] Locke argues that the family does not require civil society for its existence, as the ends of marriage may be "obtained under Politick Government, as well as in the State of Nature" (II: 83), but the state of nature is so insecure that "To avoid this State of War...is one great reason for Men's putting themselves into Society, and quitting the State of Nature" (II: 21). The potential state of war implicit in the state of nature undermines the achievement of the ends of the family. Common property generated to preserve the young is radically insecure in a condition in which there is no common force to restrain "the partiality and violence of Men" (II: 13). Thus if patriarchy is a feature of the state of nature, the transition to political society signifies the utter inadequacy of the patriarchal family as an institution designed to secure the lives and possessions of its members. In light of the historical

---

[39] Grant correctly observes that Locke believed that "what is essential for legitimate rule varies as historical conditions change," but curiously she does not apply this insight to the family as we might expect ("Locke on Women," 301).

[40] See Brennan and Pateman, "Mere Auxiliaries," 193; Clark, "Women and Locke," 16, 33; and Pateman, *Disorder*, 93.

origins of patriarchy, we might also ask if the family is altered in the transition to Locke's conception of civil society.

The historical origins of patriarchy presupposed that wives and children consented to fatherly rule, which consisted in allowing one man to judge "controversies" regarding property and to punish transgressions of the rights of others. Even though Locke limits this paternal power in several ways, it appears to raise important conceptual problems for Locke's general teaching.[41] However, the transition to civil society involves two crucial changes that directly impact the natural family. First, Locke insists that it is necessary "to quit everyone his Executive Power of the Law of Nature, and to resign it to the Publick, there and only there is a Political, or Civil Society" (II: 89). Second, there must be the creation of a "common established Law and Judicature to appeal to, with Authority to decide Controversies between them" (II: 87). Civil society requires common rules of judgment and punishment. The two functions that women and children have historically granted to the father, judgment and punishment, are now, Locke argues, the functions *par excellence* of civil government. Civil society is instituted to secure the property and the lives of all of its members and as such requires, at least in a formal sense, practically exclusive power of judgment and punishment.

The idea of family is thus clearly affected by the transition from the state of nature to civil society. In the relations of husband and wife, Locke argues, the "Civil Magistrate doth not abridge the Right" to the attainment of the ends of the family, but civil government does possess the power to decide "any Controversie, that may arise between Man and Wife about them" (II: 83). But what of the man's rule as the "abler and stronger"? The problem of majority rule in spousal disputes appears supererogatory when we consider that the deciding vote in such matters may be a civil judge. Moreover, the "natural" paternal rule over family property is seriously qualified by the presence of civil government to settle marital disputes.[42] In light of this role of government, the claim of "abler and stronger" husbands appears highly contingent on prevailing conditions. What may be necessitated in the natural condition may have little or no reasonable ground for consent in an established legitimate regime. The government becomes the "abler and stronger" force that can best preserve the property of all its rights-bearing citizens. Locke even suggests that the fullest expression of

[41] Butler, "Early Liberal Roots," 145 and Waldron, "Locke, Adam, and Eve," 250–4.
[42] Compare with Brennan and Pateman, "Mere Auxiliaries," 193; Butler, "Early Liberal,"147; and Coole, *Political Theory*, 66.

proper spousal relations in civil society would not involve any particular "Power in the Husband," but rather "might be varied and regulated by that Contract, which unites Man and Wife in that Society" (II: 83).

Locke's discussion of conjugal and political society obviously has serious implications for the status of women in the family. Locke argues that civil government may settle "any Controversie that may arise between Man and Wife" because they are "*in Political Society together*," and are thus "united into one body" having a "common ... Judicature to appeal to, with Authority to decide Controversies between them" (II: 83, 87 emphasis added). Men and women may be in conjugal and political society simultaneously. The creation of conjugal and political society institutionalizes the public and private spheres of life, but rather than subjecting and insulating women in the domestic sphere, Locke distinguishes two areas of life the separation of which does not preclude the public activity or at least public representation of women. The private family, geared toward procreation and education, is primarily intended for the education and nurturing of children, whereas the public realm serves to facilitate the adult concerns of securing property and individual rights.[43] Locke's argument for the contractual understanding of spousal rights and duties suggests that it is not the separation of the public and private spheres that leads to the subjection of women but rather their historical and philosophical confounding by patriarchalists.

The complex relation between Locke's *eidetic* and *genetic* account of the family, thus hinges on his attempt to combine an observation of what is and has been with an effort to provide a normative demonstration of what by right should be. By distinguishing and contrasting what is from what should of right be, Locke tries, on the immediate level, to counter the influential providentialist doctrine that tended to conflate these two. In separating the "is" from the "ought," Locke undermines the patriarchal argument of Filmer for the divine ordination of power in politics and in the family, which held that things are as they are because God made them that way, and since God made them that way that is how they should be.[44] Locke thus reveals patriarchy to be an erroneous principle animating a flawed conception of the family, which nonetheless has proven to be a very common historical response to the penury of nature. However, on a more general level, Locke points the reader to the uniquely human capacity to equate truth with tradition. The historical prevalence of the practice

---

[43] Walsh, "Locke and Feminism," 262.
[44] For the role of divine providence as a support for patriarchalism, see Filmer, *Patriarcha*, 6–7, 11.

of patriarchy, with its alleged supports in scripture and historical custom, provides Locke with a particular example to illustrate the broader danger to natural rights philosophy posed by the all-too-frequent human tendency to abandon reason, our "only Star and Compass" (I: 58).

THE NATURAL RIGHTS FAMILY

Although Locke recognizes the subjection of women in the family as a feature of practically all previous thought and social experience, his conception of human freedom and equality suggests that this condition can and should be overcome.[45] The individualist principles that ground Locke's thought move him toward a view of the family safe for liberalism. In this way he undermines the traditional supports for patriarchy, such as arguments for greater male strength and ability, and in the process opens conceptual room for the greater equality of men and women.[46] Strength, Locke argues, does not give title to rule because people should not "live together by no other Rules but that of Beasts, where the Strongest carries it" (II: 1).[47] All manner of inequalities of age, virtue, birth, and alliance may thrive in society without justifying the subjection of anyone "to the Will or Authority of any other Man" (II: 54). Locke's new contractual family provides the theoretical framework for an arrangement in which the relations of husband and wife may be consistent with a political society based on natural freedom and equality.

One major feminist criticism of Locke's natural rights theory is that women, being subsumed in the family, do not play a role in the original contract that begins civil society. In this view, the individuals who enter civil society are fathers of families and they construct civil government to serve their exclusive interests.[48] However, as Waldron observes, it is striking that while practically every major philosophical authority of the period, such as Samuel Pufendorf and Thomas Hobbes, for instance, explicitly denied that women participate in the original contract, Locke made no such claim.[49] Moreover, Locke insists that a women's "peculiar" property rights (II: 82)

---

[45] Butler, "Early Liberal," 143.
[46] Foster, "Taming," 641 and Tarcov, *Education*, 76.
[47] Mary Shanley, "Marriage Contract and Social Contract in Seventeenth Century English Political Thought" *Western Political Quarterly*, 32, 1 (March 1979): 79–91, esp. 90.
[48] Brennan and Pateman, "Mere Auxiliaries," 185; Pateman, *Sexual Contract*, 52–53.
[49] Waldron, "Locke, Adam, and Eve," 259. Pufendorf argued: "states have certainly been formed by men, not women" (Samuel Pufendorf, *On the Duty of Man and Citizen According to Natural Law*, James Tully, ed. [Cambridge: Cambridge University Press, 1991], p. 125). For his part, Hobbes was noticeably less emphatic arguing that "for the

are, like those of her husband, subject to a power beyond the limited sphere of the family, namely civil law. By recognizing women as individual property holders, Locke presupposes that they would have the same motive for entering civil society as men, namely to secure their property and, by extension, the lives of their children. Property is both an end, as an expression of human freedom rooted in our self-ownership, and a means to the preservation of that freedom (II: 27; 18, 131). Locke implies that the creation of a public sphere allows women to preserve their property, and hence their freedom, in the event of a dispute with their husbands. Perhaps it is only in civil society, as opposed to the natural condition, that a woman would be able to protect both her particular and her family interests. Women in the family may better secure their property in civil society, where they can appeal to the law, than in the state of nature, where the husband almost imperceptibly assumes executive power. As Locke argues: "No rational Creature can be supposed to change his condition with an intention to be worse" (II: 131).

Locke's account of conjugal and civil society has been accused of creating a dichotomy of the public and private spheres that obscures the inequality of women in the family by encouraging their dependent position in the family.[50] Yet the logic of Locke's reformulation of the family on the grounds of natural rights does not insulate the private sphere from the effects of the public principles of legitimate government; rather the improved status of women in the family and political society seems to be crucial for reconstructing all social relations on the basis of these principles of legitimacy. In order to determine the depth of Locke's reformulation of the role of women in society in this respect, we need to examine the status of women with respect to what he viewed as some of the key elements of political life: property rights, labor, inheritance, and rationality.

Two questions for the natural rights family are whether women's property rights are recognized in the conjugal and political contract, and whether the formal extension of such rights provides women with meaningful control over their lives and their children's lives. Clearly, if men and women are not in a position of equality in the family, then Locke's support for a woman's freedom to contract as best she can is deeply disingenuous.[51] As we have seen, Locke's entire theory of the family and government

---

most part commonwealths have been erected by fathers, not by the mothers of families" (Thomas Hobbes, *Leviathan*, Edwin Curley, ed. [Indianapolis: Hackett Publishing, 1994], ch. 20, sec. 4, p. 129).
[50] See for example, Okin, *Justice*, 111.
[51] Coole, *Political Theory*, 64–65.

presupposes that the improvement of a self-regarding individual's position with respect to others is not only morally permissible but may be necessary for protecting individual rights and releasing the productive capacities of a nation. Significantly a case in point is Locke's argument regarding the solubility of marital union: "the Wife has in many cases, a Liberty to separate from him [her husband]; where Natural Right, or their Contract allow it" (II: 82). Arguably, Locke's great innovation was in making the marriage contract negotiable, limited, and terminable.[52] As Shanley observes, the wife's natural right to separation parallels the citizen's natural right to resist tyrannical government.[53] Locke argues that no one can consent to arbitrary rule or be required to honor a contract with a government that has become tyrannical (II: 23, 24, 204–8). Likewise, a woman's natural freedom cannot be alienated by the first act of contract with her husband. The right to separation reaffirms her natural freedom.

But does Locke's reformed family protect a woman's right not only to *own* property, but also to exercise the natural right to *acquire* property through her labor? Some feminist commentators contend that Locke's conjugal society violates this principle inasmuch as a wife's right to the property generated by her labor is presumed to be transferred to her husband.[54] The implication is that Locke cannot truly view women as naturally free beings because the ground of the right to property acquired through labor is the natural freedom of the human person. As Locke argues: "Man (by being master of himself, and *Proprietor of his own Person*, and the Actions or *Labour* of it) had still in himself the great Foundation of Property" (II: 44). Private property derives from neither civil law, nor revelation, nor even the consent of any other individual. Thus if Locke does not extend the right to acquisition through labor to women, he has denied their very humanity by implying that women either do not appropriate through labor or have no claim to ownership of what they produce through labor.

Locke's explicit references in the *Two Treatises* to the female capacity for labor are few but significant. The first direct reference arises in the course of his refutation of Filmer's argument that all title to property derives from God's original grant of Dominion to Adam. Locke points out that God's grant of "Dominion over every Living thing that moveth on the Earth (Gen.1:28)" was extended not solely to Adam but to "them," meaning him and Eve.[55] The potential significance of this for all wives is obvious: "If it be

52   Butler, "Early Liberal," 144; Shanley, "Marriage Contract," 89.
53   Shanley, "Marriage Contract," 83.
54   Brennan and Pateman, "Mere Auxiliaries," 192; Clark, "Women and Locke," 32; Coole, *Political Theory*, 73.
55   Butler, "Early Liberal," 142.

said that *Eve* was subjected to *Adam*, it seems she was not so subjected to him, as to hinder her *Dominion* over the Creatures, or *Property* in them" (I: 29). Locke disproves the absolute subjection of Eve on the grounds that it would be strange to "say that God ever made a joint Grant to two, and only one was to have the benefit of it" (I: 29). The patriarchalist assumption that marriage places a woman entirely in service to her husband ignores the basic fact of nature that every person has the right to preserve his or her self (II: 6). Buried in this patriarchalist assumption is the failure to recognize that though the family may involve an individual's concern extending to all the family members, *the root of property* is not in the service of others, nor even in the service of the self, but in the very existence of the self. This, Locke argues, is as true of Eve as of all wives. The marriage contract cannot annul this natural right to acquisition because it is not in any individual's power to renounce the right to her own preservation expressed through the natural right to property.

Locke's most direct reference to a woman's right to acquire property is contained in his chapter on conquest near the conclusion of the *Second Treatise*. This chapter is unique in two senses. First, it is Locke's only full treatment of what he considers to be a third major hypothesis about the origin of government besides that of consent and patriarchy.[56] Second, it is the only occasion in the entire *Second Treatise* in which he explicitly speaks of a wife's property acquired through her labor. Locke argues that the turbulence of human history has led many to mistake "the force of Arms, for the consent of the People; and reckon Conquest as one of the originals of Government" (II: 175). He counters that force can certainly destroy a government, "but, without the consent of the People, can never erect a new one" (II: 175). The link to Locke's theory of labor is in the reminder that just as only consent can create lawful government, it is only labor that creates the original title to property. Acorns may be bought, bartered, or inherited, but what first made them private and made a "distinction between them and the common" must have been someone's labor (II: 28). Force can account for neither title to property, nor the origins of lawful government.

The question of a woman's title to property emerges in the context of Locke's discussion of the rights of a lawful conqueror. The right of such a conqueror, who has fought in retaliation against unprovoked aggression, is "perfectly despotical" over those responsible for the war (II: 178–80). The one major restriction on the conqueror's rights is what Locke admits sounds like yet another "strange doctrine," whereby this despotism does

---

[56] Tarcov, *Education*, 214, n. 5.

not extend to "the Innocent Wife and Children" (II: 180, 182).[57] The lawful conqueror "may appropriate to make himself reparation" from the goods of the unjust aggressor, but "he cannot take the Goods of his Wife and Children; they too had a Title to the goods he enjoy'd, and their shares in the Estate he possessed" (II: 183). While the primary focus of this discussion is Locke's attempt to define rules of conquest and occupation, it also indirectly has important implications for his view of the status of women because the grounds for this restriction on the right of conquest differ as they relate to wives and children. Children have "a Title to their Father's estate for subsistence" (II: 183). The natural right of children to be maintained, as well as the family's role in continuing the species, must not be interfered with even in a just war. But with respect to wives, Locke argues that they have a title to property in their own right: "My Wife had a share in my estate, that neither could I forfeit…whether *her own Labour* or Compact gave her a Title to it, 'tis Plain, Her Husband could not forfeit what was hers" (II: 183 emphasis added). A child has a right to his or her parents' property whether he or she labors or not, but a wife's sole title to property in the event of conquest is through labor or contract.

This discussion reveals that the property generated through a wife's own labor cannot be simply subsumed into her husband's estate. Locke may even be implying that wives derive some title over family property generated during the marriage. In this way, he employs the extreme case of foreign conquest to reveal the simplistic and unjust assumption underlying the patriarchal view of the family. When the *paterfamilias* loses a war, does his family lose their right to survive? This individual natural right can never be lost through the actions of others. Just as force is the way of "beasts," in forgetting that individual rights ground any human association, the patriarchalists regard women, children, and for that matter men as mere beasts. Any family structure that denies women the right to the products of their own labor or denies them the contractual means to preserve their property is modeled on unjust conquest. The patriarchal conception of marriage is in effect a perpetual state of war. Locke, on the other hand, sets a high standard for any legitimate familial arrangement: neither force nor paternity, but only the consent of free and rational individuals can explain the origin of the family and civil society.

The issue of inheritance is another crucial aspect of Locke's theory of property and plays a central role in his reform of the family. Evidently

---

57   Locke's other strange doctrine was of course the executive power of the law of nature (II: 9). Cf. Chapter 2 above.

real equality for women would require an equal right to the disposition of family property.[58] It has been argued, however, that Locke's construction of the family simply provides the theoretical basis of the absolute right of male heads of households to pass on their property to their legitimate male heirs.[59] In order to assess this argument, we need to examine Locke's view of inheritance, particularly his attitude toward the practice of primogeniture. Locke's main treatment of primogeniture occurs in the *First Treatise* in his attack on Filmer's notion of the divinely ordained "monarchy by inheritance." Here Locke argued that in those "countries where their particular Municipal Laws give the Whole possession of Land entirely to the First Born, and descent of Power has gone so to Men by this Custom, some have been apt to be deceived into an Opinion, that there was a Natural or Divine Right of Primogeniture to both Estate and Power" (I: 91). Clearly, this passage is Locke's attempt to unlink the transmission of property through primogeniture from the patriarchal assumption of the transmission of power in the same way. As Locke argues, the distinct character of property and political rule are incommensurable since government exists for "the good of the governed," whereas property is "for the benefit and Sole advantage of the Proprietor" (II: 92).[60] Though Locke's principal aim is to attack the patriarchalist tendency to confound the inheritance of property with that of title to rule, it is notable that in the course of this assault Locke also questions the natural or scriptural justification for primogeniture (I: 91, 111–18).[61] He even implies that in those "Countries where their particular Municipal Laws" support primogeniture, there is a tendency to structure the descent of political power on the same basis (or at least the two practices are often coeval), and it is this tendency that habituates people to accept absolute monarchy. The unthinking, purely traditional practice of bequeathing property to the eldest son seems to mirror the dangerous condition in which ruler and ruled alike forget that all legitimate government rests on the consent of the governed and not on the birthright of an eldest son.

Locke's discussion of inheritance exposes a potential conflict between a child's natural right to "inherit, with his Brethren, his Father's Goods" and the parent's right to freely dispose of his or her property (II: 190). Property exists for the "Sole Advantage of the Proprietor" and is the "unquestionable Property of the Labourer" (I: 92, II: 27). Yet there is a tension between

---

[58]   Clark, "Women and Locke," 27.
[59]   Clark, "Women and Locke," 16; Coole, *Political Theory*, 70.
[60]   Tarcov, *Education*, 60.
[61]   Tarcov, *Education*, 61.

the free, rational choice implied in the parents' right to dispose of their goods and the natural right of the children to inherit them. It seems that Locke is not basing the child's natural right on any natural parental duty – as this would violate the sole proprietorship of the laborer – but rather is basing it on a parent's natural desire to continue his or her self through the child (I: 88).[62] A child's right to inherit is conditional on a parent's free will rather than a natural or divine argument for primogeniture.[63] Locke's rejection of primogeniture also reflects his skepticism about the whole notion that property belongs to a family as a whole and that the individual right – either of parents or children – is simply subsumed to serve its needs and interests. Clearly changing the way that society views inheritance is a key element in Locke's reform of the family.

What implications does Locke's argument for the reform of inheritance law have for the position of women in the family? In the chapter "Of Paternal Power" in the *Second Treatise*, Locke argued that this power does not extend to a natural dominion over a child's person, actions, possessions, or "whole Property" (II: 57). The law of nature actually reduces paternal power to "an obligation to preserve, nourish, and educate the children" (II: 5, 6). In return, a child is bound to "that honour which he ought, by the Law of God and Nature, to pay to his *Parents*" (II: 66). Significantly, Locke deliberately asserts that the duty to educate, nourish, and preserve children is actually "parental" as opposed to "paternal" because "whatever obligation Nature and the right of Generation lays on Children, it must certainly bind them equally to both the concurrent Causes of it" (II: 52).[64] Parental honor must extend to mothers because mothers as well as fathers deserve filial respect for their role in educating, nourishing, and preserving their children.

However, through the course of Locke's complex discussion of parental power, it becomes apparent that there is no natural guarantee of a child's duty to honor his or her parents. Locke's initial, and largely hortatory, claims about unconditional parental honor are followed up with the half-hearted appeal that with respect to filial duty, parental honor involves no more than "it may become his Son in many things, not very inconvenient to him and his Family, to pay a deference to it" (II: 69). Locke's less than enthusiastic endorsement of filial gratitude indicates that there actually is no natural law obligation as such for adult children to obey or honor their

---

[62] Pangle, *Spirit*, 232–233.

[63] Pangle, *Spirit*, 233.

[64] For Locke's revision of the traditional idea of paternal power into the more egalitarian notion of "parental power," see Shanley, "Marriage Contract," 89.

parents.[65] But Locke continues: "There is another *Power* ordinarily *in the Father*, whereby he has a tie on the Obedience of his Children...And this is the Power Men generally have to bestow their Estates on those, who please them best" (II: 72). He hints that "this is no small Tye on the Obedience of Children" (II: 73). The parent's power to bequeath property on those children "who please them best" emerges as the natural glue that, along with education, holds Locke's contractual family together.

Locke's theory would definitely discriminate against women if, though extending equality to women in the area of education of children, it did not also extend this equality to the distribution of property. As such, maternal honor would simply depend on the arbitrary will of the male property holder, the father.[66] However, Locke's argument suggests otherwise. Of maternal honor, Locke argues: "The Father's authority cannot dispossess the mother of this Right, nor can any man discharge his Son from honouring her that bore him" (II: 69; 1:62). Locke continues that any honor due to a father "is owing to the Mother too" (II: 70). If Locke systematically deprives women of the right to transmit property to their heirs, we would have to wonder if he is making an uncharacteristic appeal for an unconditional duty or is rather implying that mothers have a right to a share of the family estate. The inalienability of the right to maternal honor suggests that the right to bequeath property is not invariably exercised by the father (Locke says it is a power "ordinarily" and "generally" in fathers [II: 72]), but may be delegated or even exercised by the mother in her own right.

But does Locke ever address the status of unmarried women?[67] In one sense he clearly does for the argument that mothers need to possess property in order to secure the honor and support of their children must have serious implications for the position of separated and divorced women (I: 62; II: 82). The solubility of marriage in Locke's conception of the family makes any woman potentially a single mother (II: 81, 82). Locke is certainly encouraging women to protect their property under the terms of the marriage contract, but he may also be indicating that securing the right to generate property during the marriage would be any sensible woman's condition for entering marriage. Without this security, it is unclear why any woman would diligently nourish and educate children who would never be obliged to support or honor her later.

Locke's reduction of the Fifth Commandment to a child's calculated self-interest to inherit parental goods emerges as a great incentive for parents

---

[65]   Strauss, *Natural Right*, 218.
[66]   Clark, "Women and Locke," 27, 30.
[67]   This is a concern for Lorene Clark (Clark, "Women and Locke," 20).

(especially women) to accumulate property, but it also frees industrious children from filial obligations to lazy, unproductive parents.[68] One crucial consequence of this is the stimulation of the acquisitive talents of all the family members. When the enjoyment of inherited goods is a source of political obligation, inheritance also becomes a stabilizing force in political society (II: 73). But this revaluation of inheritance and parental honor also has radical implications for women's equality. Locke's equating of the motive for parental honor with a child's desire to secure property provides a rationale for the extension of property rights to women, particularly in the case of widowed or separated women. Moreover, Locke's attack on primogeniture in principle extends the right of inheritance to daughters, allowing them to negotiate their own marriage contracts more freely and on better terms. It may be a daughter, rather than her brother, who most comports with the "Will and Humour" of her parents (II: 72). By making favoritism rather than primogeniture the basis of inheritance law, Locke counters the stultifying resignation of individuals to their economic condition and the dictates of custom.[69] Rather, Locke aims to unleash the productive capacities of individuals who, relying on their own industry, are brought to recognition of the true harshness of the natural condition.

The heart of Locke's political philosophy may be summed up in the statement: "Thus we are *born free*, as we are born Rational" (II: 61). This simple but beautiful statement rests at the heart of his understanding of human nature. Of children's dependence on parents, Locke argues: "Age and Reason as they grow up, loosen them till at length they drop quite off, and leave a Man at his free Disposal" (II: 55). The democratic conception of the faculty of reason that grounds Locke's epistemology also obviously animates the egalitarianism in his ideal of parent-child relations. However, if, as some feminist scholars claim, Locke denies that women have the same rational capacity as men, would it not then make a mockery of the philosophical pretensions of Locke's democratization of mind? [70] The egalitarian credentials of Lockean political philosophy stand or fall on whether or not he included one half of the human race in his operating assumptions about rationality. If women lacked the reason characteristic of full human relations, they would be what Locke calls "Lunaticks," "Ideots," "Innocents," or "Madmen" (II: 60). If Locke believed this, he never said so. Rather we

---

[68]   Foster, "Taming," 667; Pangle, *Spirit*, 238.
[69]   Pangle, Spirit, 242; Michael Zuckert, "An Introduction to Locke's First Treatise" *Interpretation*, 8 (January 1979): 73–74.
[70]   See, for example, Coole, *Political Theory*, 75; and Brennan and Pateman, "Mere Auxiliaries," 195.

saw that in America, children are often left wholly under the "Care and Provision" of their mother (II: 65). While Locke implies that women often require men to help secure their children, especially in the state of nature, clearly he does not argue that women by nature require men to preserve themselves (II: 77–80). In Locke's view of nature, reason, like necessity, is not gender specific.

A key aspect of the debate surrounding Locke's assessment of female rationality is the act of contracting. To be a party to a contract implies rationality because the "Brutes" do not contract. As Okin and Shanley have observed, contracting is an expression of human freedom and reason, which consists of two distinct principles: the *freedom to contract*, regarding whether and with whom to contract, and the *freedom of contract* regarding the choice of terms.[71] Though a woman in the natural condition may be under strong necessity to contract with a man to secure her children, Locke indicates that in principle; it is ultimately her free choice that will decide, whether in nature or more significantly in civil society. Locke also goes very far in arguing for a woman's freedom to negotiate the terms of the marriage contract (II: 82, 83, 183). The inherent rationality of the contractual act encompasses both the political contract that can legitimately support monarchy, aristocracy, or democracy, as well as a marriage contract that supports a number of familial arrangements (II: 81–3).[72] Locke insists that the family may be ruled by a "Master" or "Mistress," or even that spousal affairs may be "varied and regulated" entirely by contract (II: 77, 83). The mutability and adaptability of either contract is restricted only to the impossibility of legitimately consenting to arbitrary rule (II: 23, 82). Neither absolute monarchy nor the extreme patriarchal family of Filmer is justified by Locke's account of human reason.

One of the most striking features of Locke's reform of the family is his emphasis on its educative role in the formation of free and equal citizens. The family, so long an enemy of liberty, will have the primary responsibility for educating children in a way consistent with their natural freedom, and do so largely independent of political supervision.[73] Of this important educative function, Locke continually emphasizes that "the mother hath an equal share" (II: 52, 53, 55, 58, 66, 67). In one fell swoop, Locke undermines the patriarchalist inference of political obligation from paternal power and

---

[71] Okin, *Justice*, 120; Shanley, "Marriage Contract," 79.

[72] Pateman, *Disorder*, 129; Walsh, "Locke and Feminism," 267.

[73] Foster, "Taming," 646; Tarcov, *Education*, 72. Although for the important public role that Locke sees in education, see Chapter 5 below.

redistributes the remaining "parental" power – namely education – into the hands of the father and mother equally. While Locke's argument for parental education could theoretically limit a father's absolute control over his children but still leave men, not women, ruling the family, it is important to recognize the way in which Locke's treatment of education undermines paternal claims to rule more generally.[74] By extending the duty of education to mothers, Locke places women in the very crown of the family's virtues. Envisioning women as powerful agents in achieving the chief moral goal of the family is a stark contrast with the patriarchal family that encouraged unthinking submission and obedience to the father alone. In failing to recognize the distinction between the family and political society, patriarchy failed to recognize that politics is the realm of mature, self-regarding adults, while the family rests on the idea of parents as educators to children.[75] The family, for Locke, is not meant to institutionalize the unequal power relations of the adult male and female, and thus if the family was properly ordered and understood, there is nothing to suggest that it would preclude the public participation of women.

The mother's role in education reaffirms Locke's argument for the inherent rationality of women. The very essence of Lockean education is the inculcation of the principles of reason in children. Parents should make the mind of the child "pliant to Reason" and encourage "such rigour and rectitude to their minds, as may best fit the children to be most useful to themselves and others" (II: 64).[76] Parental relations wherein two free and equal beings work together for a common end, without the subjection of either party, also provides an example for the moral development of future citizens of a liberal society. Perhaps the full extent of Locke's argument for women's rationality is seen in his contradiction of one of the long-cherished tenets of Aristotelian biology: "The Rational Soul...(of the yet Unformed Embrio)...if it must be supposed to derive anything from the Parents, it must certainly owe most to the Mother" (I: 55). Though Locke's materialism predisposes him to reject the superiority of form over matter, he suggests that even if one proceeds from Aristotelian terms, the generation of the rational soul would indicate the natural superiority of women, not men. Locke's reinterpretation of the generation of animals, like his reformation of family education, reaffirms his argument for natural equality.

[74] Clark, "Locke and Feminism," 22.
[75] Walsh, "Locke and Feminism," 276; Makus, *Women*, 56.
[76] John Locke, *Some Thoughts Concerning Education*, Ruth Grant and Nathan Tarcov, eds. (Indianapolis: Hackett, 1996), sec. 34 (hereafter in notes and text T and section). See also Walsh, "Locke and Feminism," 276.

While Locke's educational writings will be the focus of the following chapter, it would not be amiss to consider briefly how some aspects of his educational theory have a direct bearing on his account of gender equality. Near the beginning of Locke's *Some Thoughts Concerning Education*, he reveals a telling ambiguity: "I have said He here, because the principal Aim of my Discourse is, how a young Gentleman should be brought up from his Infancy...though where the Difference of Sex requires different treatment 'twill be no hard Matter to distinguish" (T 6). A few sections later, Locke reveals the essential similarity of the proper education of boys and girls when he proposes that regarding the education of daughters, "the nearer they come to the Hardships of their Brothers in their Education, the greater Advantage will they receive from it all the remaining Part of their Lives" (T 9). The significance of Locke's views on the education of girls is twofold. First, his encouragement of physical training for girls suggests that the presumed physical weakness of the "softer sex" may be overcome by individual effort.[77] It also implies that the pernicious effects of the concern for female fragility are the result of convention, the product of a poor education rather than any natural cause. The suggestion that girls can strengthen their bodies reminds us of Locke's argument that women may relieve the pain of childbirth "if there could be found a Remedy for it" (I: 47). As Butler has pointed out, Locke's individualist principles not only encourage women to resist succumbing to complacency in their current condition, but also stress the ability of individual women to overcome their particular obstacles.[78] Perhaps more importantly, Locke's reform of family education makes the encouragement of this belief in daughters a parental duty.

The second, and perhaps most significant, implication of Locke's view of the education of girls may be seen in the fact that in a book at least ostensibly intended primarily for the education of young gentlemen to prepare them for careers in business and politics, Locke retains only minor, nonintellectual differences for girls.[79] In his "Letter to Mrs. Clarke" Locke reveals that with respect to the mental development of boys and girls: "I acknowledge no difference of sex in your mind relating...to truth, virtue, and obedience, I think well to have no thing altered in it from what is (writ for the son)".[80] Clearly both girls and boys should be schooled in the use of reason. Locke's argument that the native intellectual potential of

---

[77] John Locke's "Letter to Mrs. Clarke, February 1685," in *Locke's Educational Writings*. James Axtell, ed. (New York: Cambridge University Press, 1968), p. 344.

[78] Butler, "Early Liberal," 149.

[79] Locke, "Letter to Mrs. Clarke," 344–345.

[80] Locke, "Letter to Mrs. Clarke," 344–345.

girls should be developed in childhood marks a revolution in thinking from the patriarchal assumptions of the natural and irremediable inequality of father and child, male and female.

Locke's argument for the essentially equal education of girls and boys casts a critical light on traditional notions of conventional sex roles in the family and politics. Locke's thoughts on education, like so much else in his work, reflect his belief that there is a pliancy in human nature that is obscured by procrustean efforts to design a rigid, differentiated education for girls and boys. Locke encourages parents toward a deeper reflection on the influences of a conventional education and the misguided assignment of individual rights and duties on the basis of sexual difference.[81] His theory of education raises new possibilities for an understanding of the moral and intellectual development of children that would reduce the inequality of men and women in the public and private spheres.[82] Locke hints at the potential for revolutionary change in human relations near the end of this work on education when he expresses his hope that "it may give some small light to those, whose Concern for their dear little Ones makes them so irregularly bold, that they dare venture to consult their own Reason, in the Education of their Children, rather than wholly to rely upon Old Custom" (T 216).

LOCKE'S LEGACY ON THE FAMILY

Locke points to the natural rights family as the end product of his critique of patriarchy. However, this begs the question about his reluctance explicitly to follow through on the more radical implications of his natural rights argument as it pertains to women's status in the family and society. As we have seen, much of Locke's argument for sexual equality and reform of the family has to be pieced together from fragmentary discussions strewn throughout his political and educational writings. But why does Locke consider the problem of the inequality of women in the family only in the context of his broader battle with the extreme patriarchalism of Filmer and not treat the issue of sexual equality as a central and systematic theme in his political theory? Why, in other words, did Locke not write a work like John Stuart Mill's *On the Subjection of Women*?

One plausible explanation is rooted in the political and historical context in which Locke worked. The *Two Treatises*, which contains his

---

[81]   Butler, "Early Liberal," 149.
[82]   Walsh, "Locke and Feminism," 277.

clearest attack on patriarchy, is a work of constitutional theory, as well as a work of political philosophy. Because it is, on the immediate level, a constitutional tract intended to combat the monarchist arguments in the Exclusion Crisis of 1679–1681, Locke presumably had to be cautious in illuminating the full implications of his natural rights theory for fear of losing support for the Whig constitutional position from socially conservative men concerned primarily with the political balance of power between king and parliament, which was the focus of the immediate controversy.[83] Locke addresses this very fact in the Preface to the *Two Treatises* when he appeals to any "Englishman, much less a Gentleman" who would display the "generous Temper and Courage of our Nation" in the struggle against absolutism (I: 1). It is highly dubious that the typical "Englishman, much less a Gentleman" of Locke's time steeped in a pervasive patriarchal culture would be receptive to a radical reformulation of the family and of women's role in society.

A second possible explanation for Locke's reluctance to articulate and promote explicitly the more radical elements of his argument is rooted in the premises of his political philosophy itself. His conception of nature holds the promise of sexual equality, but it also reveals considerable fragility at the core of the idea of the human family. His insistence on the need to preserve a stable conjugal unit in the face of the harshness of nature is rooted in his empirical observation that human biology makes children vulnerable longer than the young of other animals. Moreover, Locke also suggests that a properly structured family can act as a spur to economic growth, which will redound to the benefit of a whole society by encouraging the industry of parents to accumulate property in order to pass it on to their children.[84] The family can become a vehicle for the conquest of harsh nature, which by itself provides "little more than nothing" (II: 42). Locke was perhaps inclined to view the family as a rather fragile institution still somewhat limited in its capacity for change by the economic, technological, and material reality of the seventeenth century. But with greater economic development and technological advance, he may very well have been inclined to see a much more egalitarian family structure as not only desirable but also more

---

[83] Grant, "Locke on Women," 298. For discussions of the historical and political context of the *Two Treatises* in the Exclusion Crisis and later Glorious Revolution, see Richard Ashcraft, *Revolutionary Politics and Locke's Two Treatises of Government* (Princeton: Princeton University Press, 1986), esp. Ch. 5 and Ward, *Politics of Liberty*, chs. 8–10.

[84] Makus, *Women*, 81.

socially viable than traditional patriarchy. The conquest of physical nature through human labor and technology does not require the conquest of or the liberation from the family, but rather it requires the destruction of a particular kind of family, namely the patriarchal model of the family. It is the gradual reform of the family, rather than a sudden and violent revolution in the relations of men and women and parents and children, that Locke held to be meaningful change within his society's grasp.

However, this is not to diminish the long-term radical implications of Locke's natural rights family. In arguing that the traditional sources of the subjection of women, namely the family and civil society, are human institutions capable of improvement, Locke desanctified and denaturalized the inequality of women. Thus in many ways, Locke's critique of patriarchy began a gradual revolution in thinking that made modern feminism possible. He systematically undercut the core patriarchalist assumptions that had marked, to varying degrees, virtually all pre-modern political thought. Like many feminists today, Locke recognized the importance of language and custom as either a source of subjection or a vehicle for emancipation. Locke may even be said to have laid the foundation for the rhetoric of women's liberation when in the course of trying to articulate the distinction between paternal and parental conceptions of authority, he argued that finding "fault with words and names that have obtained in the World...it may not be amiss to offer new ones when the old are apt to lead Men into mistakes" (II: 52–3). In the end, though, Locke was not naive about the immediate prospects for change in all areas of his teaching as "this mistake of words...remaining firm in their minds, it is no wonder that the wrong notions annexed to them should not be removed."[85] He suggests that with respect to deeply rooted customs in an institution like the family, which affects practically every human being, it will take a long time to overcome the errors of the past. At one point in the *Second Treatise*, Locke compares the "Humane" tenderness in parental love of children to God's paternal rule of the Israelites in *Deuteronomy* 8:5 (II: 67). When we look at this biblical passage we realize that God's love involved the death of an entire generation of people after forty years in the desert before reaching the Promised Land. This is perhaps a poignant image to describe Locke's own awareness that it would also require many years and much pain before women can achieve equality in the family and society.

[85]   Locke, ECHU 3.10.16.

5

Locke's Liberal Education

The issue of education emerged in the *Two Treatises* as an element in Locke's broader project to undermine traditional patriarchy. In this way, Locke's critique of patriarchy involved reexamining and reforming the conventional understanding of both marriage and parenting. With respect to the latter, Locke insisted in the *Second Treatise* that one way to topple the patriarchal support for Filmerian divine right monarchy was to reinterpret paternal authority in terms of the parental duty to educate a child rather than a child's unconditional obedience to the presumed biological source of his or her being.[1] Locke's reformulation of political power not only placed the primary burden of moral obligation on parents rather than offspring, but also advanced a conception of human freedom according to which the undeniable dependence of children on parents in no way diminished the ultimate goal of rational autonomy and full independence upon reaching the age of maturity: "Care and Reason as they grow up, loosen them [the Bonds of Subjection] till at length they drop quite off, and leave a Man at his own free Disposal" (II: 55).[2]

However, in the context of the *Two Treatises*, Locke had little to say about the pedagogical approach and specific content of the education parents are morally required to provide for their children. This was due both to the narrow political purpose of this discussion of education as an antidote to patriarchal political pretensions, and to the fact that Locke's main focus in his account of the family in the political writings was to radically reform

---

[1] John Locke, *Two Treatises of Government*, Peter Laslett, ed. (Cambridge: Cambridge University Press, 1988), *Second Treatise*, sec. 67 and 69 (hereafter in notes and text Treatise and section).

[2] See also II: 59, and 61.

marriage and the relations of adult women and men. Indeed, Locke's primary appeal to novelty in his treatment of the family in the *Second Treatise* had to do with his insistence on the legitimate involvement of mothers in parental, as opposed to traditionally paternal, authority over children.[3] The societal goal of reforming parenting to support the education of citizens of a liberal polity was thus inextricably connected to the directly political goal of advancing the rights of women in marriage.

The issue of educational reform, always somewhat peripheral in the *Treatises*, becomes a sustained and systematic central theme only in Locke's two major educational writings, *Some Thoughts Concerning Education* (1693) and *Of the Conduct of the Understanding* (1697).[4] The core insight of Locke's critique of patriarchy, namely that the family is a very human, and in crucial respects conventional, institution capable of better and worse design provides an important source of continuity between the political and educational writings. Both the *Thoughts* and the *Conduct* are saturated with the language of novelty and a reformist impulse. Locke's most celebrated reforms, such as the discouragement of corporal punishment, abandoning the system of education based on memorization of rules and deemphasizing the teaching of formal logic and ancient languages, as well as his call for improved education for girls, pit Locke firmly against the traditional model of education dominated by humanist philosophy and the pedagogy of the grammar schools in his time.

The main thrust of Locke's reform proposals was to conceive of early childhood education as primarily socialization rather than the inculcation

---

[3] See II: 52, 53, and 65.

[4] The *Thoughts* was expanded considerably for the 1695 edition. There is strong evidence to suggest that Locke initially intended that the *Conduct* would be one of the major additions to the fourth edition of the *Essay* along with new chapters "Of Enthusiasm" in Book IV and "Of the Association of Ideas" in Book II. In a letter to William Molyneux in April 1697, Locke spoke of proposed additions to the fourth edition, including a chapter the title of which "will be Of the Conduct of the Understanding, which, if I shall pursue, as far as I imagine it will reach, and as it deserves, will, I conclude, make the largest chapter of my *Essay*" (John Locke, *The Correspondence of John Locke, Volume VI*, E. S. de Beer, ed. [Oxford: Oxford University Press, 1981] Letter no. 2243, p. 87). Unlike the chapters on enthusiasm and the association of ideas, the *Conduct* for some reason was never incorporated into the *Essay* and was only published posthumously in 1706. However, inasmuch as Bk. 4, ch. 20 of the *Essay* "Of wrong Assent, or Errour" covered much the same ground on error but did not include the discussions of mental training that appear in the *Conduct*, we might speculate that Locke decided at some point to approach the *Conduct* as a standalone educational treatise. For a good discussion of the context of the *Conduct*, see Paul Schuurman, "Locke's Way of Ideas as Context of His Theory of Education in *Of the Conduct of the Understanding*" *History of European Ideas*, 27 (2001): 45–59, esp. 45–47.

of knowledge. While the private family is the primary educator in both the political and educational treatises, Locke insists that education has profound political and social consequences. Improving education will not only enhance the "welfare and prosperity of the nation" by producing more rational and intelligent citizens, but educational reform also promises to undermine the traditional social structures that have historically reinforced authoritarian politics.⁵ Locke's target audience, including the general reading public and, more specifically, middle and upper class parents of young children, is intended to reflect upon both the nature of education and the changing way society understands the function and political meaning of the family. Locke assumes that liberalizing the institution of the family requires revolutionizing the thinking of its constituent parts.

In order to understand the full scope and range of Locke's educational reforms, we will need to consider the relation of the educational writings to the *Two Treatises* and the *Essay,* on the one hand, and the relation of the *Thoughts* and the *Conduct* to each other, on the other hand. The intellectual nerve linking the *Second Treatise* and the educational writings is the foundational principle of natural equality. At the very beginning of the *Thoughts,* Locke signals the enormous public importance of education in a natural rights-based society: "I think I may say that of all the men we meet with, nine parts of ten are what they are, good or evil, useful or not, by their education. 'Tis that which makes the great difference in mankind" (T 1). The significance of education highlights the relative equality of natural intellectual faculties that was such a central theme in the *Two Treatises.* While the explicit focus of the *Thoughts* is on the sons of the politically vital gentry class, Locke emphasizes the far-reaching implications of his educational proposals for girls and indeed potentially for all classes in the nation. As we shall see, in his considerations on poor relief written in his role as a public servant, Locke even envisioned a system of publicly funded "work schools" for poor children that incorporated some of the key insights of his pedagogical theory. The possibility for broad public application of his educational reforms is both implicit in his recommendations for the private family and reflective of the public acknowledgment of basic equality of intellectual capacity Locke marks as one of the salient features of modern society. From the egalitarian principles of natural rights philosophy, Locke

---

5 John Locke, "Some Thoughts Concerning Education," in *Some Thoughts Concerning Education and Of the Conduct of the Understanding*, Ruth Grant and Nathan Tarcov, eds. (Indianapolis: Hackett, 1996), "Dedication" to *Thoughts,* p. 8 (hereafter in text and notes T and section).

deduced that providing educational opportunity on a massive scale could become a legitimate policy objective of government arguably for the first time in history.

The unifying principle linking the *Essay* and the educational treatises is the notion of education involving training in certain methods of mental activity. The democratic implications of the *Essay's* focus on a novel empiricist epistemology and the "way of ideas" illuminating the internal operations of the human mind deeply inform Locke's proposals for educational reform.[6] Indeed, perhaps the most tangible and practical manifestation of the democratization of mind arises in the context of Locke's educational writings. The practice of suspending desires and forming reasoned judgments, which Locke identifies in the *Essay* as the source of intellectual freedom, is the philosophical touchstone for Locke's account of both early childhood and higher education. With respect to the means for establishing the proper mental habits of a rational being, Locke conceives of the relationship between his epistemological and educational writings in the following terms: In the former "ground clearing" work he identified the problems plaguing human understanding and in the later educational writings he proposed concrete steps to address and remedy these problems.[7] However, Locke's prescriptions take a different form in each of his two major educational works depending on the stage of development to which his educational method is applied.

While the goal of rational autonomy Locke advanced as the aim of education in the *Second Treatise* remains continuous throughout the *Thoughts* and the *Conduct*, he clearly distinguished primary and secondary from higher education. The focus of the *Thoughts* is on early childhood education and rests on the fundamental insight of Locke's epistemology that the

---

[6] For support for the idea that Locke's educational theory is closely connected to his philosophy and epistemology, see also Schuurmann, "Locke's Way of Ideas," 47–50; Jay Fliegelman, *Prodigals and Pilgrims: The American Revolution against Patriarchal Authority 1750–1800* (Cambridge: Cambridge University Press, 1982); and Peter Gay, "Introduction," *John Locke on Education*, Peter Gay, ed. (New York: Columbia University, 1964), pp. 1–14, esp. p. 5. Fliegelman in particular puts it nicely when he states that Locke's pedagogy "derived logically and consistently from his psychology" in the *Essay* (p. 12).

[7] Compare John Locke, *An Essay Concerning Human Understanding*, Peter Nidditch, ed. (Oxford: Oxford University Press, 1975), bk. 2, ch. 33 (hereafter in notes and text E bk, ch, sec, p.) and John Locke, "Of the Conduct of the Understanding," in *Some Thoughts Concerning Education and Of the Conduct of the Understanding*, Ruth Grant and Nathan Tarcov, eds. (Indianapolis: Hackett, 1996), sec. 41 (hereafter in notes and text C and section).

key to proper education is paying close attention to how one learns rather than the content of what one studies. The emphasis in the *Thoughts* is on learning through experience and the development of habits encouraging rational self-control of one's appetitive desires. Locke presents the establishment of these mental habits in youth as both a preventative measure to avoid the unfounded association of ideas in error and prejudice, and as originally relatively unreflective practices that hopefully will develop over time into the basis for rational, conscious activity. The *Thoughts* allows wide scope for external influences, primarily parents and tutors, on the child's development, but Locke insists that these formative influences are properly self-limiting by being carefully calibrated to the age and abilities of the child. The fundamental egalitarianism of Locke's educational method thus lies in both its potentially universal application and the notion that in most cases there is, in principle, no natural obstacle to the improvement of understanding culminating in an autonomous, self-directed individual.

For its part, The *Conduct* focuses on the application of Locke's method to adults. Perhaps one of the most revolutionary, but rarely noticed, aspects of Locke's educational writings, which span the topics of early childhood education in the *Thoughts* to a call for reform of university curricula in the *Conduct*, is his foreshadowing of contemporary approaches to education that seek to adjust pedagogical methods and content to the capacities of the student in a framework integrating preschool, primary, secondary, higher education, and even continuing education. The *Conduct* represents Locke's attempt to replace the formal logic and traditional curricula of the universities with a new mode of instruction informed by experimental science and the fundamental insights of the Cartesian method of "clear and distinct ideas". However, the scope of the *Conduct* extends beyond formal education to include recommendations for continuing education among the reading public more generally, as well as instruction designed to be useful for the improvement of understanding in all social classes. Locke's educational reform directed to the goal of rational autonomy has its foundation in the habits and practices established in childhood, but he is emphatic that its full societal impact both produces and reflects a broader cultural commitment to the ideals of an open and intellectually vibrant modern society. Rational autonomy, so much the promise of early education, culminates in the ideal of the individual's examined relationship with the community and its beliefs in a continuous process of self-reflection upon issues of religion, politics, science, and morality that are unsuited to the capacities of children but comprise the very essence of citizenship in liberal society.

THE *THOUGHTS*: EDUCATION AS SOCIALIZATION

Locke opens the *Thoughts* with the admission that his collected reflections on education were not originally intended "for public view," but he came to the decision to publish them only once he became convinced that they "might be of some use if made more public."[8] From the private correspondences with his friend Edward Clarke, in which he proposed an educational regime for that gentleman's son, Locke concluded that the "method here proposed" may have much more general application than that for which it was initially designed. What is perhaps most striking about this method from the outset is the extent to which Locke emphasizes the deep underlying connection between physical and mental education: "A sound mind in a sound body is a short but full description of a happy state in this world" (T 1).

Locke first introduces the subjects of habituation and rational self-control that would be the hallmark of his educational proposals in the context of the lengthy opening discussion of health. This initial foray into physical education immediately sets a democratic tone that permeates through the entire treatment of early education. All children should be trained to endure physical hardship so as to be hardy and adaptable adults later in life. Effeminacy, morbidity, and valetudinarianism are presented by Locke as the pernicious effects of physically corrupting habits acquired in youth. Much to the anticipated horror of "fond mothers," Locke insists that the young gentleman's "bed should be hard," and he should be brought by insensible degrees of change when still an infant to become accustomed to wearing wet shoes and light clothing (T 22, 7). With perhaps more than a hint of democratic *ressentiment*, Locke insists: "gentlemen should use their children as the honest farmers and substantial yeomen do theirs" (T 4). Locke amplifies the jarring novelty of this reverse snobbery by extending the recommendation for robust physical exercise to include the daughters of the gentry as well as their sons. Indeed, it is in the context of suggesting measures for strengthening the physical constitution of children that Locke implies the potentially far-reaching and radical effects of his educational system for gender relations when he insists that the nearer girls "come to the hardships of their brothers in their education, the greater advantage will they receive from it all the remaining part of their lives" (T 9).[9] By forcing

---

[8] *Thoughts*, "Dedication," p. 7.

[9] As we observed in the previous chapter, in addition to the significance of advocating similar physical education, Locke never indicates any area of intellectual development or academic training that would be any less suitable for daughters than it is for sons.

parents to confront their own deeply rooted prejudices about gender, Locke seeks to encourage an open-minded attitude as the natural default position of parents and teachers concerned with education more generally.

Locke's response to the predictable objection from concerned parents that his proposal for training the child's body for hardship is indistinguishable from sadism is twofold. First, he insists that a system of plain diet and rigorous exercise is conducive to health and vital to long-term development of sound mind and body (T 14). More importantly, however, Locke employs this discussion of health to introduce his reflections on the power of habit and custom. A central theme of this discussion of physical education is Locke's effort to demonstrate the malleability of human understanding through examining the interconnection of mind and body. By changes introduced in gentle and insensible degrees "we may bring our bodies to anything without pain" (T 7). The great extent to which education contributes to making people "what they are" apparently applies as much to their physical as to their mental well-being. Insofar as habituation plays an important role in education, the key for success lies in correctly deciding "what habits you settle" in the child (T 18). Locke spares no occasion to excoriate what he takes to be the many ill-conceived and pernicious customs of childrearing among English gentry relating to poor diet, constrictive clothing, and enforced physical delicacy. Parents are encouraged to promote mastery of desires in children by responding only to clear physical needs rather than fanciful wants (T 106).

However, the ultimate effect of this external influence on a child's development is not simply to accustom the body to hardship, but rather to begin the process of habituating the mind to rational control of the desires by reducing their number and intensity. Inuring a child to the effects of cold and wet through habit is the earliest and wholly somatic practice in developing the cognitive capacity of suspending desires that grounds Locke's account of intellectual freedom in the *Essay*.[10] Freeing a child from an impulsive response to pain and discomfort is the first step in somewhat removing him or her from the mechanism of natural sensation.

The solid foundation of a sound body trained to endure physical hardship provides support for Locke's later recommendations for a general method of education. However, whereas the key for physical development is to avoid corrupting customs that encourage delicate sensibilities, Locke indicates that the most important, and potentially dangerous, issue in mental development relates to proper punishments and rewards. Use of incorrect

---

[10]   ECHU 2.21.47.263.

rewards and punishments will undermine any system of education, much like proper rewards and punishments are the irreplaceable instruments for correct socialization. The main thrust in Locke's effort to direct early education toward proper socialization involves replacing the ubiquitous practice of corporal punishment with a new system of incentives based on esteem and disgrace. Locke rejects the "rough discipline of the rod," which is the "ordinary way of education" in the grammar schools as well as with private tutors, on the grounds that it provides no positive reinforcement for good conduct and the inculcation of good habits (T 74). Children who are whipped for failing their lessons will simply hate and resent the books and subjects (as well as the teachers) that are the cause of their torment (T 37, 47). Moreover, corporal punishment contradicts the physical education directed to training endurance toward hardship. Indeed, children raised with a Lockean system of physical education would be least responsive to corporal punishment precisely because they have been trained since infancy to see pain as not being a great, or at least not the greatest, evil.

Cultivating a child's sensitivity to esteem and shame is the lynchpin of Lockean socialization. He calls this "the great secret of education" because praise and disgrace are "the most powerful incentives to mind, when once it is brought to relish them" (T 56).[11] One commentator observes that Locke's identification of esteem as what we might call "soft power" meant to supply the motivation for virtuous action marked a "dramatic shift in the history of moral thought."[12] Unlike the "hard power" expressed in corporal punishment, shame and esteem appeal to a child's nascent sense of oneself as a rational being. The novelty in Locke's use of the idea of esteem lies not so much in his sense of its applicability to explaining human motivation, but rather his conviction about its usefulness as a concept applied to very young children. He does not argue that the desire for esteem is natural in the strict sense, as is for instance the problematic desire to dominate others that is exhibited in the cradle (T 103). His point rather is that sensitivity to one's estimation in the eyes of others emerges much earlier than is typically supposed (T 35, 57). The mental aspect of the hedonic principles woven into the fabric of human understanding produces even in very young children an enjoyment in possessing a "state of reputation" (T 59). Locke insists that even in the very rare cases of extreme rebelliousness in which corporal

---

[11] Ian Harris identifies Nicole and Bayle as potential sources for Locke's sensitivity to the educational and social power of opinion (*The Mind of John Locke* [Cambridge: Cambridge University Press, 1994], pp. 281, 287).

[12] P. J. Crittenden, "Thoughts about Locke's Thoughts about Education" *Journal of Philosophy of Education*, 15, 2 (1981): 155.

punishment may be justified (T 78), it should only be employed after all efforts at using praise and shame have been exhausted.

Locke admits that his call to reason with even small children is novel and will be "wondered at," but he maintains that "gentle persuasion" is almost always more effective in shaping behavior than compulsion (T 80). The key for Locke lies in not confusing the desire for being thought reasonable with the actual state of being fully rational. While these two phenomena are related, Locke clarifies that it is the desire or passion to be esteemed as rational that needs to be cultivated: "They love to be treated as rational Creatures...'Tis a pride should be cherished in them" (T 81, 34). The reason guiding young children is properly speaking that of the parent or teacher; however, the child's willing participation in this superintending *nous* is itself both an indication of nascent rational faculties and an exercise in their gradual development.

Does Locke's use of disgrace and esteem as tools of socialization undermine or contradict the goal of achieving rational autonomy? While it clearly requires a dependence on external rational forces to direct a child's behavior, Locke sees no obvious contradiction between the means and end of his educational proposal. He suggests that a system of reward and punishment based on esteem and shame encourages a general climate of respect for reason to surround a child as it places a burden on parents and teachers to teach through example by taking care to ensure that they always maintain a calm and rational demeanor in their children's presence (T 81). In this sense, Locke's proposal is as much about the conduct of educators as it is about children.

But is concern for esteem really not just slavery to the opinions of others? Locke admits that there is some truth to this; however, the key is to employ concern for reputation as a way to begin the process of making children reflect upon their own actions. Locke rejects the idea of reputation as a means to reinforce class prejudice by excoriating pretentious affectation in children, and instead seeks to lead them to savor a decidedly democratic taste in which concern for one's repute serves to confirm one's sense of the moral worth of others.[13] He pointedly extends this concern for how one appears to others beyond narrow class confines to include how the child sees oneself in the eyes of the public more generally, or at least to the tutor, servants, and local people that inhabit a child's social world. The most important feature of Locke's account of esteem is his insistence that it is not

---

[13]   Nathan Tarcov, *Locke's Education for Liberty* (Chicago: University of Chicago Press, 1984), p. 104.

the true source of virtue but rather the best method suited to the capacities of children. Locke's emphasis on worldly reward and near-total silence about theological support for virtue through divine reward and punishment is primarily a function of the fact that he does not believe theological doctrines are suited to the capacities of children and therefore are not the proper method of education for young children. Concern for reputation can encourage a child to proper conduct, but it is a method of instruction pointing beyond itself to a fuller, more reflective intellectual process at a later stage of development when "they grow able to judge for themselves and to find what is right by their own reason" (T 61). The real question is, of course, how does Locke propose to make this move from desire for reputation to independent judgment and critical reason?

Habituation is the conceptual bridge linking the desire for esteem and rational autonomy in Locke's theory of early education. The foundation of the method of education is early training of the mind to act in a rational way. Esteem and disgrace are the quasi-natural, hedonic basis of a system of reward and punishments that supports preliminary efforts to make a child's mind "pliant to reason" even if at first this is the reason of others (T 34). Locke presents habituation as a means to bring a child closer to the achievement of rational control over desires. Esteem without habit requires constant reaffirmation by external agents; good habits without the need for constant praise is a vital milestone on the path to rational autonomy. However, Locke is careful to distinguish good habits from merely prevailing customs. The inculcation of good mental and physical habits originating in the supervening reason of parents and teachers is required at least in part as a means to prevent bad habits or customs from being implanted in a child's mind. Locke practically equates custom with bad habits rooted in the mind's early acceptance of erroneously associated ideas at a period when the child has not yet fully developed his or her critical faculties. For example, while there is no natural connection between the ideas of darkness and fearful apparitions such as goblins, frightful and fanciful tales can implant these ideas in the mind of a child. In order to counter irrational fearfulness and superstition, a parent should get the child into the habit of playing at night without fear and avoid telling ghost stories (T 138). Locke's point is that it is better to form a correct association of ideas without conscious, rational activity than it is to allow unreasonable customs to ossify in a young mind.

In addition to the prophylactic dimension of habituation, Locke also sees a more constructive element in it. For Locke, habit stands as a kind of midpoint between custom and critical thinking. In this respect, his notion of habit is a departure from the traditional Aristotelian idea of the role of habit in ethical training. In Aristotelian ethics, good habits originate in a conscious activity that gradually over time becomes practically natural or a kind of second nature embedded in one's character. Thus an individual learns to be courageous, for instance, by deliberately experiencing dangers in battle.[14] One cannot learn to be courageous by playing football or climbing tall trees.[15] For Aristotle, the serious business of ethical training only gradually, and perhaps only in rare cases, becomes genuinely pleasant once the individual has developed a powerful predisposition toward the beauty and nobility of morally virtuous action.[16]

However, Locke's education operates on the basis of a different understanding of habit and experience. He maintains that early education is advanced by making all tasks a form of play: "I have always thought learning might be made play" (T 147). By employing the hedonic motivation natural to children, Locke suggests parents and teachers can teach them to read more effectively by making it a game than through dry memorization and beatings (T 155–8). Locke's innovative proposal, familiar to a generation of parents and children reared on Sesame Street, extends to a general disapproval of the traditional model of education as rule-based and repetitive. In contrast to Aristotle, Locke sees habituation originating in unreflective and even pleasant activity that only gradually becomes more self-conscious and less intrinsically pleasant over time. For Locke, what originally seems natural and pleasant, such as learning to read through games, only gradually over time becomes a more conscious and deliberate activity such as reading a particular book on a certain subject.

Does Locke's account of habituation involve a considerable degree of manipulation? Clearly it does, but his point is that successful education can only proceed with an awareness of the important biological and physiological limits placed on instruction. Early education must always be suited to the capacities of children in their state of development. However,

---

[14] Aristotle, *Nicomachean Ethics*, Martin Ostwald, translator. (New York: MacMillan Publishing, 1962), Bk III, chs. 6–9. See also Lee Ward, "The Problem of Courage in Aristotle's *Nicomachean Ethics*" *American Political Science Review*, 95, 1 (March 2001): 71–83.

[15] In this respect, note Aristotle's insistence that ethical training is emphatically not for the young (*Ethics*, Bk I, ch. 3, 1095a2–7). While Locke does not disagree with Aristotle that immaturity makes full understanding of virtue virtually impossible, he does place an emphasis on appealing to the nascent rationality of even very small children that seems, if not incompatible with Aristotle, at least to have been philosophically uninteresting to the ancient master.

[16] Aristotle, *Ethics*, Bk. II, ch. 3, 1104b5–12.

these limits still point to the nascent sense of autonomy even in very young children. Locke presents the manipulation of children's desire for play or esteem by the reason of adults as a preparation for the conscious activity of giving consent. Physical and mental education differs in this regard. Habituating a child to physical hardship may be eased somewhat through introduction by degrees; however, wetness and coldness are not naturally pleasant (at least with respect to shoes and clothes), and thus there is no real trickery involved. Children are compelled to bear with discomfort in order to become gradually inured to hardship. However, turning study into play involves an implicit recognition that a child cannot be made to learn in the same way you can harden the body. In keeping with Locke's contention that the first sparks of subjectivity emerge very early in children, the pleasant supplies a simulacrum of consent without which early education is often a tortuous and self-defeating experience for teacher and pupil alike. The basic intellectual freedom that grounds Locke's political doctrine of consent and his epistemological principle of assent is thus not only present in immature form in children, but also must be cultivated in their early education.

This is not to suggest Locke's educational theory presupposed, or even entertained, the possibility of the perfectibility of human reason or social institutions. Some commentators, most notably Passmore, greatly exaggerate Locke's sense of human malleability when they claim that he had confidence in the possibility of moral improvement "to an unlimited degree by education and other forms of social action."[17] While Locke's philosophy completely rejected the doctrine of innate ideas, it did not deny the variability of innate capacities and temperaments. As Locke admits, there are limits to what even a good education can achieve: "God has stamped a certain character upon men's minds, which, like their shapes, may perhaps be a little mended but can hardly be totally altered and transformed into the contrary" (T 66). Every child, and for that matter every adult, has a "natural genius and constitution" to which their education must be to some extent calibrated. Moreover, Locke identified native propensities such as the "love of power and dominion" (T 103) that appeared for all intents and purposes to be woven into the moral economy of human psychology. Clearly Locke assumed that there were some potentially nasty skeletons hiding in the "empty Cabinet" (E 1.2.15.55) of even the yet unformed mind.

---

[17] John Passmore, *The Perfectibility of Man* (New York: Charles Scribner's Sons, 1970), pp. 59–63. For a solid critique of Passmore's position about Locke's belief in perfectibility, which emphasizes Passmore's failure to appreciate Locke's recognition of the importance of natural temperament and innate capacities as a limit to perfectibility, see Crittenden, "Thoughts about Locke," 149–160, esp. 150–154.

The radical thrust of Locke's educational theory lies then not in the utopian dream of totally transforming human nature, but rather in the more sober, but still aspirational, claim that many of the obstacles to moral and intellectual improvement can be overcome with great results through education.

Locke's basic premise that habituation, in unreflective desire for pleasure and esteem, prepares for gradually greater self-conscious mental activity has prompted objections from several commentators who view Locke's education as essentially socialization to obey authority. They often see a radical disconnection between habituation and the stated goal of rational autonomy.[18] Carrig even suggests that Locke's claim that if a father wants his "son obedient to you when past a child" you must "imprint" awe of you in his infancy (T 40), demonstrates that Lockean liberalism simply "reproduces traditional patriarchal stereotypes," thus making the idea of legitimacy in liberal politics "nothing more than a chimera."[19] While it is correct to observe the importance of habituation for Locke as formative experience, much of Carrig's criticism is off the mark. First, it is useful to recall that unlike traditional patriarchy, Locke seeks to more or less eliminate force and compulsion from parental authority.[20] He encourages parents and teachers to be the models of rationality imbibing good habits to children through calm approval or disapprobation rather than being creators and enforcers of rules: "Let therefore your rules to your son be as few as possible" (T 65). Thus the source of "awe" Locke refers to is based on the child's impression of the father, and in principle the mother and tutor, as not only a providential figure but also as an eminently rational being. By learning to appreciate a parent's reasonableness, the child learns to see him or herself as a rational being.

More importantly, however, this objection does not take seriously enough Locke's insistence that education must be calibrated to the child's capacities. The natural fact of human biology means that external influences

---

[18] See especially Joseph Carrig, "Liberal Impediments to Liberal Education: The Assent to Locke" *Review of Politics*, 63, 1 (Winter 2001): 41–76 and Uday Singh Mehta, *The Anxiety of Freedom: Imagination and Individuality in Locke's Political Thought* (Ithaca: Cornell University Press, 1992), esp. pp. 143–147. Perkinson goes even further to conclude that the *Thoughts* represents an "authoritarian educational theory" born out of Locke's fundamental desire for security and fear of disorder (Henry J. Perkinson, *Since Socrates: Studies in the History of Western Educational Thought* [New York: Longman, 1981], p. 126).

[19] Carrig, "Liberal Impediments," pp. 42, 44–45. For a contrary reading of this passage in the *Thoughts* that is closer to mine, see Fliegelman, *Prodigals and Pilgrims*, 14.

[20] For the typically enthusiastic endorsement of paternal coercive power, see Robert Filmer, "Patriarcha" in *Patriarcha and Other Writings*, Johann P. Somerville, ed. (Cambridge: Cambridge University Press, 1991), p. 18.

on children are inevitable and yet are not antithetical to mental training directed toward autonomy.[21] Locke is clear that the same qualification that applies to concern for reputation applies to awe of parents. Awe, like esteem, prepares the mind for more reflective mental activity, which Locke associates firmly with egalitarian sentiments. He charges parents to ensure that as a child grows older, "admit him nearer to your familiarity" by involving the child in family decision making (T 40). While the natural dependence and physical weakness of small children means that some measure of fear provides "the first power over their minds," Locke's point is to encourage egalitarian sympathies and expectations in the family so that it is "love and friendship" that will anchor the parent-child relation in "riper years" (T 42). Clearly Locke imagines that the earliest effects of education establish a kind of power over a child's mind, but this influence is hardly impervious to rational examination, nor is it meant to be.

A more perceptive objection to Locke's account of habituation is not that it simply replicates traditional patriarchy in liberal guise, but rather that Locke aims to socialize children to trust and obey authority more generally, and this undermines the libertarian ethos of a rights-based society.[22] There is clearly some truth to the suggestion that Locke sought to socialize children to obey authority insofar as it embodies reason. But this hardly need be slavish or permanent. Locke's idea of early education as socialization assumes that robust individuality is hardly to be expected in children whose cognitive capacities are still quite limited. His primary concern is to prevent the settling of bad habits and to counter the natural willful desire to dominate others by encouraging submission to reason, preferably through gentle means. Locke's sensible assumption seems to be that with maturity and the greater intellectual and moral demands of citizenship, the individual will confront issues relating to politics, morality, and religion that are rooted in interests and beliefs that have an inescapably individualist basis and will at times resist the pressure to conform to society. In this sense, children will inevitably be as free to choose their faith, form of government, or economic interests as their parents and teachers before them.

THE THOUGHTS: TRAINING IN VIRTUE

Given the emphasis on experience and radical diminution of the importance of rules in Locke's account of socialization in early education, it is perhaps

---

[21]   Alex Neill, "Locke on Habituation, Autonomy, and Education" *Journal of the History of Philosophy*, 27, 2 (April 1989): 241.
[22]   Mehta, *Anxiety of Freedom*, pp. 143–147.

not surprising that Locke presents virtues as mental habits that, like foreign languages, should be learned by children through experience rather than as academic studies. There are two prominent features of Locke's treatment of virtue. First, each of the virtues he considers in detail, including liberality, courage, and humanity, are eminently practical, geared to the age and capacity of the student, and are understood to be in service of the general educational goal of socialization. Second, the virtues are presented to the educator less as goods in themselves than as learned behavior designed to counteract certain natural vices or antisocial propensities. The obverse of the natural love of liberty and desire to be treated as a rational being is, according to Locke, the even more basic "love of power and dominion," which shows itself practically in the cradle as children try to bend those around them to their will through "peevish" crying (T 103). The second and related natural vice is the covetous "desire of having in our possession and under our dominion more than we have need of." This natural "wanting more" Locke identifies as "the root of all evil" (T 106).

Locke's remedy to the problem of natural vice is a method of inculcating virtue that relies on a curious blend of hedonism and self-control. On the one hand, Locke insists that parents and teachers should never submit to the imperious demands of children. While parents must always be attentive to a child's genuine needs, one should never satisfy their superfluous desires for specific things (T 106). The aim is to inculcate mental habits of self-control so that children become accustomed to master their desires and learn to consult their reason. Self-denial, which Locke admits is "so contrary to unguided nature," must initially be imposed on children with the expectation that it will gradually become habitual. Locke maintains that without this capacity to suspend desires prior to forming judgment about action, they can never have virtue (T 45). On the other hand, Locke's account of virtue also emphasizes the need to make virtuous action as pleasant, or at least as painless, as possible. For instance, children are to be taught courage by exposing them only "by gentle degrees" to things that frighten them so that these frightful things gradually become familiar and inoffensive (T 115). Locke is prepared to make other even greater concessions to children's natural propensities. In order to teach liberality, children should not only be conspicuously esteemed for freely sharing or parting with what they have, but parents and teachers should always ensure that a child loses nothing by his or her liberality: "Let all the instances he gives of such freeness be always repaid, and with interest" (T 110). The key to developing habits of liberality as an antidote to natural covetousness is to make virtue appear to be both easy and as a reward in itself. Liberality is thus distinct from, but prepares for, the virtue of justice, which requires respecting the property of others, and is thus perhaps the example of self-denial *par excellence*.

By linking liberality with worldly happiness in this way, Locke's early education requires that training in virtue at least initially abstract from any notion of virtue as instrumental for self-preservation.[23] The virtue of humanity, which includes both encouraging children to show civility toward social inferiors and inculcating an "abhorrence" to cruelty "toward all sensible creatures," relies less on material reward than reinforcing what Locke takes to be a quasi-natural sentiment of compassion that can be corrupted by a "foreign and introduced disposition" (T 116–7).[24] Thus, while self-denial constitutes the root of virtue, Locke maintains that in developing habits of virtue, it is typically best to follow the path of least resistance and in this way try to encourage liberal and humane sentiments with a system of rewards designed to accentuate native empathy, and thus make virtue, at least initially, seem both natural and pleasant.

One striking feature of Locke's treatment of virtues is the extent to which he deemphasized the role of religion in encouraging good moral habits in children.[25] While Locke claims that the foundation of virtue requires imprinting "very early" on the mind "a true notion of God" who "loves us and gives us all things," he is silent as to how this providentialist disposition assists in making a child liberal, courageous, just, or humane (T 136). Locke's religion in the *Thoughts* is a simple nondogmatic creed

---

[23] In this respect, Michelle Brady exaggerates the importance of the natural desire for self-preservation in Locke's early education ("The Nature of Virtue in a Politics of Consent: John Locke on Education" *International Philosophical Quarterly*, 45, 2 [June 2005]: 157–173). As she observes (p. 168), Locke only mentions self-preservation once in passing in sec. 115. Given Locke's aim to promote virtue indirectly through experience and habit rather than harsh reminders of one's mortality – a concept Locke doubts is accessible or appropriate for children – it is perhaps fair to say that he seeks to radically deemphasize, if not entirely eliminate, preservationist concerns in early education.

[24] While Locke identifies certain natural vicious habits flowing out of the desire to dominate, he does not appear to consider cruelty to be "ordinary and natural" (T 103).

[25] As Fliegelman demonstrates, Locke's educational proposals for children were much less pietistic than the pedagogy of later English moralists like Defoe and Watts, who were in other respects deeply indebted to Locke (*Prodigals and Pilgrims*, 17–23). See also Mehta, *Anxiety of Freedom*, 128; M. V. C. Jeffreys, *John Locke: Prophet of Common Sense* (London: Methuen & Co, 1967), p. 53; Thomas Pangle, *The Spirit of Modern Republicanism* (Chicago: University of Chicago Press, 1988), p. 203; and Tarcov, *Education for Liberty*, 87. In this respect, Harris (*Mind of Locke*, 283, 289) and James Tully tend to exaggerate Locke's sense of the importance of religion as a practical support for training young children in virtue ("Governing Conduct," in *An Approach to Political Philosophy: Locke in Contexts* [Cambridge: Cambridge University Press, 1993], pp. 231–232).

with an at-best inchoate notion of a providential God suited to the capacities of children. There is no notion of an Afterlife with eternal rewards and punishments, and indeed Locke explicitly discourages the "promiscuous" reading of Scripture by children (T 158). The vague sense that there is a God who knows everything and does "all manner of good to those that love and obey him" suffices for children (T 136). Locke's aim here is not to undermine the traditional Judeo-Christian connection between religion and moral education, but rather to reinforce his contention that any form of education – including moral education – must be suited to the age of the pupil.

Locke makes this point explicitly in his treatment of natural philosophy toward the end of the *Thoughts*. Here he argues that older students should be introduced to metaphysics prior to beginning the study of natural science. His reasoning is that careful introduction to biblical religion instills a notion of spirits in a student that expands the mind toward a fuller understanding of the intellectual world (T 190–1). Locke insists that this is "good preparation for the study of bodies," not because it encourages any specific moral behavior, but rather inasmuch as developing in the student a sense of the possibility of the existence of spiritual beings may check the potential excesses of the materialist bent natural to the human mind, which is of course supplied with much of the material for knowledge by the senses (T 192).[26] In one sense then, Locke's training in virtue for youths effectively reduces religion to an ancillary role as a heuristic device intended to prepare the mind for the study of natural bodies. However, Locke's characterization of this ascent to natural philosophy through rudimentary metaphysics also serves the purpose of harnessing the synergies of natural and moral philosophy by encouraging openness to both science and theology in later stages of academic development.

It is *breeding* that replaces religion or metaphysics as the practical foundation of virtue in Locke's proposals for early education. He distinguishes "breeding" or "civility" from virtue, for breeding is a character trait that "sets a gloss on virtues" in a social context (T 145, 93). Breeding is both the superintending principle of all the virtues and the social manifestation of the virtue of humanity in particular. Breeding supples "natural stiffness" and "softens men's tempers" so that without it courage appears as brutality, learning becomes pedantry, and wit mere buffoonery (T 143, 93). The well-bred individual makes those he "converses with easy without debasing himself" (T 143). In a remarkable revaluation of a traditionally aristocratic

[26] Compare with E 2.1.2–3.104–105.

prejudice, Locke interprets the idea of breeding to involve inculcating deeply egalitarian sympathies. Breeding means avoiding showing contempt for anyone in conversation and indeed teaching children "to love and respect other people" (T 144). It involves more than just good manners, although this is clearly a part of it. Instilling good breeding essentially involves the encouragement of democratic sentiments and humane impulses. This is Locke's quasi-conventional supplement to natural compassion. Breeding not only bridges the concerns of the self-regarding individual to his or her community in the immediate social context; Locke presents breeding, rather than religion, as the first practical manifestation of a child's growing awareness and experience of universality and membership in a common humanity.[27] Locke's reinterpretation of breeding is then meant to support the later development of the more sophisticated philosophical and theological commitment to equality that is the moral core of his vision of a natural rights-based society.

Locke's account of early education presents a series of tensions at the heart of his pedagogical project. The child is supposed to become sociable and accommodating but also enjoy a hardy self-reliance; to practice self-control and yet be active and free; and to develop good habits of mind and body while remaining directed toward the goal of rational autonomy marked by freedom from unreflective custom and habit.[28] Moreover, the child must be trained in virtue, but through an educational method that deemphasizes the use of books, formal rules, and physical punishment. Indeed, Locke admits that his reader will wonder that he relegates the traditional idea of learning to be "the least part" of education (T 147). It is in this context of education by experience that the teacher, as opposed to the specific content of the teaching, assumes special significance for Locke. In what Locke calls a crucial digression from "our method," he directs his audience of concerned parents to reflect upon the vital question of who should teach their children. While Locke operates from the assumption that families should retain a tutor for their children, he is at pains to express his conviction that a good tutor is exceedingly rare. Parents should spare no expense in securing such a precious commodity and they should always show utmost respect to the tutor as a valued member of the household: "As to the charge of it, I think it will be the money best laid out that can be

---

[27] While Steven Forde sees breeding as a bridge between the interests of the individual and membership in the community ("What Does Locke Expect Us to Know?" *Review of Politics*, 68, 1 [2006]: 252–254), I argue that Locke extends this sentiment into a nascent identification with a broader sense of humanity.

[28] Tarcov, *Locke's Education*, 104.

about our children" (T 90, 88). The only real concern for parents, according to Locke, is the immense difficulty in finding an individual willing and capable of doing this important job.

One effect of Locke's insistence on the need to find a good tutor is perhaps paradoxically to highlight the important role of parents in their children's education. Locke's candid assessment of the great potential expense of education reinforces his conception of the family as an economic unit and provides additional incentive to encourage industry and acquisitiveness in parents. Perhaps more importantly, parents who heed Locke's warning to be very careful about who teaches their kids are going to be preoccupied with education. They will see providing for education as probably the primary part of their parental duty and presumably will be open to promising new proposals such as those of Locke. Parents, in particular, who grasp the experiential basis of learning in Locke's new method will pay special attention to the company that their children keep and the example set for them by parents, tutors, servants, and others with whom they come in regular contact (T 67). Locke appeals to the judgment and critical faculty of parents who must already have certain clear and distinct ideas about education before they can properly select a good tutor. That is to say, if a parent has thought seriously about the qualifications of a tutor, he or she has moved a considerable distance toward being able to do the task themselves, or at least to be a constructive partner in their children's education.

Locke argues that the primary qualification of a tutor is good breeding and knowledge of the world. He does not expect a good tutor to have expertise in an array of academic subjects. The tutor's role in the academic element of education is simply to introduce the student to the basics of history, geography, arithmetic, and such. The main job of the tutor is to develop good breeding. Breeding is not taught from books but by good example, therefore the tutor must himself be well-bred (T 93). By knowledge of the world, Locke means the tutor's familiarity with a variety of social contexts and the diversity of human types. This supports the teaching of breeding because it allows the tutor to impart to the student through habit and use the proper and free composure of language, look, motion, and posture suited to conversation with various people and occasions. The fundamental problem in private education in the family is the natural tendency to a certain parochialism, which, Locke maintains, a good tutor can reduce by introducing a worldly and urbane element into an otherwise potentially quite insular institution (T 70). Parents, of course, are charged to reinforce their children's good manners assiduously.

While the primary focus of the tutor is "to fashion the carriage and form the mind" of the student by proper breeding rather than academic study, Locke insists on laying out certain criteria for learning (T 94). Given that the gentleman's probable calling is to be a "man of business" and not a scholar, Locke insists that the curriculum must be designed to meet the practical needs of the gentry. The fundamental principle of instruction should be to encourage a taste for "method and order" in the student's mind (T 175–6). Locke more or less abandons the teaching of classical languages and rhetoric, the cornerstones of humanist education with its pedagogic system of rules, drills, and memorization. Instead he recommends focusing on modern languages, such as French, that can be learned through experience and will be of practical use in future life (T 163). Among the list of subjects Locke considers, history and math stand out in significance.

Studying history supports the tutor's goal by increasing a child's experience of the world, but it is with respect to learning about the laws and history of one's own nation that Locke sees the primary advantage for a gentleman's future role in public life (T 182). Notably, it is in the context of the study of civil law that Locke encourages the reading of the classic works of natural jurisprudence by Grotius, Pufendorf, and his own *Two Treatises*, hereby confirming the practical character of his natural rights philosophy (T 186).[29] Locke expects that educated people will treat political philosophy not as an abstract and speculative study, but rather as a familiar and necessary element of their civil life. He also emphasizes the practical utility of arithmetic as an introduction to the most basic sort of abstract reasoning that "is of so general use in all parts of life and business that scarce anything is to be done without it" (T 180). As civil and legal history, political philosophy, and basic accounting are elevated in Locke's curriculum, the traditional military and aristocratic virtues encouraged by practice in horsemanship and fencing are seriously diminished (T 198–9).[30] The seeds of the virtues and attitudes specific to a commercial republic are adapted to flourish in the fertile soil of Locke's program for early education.

Locke's account of the qualifications and pedagogic duty of a tutor represents a kind of theoretical peak in his treatment of early education. The tutor's task encompasses the full scope of Locke's new method of education with its combination of socialization and communication of ideas. The

[29] See also Locke's "Some Thoughts Concerning Reading and Study for a Gentleman" in John Locke, *Political Essays*, Mark Goldie, ed. (Cambridge: Cambridge University Press, 1997), pp. 351–352.
[30] See Pangle, *Spirit*, 226–227 and Tarcov, *Locke's Education*, 164–167.

great secret of education is to develop strategies geared to the optimum effect possible given the student's temperament, abilities, and level of maturity. Thus, the "great skill of a teacher" lies not in filling the mind with wisdom, but rather "to get and keep the attention" of the student through carefully devised activities (T 167). The tutor then is an integral element of Locke's overarching theme in the *Thoughts*, which amounts to a call to standardize or even professionalize a new method of childhood education with a focus on adapting learning to the capacities of the students and designing a sensible curriculum that helps prepare students for their life and career. As such, the *Thoughts* points beyond itself to the outline of a graduated system of education extending from primary right through to higher and continuing education.

HIGHER EDUCATION: THE CONDUCT

In the introduction to the *Conduct of the Understanding*, Locke signals that this book on education has a different purpose and intended audience than his earlier *Thoughts*. While the argument of the *Thoughts* registered some movement from very early education through to introductory level studies of the various disciplines, Locke's focus in this work was primary and secondary education. The *Conduct*, however, is focused exclusively on higher education. In particular, Locke highlights what he takes to be the need to replace the system of "logic now in use…in the Schools" with a new method of higher learning (C 1). He appeals to the legacy of no less an authority than Francis Bacon who many years earlier criticized England's universities for failing to provide a model of education that would support the promising new experimental science (C 1). The *Thoughts* and the *Conduct* are thus the root and branch of Locke's larger program of educational reform. In order to appreciate the full scope of Locke's revolutionary proposal, we need to begin by considering the relation between these two works.

   The goal of rational autonomy remains continuous throughout Locke's educational writings. However, while he locates the foundation of this project in early education, its culmination requires further and a very different sort of training in maturity. In the *Thoughts*, childhood education amounts to methodical application of certain physical and mental habits geared toward training the student's capacity for self-denial and suspension of desires. At this stage, external influences are formative both in the sense that the good habits instilled by the reason of others are meant to avoid the entrenchment of bad habits and error, and in the sense that learning through experiences designed by adults constitute the kind of instruction better suited to the capacities of children than formal academic studies. In the *Conduct*, however, Locke's aim is to replace habituation with conscious activity and to progress his methodology toward practice in critical thinking, an activity not to be expected in children. The *Conduct* operationalizes the vision of rational or "epistemic" autonomy undergirding but largely nascent in the *Thoughts*.[31] In a sense, Carrig is correct to observe that the model of critical reason in the *Conduct* is a kind of rebellion against the habituation advocated in the *Thoughts*.[32] However, it is important to recognize the deeper underlying unity between the two works, as well as what precisely Locke's later endorsement of critical reason was directed against.

In Locke's conception of epistemic autonomy, the individual is required first to achieve some kind of mastery over physical necessity and untrained natural desires, but the realization of this project involves gradually increasing autonomy vis-à-vis the community and received opinion to which one has previously been socialized. The flower of the seed planted in early education is the promise of forming a rational individual possessing the "vigor of mind to contest the empire of habit" and able to resist accepting "their teachers notions and tenets by an implicit faith" (C 41). In transferring his method from the early goal of freeing children from the mechanism of nature to the more advanced development of the complex mental operations involved in critical reason, Locke replaces socialization and habituation with an inherently individualist and skeptical attitude that ceases to be habitual precisely by virtue of its self-conscious character.

The philosophical foundation of Locke's method in the *Conduct* is identical to that of the *Thoughts*, namely the new democratic epistemology of the *Essay*. Both the foundation and objective of his educational methods are deeply egalitarian. Not only do the natural capacities of human beings differ little in "the woods of America, as well as the schools of Athens," but Locke insists that "we are born with faculties and powers capable of almost anything" (C 2, 4). The fundamentally leveling effect of Locke's teaching is reflected in his assumption that it is the application of correct or incorrect methods of thinking that create significant intellectual differences among people, not their natural abilities. Whereas the *Thoughts* distinguished the proper means to educate and socialize an ordinary "man of business" from

---

[31] "Epistemic autonomy" is the useful term employed to describe Locke's practical goal of education by Neill, "Locke on Habituation," 227 and Peter Schouls, *Reasoned Freedom* (Ithaca: Cornell University Press, 1992), pp. 26–27.

[32] Carrig, "Liberal Impediments," 64.

the production of scholars or prodigies, the *Conduct* consistently blurs the distinction between the scholar and the ordinary citizen. Locke attacks the narrow-mindedness and intellectual laziness of the English gentry and asserts that contrary to custom, reading and study should be the proper business of a gentleman (C 3). Indeed, in the *Conduct*, Locke extends his focus beyond the gentry class by attributing to all adults the duty and capacity to expand their intellectual horizons through rigorous reflection on issues of political legitimacy and religious salvation that are, in principle, accessible to and impact all (C 19). With this, Locke presents epistemic autonomy not as a realistic goal only of a few, but as a cultural expectation of liberal society.

The evil twin of relative equality of natural capacities is, according to Locke, the all-too-natural temperamental and intellectual defects common to human understanding. First, there is the disposition toward intellectual laziness in which one is content to rely uncritically upon the opinions of others in important practical and speculative matters (C 3). In other words, the natural and healthy default position of early education becomes inherently problematic in adults. Second, Locke identifies the problem of partisanship displayed by individuals who put "passion in the place of reason" when confronted by an issue that affects their humor, interest, or party (C 3). Locke suggests such people are capable of being open-minded on matters that do not touch their interests but are incapable of critically examining their own most deeply rooted prejudices.[33] The third defect, and the one that elicits Locke's lengthiest treatment by far, is partiality or pride in one's own reason. Locke concedes that it is impossible for one individual to examine any issue from all perspectives: "From this defect I think no man is free" (C 3). However, the defining characteristic of the intellectual sectarian is the failure to recognize that one's basic principles and commitments are but a part of a complex reality. It is all too common for even, or perhaps especially, intellectually inclined individuals to converse with only one sort of person and read only one sort of book, for they "will not venture out into the vast ocean of Knowledge." Unwilling to engage in meaningful contact with diverse ideas and opinions, they think there is "no truth but in the sciences that they study, or the books they read" (C 3).

Locke's intellectual method in the *Conduct* is designed to liberalize higher education by encouraging scholars and the broader educated class not only to recognize the intellectual defects and sectarianism endemic in

---

[33] See Schuurman, "Locke's Way of Ideas," 51–52 for a good discussion of passion as a major source of error in the *Conduct*.

the current system, but also to remedy these problems. He seeks to respond
to these natural intellectual defects by combining a new awareness of the
internal operations of mind with an attitude encouraging direct and systematic engagement with a variety of studies and texts. The cardinal virtue in Locke's new system of higher education is probity. Probity is both
the enemy of habit and, paradoxically, the final product of habituation to
self-control instituted in childhood. It is important to recall that Locke
always maintained throughout his account of early education that knowledge is distinct from habit.[34] Knowledge properly speaking presupposes
what Locke calls "indifferency," which is not passivity but rather a form of
mental activity that makes possible self-examination of one's own opinions
(C 10–1). Indifferency addresses, without entirely neutralizing, the natural
problem of perspectivalism. By achieving a condition of mental equanimity
in which one "must not be in love with any opinion, or wish it to be true,"
the individual can be confident that only genuine evidence and rational
examination can secure one's assent to any proposition (C 11, 34). Herein
lies the ambiguous status of pride in Locke's account of education. Insofar
as pride or love of one's own opinions contributes to intellectual sectarianism, it is a problem to be guarded against carefully. However, Locke's intellectual method, epistemologically rooted in indifferency, is also meant to
encourage a kind of epistemic egoism by which the individual takes pride
in his or her probity. In some sense, rational autonomy is premised on the
perhaps unrealistic expectation that an individual is capable of attaining
any part of knowledge to which one applies oneself.

In contrast to the syllogistic reasoning characteristic of the formal logic
of the universities, Locke's new method focuses on the mind's ability to
control its own internal operations. The first stage involves developing the
"habit of attention and application" required to focus the mind on the connections in a train of ideas (C 30). Locke insists that the ability to direct
the train of ideas may be one of "the great differences that carry some
men in their reasonings so far beyond others" (C 30). In order to facilitate this practice, Locke suggests that the individual needs to adopt the
Cartesian methodology of reducing every argument to "clear and distinct
ideas" (C 29). Locke is fully aware that this induced decompositionalism
runs directly counter to the more natural tendency of the human mind to
construct composite ideas in order to make the world intelligible to us,
however unexamined or erroneous our judgment of the association of these
ideas may prove to be.[35] Much as Locke's proposals for physical education

---

[34]   Neill, "Locke on Habituation," 238.
[35]   Locke, ECHU 2.12.1–2.163–164.

strove to make play out of necessity for children, similarly his method of higher education appeals to an individual's epistemic egoism to encourage a relish for mentally deconstructing arguments and opinions.

One of the most important aims of Locke's method is to develop what he calls the practice of "bottoming." Whereas his early education was designed to enhance the natural taste for reason by encouraging children to participate in problem-solving exercises with parents and teachers, it is only with maturity that the individual is capable of reaching the bottom of problems by self-directed mental activity. Bottoming is a complex process in which an individual reduces one's beliefs or the elements of a particular question down to their clear, distinct, and self-evident propositions.[36] Once the mind has reached this foundational principle, or bottom, it "clears the doubt, and gives an easy solution of the question" (C 44). By carefully examining each link in the chain associating a number of ideas and tracing them to their self-evident source, the individual is then in a position to reconstruct the logical connections in a proposition on more solid epistemological ground. If an opinion does not reach its bottom in a foundation of certain, self-evident principle, then it should be radically reconsidered or rejected. This process of mental deconstruction and reconstruction requires a form of skepticism related to indifferency, but it is a limited skepticism informed by the possibility, and indeed necessity, of grounding arguments on self-evident propositions. Significantly, Locke's example *par excellence* of bottoming involves reducing particular questions of political legitimacy to the certain principle that "all men are naturally equal" (C 44). From this premise, Locke insists all manner of debates concerning the rights of individuals in society can be resolved.

Locke is obviously fascinated by the extent to which the human mind can control its own internal operation. Bottoming is not simply a dogmatic assertion of principle. It is rather a difficult, even painstaking, process by which the mind carefully examines the evidence before it, the agreement or disagreement of ideas, and their compatibility or inconsistency with self-evident propositions. Implicit in this process is, of course, the suspension of desire and judgment that Locke made the source of intellectual freedom in his epistemology. The individual must control his or her desire simply to validate a certain favored conclusion.

Locke's emphasis on the mind's ability through training to become conscious of, and thus capable of directing, its own activity is perhaps even more apparent in the mental activity he terms "transferring." Transferring

---

[36] See Schouls' good discussion of "bottoming" at *Reasoned Freedom*, 218–219.

involves conscious exercise of the "habits of attention and application" by which the mind learns to transfer its thoughts from one subject or idea to another without distraction or loss of focus. Practice in transferring tests the extent of an individual's "full power over his own mind," and helps establish mental processes that will be of "great use both in business and study" (C 45). The radical implication of Locke's argument is that complex mental activities such as bottoming and transferring are not natural intellectual gifts enjoyed by a lucky few. Rather as integral features of the epistemological democratization of mind, they are products of training and the application of a method capable of improving the understanding of practically anyone, regardless of their calling or natural disposition.

The universalist thrust of Locke's methodology reflects his assessment of the natural, and in some respects surprisingly egalitarian, distribution of the defects that plague human understanding. Narrow-mindedness and commitment to unexamined opinions are problems that transcend class. The intellectual sectarians in the universities and pulpits are as prone to these mental limitations as the day laborer in the field, even if for somewhat different reasons. With those of "low and mean education" who have never looked beyond the "ordinary drudgery" of physical labor, the problem is mainly lack of exposure to diverse ideas and lack of leisure to consider them to their bottom (C 6). Among scholars and the educated classes, Locke identifies a tendency to commit to unexamined "airy useless notions" and a disdain for descent "to the mechanical drudgery of experiment and inquiry" (C 43). The problem in both cases, whether caused by necessity or undisciplined speculation, is the "custom of taking up with principles that are not self-evident and very often not so much as true" (C 6).

For Locke, the application of the method relates primarily to reading and study. One crucial difference between the *Thoughts* and the *Conduct* is the emphasis on books in the latter. Early education based on experience and a general deemphasizing of book learning now, in adulthood, becomes education through the experience of reading, or more properly learning how to read carefully. In a small but important digression in the *Thoughts*, Locke suggests that those training to become scholars should follow La Bruyere's recommendation to ground their education on close study of "the original texts" (T 195).[37] Locke endorses Bruyere's textualism not only because it allows insights into a given author or text, but also, and even primarily, because it accustoms the mind to method and order by reducing arguments to "the simplest and most uncompounded parts it can

---

[37]   Locke quotes a passage from Bruyere's *Mouers de ce siecle* (1696).

divide the matter into" (T 195). In the *Conduct*, Locke systematizes this call for close study of original texts and offers it as an alternative to the study of formal logic as the basis of higher education. He is far from insouciant about the advantages of reading: "there is no part wherein the understanding needs a more careful and wary conduct than in the use of books" (C 24). Locke warns vociferously against the dangers of adopting opinions on the basis of sloppy, hasty, or prejudiced reading. However, with due attention to the requirement of indifferency, close reading of original texts is the ideal training ground for the development of methodical reasoning. Locke maintains that by studying original texts, the young scholar can learn to follow an author's train of reasoning, to observe the strength and clearness in the connection of ideas, and to examine upon what proposition it bottoms. He redefines the value of reading from being the imparting of knowledge to being an exercise in critical thinking: "Reading furnishes the mind only with materials of knowledge; it is thinking makes what we read ours" (C 20). Reflecting upon the structure, design, and logic of an argument in a text does more to develop the understanding than the bare collection of facts or mechanical memorization of axioms. Textualism amounts to the higher education equivalent of Locke's insistence that early education be based on learning through experience.

The application of methodical reasoning to reading is the hallmark of Locke's treatment of the various studies to which the adult individual, and especially the university student, should aspire. He strongly recommends an interdisciplinary approach as an antidote to the problem of restricting the understanding to "narrow bounds," and not "looking abroad into other provinces of the intellectual world" (C 22). However, two subjects stand out in Locke's account. First, Locke expands on his earlier recommendation to study mathematics in the *Thoughts*. The value of math is twofold. On one level, it makes the assumption of indifferency much less problematic than in moral, political, or religious studies that more naturally produce a passionate or emotional response. More importantly, however, Locke sees studies in math as a way to train the mind of a scholar in following a chain of ideas and examining their connection. The aim is not to make everyone a mathematician, but rather to help "make them reasonable creatures" (C 6).[38] The great value of math lies in its general application: "in all sorts

---

[38] Mehta is incorrect to assert that Locke saw no practical importance in mathematics as a spur to speculative knowledge (*Anxiety of Freedom*, 101). As Locke made clear with his praise of Newton (T 194), he saw great promise that practical application of math to scientific questions would yield astonishing discoveries. However, of course, Locke did not believe every one can be another Newton.

of reasoning, every single argument should be managed as a mathematical demonstration" (C 7). As we saw in Chapter 1, Locke did not mean by this that all aspects of intellectual experience can be reduced to mathematical certainty. Rather his point here is that mathematics accustoms the mind to the useful practice of thinking in terms of probability and weighing the merits of various pieces of evidence before giving assent to a proposition (C 7). Similarly, Locke praises textualism for its application beyond scholarship as it encourages a method of reading that "may be of use to gentlemen too, when at any time they have a mind to go deeper than the surface and get to themselves a solid satisfaction and masterly insight into any part of learning" (T 195). Mathematics and close reading of texts both accustom the mind to thinking consciously about thinking clearly.

The other study that assumes great significance in the *Conduct* is religion. While in the *Thoughts*, in-depth study of theology and questions of divine reward and punishment were seen as beyond the capacity of children, these concerns become essential elements of the mature individual's efforts toward rational autonomy. Locke's foundational principle of the relative equality of natural cognitive capacities assumes greater priority with respect to religion than possibly in any other subject to which his method can be applied. From this "bottoming" principle, Locke asserts that every adult has an intellectual interest in two things: in their particular calling and in the "concern of a future life" (C 8). Soteriological concerns are, if not wholly natural, at least a basic function of human cognition rather than advanced education. Locke refers to instances of "very mean people" who have raised their minds to a "great sense and understanding of religion" (C 8). The primary significance of Locke's method with regard to religion is its encouragement to all people to think more clearly and rationally about morality and salvation. He excoriates the English gentry in particular for their notoriously bigoted and unreflective religious attitudes and suggests that they would benefit greatly from embracing a stance of intellectual indifferency and probabilism on religious matters rather than assertions of dogmatic certainty (C 3). Theology emerges for Locke as the democratic study *par excellence*, as a "noble study which is every man's duty," because in principle, questions of salvation are every individual's concern (C 23). The egalitarian basis of Locke's method ensures that the value in close reading of texts, especially Scripture, extends to all classes. The goal of epistemic autonomy thus is more than just a scholarly or elite concern, but in effect becomes the basis of an argument for the broad diffusion and application of Locke's educational method on a scale far beyond the university.

EDUCATION AND THE PUBLIC

We have seen that Locke's educational proposals in the *Thoughts* and the *Conduct* address issues relating to pedagogical concerns ranging from primary to higher education and even include recommendations for continuing education not only for gentlemen, but also for common people inspired to reflection and examination of political, moral, and religious beliefs. We have also seen that Locke's educational method rests on a profoundly egalitarian epistemological foundation. This is not to say Locke believes that human beings can achieve absolute intellectual equality, but rather that he is confident that the range property of human mental capacities is relatively narrow, and all individuals are able to improve their understanding by virtue of enhanced educational methods.

Natural equality and a new democratic epistemology are thus the core philosophical ideas underlying Locke's teaching on education. However, as some commentators have observed, there are at least two aspects of Locke's argument in the *Thoughts* that seem to conflict, or at least be in tension, with the egalitarian premises of his natural rights philosophy. First, Locke directs his pedagogical ideas in the *Thoughts* not at all children, but rather primarily at the sons and daughters of gentlemen.[39] Second, Locke's recommendations seem to presuppose that a proper education can only occur in the private family under the instruction of a personal tutor.[40] Together these propositions suggest that Locke's pedagogical theory was based on certain assumptions about class and social conditions that meant in practice, his conception of education had little application to the public more generally.

From the very opening lines of the *Thoughts*, Locke suggests a certain ambiguity in this respect. He admits that he only agreed to publish his private thoughts on education for a gentleman friend's son once he has concluded that these ideas may be of use to the public. But who does Locke think are the public and how does he arrive at this determination? It is certainly surprising that Locke, the great opponent of patriarchy in the *Two Treatises*, appears in the *Thoughts* to assign the crucial function of education to the private family, at least with respect to the gentry. Moreover,

---

[39] Robert Horwitz, "John Locke and the Preservation of Liberty: A Perennial Problem of Civic Education," in *The Moral Foundations of the American Republic*, 3rd ed., Robert H. Horwitz, ed. (Charlottesville: University Press of Virginia, 1986), pp. 136–164, esp. 141. Schuurman extends this notion of Locke's class prejudice rather less plausibly to the *Conduct* as well ("Locke's Way of Ideas," 57).

[40] Tarcov, *Locke's Education*, 3–4.

it is noticeable that unlike Hobbes, for instance, who charged the political sovereign with the job of reforming and monitoring the universities, Locke appeals with respect to reform of both primary and higher education to a rather vague societal force that can perhaps best be described as the "reading public."[41] While Locke's novel proposals for early education are clearly developed in the context of a new understanding of the natural rights family, does his appeal to the public importance of education suggest certain limits in the family's capacity to perform a function with such vital public importance? On the face of it, the answer would appear to be no, given Locke's endorsement of the private education of gentlemen's sons and daughters in the family. However, Locke's reasoning on this issue is worthy of further examination.

To start, Locke's endorsement of private education at home has a great deal to do with his assessment of the dismal state of English grammar schools at the time. The problems he identifies in these boarding schools are manifold. Locke dismisses them as the bastions of pedagogic orthodoxy in which the curriculum is outdated, the teaching method bare memorization, and enthusiastic employment of corporal punishment is "the ordinary way of education" (T 74). Moreover, unlike tutors and parents who can mind their charges pretty much continuously, in the grammar school, "let the master's industry and skill be ever so great, it is impossible he should have fifty or a hundred scholars under his eye any longer than they are in school together" (T 70). It is in the dorms and on the playing fields that Locke fears children adopt all the tricks, raillery, and vulgar code of faux manliness that plague these institutions. In this light, education at home is another aspect of the prophylactic character of Lockean early education.

Thus, Locke endorses private tutorial in the family, but it is hardly a ringing endorsement of private home schooling per se. Given the primitive state of transportation and the diffusion of population in preindustrial and largely rural society, it is not surprising that Locke does not in the *Thoughts* seriously entertain the idea of public education familiar in many liberal societies today with its division of labor between formal day schooling and parental supervision at home. But is Locke's advocacy of private education at home incompatible with this modern system of education? It can be argued that Locke's account of the importance of the choice of tutors contains an implicit element of public involvement in education. As we have seen, Locke expressed concern about the problem of parochialism

---

[41]   Tarcov, *Locke's Education*, 3–4. See also Thomas Hobbes, *Leviathan*, Edwin Curley, ed. (Indianapolis: Hackett Publishing, 1994), ch. 30, sec. 14, pp. 225–226.

in familial-based education. Patriarchy is perhaps only the extreme logical, and politically most deleterious, extension of this parochialism. The tutor is charged by Locke with providing the student "knowledge of the world," and is, if not a representative of the public strictly speaking, at least a prominent intermediary between the child and his or her parents. The importance Locke assigns to employing a good tutor thus demonstrates that the problem of familial parochialism is only partly alleviated by a more enlightened reading public and more equal gender relations in the family. Locke suggests that it is to the advantage of the family to welcome this quasi-public element into the household, at least when the tutor embodies the progressive principles of educational reform Locke advocates. Perhaps the very least we can say, therefore, about Locke's attitude toward the possibility of introducing day schools informed by new pedagogic methods and positive parental involvement and reinforcement at home, is that it would present a different set of problems than the grammar schools then in place.

However, does Locke's endorsement of private education in the family reveal a deeper class prejudice that inevitably diminishes the public application of his educational reforms? On an even more fundamental level, might we not conclude that Locke's effort to contrast his scientific method of reasoning with "ordinary reason" requires, or at least justifies, the political and social disqualification of the many people who do not benefit from his new education? The charge that Locke endorses a theory of "differential rationality" that privileges the emerging bourgeoisie and effectively undermines the egalitarian premises of his natural rights philosophy has been a theme among Locke scholars at least since C.B. McPherson's influential presentation of the theory of possessive individualism.[42] In order to examine these issues in the context of Locke's educational writings, it is important to consider a number of things.

First, Locke insists that the errors of human understanding are natural, in some respects transcend class difference, and can be remedied by disciplining the mind in the manner he recommends.[43] His emphasis on the importance of education rather than supposed natural cognitive differences reflects his assumption that education can be a means for both individual

[42] C. B. McPherson, *The Political Theory of Possessive Individualism* (Oxford: Oxford University Press, 1962), ch. 5. See also Ellen Meiksins Wood, "Locke against Democracy: Consent, Representation and Suffrage in the *Two Treatises*" *History of Political Thought*, 13, 4 (Winter 1992): 657–689, esp. 671 and 685–689.

[43] See Jeremy Waldron, *God, Locke and Equality* (Cambridge: Cambridge University Press, 2002), pp. 88–91.

social mobility and for improving the general level of understanding in society as a whole. The difference between the understanding of the leisured class "who by the industry and parts of their ancestors have been set free from a constant drudgery," and the lower classes is, Locke insists, very real (C 6–7). However, the source of the distinction lies not in "the want of natural parts" among the poor, but rather "for want of use and exercise" of their rational faculties (C 6). Locke maintains that the benefits of expanding instruction in even rudimentary mathematics, for instance, are potentially enormous: "Among the children of a poor countryman, the lucky chance of education and getting into the world gives one infinitely the superiority over the rest, who, continuing at home, had continued also just the same size with his brethren" (C 6). Clearly then, the question of Locke's supposed assumption of a differential rationality is something of a moot point inasmuch as while he unhesitatingly endorses a new method of scientific or mathematical reason to replace traditional custom, the social and political imperative this suggests is the need to improve education generally, not the development of a system of mass disqualification. That is to say, Locke subscribed to the view, uncontroversial today, that there is a general educational requirement for successfully establishing liberal societies, but he did so at a time when this view was hardly common, to say the least. McPherson and others completely miss this radical dimension of Locke's attitude toward differential rationality.

A second aspect of Locke's educational theory that most versions of the theory of possessive individualism simply do not take seriously enough is Locke's consideration of the importance of religion as a support for educational reform. An important connection between Locke's epistemological and educational writings is his aim to inject rationalist principles into religion, in many respects the traditional bastion of orthodoxy. As we have observed, Locke expresses some of his most egalitarian sentiments in relation to the cognitive properties of faith.[44] However, it would be a mistake to conclude as has Waldron that Locke hereby advanced a "profound validation of the claims of the ordinary intellect" in contradistinction to scientific reason.[45] Rather Locke's point is that adult concern for salvation properly understood is a spur for the radical expansion of his new method of education. Locke's endorsement in the *Thoughts* of including instruction in current scientific theories, especially those based on "rational experiments and observation" rather than speculative systems, as a form of study "convenient

---

[44]   Compare E 4.18 with C 8 and 23.
[45]   Waldron, *God, Locke and Equality*, 105–106.

and necessary to be known by a gentleman," should be understood as being in essential unity with his argument for the rationalist and probabilistic basis of faith in the *Essay* (T 193). In both instances, Locke's aim is to encourage a broad cultural attitude of openness to scientific research.

The thrust of Locke's epistemological and educational writings is to persuade the believer that the compelling logic of soteriological concerns need not be an apology for obscurantism; they can rather encourage a taste and motivation for developing critical thinking that speaks to the aspirations of individuals in any class. Broad-based instruction in basic literacy need hardly exhaust the educational possibilities desired by a society awakened to the connection between education and well-grounded religious belief. It is in response to the complaint that common religious believers do not examine the principles of their faith that Locke insists this is often due to the "want of use and exercise" of their faculties produced by a life of "constant drudgery," rather than for "want of natural parts" (C 6). To the extent that Locke concedes the practical existence of differential rationality, the motivation for improving education supplied by religion is deeply subversive of the continuation of this educational inequality over the long term.

The public dimension of Locke's educational reforms comes perhaps most clearly into focus in his famous policy recommendation to the Board of Trade in 1697, generally known to history as "An Essay on the Poor Law." This policy paper devised in Locke's role as a senior civil servant in the post-Glorious Revolution government, and written more or less contemporaneously with the *Conduct* and just a few scant years after the *Thoughts*, is often castigated as a draconian, insensitive, and elitist piece of work meant to encourage paternalistic state control over the behavior of the poor and working classes.[46] I submit that this interpretation misses the real significance of this essay, which lies in the assistance it provides in acquiring a fuller understanding of the potential role of the public in Locke's educational program. The core argument of Locke's report is that the problem of poverty must be addressed through the broad application of public power to educate poor children. The philosophic premise underlying this policy is, of course, natural equality.

Locke insists that the key to tackling the problem of poverty is persuading governments at the national and local level that the poor may be made

---

[46] See, for example, Gay, "Introduction," 12–13; W. M. Spellman, *John Locke and the Problem of Depravity* (Oxford: Oxford University Press, 1988), p. 207–208 and McPherson, *Possessive Individualism*, 223.

"useful to the public."[47] With respect to adult behaviour, Locke admittedly displays a quasi-Victorian moralism in his identification of the social causes of poverty to be "the relaxation of discipline and corruption of manners" in *fin de siècle* England.[48] And his proposals for dealing with vagrancy and begging are hardly gentle as he suggests that dealing with these problems requires "restraint on their debauchery by a strict execution of the laws" with punishments including beatings, mutilation, and impressments in the navy.[49] Corporal punishment, more or less abandoned in Locke's account of the modern family and childhood education, returns with surprising *éclat* in his treatment of civil law. Where the truly enlightened and progressive aspect of Locke's proposal emerges is with respect to his ideas regarding the children of the poor. For the poor, as opposed to vagrants and beggars, Locke argues, relief "consists in finding work for them."[50] The most innovative element of this project is his call for the establishment of "working schools" for poor children between the ages of three and fourteen. The basic idea is that for part of the day the children will work in the factory spinning textiles from material supplied by local ratepayers, and for the rest of the day the children will attend school on-site.[51] In effect, poor children will, through their labor, defray at least part of the cost of an education provided largely by the public.

Before simply dismissing this proposal as a Dickensian nightmare, it is important to consider Locke's reasoning in the "Essay on the Poor Law." Besides the obvious advantage of dramatically expanding public access to education, Locke identifies several other benefits from this proposal. First, he argues that the establishment of public education will alter the family's role as a traditional obstacle to social, economic, and academic advance among the poor. Significantly, Locke's "working schools" are not orphanages. They are intended for poor children who "live at home with their parents."[52] Coming from families lacking the means to afford private instruction at home or to attend boarding schools, these children

---

[47] John Locke, "An Essay on the Poor Law," in *Political Essays*, Mark Goldie, ed. (Cambridge: Cambridge University Press, 1997), p. 183.

[48] Locke, "Poor Law," 184.

[49] Locke, "Poor Law," 184–187. It is also only fair to point out that in this essay, Locke also recommended a publicly supported system of long-term care for invalids "who are not able to work at all," and he insisted that "if any person die for want of due relief in any parish," the parish should be fined by the national government according to the circumstances of the case and the "heinousness of the crime" ("Poor Law," 197–198).

[50] Locke, "Poor Law," 189.

[51] Locke, "Poor Law," 190.

[52] Locke, "Poor Law," 190.

are destined to have little or no formal education. The goal is to partially
remove children from their families by supplying educational possibilities
independent of their family circumstances, rather than providing money
directly to the father and head of household, who Locke suspects would
spend it "on himself at the alehouse."[53] The effect, he claims, would be to
undermine patriarchy more generally in poor families inasmuch as relieving
poor mothers of childcare duties during the workday will allow a woman
"more liberty to work" herself.[54] In Locke's working school proposal, we
can perhaps see the germ of a primitive public day care system.

The main aim of the working school is, of course, to get poor children to
attend school. A daily supply of a "bellyful of bread" provided by the public
is both a way to improve health for poor children and an incentive for poor
parents to send their little ones to school.[55] The work school is the means by
which Locke envisions applying his method of education as far as feasible to
the broadest possible spectrum of society. While Locke offers no suggestions
as to how working the loom can be made child's play, he does insist that the
local ratepayers hire teachers to "be paid out of" local taxes.[56] The "working
school" teacher substitutes for the tutor in the gentry by playing a similar
role as both instructor and social intermediary between the parents and their
children. The logical outcome of the broad implementation of this proposal
would be the creation of a new class of public teachers, presumably informed
by Locke's novel method of education. Locke argues that this democratization of education would include boys and girls being taught together and even
would allow uneducated poor adults to attend the work schools "to learn"
through a program of continuing education.[57] The effect on public morality
is also a consideration for Locke. With improved education, he claims, poor
children will be brought to the better "sense of religion" that comes with
a certain freedom from the prejudices and deprivations of their families.[58]
While notably Locke founds his educational reform for the poor on a secular,
publicly supported institution rather than the churches, he tries to soothe
ruffled sensibilities by stressing that a public system of education would support, instead of threaten, the religious institutions of civil society.

Locke's revolutionary proposal for reform of the poor law outlined an
early system of public education that proved to be far too radical for the

---

[53] Locke, "Poor Law," 190.
[54] Locke, "Poor Law," 190.
[55] Locke, "Poor Law," 191.
[56] Locke, "Poor Law," 192.
[57] Locke, "Poor Law," 192–193.
[58] Locke, "Poor Law," 191.

narrow oligarchy ruling England after the Glorious Revolution, and was thus promptly dismissed by the powers that were. While this plan would have produced a system of public schools for the poor coexisting with an unofficial private system including home schooling and boarding schools for the affluent, when viewed in tandem with his proposals in the *Thoughts* and the *Conduct*, it is clear just how progressive and innovative Locke's "Essay on the Poor Law" really was. Even in the *Thoughts* Locke suggested that although his audience was primarily gentlemen, he believed that these reforms would have a positive impact on society generally: "For if those of that rank are by their education set right, they will quickly bring all the rest into order."[59] By this he meant primarily that improving the principles of education for gentlemen would be a key ingredient in the project of enlightening this politically vital class whose members will some day be in a position to introduce policies, and perhaps reforms, affecting society as a whole. The emphasis on practicality and teaching how to think, rather than memorizing dead languages, is a common link between Locke's recommendations for both poor children in their "working schools" and for those to the manor-born. The ultimate effect of Locke's various proposals is a movement toward the greater homogenization of education across class lines with a common method and similar curricula. On this basis, it is perhaps possible that the system of education familiar to us today, with publicly supported day schools, professional teachers, and an important role for aware and engaged parents, would not be far from a kind of Lockean ideal.

The "Essay on the Poor Law" indicates Locke's willingness to consider the use of public power on a massive scale to combat the social ill of poverty. In this regard, Locke points to a whole new field of public policy. The parallel development to his call for expanded economic opportunity in a new acquisitive ethos is the possibility for expanding educational opportunity on a scale unimaginable previously in human history.[60] This idea of

---

[59]   T "Dedication," p. 8.
[60]   Public education was not, of course, unheard of prior to Locke. The ancient Greek cities clearly had such an idea and frequently implemented it. However, perhaps the differences between the classical ideal and what Locke proposes are more significant than any superficial resemblances. First, the Greeks typically saw only the education of male children of citizens as a public duty – excluding women, slaves, and foreigners – whereas Locke extends public education to girls and to the children of manual laborers who would most likely have been slaves in antiquity. Second, whereas Locke's proposal has its philosophical premise in natural human equality, the ancient Greeks saw this public duty toward education as a function of their conception of citizenship and moral training. For a good account of the classical ideal of civic education that reveals how profoundly it differs from the modern view pioneered by Locke, see Paul Rahe, *Republics Ancient and*

employing public power to modernize, and in a fundamental sense democratize, society derived from principles of natural equality implicit in the very "bottom" of his proposals for the sons and daughters of gentlefolk in the *Thoughts* and for scholars in the *Conduct*. The danger of replacing traditional patriarchy and political and religious authoritarianism with a new kind of state paternalism, that would concern later libertarians, may perhaps have been a risk Locke was prepared to take, at least at the beginning of the modernization process in England. However, it is more likely that Locke anticipated that the free institutions of civil society would flourish with the support of his new, more public approach to education. The prospect of creating a society imbued at all levels with the principles of respect for the ideal of individual autonomy, cultural openness to scientific advance, and critical discourse seemed in Locke's view to set a progressive course that would gradually define the nature and limits of the liberal state. At the very least, Locke strove to encourage citizens of a natural rights polity to think critically about modern education and "to consult their own reason in the education of their children rather than wholly to rely upon old custom" (T 216).

The impact of Locke's pedagogical writings on the development of modern educational theory is difficult to overstate. For instance, the influence of the *Thoughts* on later classics of educational theory, such as Rousseau's *Emile* or Mill's *System of Logic*, is well known, as is the astonishing popularity of Locke's *Thoughts* in the American colonies in the years prior to the rebellion against British imperial rule.[61] It seems to have been well understood by many of the most discerning minds in the eighteenth and nineteenth centuries that there was something truly revolutionary about Locke's approach to the whole issue of education. That is to say, there was a democratic aspect of Locke's educational theory that was deeply subversive of practically all the traditional forms of authority political, familial, and religious inherited in the West from pre-modernity. As Helvétius, great French *philosophe* and a keen follower of Locke, would pronounce many years after the death of his English master: "It may not be possible to make

---

Modern: *Classical Republicanism and the American Revolution* (Chapel Hill: University of North Carolina Press, 1992), esp. Vol. I.

[61] For Locke's influence on Rousseau (even if often as an opponent), see Jean-Jacques Rousseau, *Emile, or On Education*, Allan Bloom, trans. (New York: Basic Books, 1979), pp. 33, 89–90, as well as Bloom's "Introduction," pp. 5, 13, 18, 25; and for the Lockean themes in Mill's educational writings, see Perkinson, *Since Socrates*, 165–171. For the popularity of Locke's *Thoughts Concerning Education* in the American colonies prior to the Revolution, see Fliegelman, *Prodigals and Pilgrims*, 38–40.

any considerable change in public education without making changes in the very constitution of the state."[62] Locke's entire educational project presupposed that changes in one social sphere, especially those as formative as the family and education, would have important effects on other seemingly unrelated spheres of civil life. Thus not surprisingly, Locke's educational theory, as can be said of his political philosophy generally, displays an acute awareness, perhaps inspired by the discoveries on a very different plane made by his friend Isaac Newton, that immediate and palpable effects often have very distant and abstruse causes.

[62] Helvétius quoted in Fliegelman, *Prodigals and Pilgrims*, 13.

6

The Church

The idea of toleration is inextricably connected with the history of liberalism. Arguably liberal political theory's first direct encounter with the conceptual problems posed by legal discrimination and unequal treatment of minorities emerged from the religious controversies of the early modern period.[1] It is in this context that John Locke emerges as an important but controversial figure in the history of political thought. On the one hand, it is widely acknowledged that it is with Locke that the argument for religious toleration made one of its first, and still most celebrated, appearances. On the other hand, some scholars question whether Locke's notion of toleration was too narrow and limited, and too dependent on seventeenth-century theological assumptions to have any real purchase in diverse modern liberal societies today.

For instance, Jonathan Israel in his important recent works on Enlightenment Philosophy highlights Locke's toleration theory as prime evidence for relegating him to the status of an "essentially conservative" thinker who played little or no role in the revolution in philosophy led by Spinoza, which produced the modern world we know.[2] For Israel, the chief defects in Locke's account of toleration were his notorious exceptions to toleration, most notably atheists and Roman Catholics, as well as what Israel takes to be the fundamentally theological orientation of Locke's argument

[1] See, for instance, the importance Rawls attributed to toleration as a paradigmatic liberal concept (John Rawls, *A Theory of Justice* [Cambridge: Harvard University Press, 1971], pp. 211–221 and John Rawls, *Political Liberalism, Expanded Edition* [New York: Columbia University Press, 2005], pp. xxiv, 10).

[2] Jonathan Israel, *Radical Enlightenment: Philosophy and the Making of Modernity 1650–1750* (Oxford: Oxford University Press, 2001), pp. 259, 265–267 and Jonathan Israel, *Enlightenment Contested: Philosophy, Modernity, and the Emancipation of Man 1670–1752* (Oxford: Oxford University Press, 2006), pp. 52, 57–58.

for toleration and his larger worldview. In contrast to radical enlightenment thinkers such as Spinoza, who publicly advocated complete toleration and freedom of thought and speech, Israel's version of Locke supported toleration only for the sake of saving the souls of sincere believers, not to promote the value of individual freedom.

This chapter aims to demonstrate that this interpretation of Locke's toleration argument barely scratches the surface of his complex teaching on the relation of religion and politics the full range of which was contained not only in the *Letters Concerning Toleration*, but also in the *Essay Concerning Human Understanding* and *The Reasonableness of Christianity*. We will argue that it is impossible to understand Locke's argument for toleration unless one first appreciates the central importance he attached to individual freedom as the central organizing principle of modern life.

The *ancien régime* in early-modern Europe rested on an interlocking series of deeply held and widely supported beliefs about the source of political authority, the nature of government, the relations of men and women, the meaning of education, and the relation of the sacred to the mundane. As the central representatives of the divine on Earth, the churches stood as uniquely integral institutions with influence that pervaded practically every aspect of life including politics, the family, and education. In England through much of the seventeenth century, the debate over the role of the church in society, and the relation of religion and politics generally, was extremely contentious producing everything from civil strife to severe persecution. Coming of age in Restoration England, Locke's generation internalized the central lesson of their country's recent history, namely that religion as traditionally conceived was a political problem. The nation Locke inherited was the England of the Clarendon code, a collection of statutes designed by the Cavalier Parliament to reestablish the Church of England and to impose religious uniformity on the dissenting sects it blamed for the religious extremism that had caused the country's long and bitter civil wars.[3] Thus, unlike Spinoza who was in the fortunate (but, by the 1670s, increasingly tenuous) position of defending religious pluralism in a Dutch Republic with a long tradition of toleration, Locke faced the more daunting challenge of trying to establish the principle of toleration in

---

[3]   The Clarendon code was essentially three statutes passed by the Restoration Parliament including the *Uniformity Act* (1662) requiring Episcopal ordination of all clergy and mandatory use of the Book of Common Prayer, the *Conventicle Act* (1664) forbidding all religious meetings outside of the established church, and the *Five Mile Act* (1665) which banned dissenting ministers from corporate towns. These laws carried penalties including fines, imprisonment, and restrictions on educational and employment opportunities.

a regime in which a history of religious conflict made legal persecution of dissenters an immediate and palpable political reality. In this context, it is hardly surprising that Locke's argument for toleration took on a different tone and texture than that of Spinoza.

However, to consider Locke's toleration argument simply in terms of the immediate historical and cultural context from which it emerged is to fail to recognize the depth and complexity of his radical reinterpretation of the significance of the church and the role of religion in political society. Toleration was an important part of Locke's larger philosophic project, which aimed to critically examine all of the authoritative institutions of early-modern life in light of the fundamental principle of human freedom. But Locke recognized that the church was an institution with unique properties – one foot in Heaven and one foot on Earth – that established a distinct set of conceptual criteria and interpretive difficulties. Thus, one aspect of Locke's toleration argument examined the church from a theological perspective and sought to reevaluate the purpose of the church as the collective expression of humanity's highest and immortal aspirations by reconsidering this purpose in terms of his philosophic discoveries about the intellectual properties of the human mind. Locke's complex analysis of the epistemological and cognitive subjectivity characterizing faith and individual soteriological concerns produced a much deeper and richer philosophy of religion than Israel suggests. In seeking to ground the relation of the sacred to the human on a philosophical and rational foundation, Locke cannot be accused of taking for granted received theological assumptions. Rather he inquired perhaps more rigorously and with greater penetration into questions about the naturalness of religion, the authority of the church, and the relation of reason and faith than arguably any of his predecessors and contemporaries in the history of political thought.

Locke also, however, approached the issues raised by toleration from a more broadly political, and even societal, perspective. On this level, Locke's thoughts on the church were a reflection of his wider treatment of the relations of government and the institutions of civil society. In defining the church as an "absolutely free and spontaneous" form of "voluntary society," Locke not only sought to inject individualist principles into one of the traditional bastions of orthodoxy, but also sought to transform the relation of government and society by positing the church and government as distinct venues of moral discourse.[4] In contrast to Israel's characterization of

---

[4] John Locke, *A Letter Concerning Toleration*, James H. Tully, ed. (Indianapolis: Hackett, 1983 [1689]), pp. 28–29 (hereafter in notes and text simply page number).

Locke's toleration argument as an essentially negative principle primarily intended to defuse religious controversy and discourage futile public debate about religion and morality, in actuality Locke's toleration theory was part of a larger theoretical ambition to support freedom of thought and freedom of speech in order to encourage an inclusive conception of the public sphere that would provide for robust debate about morality and the public good among the institutions of civil society. While it is arguable that Locke's account of toleration foreshadowed many central preoccupations in contemporary political theory, such as an emphasis on noncoercive treatment of diverse claims, as well as an aspiration toward broadly inclusive deliberations in civil society, we must be mindful not to ascribe current debates to a much earlier thinker who did not share identical concerns relating to "recognition" and cultural identity.[5] However, it is accurate to suggest that Locke viewed toleration as a means to allow for the articulation of diverse beliefs and opinions in a framework of conscientious dissent and debate that would benefit both society as a whole and the minority religious groups contained in it. But in order to understand the revolutionary character of Locke's teaching on toleration and the church, we need to return once again to the ground zero of Locke's political philosophy – the complex mental world of human understanding.

THE EPISTEMOLOGY OF FAITH

In Chapter 1 we considered the relation of faith and reason as a purely epistemological question and found that Locke's theory of knowledge assigned many moral ideas to the cognitive realm of probability that is both distinct from, and less certain than, knowledge strictly speaking. When we return to this issue from a different perspective with a view to Locke's eidetic account of the intellectual properties of the church, a different set of questions come into view. What kind of mental activity does the church or churches reflect? Does Locke's theory of knowledge presuppose that religious faith,

---

[5] For perhaps the definitive account of the "politics of recognition," see Charles Taylor, "The Politics of Recognition," in *Multiculturalism and "The Politics of Recognition,"* Amy Gutmann, ed. (Princeton: Princeton University Press, 1993): 25–73. Galeotti argues persuasively that much of the contemporary debate about difference and inclusion owes something to a conceptual framework emerging from early-modern debates about religion and toleration (Anna Elisabetta Galeotti, *Toleration as Recognition* [Cambridge: Cambridge University Press, 2002]). But for a more skeptical assessment of the attempt to interpret contemporary ideas about inclusion in light of the older idea of toleration, see Peter Jones, "Toleration, Recognition and Identity" *The Journal of Political Philosophy*, 14, 2 (2006): 123–143.

as opposed to belief or opinion simply, is a permanent feature of human life in the sense that the mind is naturally drawn or somehow compelled to reflect upon issues of morality and eternal salvation?

In order to address these questions, we need to return to Locke's treatment of the relation between faith and knowledge in the *Essay*. There the texture of Locke's argument about religion combined elements of universality and particularity in a pattern characteristic of his general approach to epistemology. Faith is a universal phenomenon in two senses. First, while Locke insists that the idea of God is not innate, for there are no innate ideas, he does indicate that ideas about God and our moral duties are embedded in human cognitive capacities. The mind must work toward moral knowledge, but God has supplied all individuals with intellectual faculties to do so. Locke maintains that "the Candle of the Lord" provides "light enough" for us to learn our moral duties.[6] Second, religion is at least theoretically a universal experience because understanding God is the core of the human *telos*: "The knowledge and veneration of Him, being the chief end of all our Thoughts, and the proper business of all Understanding" (E 2.7.6.131). On this matter, the distinction Locke draws between moral and natural philosophy could not be starker. Whereas real knowledge about natural bodies eludes the grasp of all but a few rare geniuses, moral knowledge is accessible to all and, he deduces, must therefore be the proper mission of all:

For 'tis rational to conclude that our proper Imployment lies in those Enquiries, and in that sort of Knowledge, which is most suited to our natural capacities, and carries in it our greatest interest, i.e. the condition of our eternal estate. Hence I think I may conclude, that Morality is the proper Science and Business of Mankind in general; (who are both concerned, and fitted to search their *Summum Bonum*). (E 4.12.11.646)

Locke's evocative use of the concept of a highest good or *summum bonum* puts theological inquiry into the laws of God in the place formerly reserved for speculation about the good or full human life once firmly planted in the classical *polis*. In this respect, Locke appears to adhere to a teleological conception of human rational and moral purpose dating back to Aquinas and others in the medieval period. Moreover, Locke insists that human frailty and social realities are no excuse for failing to pursue this "proper Imployment" of our rational faculties. Given the relative equality of faculties distributed among humankind, even the least among us has the

---

[6] John Locke, *An Essay Concerning Human Understanding*, Peter Nidditch, ed. (Oxford: Oxford University Press, 1975 [1690]), bk. 4, ch. 3, sec. 20, p. 552 and bk. 1, ch. 1, sec. 5, p. 45 (hereafter in notes and text E bk, ch, sec, and page).

time and ability to learn what is required to secure our "eternal estate" (E 4.20.3.708). Thus in one sense, religion stands for Locke as perhaps the most natural intellectual experience imaginable.

However, in another important sense, Locke's treatment of faith assumes the considerable particularity we would expect to flow from his democratization of mind. By virtue of its epistemological status as a form of judgment falling short of knowledge, faith is a reminder of the inherent limits of human understanding. It is in this sense of the limits of knowledge that grounds the individualist principles of Locke's theory of understanding. The "candle of the Lord" is emphatically not a floodlight, and Locke insists that on matters of faith we must usually be content to operate in the shadowy "twilight" of probability (E 4.14.1.652). Thus the cognitive properties of faith are influenced by the same external factors that characterized Locke's account of human freedom. There may be universal necessity *to prefer* (that is an intellectual compulsion toward soteriological matters), but individuals exercise their freedom regarding *what to prefer* on the basis of internal reflection on evidence and the mind's free assent to various proofs. Locke is well aware that judgments about the requirements of salvation will not hold the kind of logical self-evidence one would expect from conclusions deduced about the properties of a triangle. Diversity is the natural condition regarding religious belief for on matters of probability, "it is unavoidable to the greatest part of Men, if not all, to have several Opinions, without certain and indubitable Proofs of their Truths" (E 4.16.4.659). Thus, important elements of freedom and subjectivity are built into Locke's account of religion and universalist considerations about human flourishing.

Locke's examination of the cognitive properties of faith cannot, however, be understood simply in terms of universals and particulars. Locke is not guilty of presupposing the existence of the very thing – that is eternal life – which is most in need of demonstration. As we recall, his theory of knowledge was based on the notion that there are degrees and kinds of knowledge including intuitive, demonstrative, and sensitive in descending order of certainty (E 4.9.2.618). We are aware of our own existence through intuition, of God's existence by demonstration, and have knowledge of the external world through sensitivity. Locke insists that the limits of our knowledge not only falls short of reality, but these limits also fall short of the number of our ideas (E 4.3.4.539). We can have ideas about many things that cannot be said to constitute knowledge strictly speaking. The importance of this epistemological point with respect to religion is obvious. On the basis of our cognitive capacities we can construct ideas about things toward which we may not assume knowledge. Is the idea of an afterlife, our "eternal estate," such an idea divorced from knowing, strictly speaking?

As a purely epistemological question, Locke approaches the cognitive status of the afterlife only somewhat obliquely in the *Essay* by means of the two central ideas in his moral philosophy: the existence of God and the immortality of soul. These ideas are the cognitive building blocks of our conception of the afterlife; however, Locke deals with each of these ideas rather differently. The existence of God, he advances, is not only capable of demonstrative knowledge, he offers a demonstration himself in Book 4, chapter 10 of the *Essay*. This demonstration achieves "Knowledge by intervening proofs," and is thus less certain than intuitive knowledge of one's own existence, but it nonetheless provides such a firm epistemological foundation that Locke confidently claims: "the Knowledge of his own Mind cannot suffer a Man, that considers, to be ignorant, that there is a God" (E 4.3.4.532, 4.3.27.558). Moreover, knowledge of the existence of God is buttressed by a significant form of sensitive knowledge as well. One of the defining characteristics of our idea of God, Locke argues, is that God is or possesses "infinite Mind." The idea of infinity is not as mysterious as it first appears. According to Locke, our idea of infinite derives from an understanding of primary qualities such as space, duration, and number that are in the cognitive sense very basic (E 2.17.1.209).[7] This does not mean that we have a positive idea of what eternity actually is, but Locke does claim that we can get an idea of God in the negative sense of being able to conceive of space, duration, and number without end. For instance, simply adding numbers to infinity really amounts to perceiving the possibility of addition without end, although we can have no clear idea of what this addition would substantively produce.

Similarly, Locke argues that we can construct a complex idea of an "eternal, omniscient, infinitely wise, and happy Being" by taking our own "idea of existence, knowledge, power and pleasure," and then simply "joining all these together, with infinity to each of them" (3.6.11.445). This is not, of course, to suggest that Locke believes this gives us real knowledge about the attributes of God. God is not simply a supremely powerful expression of human qualities. However, we can acquire a perhaps hazy and obscure but nonetheless perceptible idea of God through reflection upon sensible qualities well within our mental reach. Once again, however, demonstrating the existence of God requires intellectual effort, and Locke admits that atheism is possible even on a mass, societal scale.[8] Atheism is possible, according to

---

[7] Greg Forster, *John Locke's Politics of Moral Consensus* (Cambridge: Cambridge University Press 2005), p. 67.

[8] See, for example, E 1.4.8.88 where Locke credits reports of wide-scale atheism in Siam and China, as well as expressing his own belief that there are many atheists in England who hide their beliefs for fear of public censure.

Locke, for the same reason that stunningly brutal customs blot so much of human history; namely, human beings are capable of any degradation once we abandon reason, our "only Star and Compass."[9]

Proof of the existence of soul emerges as a much more difficult proposition for Locke than the existence of God. Problematically, however, the soul is also a crucial part of Locke's moral philosophy, for it is the soul that makes sense of the obligation to perform moral duties. In Chapter 1 we examined the way in which Locke proposed the concept of self-conscious personal identity as a replacement for the traditional, and in Locke's view highly suspect, metaphysical accounts of soul. Personal identity had the advantage of being metaphysically neutral insofar as it provided a basis for punishment and obligation that neither required nor denied the immortality of soul. Personal identity supplied a convenient and epistemologically compact idea of one's present self as the same being who could be subject to punishment in the future, whether it be this life or the next. However, Locke's treatment of the cognitive basis of religion suggests that our earlier account was somewhat incomplete. In Book IV of the *Essay*, Locke is emphatic that it is knowledge of our "eternal estate," which is so deeply connected to the proper business of human understanding. That is to say, any moral theory that does not consider the immortality of soul to be a vital question will be lacking in key respects. But what, according to Locke, are the cognitive and epistemological grounds for knowledge or belief in the immortal soul?

Ambiguity riddles Locke's account of soul. On the one hand, he confidently pronounces irremediable human ignorance about the properties of soul: "He that considers how hardly sensation is, in our thought, reconcilable to extended Matter; or Existence to anything that hath no Extension at all, will confess, that he is very far from certainly knowing what his Soul is. 'Tis a point, which seems to me, to be put out of reach of our knowledge" (E 4.3.6.542). Locke roundly rejects the Platonic idea of the immortal soul based on immaterial simplicity by insisting that there is no cognitive basis for dismissing the possibility that the soul is material or that an immortal soul would necessarily be tied to the personal identity of a single individual (E 2.27.27.347).[10] The immateriality of soul is probable, Locke suggests, but

---

9   John Locke, *Two Treatises of Government*, Peter Laslett, ed. (Cambridge: Cambridge University Press, 1988 [1689]) First Treatise, sec. 58 (hereafter in notes and text treatise: section).

10   See Nicholas Jolley, "Locke on Faith and Reason," in *The Cambridge Companion to Locke's Essay Concerning Human Understanding*, Lex Newman, ed. (Cambridge: Cambridge University Press, 2007), pp. 436–455, esp. 440–441.

it is only that – a matter of probability as opposed to knowledge. However, Locke also suggests that our ignorance of soul is not total ignorance. We can, for instance, have "as clear a perception, and notion of immaterial substances, as we have of material" (E 2.23.15.305). From the ability to draw this basic distinction between material and immaterial substances, Locke claims an individual is able to know not only "that there is some Corporeal Being without me," but can also know with even greater certainty that "there is some Spiritual Being within me, that sees and hears" (E 2.23.15.306).[11] The problem for Locke's moral theory, of course, lies in determining whether this "something in us that has a Power to think" satisfies the requirements of a being subject to eternal reward and punishment. Needless to say, Locke's conclusion that it "becomes the Modesty of Philosophy, not to pronounce Magisterially," on the issue of the immortality of soul when we so obviously "want that Evidence that can produce knowledge" is not completely reassuring. The upshot of Locke's discussion is that the immortality of soul may not be demonstrable but neither is it required, for: "All the great Ends of Morality and Religion, are well enough secured, without Philosophical Proofs of the Soul's Immateriality" (E 4.3.6.542). But is this not question begging: If philosophical proofs of the immortality of soul are superfluous, what kind of proofs are necessary to establish the existence of something with such importance to Locke's account of religion and morality? Does the problem of soul put into question Locke's entire theory of moral knowledge? Or to put it another way, does Locke's admission about the inability to have knowledge of soul shed additional light on the problem of demonstrative morality?

As we have seen, the promise of a demonstrative basis of morality is something of a holy grail in Locke's account of moral knowledge in the

---

[11] Forster (*Moral Consensus*, 64–66, 68–71) suggests that Locke's aim is to purge contentious debate from consideration of soul by simply generating agreement that we have a vague sense of some spiritual being within us. This vague and uncontroversial notion of soul would serve the purpose of supplying our immediate proof that a metaphysical world exists, not actually what it is. However tempting, this interpretation has two problems. First, Locke is very clear that the soul is meant to supply a very specific kind of insight relating to the prospect of eternal reward and punishment. A dim awareness of something metaphysical out there will not do because in Locke's moral theory, the immortality of soul provides the obligatory character of the moral law. Second, Forster's argument for the very elementary cognitive requirements for the proof of the immortal soul – that there is "something in us that has the power to think" (E 2.1.10.109) – runs the danger of collapsing into something similar to a claim to a knowledge of soul that is intuitive, which, of course, Locke explicitly rejects. As an epistemological matter, Locke's account of soul is a good deal more problematic than Forster suggests, even if the political implications of Locke's account broadly follow the path Forster correctly identifies.

Essay. Forster offers an interesting and provocative approach to this issue by suggesting that we scale back the importance of Locke's claims about moral knowledge.[12] There are three elements to Forster's argument. First, by "demonstration" Locke meant it only in the technical sense of establishing the logical agreement of ideas in the archetypal pattern of mixed modes. Moral demonstration then would involve nothing more than the suggestion that we can achieve greater clarity about moral concepts, such as adultery or homicide, than we can about natural bodies. In Chapter 1 we identified this as the weaker version of Locke's argument for demonstrative morality. Second, Forster astutely observes that Locke never concludes that rational demonstration is the only form of moral reasoning available to human understanding. As we have seen in our treatment of Locke's state of nature and his account of the origin of government, Locke also identified important sensitive and empirical sources of moral reasoning. Third, Forster insists that moral demonstration was little more than a "side bar" discussion for Locke that, like his dismissal of metaphysical accounts of soul, displays that he was not preoccupied with developing a fully rational system of ethics, therefore neither should we be preoccupied with trying to find one in Locke.

The first two elements of Forster's argument are insightful and persuasive, however, they do not logically conclude in, or even support, the more radical claim that demonstrative morality was only a marginal concern for Locke. There is ample textual and extratextual evidence that Locke thought the theoretical possibility of moral demonstration was a crucial part of his philosophic project. Three times in Book 4 of the *Essay* – the book containing his most extended discussion of the intellectual properties of faith – Locke announces his belief that morality is as capable of demonstration as mathematics (E 4.3.18.549, 4.3.18.549–50, 4.12.8.643). Moreover, in private correspondence with his friend William Molyneux, Locke admitted that he tried to see if "morality might be demonstratively made out," but he suspected the task may be beyond him.[13] In addition, as Waldron, Zuckert, Grant, and others have argued persuasively, Locke's *Second Treatise* may be understood as his attempt to offer such a demonstration of moral truths.[14] This is not meant to suggest that Locke ever

[12] See Forster's good discussion in *Moral Consensus*, 97–100.
[13] John Locke, *The Correspondence of John Locke, Volume 4*, E. S. DeBeer, ed. (Oxford: Clarendon Press, 1979) Letter 1538, p. 524.
[14] See Ruth Grant, *John Locke's Liberalism* (Chicago: University of Chicago Press, 1987), p. 57; Jeremy Waldron, *God, Locke, and Equality* (Cambridge: Cambridge University Press, 2002), p. 95; and Michael Zuckert, *Natural Rights and the New Republicanism* (Princeton: Princeton University Press, 1994), chs. 8 and 9.

came to the conclusion that he, or anyone else, ever achieved a complete rational system of ethics. Rather the point is that there is strong evidence indicating that Locke believed that the archetypal dimension of demonstration was only a part, and a considerably lesser part at that, of a larger project of moral demonstration that required in addition a demonstration of the theistic elements relating to the source of moral obligation.[15]

Forster's interpretation also risks losing the texture and tone of Locke's argument regarding moral demonstration. Whatever severe difficulties Locke conceived in the path to demonstrative morality, it is misleading to suggest that he was content simply to marginalize this as a theoretical concern. Determining our moral duties, Locke claims, is our "proper business" because it relates to our highest conceivable end. Unlike mathematics, morality cannot simply be reduced to the logical agreement of ideas because morality is directly connected to action. Whether human beings understand all of the secrets of geometry is, in the grand scheme of things, not a major concern; however, a rational system of ethics would tend "entirely to the good of mankind, and that all would be happy, if all would practise it."[16] Future discoveries in mathematics will appear self-evident to us once they are discovered, but they will have no impact on our conduct or chances for salvation.

Knowledge about the immortality of soul is then the crucial missing link in Locke's account of the possibility of demonstrative morality. This would be the most important kind of knowledge, if only we had it. In yet another letter to the ubiquitous Molyneux, Locke admitted that while he feared demonstrative morality may be beyond his capacities, he was confident that the "Gospels contains so perfect a body of ethics" as to make his efforts appear somewhat redundant.[17] The suggestion that revelation provides a divine shortcut to a complete system of ethics casts the difficulties attending demonstration of moral truth in a whole new light. It is in this context that faith emerges as the pivotal intellectual concept in Locke's moral theory.

---

[15] See good discussions of the two elements of moral demonstration, understood alternatively as archetypal and theistic (Nicholas Wolterstorff, *John Locke and the Ethics of Belief* [Cambridge: Cambridge University Press, 1996], pp. 144–145) or in terms of the distinction between the existence of God and the content of the natural law (John Colman, *John Locke's Moral Philosophy* [Edinburgh: Edinburgh University Press, 1983], pp. 169–170).

[16] John Locke, *The Reasonableness of Christianity*. I. T. Ramsey, ed. (Stanford: Stanford University Press, 1958 [1695]), para. 243 (hereafter in notes and text RC and paragraph).

[17] John Locke, *The Correspondence of John Locke, Volume 5*, E. S. DeBeer, ed. (Oxford: Clarendon Press, 1979) Letter 2059, p. 595.

Epistemologically vexing questions about the metaphysical properties of soul and the afterlife can be clarified with the assurance of revelation. However, Locke insists that to understand this, we must distinguish
between knowledge and belief. In his response to Edward Stillingfleet,
Bishop of Worcester, who had roundly criticized Locke's account of faith in
the first editions of the *Essay*, Locke sought to clarify his position by stressing the importance of the distinction between knowledge and faith: "With
what assurance soever of believing, I assent to any article of faith, so that
I steadfastly venture my all upon it, it is still but believing. Bring it to certainty, and it ceases to be faith."[18] In the offending passage in the *Essay* that
fueled the good Bishop's ire, Locke distinguished between the intellectual
properties of reason and faith in these terms:

> Reason therefore here, as contradistinguished to Faith, I take to be the discovery of
> the certainty or probability of such propositions or Truths, which the mind arrives
> at by Deductions made from such Ideas, which it has got by the use of its natural
> faculties, viz. by Sensation or Reflection.
>
>   Faith, on the other side, is the Assent to any Proposition, not thus made out by
> the deductions of Reason; but upon credit of the Proposer, as coming from God,
> in some extraordinary way of Communication. This way of discovering Truths to
> Men we call Revelation (E 4.18.2.689).

For Locke, the primary distinction between reason and faith revolves around
the source of ideas and the degree of certainty pertaining to ideas. Faith is a
matter of belief and probability, while knowledge logically excludes belief.
Locke's epistemology makes knowledge and belief mutually exclusive intellectual categories, and thus by definition one cannot have knowledge about
matters of faith.[19] Belief, however, is not a simple phenomenon for Locke
because beliefs are capable of possessing degrees of assurance even if they
never attain the "visible and certain connexion" between ideas that produces knowledge (E 4.15.3.655).[20] Locke also, however, distinguishes faith
from the generic class of opinions that inhabit the epistemic zone of belief.[21]
Unlike my belief or opinion that it will rain next Saturday, which derives
from a *mélange* of murky connections between ideas of probability, ama-
teur meteorology, or just plain hunches, Locke identifies faith with opinions
deduced from a specific source, namely divine revelation. Epistemologically
speaking, faith is not just any old opinion for Locke. As Locke informed
Stillingfleet: "Faith stands by itself, and upon ground of its own."[22]

18   John Locke, *Works Volume IV* (London: Tegg, 1823), pp. 146–147.
19   Jolley, "Reason and Faith," 438.
20   See also Wolterstorff, *Ethics of Belief*, 123.
21   In this regard, I differ from Jolley, "Reason and Faith," 438.
22   Locke, *Works IV*, 146.

The subjective character of belief rests on the lack of self-evidence in its propositions and the necessarily lesser degree of universality in the apprehension of belief when compared to knowledge. Locke maintains that the faculty of judgment involved in determining probability allows us to navigate the shadowy "twilight" world of uncertainty produced by the narrow limits of human knowledge. The dependence of judgment in matters of belief also, as we have seen, leads Locke to conclude that diversity of opinions on matters of belief, including religion, is in some sense natural. But simply recognizing that Locke's epistemology narrows the range of knowledge and expands the realm of belief and opinion, while placing religion in the zone of belief or opinion, does not in itself fully explain the status of faith in Locke's theory of knowledge. Faith involves probability and judgment relating to the testimony of others offered in revelation, but what specifically does revelation tell us?

Not surprisingly, Locke frames his account of revelation in terms of the limits of reason. However, he does not exclude reason from faith. Reason is central to faith, even if faith cannot assume the rational certainty of knowledge. There are, Locke indicates, three kinds of propositions: those according to reason, those above reason, and those contrary to it (E 4.17.23.687). Monotheism, Locke claims, is according to reason, much as polytheism is contrary to it. These propositions can, in principle, be worked out and assented to or dissented from on the basis of natural reason alone. Locke's prime example of a proposition above reason is that "the dead shall rise" (E 4.18.7.694–5). Resurrection and eternal life are matters that natural reason can neither prove nor disprove conclusively. Revelation thus presents evidence for the mind's assent or dissent about matters that are, strictly speaking, beyond the capacity of reason to establish on its own.

Faith is not irrational because it crucially depends on reason being employed to test or acknowledge its own limits. Locke is not, however, saying that revelation presents a substantive argument that either persuades the mind or not. This would be characteristic of the kind of rational demonstration of morality Locke pointedly does not provide in the *Essay*.[23] His point rather is that revelation either convinces the mind of the limits of rational capacities or it does not. That is to say, superstition would be religious opinion that cannot pass the test of reason. This is the dynamic intellectual force of revelation. It does not communicate knowledge but rather commands assent to propositions that otherwise would not be apparent, or at least not compelling, to mind. Revelation is not knowledge, but it has

---

[23] For a thoughtful account of what such a Lockean demonstration would require, see Wolterstorff, *Ethics of Belief*, 142–143.

real cognitive bite according to Locke because it "carries with it Assurance beyond Doubt, Evidence beyond Exception," and thus can command assent even when reason is inclined another way: "evident Revelation ought to determine our Assent even against Probability" (E 4.18.9.695; 4.16.14.667). It is by virtue of revelation, then, that the immortality of soul and the existence of the afterlife can be believed with the highest degree of assurance, even if never actually known.

The role of reason in Locke's account of faith is thus a complex one. The term he uses to describe it is as the "regulator" of faith (E 4.17.24.687). In contrast to those Locke identifies as "Enthusiasts," who claim that all questions of religion are "a Matter of Faith, and above Reason," Locke claims that reason plays a crucial role in faith. Enthusiasm equates faith with intensity of feeling and thus presents a challenge for religious freedom: "The assuming and Authority of dictating to others, and a forwardness to prescribe to their Opinions, is a constant concomitant of this bias and corruption of our Judgments" (E 4.19.9.700; 4.19.2.698). The logical result of the complete exclusion of reason from religion is superstition, not faith. But how can we harmonize Locke's claim that reason is to be our "Last Judge and Guide in everything" with his epistemological conclusion that reason must defer to revelation on matters beyond the limits of reason?

It helps if we distinguish between the two senses in which Locke refers to reason.[24] First there is reason in its *zetetic* or discovery mode, which involves establishing certainty or probability in the connection or agreement between ideas that do not obviously display any connection or agreement. This aspect of reason cannot help us much with the proposition that "the dead shall rise," and thus we must take this as "purely a matter of faith" (E 4.18.7.691). This does not, however, mean that reason is simply dormant in matters of faith. Rather Locke insists that "Revelation is natural Reason enlarged by a new set of discoveries communicated by God, which Reason vouches the Truth of, by the Testimony and Proofs it gives, that they come from God" (E 4.19.4.698). By equating revelation with natural reason, Locke is not suggesting that revelation simply communicates truths that we could, in principle, have figured out on our own like a master geometer explaining the properties of a triangle to a mathphobe. Locke's point, rather, is that reason can also be understood in a more technical sense as the faculty involved in determining whether someone really is a master geometer and has the expertise he or she claims (E 4.18.8.694). In lieu of rationally verifiable evidence about the truth of revelation's claims,

---

[24] Here I follow Jolley's good discussion in "Reason and Faith," 442–443.

reason can play a crucial role in determining upon what authority revelation is based.

Reason is a part of faith because it allows us to achieve assurance about revelation. We can do so because we can have greater certainty about the limits of our own knowledge than we can about the positive teaching of revelation. In a crucial sense, Locke's theory of knowledge places very considerable cognitive and epistemological limits on what we can reasonably take to be genuine revelation. For instance, revelation cannot communicate any new simple ideas (E 4.18.3.690–1). The visions of St. Paul may indeed be grander than eye has seen or ear has heard, but it is precisely for this reason that scripture can only communicate this vision to us in terms apprehensible to the range of human sense experience. A more important limit, however, is Locke's insistence that revelation cannot contradict our knowledge. Probability defers to faith, but knowledge emphatically does not. This is the other dimension of Locke's claim that "revelation is natural reason," for genuine revelation cannot contradict any proposition about which we have intuitive, demonstrative, or sensitive knowledge. A revelation that contradicted the Pythagorean theorem should, Locke argues, be summarily dismissed as spurious. Locke concludes that thankfully, the Gospels contain no such contradictions, nor he insists can we reasonably draw from scripture propositions like the doctrine of transubstantiation, which contradicts intuitive knowledge of being (E 4.20.10.713). Locke's major theoretical point with respect to reason's regulatory role in faith is that we do not need revelation to be the source of all knowledge – unassisted reason can establish much of what we need to know, even perhaps with regards to morality.

One important question that we will need to pursue further in the context of Locke's argument for toleration is just how much certainty he thought we can acquire in moral matters given that religious belief appears to be both a permanent feature of human life and yet also an intellectual activity falling short of knowledge, and thus inclining toward the production of great diversity of belief. The subjective intellectual core of belief formation that flows out of Locke's democratization of mind points to what seems to be in Locke's view a fundamental disconnection between modern philosophy and modern politics. On the basis of Locke's epistemology, religious pluralism should be the natural human condition. Yet the evidence of historical experience and the legal realities of Locke's own time suggest the exact opposite. Does the idea of the church properly conceived logically require the toleration or even encouragement of numerous churches?

THE CASE FOR TOLERATION

Diversity of opinions about religion and the requirements of salvation is, Locke reasons, a natural function of human understanding. However, this fact alone does not justify the policy of toleration. Diverse beliefs may be natural in one sense, but is this diversity compatible with stable and peaceful civil society? Are these various opinions and beliefs worthy of moral respect from government and other individuals? Locke offers four main arguments in the *Letter Concerning Toleration* as to why the policy of toleration is the natural, and indeed necessary, implication from his account of the intellectual properties of faith. The first argument relates to the irrationality of persecution. According to Locke, coercion affects the will, not the faculty of understanding. Since belief is a product of understanding rather than will, penalties are "not proper to convince the mind" because it is "only light and evidence that can work a change in Mens Opinions" (27; E 4.15.365). Locke admits that civil penalties can produce outward conformity but denies that they can form or alter sincere belief. Lacking the power of religion, which consists "in the inward persuasion of the Mind (27)," civil government cannot alter belief by virtue of the coercive means available to it, and therefore it is irrational even to try.[25] Force can affect will and behavior to make an individual do something he or she does not wish to do, but according to Locke, one cannot be forced to believe something to which one's understanding will not assent: "I cannot be saved by a Religion that I distrust, and by a Worship that I abhor" (38).

Locke's second argument relates to the intrinsic fallibility of all claims to knowledge about religious truth. By this argument, the variety of religions in the world reflects a fundamental disharmony and thus recommends healthy skepticism about any government's claim to enforce the "true religion." In a world characterized by one truth but a "variety and contradiction of Opinions in Religion," individuals cannot sensibly "quit the light of their own Reason" and simply submit their chances of salvation to the determination of fallible rulers in the "places of their Nativity" (27–8). In a striking double movement, Locke's moderate philosophical skepticism retains the possibility of religious truth while simultaneously serving to undermine confidence that any individual or group can rightfully claim full possession of it.

---

[25] Creppell sees this as a reflection of Locke's "social science" awareness of human psychology and the dualism of public and private spheres (Ingrid Creppell, "Locke on Toleration: The Transformation of Constraint" *Political Theory*, 24, 2 [May 1996]: 200–240).

Third, Locke suggests that toleration is grounded in the contractual origins of government inasmuch as individuals in the state of nature delegate their natural power to government in order to secure basic rights to life, liberty, and property. However, Locke claims that the "care of souls is not committed to the Magistrate, any more than to other Men," and therefore the power to enforce or punish religious belief cannot be vested in "the Magistrate by the consent of the People" (26). Locke clarifies this basic premise with two arguments. First, he claims that religious belief in no way constitutes the kind of harm that the individual is trying to avoid by consenting to form civil society.[26] Second, Locke insists that individual belief about salvation is no less certain than the beliefs of rulers, and thus no rational individual would authorize the rulers to coerce belief, since there are no rational grounds for believing any government necessarily possesses knowledge of religious truth.[27] Given the limits of human understanding, no claim to knowledge in matters of faith can ever extend beyond the realm of fallible judgment and contestable probabilities.

A fourth argument for toleration is Locke's claim that toleration is a Christian duty and "the chief Characteristical Mark of the True Church" (23). He suggests that the spirit of "Charity, Meekness, and Goodwill" toward all people, which grounds a policy of toleration, is "so agreeable to the Gospel of Jesus Christ" that it "seems Monstrous for Men to be so blind, as not to perceive the Necessity and Advantage of it" (23, 25). With this, Locke accuses opponents of toleration of both un-Christian practice and political opportunism, of showing more concern with persecuting religious dissenters than with encouraging morality and piety among nominal members of the established church.

Several commentators have demonstrated that none of these arguments provide a knockdown case against opponents of toleration such as Jonas Proast, defender of the established Church of England and Locke's antagonist in the polemical exchange following the original *Letter Concerning Toleration*. For instance, it has been observed that the argument for the irrationality of persecution is qualified or even undermined by Locke's noticeably more voluntaristic account of understanding in the *Essay Concerning Human Understanding*, in which he admits that while belief is formed in response to evidence, judgment of this evidence can be seriously affected by inclinations of the will that are, at least theoretically, responsive to external

---

[26]   John Locke, "A Third Letter Concerning Toleration," in *The Works of John Locke, Vol. 6* (London: Thomas Tegg, 1823 [1692]), pp. 141–546, esp. 212.

[27]   Locke, "Third Letter," 144.

force.[28] Moreover, Waldron argues persuasively that Locke seems to ignore the "epistemic apparatus" that surrounds and supports belief formation such as intellectual materials made available to the understanding.[29] These emphatically are open to influence by the state through censorship of books and propaganda supporting an official teaching.

These practical objections to Locke's account of the epistemological basis of belief echo Proast's claim that moderate penalties can effectively be applied to dissenters to force them to reconsider the errors of their nonconformity.[30] However, the fundamental theoretical problem with Locke's argument is its apparent consequentialist logic. The argument for the irrationality of persecution does not rest on a right of conscience, but rather relates solely to claims about the functional limits of civil power. But what if persecution can be shown to change belief? Would it still be wrong? Even if existing governments in the seventeenth century are unable to alter belief, might not future governments be able to do so with the enhanced instruments of social control and mass psychology available to the modern state? Moreover, how would one measure "sincerity" of belief? In lieu of any convincing formulation of a natural right of conscience, a moral duty of toleration, or even a more sophisticated utilitarian argument about societal progress and human flourishing,[31] on its own Locke's argument for the irrationality of persecution reduces to a matter of unavoidably contestable and contextually bound empirical observation.

There are similar problems with Locke's skepticism argument. Once again, Proast clarified this issue by challenging Locke to answer whether the moral and epistemological rationale of toleration applied when the national church is objectively the "true religion."[32] This effective polemical strategy sought to force Locke into the awkward position of having either to deny the possibility of any religious truth, and thus being subject to the

---

[28] J. A. Passmore, "Locke and the Ethics of Belief," in *Locke*, Vere Chappell, ed. (Oxford: Oxford University Press, 1998), pp. 279–299, esp. 279–283. Vernon suggests that Locke's point is not that belief is entirely free of voluntarist aspects, but rather that religious belief is not as amenable to coercion as other ideas and forms of behavior (Richard Vernon, *The Career of Toleration: John Locke, Jonas Proast, and After* [Montreal: McGill-Queen's University Press, 1997], pp. 28–29).

[29] Jeremy Waldron, "Locke: Toleration and the Rationality of Persecution," in *Justifying Toleration*, Susan Mendus, ed. (Cambridge: Cambridge University Press, 1988), pp. 61–86, esp. 82. See also Paul Bou-Habib, "Locke, Sincerity and the Rationality of Persecution" *Political Studies*, 51, 4 (December 2003): 611–626.

[30] Locke, "Third Letter," 242–243.

[31] See, for instance, John Stuart Mill, "On Liberty," in *The Basic Writings of John Stuart Mill* (New York: Modern Library, 2002 [1859]), pp. 17–76.

[32] Locke, "Third Letter," 219.

popular stigma of complete skepticism or even atheism, or to deny only the truth of the Church of England in particular (and any other extant church) and thus implicitly concede that a hypothetical "true religion" may indeed be entitled to be intolerant because, in principle, there would be no rational grounds to question the validity of its truth claims. Caught between denying the possibility of any religious truth available to human reason, on the one hand, and admitting the intrinsic value of intolerance in the exceptional or optimal case of a true religion, on the other, Locke predictably sought refuge in the folds of his other arguments asserting the impracticality and immorality of persecution. However, even the possibility of a more thoroughgoing skepticism than Locke will admit has the potential to deflate his contention that toleration presupposes truth claims of the individual deserving moral respect by the government. Does the principle of toleration depend ontologically speaking on the very possibility of truth Locke's argument seems to undermine?

Locke's contractualist argument seems to avoid this problem by replacing absolute considerations of truth and falsity with the distinct and seductive logic of legitimacy rooted in consent. However, Proast's objection still applies in a somewhat different form. The argument that it is irrational to consent to one's potential persecution for religious reasons seems to depend on a specific conception of the consequences of skepticism. Skepticism can also, of course, lead to authoritarian conclusions. For instance, could an individual not consent to the creation of an intolerant national religion on the logical ground that one can legitimately authorize one's own future persecution, if one should later dissent? Why is it intrinsically irrational to consent to be potentially coerced by another agent when the other agent has no better, but also no less, chance of discovering the "true religion" than I do? The individual could authorize government to make and enforce laws relating to religion out of a concern for public peace and order, and herein produce no arbitrary injury to the rights of others who presumably consent to government on identical terms.[33] This is precisely what the individual does in the transition from the state of nature to civil society when he or she authorizes a whole range of punishments for violating civil law. Given Locke's account of the inherent mysteries in the lottery of eternal life and his skepticism about any religion's claim to the whole truth, there appears

[33] As is well known, twenty-five years prior to the *Letter*, Locke made a similar argument against toleration in the *Two Tracts of Government* (John Locke, *The Two Tracts of Government*, Philip Abrams, ed. (Cambridge: Cambridge University Press, 1967 [1661]) that displayed the powerful influence of Hobbes. See, for instance, Thomas Hobbes, *Leviathan*, Edwin Curley, ed. (Indianapolis: Hackett, 1994 [1651]), pp. 113, 188.

to be no logical reason that necessarily precludes the rational individual from delegating to government authoritative decisions about religion. In order to demonstrate not only that government is incapable of altering belief, but in addition that it is logically and morally prohibited from even attempting to do so, Locke would need to show how the essential properties of the political realm differ from the epistemological and theological premises of the institutional expression of religious belief. That is to say, the liberal idea of the state based on consent required a new philosophical account of the church.

The problems with Locke's final argument for toleration, namely that intolerance is incompatible with Christianity, are fairly obvious. To start, the proper interpretation of Christianity and the church is precisely what is at issue between Locke and opponents of toleration. How can Locke's argument be anything other than an arbitrary interpretation of Christianity, especially since evidence for this interpretation may require extensive theological reflection largely absent in the *Letter*? Moreover, by limiting toleration to Christian principles, Locke undermines the possibility of a natural right of conscience with universal validity. Why should non-Christians embrace toleration if it is not part of their religious duty? The deeper problem with this argument, however, is that it does little to inform us about what Locke means by a church or how the nature of a church differs from civil government. Thus, on the one hand, Locke's claim that the true church supports toleration is on its face perhaps the most contestable aspect of his toleration argument. Yet, it is also possibly the most important argument of them all because if Locke can demonstrate that there is something in the nature of religion and the church that excludes the very possibility of their legal expression or makes such expression unintelligible, the problematic features of the arguments from consent, skepticism, and the irrationality of persecution lose much of their political salience.

THE PROBLEM OF A NATIONAL CHURCH

In the historical and intellectual context of seventeenth-century England, Locke's various arguments for toleration are united by the theoretical requirements of a response to the problem posed to his account of religious belief by the idea of an intolerant national church. The central issue animating the *Letter* and the extended polemic between Locke and Proast that followed was the legal establishment of religion. In Locke's view, this is the classic form of the theologico-political problem, which sees the fusion of religion and politics under civil supremacy. While Locke objects to the notion of a national church because it "jumbles Heaven and Earth together" in an "unhappy Agreement" of intolerant religion and authoritarian politics (33, 55), he is clear that the core of the problem is political control and misuse of religion. At its most basic level, Locke traces the theologico-political problem back to its psychological roots in the natural desire for "Power and Empire" (23).[34] The "Spirit of Persecution" and the establishment of religion are thus inseparable for Locke precisely because they derive from the same origin in the natural economy of the human passions.

The politicization of religion is a theme not only in Locke's toleration writings, but also famously in the *Two Treatises of Government* in the Preface of which he singles out elements of the Anglican clergy, "the Drum Ecclesiastick," for blame as the chief proponents of divine right monarchy in England.[35] For Locke, the essence of the theologico-political problem is not the fragmentation of authority caused by sectarianism, but rather the consolidation of religion and politics in absolutist government. The source of the problem, which Locke seeks to correct in the *Letters*, is that neither the church nor government has hitherto been properly defined. The liberal idea of the state based on consent corresponds with a new definition of the church.

In terms of its intellectual basis, Locke presents the idea of the church properly defined as the product of a unique historical moment in which the original promise of Christianity finally comes to fruition with modern natural rights philosophy. However, Locke's genetic account or his natural history of religion and the church tells a very different story. He claims that prior to Christianity, political control of religion was the natural human condition. For example, among the ancient pagans, religion meant simply the encouragement of superstition and empty rituals by priests who served their political masters by employing religion to support civil law, and thus "tie men together in subjection" (RC 238, 241). The regime produced by the Mosaic Law, Locke identifies as an "absolute theocracy" (44) of which the political teaching, as opposed to the purely moral teaching, holds no obligation for Christians (RC 22–3). For Locke, it is only with the coming of Christ that the principle of separating religion and politics first appeared.[36]

---

[34] Recall Locke's account of the psychological roots of the desire to dominate expressed in early childhood (see John Locke, *Some Thoughts Concerning Education*, Ruth W. Grant and Nathan Tarcov, eds. [Indianapolis: Hackett Publishing, 1996], p. 76).

[35] Locke, *Two Treatises*, "Preface," p. 138. See also II: 92.

[36] Joshua Mitchell, "John Locke and the Theological Foundations of Liberal Toleration: A Christian Dialectic of History" *The Review of Politics*, 52, 1 (Winter 1990): 64–83, esp. 71–73.

He insists that the antinomian character of the early church is vouchsafed by Scripture, which requires neither a particular church structure nor a specific form of civil government (29, 56).[37] For Locke, the Gospel indicates that there is "no such thing as a Christian Commonwealth" (44). The Christian church in its earliest and, Locke insists, truest form is simply a loosely associated group of believers united by a few simple articles of faith and worship.

The development of Christianity is then largely the story of hardening orthodoxy and the absorption of the church into authoritarian political structures. For Locke, the historical Catholic Church embodied the loss of primitive Christianity with the establishment of hierarchy, the consolidation of dogma, and the political pretensions of the doctrine of papal plenitude of power.[38] The Reformation is philosophically and theologically more interesting for Locke because of its ambiguous legacy. On the one hand, Locke praises reformed religion for its unique insights about human freedom, especially the primacy of individual conscience. Moreover, Locke recognizes a semblance of early Christianity in the preference of many Protestants sects for doctrinal simplicity and the emphasis on faith (56). On the other hand, Protestantism in the erastian form represented by his opponents, such as Proast, produced a fusion of religion and politics even more rigorous than Catholicism because it held the principle that every country has the right to establish its own national church as one of the great achievements of the Reformation.[39] It is against these conceptions of the church that Locke set his sights in the *Letters*.

---

[37] Eldon Eisenach, *Two Worlds of Liberalism* (Chicago: University of Chicago Press, 1981), p. 77.

[38] See, for instance, John Locke, "Catholic Infallibility," in *Political Essays*, Mark Goldie, ed. (Cambridge: Cambridge University Press, 1997 [1675]), pp. 226–230.

[39] Locke, "Third Letter," 220–221. While it is beyond the scope of the present study to provide a historical account of the development of Locke's ideas on toleration or to offer a definitive statement on his attitude towards the Church of England, it is fair to say that my reading largely follows that of Gordon Schochet ("John Locke and Religious Toleration," in *The Revolution of 1688–89*, Lois Schwoerer, ed. [Cambridge: Cambridge University Press, 1992], pp. 147–164, esp. 148) who sees Locke's argument as fundamentally hostile to the established Church of England, and is thus contrary to others who see Locke supporting the idea of a latitudinarian national church (David McCabe, "John Locke and the Argument against Strict Separation" *The Review of Politics*, 59, 2 [Spring 1997]: 233–258), or as Harris puts it, Locke's "erastianism without tears" (Ian Harris, *The Mind of John Locke* [Cambridge: Cambridge University Press, 1994], p. 163). For a remarkable account of the development of Locke's idea of toleration and his complex attitude toward the Church of England, see John Marshall, *John Locke: Resistance, Religion, and Responsibility* (Cambridge: Cambridge University Press, 1994).

Locke defines a church as "a voluntary society of men, joining themselves together of their own accord, in order to the publick worshipping of God, in such manner as they judge acceptable to him, and effectual to the Salvation of their Souls" (28). Given the "free and voluntary" nature of this society, Locke insists: "Nobody is born a member of any Church" (28). Remarkably, Locke claims that church discipline, articles of faith, and forms of worship derive from the same voluntary principles as the rules governing any other association such as a learned society or a chamber of commerce. As members of "absolutely free and spontaneous" societies, church members are free to join or leave at their own volition (29).

This definition of a church is a striking departure from traditional understandings. One such view, which Locke identifies explicitly in the *Letter*, is the conception of a church as a "Convention of Clergy-men making Canons" (37). The underlying premise of this definition is that the church is a divinely constituted organization. Not surprisingly this is the fundamental assumption of Locke's opponents in the toleration debate and a position with considerable pedigree in the history of the Church of England. Anglican authorities of no less stature than Hooker, Cranmer, and Bishop Overall's *Convocation Book* spoke of the divine grace that binds the church into "one mystical body of Christ" under Episcopal government.[40] The theoretical and practical implications of this conception of the church are manifold. First, in contrast to Locke, it asserts that church structure and discipline are divinely established rather than the product of voluntary agreement. Second, it stigmatizes any serious dissent as heresy or schism, the suppression of which by government becomes practically a moral duty. In this venerable conception of the Church, civil government represents the temporal sword of God's church on Earth.

Locke is careful, however, to distinguish his voluntary conception of the church from the form of congregationalism familiar to his seventeenth-century English audience. He presents the church properly understood not as a particular species of independent sectarian belief, but rather as the logical outgrowth from modern natural rights philosophy. Locke's voluntary church is thus at least in part deduced from a natural rights-based conception of civil government deprived of direct supervision over religion. He defines "Civil Interests" as "Life, Liberty, Health, and Indolency of Body; and the Possession of outward things, such as Money, Lands, Houses, Furniture and the like" (26). The distinction between civil and religious interests relates both to their different purpose or end and to their

---

[40] Harris, *Mind of Locke*, 165–167.

differing origins. For Locke, civil government cannot extend to concern for "the Salvation of Souls" (26) because this is not one of the purposes for which individuals consent to government. This argument rests on the twin assumptions that individuals do not need civil government to assist in salvation and that the speculative opinions of others constitute no conceivable harm against which one would sensibly intend government to provide. While voluntary national churches may be compatible with natural rights, Locke indicates that intolerant national churches clearly do not logically deduce from individuals in the state of nature.

Locke charges that proponents of religious uniformity fail to recognize differentiated forms of association. Proast, for instance, argued that civil government is instituted for the sake of a good end, and since eternal life is a good end, the responsibilities of civil government must include promoting the true religion that will secure the possibility of eternal life for its members.[41] Locke assails Proast's assertion of the architectonic character of civil government on several fronts. First, with characteristic skepticism he challenges the assumption of any government's claim to comprehensive religious knowledge: "Neither the right, nor the Art of Ruling, does necessarily carry along with it certain knowledge of other things; and least of all of the true religion" (36). More importantly, however, Locke attacks the false premises of Proast's conception of undifferentiated power: "By which account there will be no difference between church and state, commonwealth and army, between a family and the East India Company; all of which have hitherto been thought distinct sorts of societies, instituted for different ends."[42] Every association may be directed to a certain notion of the good, but they are not all directed to the same good, otherwise "one end of the family must be to preach the Gospel."

Locke claims that the notion of a national church is problematic both theologically and logically. As a theological question, he appeals to the antinomian character of the Gospels and the original Christian community to support his contention that "religion established by law is a pretty odd way of speaking in the mouth of a Christian."[43] The logical difficulty of any national church – including a voluntary one – lies in the problem of collapsing distinct interests with their own unique properties into a disarticulated

[41] Locke, "Third Letter," 216.
[42] Locke, "Third Letter," 216. As Vernon (*Career*, 14) observes, with this argument Locke cleverly exposes how seriously Proast's logic endangers the integrity of the church he means to defend. How precisely the "true church" could resist the pretensions of a bad or even hostile ruler such as James II, Proast never adequately explains.
[43] Locke, "Third Letter," 227.

expression of raw power that "Jumbles together Heaven and Earth" (33). However, the principle of a legally established religion that compels uniformity not only constitutes a denial of the voluntary character of a genuine church, it also fails to identify the true nature of law. Salvation is an end beyond the competence of legislation, and thus the formal claims of an established church are essentially just the political interests of a dominant faction trying to justify the persecution of opponents under the veil of law. Intolerant national churches violate the civic principle of impartial execution and equal application of law, so central to Locke's idea of constitutional government, precisely because they are nothing more than "established sects under the specious names of national churches."[44] As Michael Walzer astutely observes, with his definition Locke condemns all churches to a sectarian existence.[45]

Whereas Locke's account of the different purposes or ends of civil government and churches has received much attention, his consideration of their distinct "Original" has typically received less focus.[46] The reason is most likely because on the face of it, Locke's church and civil government appear to have the same original, namely in the consent of individuals. However, while Locke elsewhere defines civil government as a "voluntary association" (II: 102, 173; 1823: 212), in the crucial passages in the *Letter* relating to the definition of a church he reserves this designation for churches and omits any reference to the consensual origin of civil interests.[47] While both churches and civil government originate in consent, Locke subtly suggests that they may represent distinct forms of voluntary agreement the differences of which hold important implications for church-state relations.

Civil society, according to Locke, is a voluntary agreement by which individuals leave the "loose state of nature" and form one distinct body governed by a legislature set apart from the "great and natural Community" of humanity (II: 211, 128). The sole purpose for which individuals surrender their natural power to execute the law of nature and submit to civil law is for the "mutual Preservation of their Lives, Liberties, and Estates" (II: 123).

---

44 Locke, "Third Letter," 239.
45 Michael Walzer, *Toleration* (New Haven: Yale University Press 1997), p. 81.
46 Notable exceptions are Waldron, *God, Locke and Equality*, 211–213; Harris, *Mind of Locke*, 185–190; Ian Harris, "Tolérance, église et état chez Locke." *Les fondements philosophiques de la tolerance en France et en Angleterre au xviie siècle, 3 vols.* Yves Charles Zarka, Franck Lessay, John Rogers, eds. (Paris: Presses Universitaires de France, 2002). Vol. 1: 175–218; and Judd Owen, *Religion and the Demise of Liberal Rationalism* (Chicago: University of Chicago Press, 2001), p. 157.
47 Compare Locke II: 102, 173 and Locke, "Third Letter," 212 with the *Letter*, 26 and 28. See also Waldron, *God, Locke and Equality*, 211.

The form and substance of consent operating with churches is rather different. According to Locke, the epistemological basis of faith means that salvation is not the kind of interest for which an individual requires civil government to secure. His claim that individuals who lack a common legislature are still in a state of nature "however associated" (II: 87) suggests that churches may, like families, be the kind of association that preexists and survives independently of civil government. This does not, of course, mean that protection from injury directed against oneself because of religion may not be one of the reasons an individual would consent to the protection of laws. Rather Locke's major theoretical point is that the difference between the operation of consent in religion and in political society lies in the distinct character of the rights to which each properly relates.

The distinct political and religious dimensions of Locke's rights theory are evident in his account of the forfeiture of natural rights and his theory of political obligation. Perhaps the two most important Lockean natural rights for our purposes are the "right of conscience" (51, 55) and the right of "Self-preservation" (I: 86). Locke argues that the right of self-preservation is inalienable; however, it can be forfeited both in the state of nature and in civil society due to actions punishable under the law of nature (II: 10, 11, 16, 23–4). Civil government is created by individuals to ensure self-preservation, but this form of consent includes an implicit recognition that the right of self-preservation may be forfeited to civil governments, which he insists must have had transferred to them a "Right of making Laws with Penalties of Death" (II: 3). Clearly Locke's idea of the rationality of consent includes acceptance of the right to be punished, even to the point of death, under a law to which one freely submits. Strikingly Locke presents no parallel discussion of the forfeiture of the right of conscience. Criminals may be legitimately deprived of their life and even be reduced to a form of slavery sanctioned by the law of nature (II: 23–4), but apparently even the greatest malefactors may not be stripped of their right to hold a certain faith or to belong to any church that will accept them. Locke never so much as hints that consent to government logically or morally includes the juridical possibility of a forfeiture of the right of conscience. Thus, in the complex structure of Locke's rights theory, the right of conscience appears to be even more durable than the right to life itself.

The political implications of Locke's nonforfeitable right of conscience can be seen in the differing notions of rational consent underlying his accounts of political obligation and religious communion. In one sense, the voluntary basis of the church and civil government produces an identical result, namely that one is not born into either (26; II: 113). Locke admits, however, that political obligation may arise in one of two ways, either by express or tacit consent. Tacit consent means that by accepting an inheritance or enjoying the protection of property, one tacitly consents to the authority of the government that regulates the property in that territory (II: 117, 120, 122). Whereas one's express consent typically cannot be reversed (II: 121), Locke insists that individuals may withdraw tacit consent and end their political obligation by leaving the territory in which they reside. However, individuals cannot take their landed property with them because commonwealths cannot permit "any part of their dominions to be dismembered" (II: 117) as a result of the cessation of individual political obligation. The Lockean theory of political obligation thus produces considerable legal and normative restraints on individual freedom depending on the type of consent and the nature of the institution involved.

In contrast, the "spontaneous" nature of church membership is immune from any association with tacit consent and it most emphatically includes an unconditional right of secession. A church may excommunicate whomever it chooses; however, Locke asserts that no church can compel individuals to remain in it when they no longer believe simply for fear of losing their property (28). Locke hereby severs the normative connection between faith and civil law assumed by those defenders of religious uniformity who supported the civil punishment of nonconformity. Freed from the structural and logical constraints placed on political obligation by the issue of property, the church is more purely voluntary and hence arguably a freer association than political society. Locke's idea of religious communion thus reflects more radical individualist principles than even his theory of political obligation can allow.

How then does Locke's account of the differing forms of consent in civil government and the churches respond to the counterargument about the consensual basis of national churches famously proposed by Thomas Hobbes and advanced by Locke's early work on toleration? In the *Two Treatises*, Locke acknowledges a broad scope for prudential or utilitarian considerations with respect to the consensual basis of government, especially as these considerations help explain the transition from the state of nature to civil society. However, by restricting the institutionalization of religious faith to churches lacking civil power, Locke's toleration writings indicate that one of his fundamental theoretical aims was to distinguish the intellectual and volitional dimensions of consent. It is by virtue of the intellectual or epistemological, as opposed to purely volitional, aspect of consent that Locke sets stricter limits than does Hobbes with respect to what individuals can legitimately consent to in forming civil society.[48] However, Locke also proposes that the constitutive dynamic of rational consent involves both a range of degrees of forfeiture, and in addition a complex interaction of intellectual and volitional faculties operative in distinct ways in the formation of churches and civil governments. It is the unique intellectual properties of consent in its religious aspect that provides the Lockean church with its most characteristic features.

RELIGION AND MORALITY IN THE *REASONABLENESS*

In order to understand the intellectual foundation of the Lockean church, we need to consider the rationalist theological principles Locke proposed as the basis of voluntary religious association. Central to this rational theology is the relation between his arguments in the *Essay Concerning Human Understanding* and the *Reasonableness of Christianity* about the noetic properties of faith and how faith informs both religion and morality. Locke's rational theology hinges on the way faith relates to knowledge on the one hand and to works on the other. As we have seen in the *Essay*, Locke deals with the relation of faith and knowledge by advancing the idea that given the intrinsic limits of human understanding, religious beliefs can never be knowledge, which is deduced from "self-evident" propositions and is capable of demonstration, but rather must be understood to be an "assurance of faith" based on the probabilities of judgment to which the mind gives a range of degrees of assent: "This is the highest the nature of the thing will permit us to go in matters of revealed religion, which are therefore called matters of faith: a persuasion of our minds, short of knowledge, is the last result that determines us in such truths."[49] Faith is thus distinct from knowledge because of the very stringent epistemological standard Locke sets for what constitutes knowledge. He emphatically does not sever faith from reason; indeed they are inseparable.[50] Locke's basic assumption is that salvation is properly the subject of rational examination by the religious believer, even as the conclusions of faith can never be more than the products of fallible human capacities.

This rationalist account of faith in the *Essay* provides the proper context necessary for approaching Locke's treatment in the *Reasonableness* of the relation of faith and works to salvation. The nature of this relation was,

[48] See Alex Tuckness, *Locke and the Legislative Point of View* (Princeton: Princeton University Press, 2002), pp. 76–77.
[49] Locke, "Third Letter," 144 and E 4.15.2–4.654–656.
[50] Forster, *Moral Consensus*, 85.

of course, one of the great questions dividing early modern Christianity not only between Catholics and Protestants, but also among the various Protestant sects and national churches. While Locke clearly distinguishes faith and works, the underlying thrust of his argument is to unify the diverse elements of Christianity in a common ideational framework by bridging the chasm between the extremes of justification by faith alone on the one hand and of works on the other. He does so by consistently blurring the distinction between the morality of works and the beliefs required for salvation. Locke claims that the central article of faith that unites all Christians is the belief that Christ is the Messiah who came to bring salvation (RC 26–7). In this minimalist creed, eternal life is the core of Christianity, much as the mind's assent to the evidence of Christ's miracles is one of the necessary elements of salvation. He emphasizes the egalitarian implications of this conception of Christianity, which he calls a religion suited to "the apprehensions of the vulgar, and mass of mankind," remarkably even identifying miracles like the resurrection as "matters of fact, which they can without difficulty conceive" (RC 241, 243).[51] Locke also stresses that belief in Christ's Messiaship is the only article of faith that is absolutely required by scripture in order to make one a Christian; practically all the other articles of faith propounded by the various churches and sects one may "disbelieve without danger to his salvation" (RC 251).

With this doctrinal minimalism at its core, it is not hard to conceive of Locke's argument for toleration extending far beyond latitudinarianism and mere comprehension in the Church of England. Here he embraces a vision of Christianity that for all intents and purposes strips the notion of heresy of any political significance.[52] If, as Locke claims, heresy is a division over "opinions not contained in the express words of Scripture (56)," then practically every extant Christian church is heretical insofar as they all add articles of faith or forms of worship not expressly stated in the Gospel. For Locke, moral vice relates primarily to action rather than beliefs or errors in understanding precisely because the beliefs required for salvation are so basic.

---

[51] For some of the problems with Locke's account of the apprehensibility of miracles, see Michael Rabieh, "The Reasonableness of Locke, or the Questionableness of Christianity" *The Journal of Politics*, 53, 4 (November 1991): 933–957, esp. 950–951 and Michael Zuckert "John Locke and the Problem of Civil Religion," in *The Moral Foundations of the American Republic*, 3rd ed., Robert H. Horwitz, ed. (Charlottesville: University Press of Virginia, 1986), pp. 181–203, esp. 198.

[52] Sanford Kessler, "John Locke's Legacy of Religious Freedom" *Polity*, 17, 3 (Spring 1985): 484–503, esp. 488–490.

The centrality of faith does not, however, reduce the importance of works. Locke states definitively: "Faith without works is not sufficient for salvation" (RC 179). The problem of extreme fideism is the attendant lack of concern for morality.[53] Locke draws scriptural support for the value of works in the "moral part of Moses' Law," as well as in Christ's works and calls for repentance in the Gospel (RC 23, 166–72). The "standing law of works" is "knowable by reason" and thus obliges not only Christians, but rather "all men everywhere" (RC 23). While the "law of faith" compensates for human frailty that makes us unable to offer perfect obedience to the "law of works," Locke nonetheless insists that good works are an essential part of salvation: "All the places where Our Saviour mentions the last judgment…everywhere the sentence follows, doing or not doing; without any mention of believing, or not believing" (RC 227). Locke's point is that Christianity properly understood is deeply concerned with morality and supports the purpose of civil society by encouraging right conduct towards others. Toleration then is perfectly intelligible as, although not simply reducible to, a quasi-religious duty flowing from the moral injunction to show "Charity, Meekness, and Goodwill in general towards all mankind" (23). In his effort to account for the importance of both faith and works, Locke's natural theology interprets toleration as a universally recognizable morally good work rather than a sectarian article of faith.

The political implications of Locke's argument about religious support for morality are made apparent in his account of the problem of ancient ethics. Among the ancients, Locke claims the "superstitious and idolatrous rites" of religion were generally "distinguished from and preferred to virtue" (RC 241, 245). Only among a few philosophers, "the rational and thinking part of mankind," did the "spark of divine nature" uncover the rational basis of morality (RC 238, 231). However, Locke insists that ancient ethical theory failed to produce a firm foundation for morality for two primary reasons. First, even these few philosophers were unable to determine the full extent of moral duties and were spectacularly unsuccessful at teaching virtue to the superstitious many prone to manipulation by their religious and political leaders (RC 241–2). Second, and more importantly, the ancient philosophers were unable on the basis of reason alone to deduce the real source of moral obligation. The moral philosophy of the

---

[53]   This is exemplified for Locke by the orthodox Calvinist ideas of predestination and original sin, which he claims "shook the foundations of all religion" by condemning untold millions "to eternal infinite punishment" regardless of their good behavior (RC 1). As Stanton observes, Locke's natural theology also dramatically minimizes the significance of original sin and the Fall (see Timothy Stanton, "Locke and the Politics and Theology of Toleration" *Political Studies*, 54, 1 [March 2006]: 84–102, esp. 97).

ancients, "however excellent," showed "the beauty of virtue" but left it "unendowed" (RC 242, 245). They viewed "laudable practices" as functions of character or in terms of social utility, but they could not explain the intrinsic connection between virtue and happiness, on the one hand, and individual and common good, on the other (RC 243). Lacking any notion of a divine "lawgiver" who knows all private thoughts and sees all actions, and who has the power to dispense eternal punishments and rewards, the ancient philosophers could not demonstrate convincingly why individuals should act morally in all cases, even when it is against one's calculated temporal self-interest to do so. The heart of the problem, according to Locke, is that the ancients had no clear notion of an afterlife (RC 245). The chief moral significance of Christianity then is the promulgation of a clear "doctrine of a future state" and divine judgment that is apprehensible and persuasive to a wide range of intellects. For Locke, eternal life is the great "encouragement for virtue" and "upon this foundation, and upon this only, morality stands firm" (RC 245).

What implications does the Christian revelation about the afterlife have for the possibility of establishing a rational system of ethics as ancient philosophy sought to do? On the face of it, Locke's response is that the implications are enormous. In one of the most striking passages in the entire *Reasonableness*, Locke declares:

> The greatest part of mankind want leisure or capacity for demonstration, nor can carry a train of proofs, which in that way they must always depend for conviction, and cannot be required to assent to till they see the demonstration...And you may as soon hope to have all the day-labourers and tradesmen, the spinsters and dairymaids, perfect mathematicians, as to have them perfect in ethics this way: hearing plain commands, is the sure and only course to bring them to obedience and practice. The greatest part cannot know, and therefore they must believe (RC 243).

This passage has occasioned great interest among Locke scholars striving to grasp his understanding of the relation between religion and morality. Much of this attention revolves around two issues. First, some such as Waldron argue that Locke's admission that the "greatest part" cannot know moral truth and thus must believe indicates a partial retreat from his earlier promises about the possibility of demonstrative morality in the *Essay*. In this view, Locke's "pessimism" about the efficacy of reason in the *Reasonableness* reflects his gradual, and perhaps reluctant, admission that philosophy is incapable on the basis of unassisted reason of establishing either the content or source of obligation of the moral law.[54] Others extrapolate

---

54 Waldron, *God, Locke and Equality*, 99.

from this a discontinuity between the *Essay* and *Reasonableness* that raises doubts as to the compatibility of the *Essay* and the *Reasonableness* in Locke's larger philosophic project.[55] A second interpretive model drawn from this passage is that of MacPherson who finds in Locke's disparaging remarks about the rational capacities of "day-labourers and tradesmen" a deeper teaching about differential rationality among the classes.[56] In this view, Locke's elitist assumptions about the vast cognitive gulf between the rational few (bourgeois property owners) and the irrational many (propertyless masses) makes a mockery of his formal commitment to equality and natural rights.

Both of these interpretations raise important questions about the purpose and coherence of Locke's teaching on religion and thus require some attention. First, to Locke's presumed elitism. It is well known that one of the central planks in MacPherson's theory of possessive individualism was his claim that Locke believed that there existed a deep and politically relevant intellectual inequality between the "Industrious and Rational " economic elites and the idle, "Quarrelsome," and we might add irrational, propertyless masses (II: 34). Locke's account of the relation between religion and morality in the *Reasonableness* thus seems to be perfect grist for MacPherson's mill. Reflecting on the hypocrisy of Locke's rational religion, MacPherson argues:

Locke's point is that without supernatural sanctions the labouring class is incapable of following a rationalist ethic. He only wants the sanctions made clearer. The simple articles he recommends are not moral rules, they are articles of faith. They are to be believed.[57]

From this MacPherson concludes that "Locke assumed in his own society a class differential in rationality which left the labouring classes incapable of a fully rational life, i.e. incapable of ordering their lives by the law of nature or reason."[58]

---

55 John Dunn, *The Political Thought of John Locke* (Cambridge: Cambridge University Press, 1969), p. 192. It should be noted that Waldron tries to distinguish Locke's "pessimism" in the *Reasonableness* from the issue of the discontinuity between this work and the *Essay*. He claims rather implausibly that the pessimism he detects in the *Reasonableness* is "adumbrated" in the *Essay* (*God, Locke and Equality*, 99). But the passages he cites in the *Essay* relating to Locke's concerns about the difficulty involved in correct moral reasoning do not speak to Locke's claims about the theoretical or logical possibility of demonstrative morality, only its practical applicability.

56 C. B. MacPherson, *The Political Theory of Possessive Individualism: Hobbes to Locke* (Oxford: Oxford University Press, 1964), pp. 194–262.

57 MacPherson, *Possessive Individualism*, 225.

58 MacPherson, *Possessive Individualism*, 232.

This is a curious misreading of Locke's intention in the *Reasonableness*, in which MacPherson gives both too much and too little weight to Locke's claims about rational morality. He gives it too little in the sense that he greatly understates the importance Locke attached to revelation as an instrument of faith the significance of which transcends classes. Locke insists that one of the surest indicators of the divine source of the gospels is the capacity for its message to resonate with a variety of classes and human types: "As it suits the lowest capacities of reasonable creatures, so it reaches and satisfies, nay enlightens the highest" (RC 243).[59] Moreover, Locke's actions in his own life belie MacPherson's suspicions about his religious sincerity as there is plenty of evidence suggesting that Locke expended a great deal of his own philosophic energies trying to expound the meaning of scripture.[60] MacPherson also gives rather short shrift to some of the astonishingly egalitarian features of Locke's account of religion. For example, Locke insists that the deepest mysteries of Christianity are intelligible to the faithful precisely because their cognitive requirements are so basic. Christianity, Locke claims, is a religion suited to the "vulgar capacities" of the uneducated masses. But as we know from Locke's account of the epistemological grounds of faith, his point here is not to diminish Christianity's profundity. Rather he means to reaffirm the distinction between knowledge and belief. As Locke presents it, the Gospels derive their authority in the following manner: Once the individual is persuaded that Christ was sent by God, then "all his commands become principles," and thus one only needs "but to read the inspired books to be instructed; all the duties of morality lie there clear and plain, and easy to be understood" (RC 243).

But how, according to Locke, does one become convinced that Christ was sent by God? By the evidence of Christ's miracles in Scripture: "The healing of the sick, the restoring of sight to the blind by a word, the raising, and being raised from the dead, are matters of fact, which they can *without difficulty conceive*" (RC 243, emphasis added). Needless to say, this is an astonishing claim on Locke's part. To maintain that the resurrection is intelligible to the "ordinariest apprehension" is in one sense clearly to deny the traditional Christian teaching about the need for divine grace

---

[59] Even MacPherson begrudgingly concedes that "Locke was, of course, recommending the simplified Christianity for all classes" (*Possessive Individualism*, 225). See also Wolterstorff, *Ethics of Belief*, 147–148.

[60] In addition to his extended scriptural exegesis in the *First Treatise*, the *Reasonableness* and the various *Letters Concerning Toleration*, there is also the vast and uncompleted *Paraphrases and Notes on the Epistles of St. Paul*, which consumed the latter years of Locke's life.

as the vital supplement to belief. We would perhaps expect, following MacPherson's lead, that Locke would declare that the mystery of the resurrection is beyond reason and thus purely a matter of faith. However, this is not exactly what Locke does. Rather he assumes that regarding its basic cognitive elements, the resurrection is, epistemologically speaking, child's play. In order to understand the moral significance of Christ's resurrection, one need only be able to understand the distinction between "sick and well, lame and sound, dead and alive" (RC 243). *Pace* MacPherson, what is most striking about Locke's treatment of rational religion is the extent to which he is willing to minimize the intellectual requirements for apprehending the deepest mysteries of faith. Locke leaves us to wonder why even the "vulgar" masses ever needed the Gospels at all.

In another sense, MacPherson places too much weight on Locke's claims about rational religion. He assumes that Locke expected the industrious, propertied few to live by a rationalist ethic almost effortlessly because Locke's rational religion amounted to being basically a celebration of bourgeois virtues they already possess. However, Locke's treatment of religion is more skeptical than this. He excoriates the intellectual laziness of privileged elites who are particularly vulnerable to the illusion of moral self-sufficiency. With logic familiar to us from Locke's pedagogical approach in the *Conduct of the Understanding*, he worries that those familiar with Christian revelation "from the cradle" are prone to minimize the difficulty involved in fully understanding these moral truths. Locke compares the complacent believer to a traveler on the road who:

Applauds his own strength and legs, that have carried him so far in such a scantling of time, and ascribes all to his own vigour, little considering how much he owes to their plans, who cleared the woods, drained the bogs, built the bridges and made the ways passable (RC 243).

On one level, this simply reaffirms the problem of ancient philosophy's effort to produce rational ethics and highlights the moral advantages for a Christian people. However, the similarity in tone and imagery to Locke's description of his own philosophic activity in the "Epistle" to the *Essay* is unmistakable.[61] Christian moral philosophers – the intellectual elites in European society – are as much the target of Locke's attack as anybody precisely because they take scripture for granted without examining it before the bar of reason as fully as they ought.[62] It is this lack of probity

---

[61] There Locke described himself as an intellectual "Under-Labourer" whose job was to clear the "Rubbish" on the road to knowledge.

[62] Waldron, *God, Locke, and Equality*, 106.

that makes them prone to zealotry, partisanship, sectarianism, and passion for persecution. Contrary to MacPherson's argument, among those Locke thought desperately needed a rationalized account of faith, the elites were not exempt.

When we turn to the argument of those who identify a palpable "pessimism" in the *Reasonableness* about the prospects for rational morality, a different set of interpretive problems emerge. It is suggested that evidence for Locke's pessimism lies in his admission that prior to Christ, natural reason was only ever able to produce "defective" morality. The variety of contradictory moral rules across sects and nations derived from the fact that in absence of Scripture, natural reason was unable on its own to form a clear and distinct idea of a lawgiver God who rewards and punishes in the afterlife. Even if the existence of God is theoretically demonstrable, the certainty that God is concerned with morality is not, and thus "Philosophy spent its strength" in a futile effort to ground a system of morality lacking divine support (RC 243). This interpretation of the *Reasonableness* raises two fundamental issues relating to both the content and the presentation of Scripture.

As to the content, Waldron argues that Locke's partial withdrawal from his earlier optimism about rational morality in the *Essay* indicates Locke's recognition that there is no way to uncover the basis of morality apart from Scripture: "There is no philosophical demonstration of morality."[63] For proof, Waldron appeals to Locke's own words:

Experience shows that the knowledge of morality, by mere natural light (how agreeable soever it be to it), makes but a slow progress, and little advance in the world. And the reason of it is not hard to be found in men's necessities, passions, vices, and mistaken interests...Or whatever else was the cause, 'tis plain in fact, that human reason unassisted, failed men in its great and proper business of morality (RC 241).

Philosophy and faith then, according to Waldron, cannot be two alternative paths to the same goal of moral truth, because unassisted reason has never formed a complete science of morals.[64] The completeness of the Gospel's moral teaching simply surpasses anything possible by unaided reason.

While Waldron is correct to acknowledge Locke's concerns about the epistemological limits of human understanding, he also unfortunately loses touch with the tone and complexity of Locke's argument about

---

[63] Waldron, *God, Locke, and Equality*, 105.
[64] Waldron, *God, Locke, and Equality*, 103. See also Wolterstorff, *Ethics of Belief*, 148.

ancient philosophy. Locke never states as clearly as Waldron suggests that Scripture is the only way to grasp moral truth. In the crucial passage to which Waldron refers, Locke clearly states that the "greatest part" cannot know and therefore must believe. But the "greatest part" logically implies that a smaller part can in principle know moral truth. For a writer as concerned with precise and logical reasoning as Locke was, we can only expect that he saw this conclusion as self-evident. In one sense, Locke's admission that the "greatest part" cannot know moral truth belies his suggestion in the *Second Treatise* that the moral law is "intelligible and plain"(II: 12) to all, but this contradiction applies only when we assume the absence of Scripture. With the support of scripture, it is possible, in Locke's view, that the moral law can be "plain" to all, as opposed to just a few.

Perhaps sensing that he goes too far when he claims that Locke completely abandoned the possibility of demonstrative morality, Waldron later qualifies his position somewhat: "What has become, on account of Christian revelation, widely dispersed moral common sense is the only reliable mode of access" to moral truth.[65] However tempting it may be, this argument will not do. Unlike later Scottish thinkers such as Adam Smith and Francis Hutcheson, Locke never speaks of anything like a "moral common sense," nor, given his attack on innate ideas and the epistemological properties of faith would we expect him to. Perhaps Waldron means that Locke believed that since the appearance of the Gospels, there is a definite cultural expectation toward a true understanding of the requirements of morality in Christian lands. If this is the case, Locke never said so. Indeed, how would we then make sense out of Locke's frequent attacks on the immorality of Christian societies (especially their persecutorial zeal), the supposed beneficiaries of this "moral common sense"? As to revelation being the only "reliable" mode of access to truth, Waldron's formulation of the issue evades the very point most at issue; namely, reliable for whom? The "greatest part" or more radically for all?

When we consider Locke's account of revelation from the perspective of its form of presentation and its general apprehensibility, then Waldron and others seem to be on firmer ground. Locke declares in no uncertain terms: "the instruction of the people were best still to be left to the precepts and principles of the gospel" (RC 243). Locke intimates that there is something about the revelatory status of the gospel that gives it more authority among "the people" than "abstract reasonings" (RC 243). But we should observe that Locke's assessment that knowledge of morality made

[65] Waldron, *God, Locke and Equality*, 106.

"slow progress" in the world prior to Christ does not mean that there was no progress at all. The obstacles to progress Locke adduced are mainly passions, interests, and necessities; that is to say, they are in large measure political problems, not intractable epistemological limits on human understanding. It is precisely the relation of politics and morality that Locke tries to work through in the *Letter on Toleration*. It is remarkable that even in a passage in the *Reasonableness* in which Locke affirms the authority of Scripture, he remains extremely reluctant to foreclose entirely the possibility of formulating rational ethics, despite the many apparent obstacles to doing so.

This is not to suggest that Locke believed scripture's greater authority to be simply a matter of better rhetorical presentation, although that is clearly a part of it. The authority of scripture points us back to the problem of ancient philosophy, and by extension to the problem of pagan religion. The real problem facing ancient morality, deeper even than the lack of authority attending unassisted reason, was that ancient religion "little concerned itself" with the morality of the people (RC 243). The priests who did speak with authority about the divine, "spoke little of virtue and a good life" (RC 243). For their part, the philosophers who relied on reason, "which contains nothing but truth," made no "mention of the deity in their ethics" (RC 243). Let's take a moment to unpack Locke's argument here.

Ancient philosophy was too reliant on reason. But observe the source of Locke's concern about this: "Yet some parts of that truth lie too deeply for our natural powers *easily to reach*, and make *plain and visible*, without some light from above to direct them" (RC 243, emphasis added). It is the lack of ease with which moral truths can be made "plain and visible" that concerns Locke in this passage, not the ability of unassisted reason to uncover the substantive content of the moral law, even if only with immense difficulty and perhaps not for all.[66] Neither Waldron nor anyone else, to my knowledge, has ever shown what specifically Locke thought the Gospel added to the content of morality – that is, what was not already available to natural reason – apart from the idea of moral obligation based on divine reward and punishment in the afterlife. Recall Locke's conclusion that a Christian can know his or her moral duties by studying the "moral part of Moses' Law," a law based on divine rewards and punishments surely, but of a temporal nature (RC 23, 166–72). The content of the Mosaic Law was not a primary concern for Locke. The real problem

---

[66] Thus I agree with Harris that it is the "obligation rather than the content of the natural law" that Locke believes is fundamentally lacking without revelation (*Mind*, 309).

of ancient ethics, or for that matter the Old Testament, seems then to be a matter of obligation.

This forces us to reconsider the meaning of Locke's indictment of ancient philosophy. In antiquity, the priests who spoke with authority about the supernatural were not concerned with ethics. Note that Locke never denies that there were those in antiquity who spoke with authority about the divine. The problem was they had no, or perhaps no rational, moral teaching. The problem of ancient philosophy is then inseparable from the defects of pagan religion. Ancient philosophers erred by allowing religion to become mere superstition orchestrated by the priests and their political masters. Ancient philosophers assumed mistakenly that religion and reason were inevitably antagonistic. In stark contrast with Locke's own philosophy, ancient philosophers doomed their moral teaching to practical irrelevance by not directly confronting superstition, or what Locke would identify later in a somewhat different context "enthusiasm." Ancient philosophers allowed a debased, irrational religion to constantly undermine the rational basis of moral obligation because they did not see philosophy as having a public role to play in testing pagan religion at the bar of reason. As Locke was well aware, this is not an entirely fair charge against ancient philosophy. After all, Socrates was executed at least in part for impiety. At this level, one of the major problems with ancient moral philosophy for Locke really does seem to involve rhetoric. In antiquity, philosophic efforts to purge superstition out of religion, such as in Books II and III of Plato's *Republic*, which not coincidentally also advocated expelling the poets from the city in a speech, were exceedingly complex moral demonstrations. A Platonic dialogue or an Aristotelian metaphysical treatise is no easy beast to master, even for the thoroughly initiated. In its contest with a debased religion and the poets who supported it, ancient philosophy was perhaps guilty of trying too hard – that is, trying to rationalize religion on the basis of a long chain of moral reasoning that presupposed the whole complex apparatus of philosophical examination. The only people convinced by the philosophic efforts to rationalize religion and moral duty were other philosophers.

There is thus strong evidence in the *Reasonableness* that Locke never abandoned the possibility of rational morality or departed significantly from his position in the *Essay*. The account of ancient philosophy in the *Reasonableness* does, however, highlight Locke's estimation of the immense difficulty in making rational morality an authoritative teaching, as opposed to a rationally apprehensible set of rules. The great importance of revelation was its introduction of soteriological concerns into theories of moral obligation. By stimulating reflection upon the conceptual problems traditionally plaguing philosophic accounts of moral obligation, Scripture brings greater clarity to the examination of the contents of a sound moral theory.

In this context, it is important to recall that while the prospect of eternal life appears to be crucial divine support for morality, Locke acknowledges that the ancient philosophers were able to discover and inculcate rules of virtue, albeit imperfectly, without the support of eternal life. Indeed, he never suggests that the content of moral duty is inaccessible to unassisted human reason as such, only that reason alone lacks authority among the considerable part of mankind who are not reliably rational, and sometimes against the inclinations even of those who are. This ambiguity with respect to the possibility of determining rational morality is also apparent in Locke's discussion in the *Letter on Toleration* of the sources of moral knowledge in which he associates the "Moral actions" required for a "good life" with both religion and civil government, both "the Magistrate and the Conscience" have a role to play in moral education (46). The two most important features of "moral actions" as Locke conceives them are that they can be understood without proof of the immortality of the soul and that they are a function of the morality of works rather than faith.[67] The emphasis on the importance of works brings morality, at least to some degree, firmly within the orbit of responsibilities apprehensible to civil or unassisted reason. Moral action requires the obligatory character of law and punishment, but Locke insists that such laws and punishments may derive from several sources including not only divine power, but also two other potent forces of moral suasion, namely civil power and the social power operating in the "Law of Reputation" (E 2.28.4–6). Indeed he claims that the variety of moralities in the world is due to the "different sorts of happiness" and different punishments relating to these types of law (E 1.3.9.69).

If we follow this important, albeit somewhat muted, line of argument to its conceptual source, it is clear that despite his assessment of the limited ability of purely rational ethics to provide a universally compelling account of moral obligation, Locke's rational theology allowed considerable scope for natural reason to provide a theoretical basis for morality in a civil context. This is exemplified dramatically in the course of Locke's discussion of the possibility of peaceful civil relations among Christian settlers and native peoples in colonial America. Locke frames this discussion in

---

[67] See Forster, *Moral Consensus*, 66 and Eisenach, *Two Worlds*, 78–79.

terms of toleration and claims that the two groups can live in civil union because "these innocent Pagans" may be "strict observers of the Rules of Equity and the Law of Nature" (43; II: 123). Locke assumes that they are capable of sufficient moral reasoning without deducing their moral obligations from a revealed religion with a clear doctrine of a future state. These non-Christians have "light enough" and can in effect grasp some of the basics of the law of nature because in principle the moral requirements of political association *qua* political association produces normative claims on the rational individual that are comprehensible independent of theological speculation, or even an awareness of the contents of revelation. Locke thus indicates that moral actions required for a good life in civil society are available without direct religious support or any greater moral obligation than civil law and a sense of common "Humanity" with one's neighbors (43; II: 14).[68] More importantly for the issue of toleration, Locke indicates that government can play a legitimate role in promoting morality without imposing on society a single authoritative conception of theological truth.

Thus Locke's claim about natural theology by no means precludes the possibility of a secular version, or at least expression, of rational morality. The "good life" of concern for civil society, is conceptually intelligible without revealed religion, even as religion provides morality, and by extension government with divine support for justice that natural reason cannot itself reliably provide. For Locke, both the churches and government are concerned with, and have a partial claim to, moral knowledge but are denied access to the encouragements and punishments available to the other: Properly understood, churches lack civil penalties, and the state has no control over belief about salvation. Reason in both its religious and civil manifestation establishes distinct kinds of moral judgment, thus the churches and government emerge from Locke's treatment of religion and morality as complementary, but also potentially competing, sources of moral authority. Much as Locke's familiar constitutional theory is marked by the diffusion of power and the difficulty of locating institutional sovereignty, Locke's account of religion and morality suggests a vision of political life characterized by multiple moral referents, the creative tension among which would prove vital for modern liberal society.

---

[68] Wolfson astutely observes that Locke at some points appears to collapse "true religion" with what he calls "natural religion," which is deducible from natural reason and thus available to all including pagans (Adam Wolfson, "Toleration and Relativism: The Locke-Proast Exchange" *The Review of Politics*, 59, 2 [Spring 1997]: 213–231, esp. 220–224). See also Locke, "Third Letter," 156.

THE POLITICS OF TOLERATION

Locke's account of the relation of religion and morality in the *Essay* and the *Reasonableness* supports a vision of civil society in which the churches are pivotally situated as the voluntary and exclusive institutional expression of the soteriological concerns Locke believed were embedded in the cognitive capacities of human understanding. In the context of his toleration argument, this obviously requires a considerable degree of legal separation between church and state, and the public and private more generally. However, it would be misleading to portray Locke's account of toleration as a purely negative principle intended solely to defuse religious controversy and remove moral debate as far as possible from the public sphere. Far from precluding robust discourse, Locke's conception of toleration envisions the churches and civil government in a process of discursive engagement relating to the nature of the public good and the proper scope of state power. As such, even Locke's famous limits on toleration, often seen as a civil trump over religious freedom and an expression of his condemnation of futile and corrosive theological controversy, can be reconsidered as an effort toward inclusion and encouragement of productive, practical inquiry about potential conflicts between individual rights and the public good. Thus on the practical level, toleration can be justified at least in part because it reflects the importance Locke attributes to the role of the churches in the formation of what one commentator aptly describes as the "moral consensus" underlying Locke's vision of civil society.[69] In this respect, Locke's toleration argument presupposes that the churches are institutions with a vital role to play in a free society as both a support for the moral foundation of civil society and as a salutary counterweight to the potentially overweening claims of the state and political sovereignty.

The kind of politics Locke expects to flow from his toleration argument is a function of the broadly inclusive possibilities revealed by the principle of toleration. While the voluntaristic church embodies a radically individualist premise, the churches themselves as institutions are subject to civil law, even if they are not created by it. Locke argues that the churches are not only absolutely denied civil power over their members, but also enjoy no jurisdiction over one another, and the clergy must never exercise political power (32–3). With respect to the determination of articles of faith and forms of worship, Locke insists that churches enjoy complete autonomy. Excommunication, the ultimate disciplinary measure of the church, is likewise the sole purview of the church except for the condition that it must

---

[69] Forster, *Moral Consensus*.

never entail injury to an individual's civil rights or even involve "rough usage, of Word or Action" (30).

Does Locke's argument for the legal separation of church and civil government require the public authorities to condone internally intolerant groups? In one sense it clearly does inasmuch as the civil government has no control over whom a church may or may not admit to its communion. However, in another sense it does not, for Locke insists that the principle of toleration extends to a broader concern for the pernicious effects of religious discrimination generally. Locke affirms: "No private Person has any Right, in any manner, to prejudice another in his Civil Enjoyments, because he is of another Church or Religion" (31). The key here is the connection between religious beliefs and "civil enjoyments." Toleration seems to require, or at least encourage, government enforcement of a legal regime of nondiscrimination by private individuals and groups insofar as such treatment impacts civil interests such as the franchise, employment, commerce, or holding public office.[70] Moreover, the concern for discrimination may, Locke insists, extend to matters that would touch not only upon religion but also upon other distinctions "made between men and men" such as those due to "different Complexions, Shapes and Features" (52).

Perhaps the clearest indication of Locke's concern about the problem of legal protection of intolerant groups is his insistence that toleration places a positive duty on the churches themselves. He envisions a crucial role for the churches to encourage the virtue of toleration: "It is not enough that Ecclesiastical Men abstain from Violence and Rapine, and all manner of Persecution. He...is obliged also to admonish his Hearers of the Duties of Peace, and Goodwill towards all Men; as well towards the Erroneous as the Orthodox" (33–4). Locke's rationale in this respect is twofold. First, preaching the virtue of toleration is perhaps the only sure proof that the clergy have no political ambitions, or more accurately will not allow themselves to be controlled by political factions. Second, by locating toleration firmly within the orbit of the "law of works" relating to moral action, Locke gives the churches a vital role as a support for toleration. Given the centrality of punishment in Locke's theory of moral obligation, churches committed to toleration serve to provide believers with a powerful motivation of the promise of eternal reward and punishment necessary to reinforce individual ethical obligation or fear of coercion.[71] By law, the state

---

[70] I believe Locke's emphasis on nondiscrimination as an integral feature of his toleration argument parallels what Tuckness identifies in a somewhat different context as Locke's "legislative point of view" (Tuckness, *Legislative Point of View*, 74–84).

[71] Wilhelm makes a persuasive case that Locke also saw educational reform as support for the formation of character suited to a tolerant society (Anthony G. Wilhelm, "Good

can enforce a policy of neutrality and even antidiscrimination, but Locke suggests that civil law alone will have great difficulty establishing a tolerant regime unless the churches place the great incentive of divine judgment behind the cause of toleration rather than against it.

The requirements toleration places on government primarily relate to assuming a non-discriminatory stance with respect to the various beliefs and practices deemed necessary for salvation. Civil government must neither establish any articles of faith nor proscribe those maintained by any church. These "Speculative Opinions" do not affect civil interests because they relate to soteriological matters of individual conscience that "terminate simply in the Understanding" and do not "influence the Will and Manners" (46). On this basis, the speculative opinions of practically every recognizable religious group would be, in principle, tolerable from the perspective of government. Notably here Locke adduces the examples of Catholics, Jews, and "Heathens" (46). The belief in transubstantiation and even the denial of the Messiahship of Christ do not cast a church beyond the pale of toleration because these beliefs as beliefs do not directly impact the ends of government. The strictness with which Locke maintains the separation of religion and government is thus largely a function of the distinct types of voluntary agreement they reflect.

The major caveat Locke places on strict neutrality and noninterference is that nothing that is illegal in the ordinary course of life can be permitted on grounds of religion. The example he gives is human sacrifice. In this case, government restriction is perfectly compatible with the voluntary basis of both church and state. By stipulating that temporal good is the "Sole Reason" (48) for creating civil society, Locke establishes that government has no obligation to ensure all practices deemed necessary for salvation.[72] However, according to the terms upon which individuals reasonably consent to government, it is authorized to punish practices violating the natural law duty to protect life. A church of human sacrificers would thus be in a contradiction by authorizing government to proscribe the very practices they deem necessary for salvation. In this instance, it would be persecution that is rational and the consent that is irrational! The limit on religious practices that contravene the very logic of political society is compatible

---

Fences and Good Neighbors: John Locke's Positive Doctrine of Toleration" *Political Research Quarterly*, 52, 1 [March 1999]: 145–166, esp. 158–162).

[72] Wilhelm perhaps goes too far when he argues that Locke believed the magistrate had a positive duty to defend the right of conscience. Locke clearly envisions situations in which the public good and the right of conscience will be in legitimate conflict ("Good Neighbors, 150–151).

with strict separation precisely because herein government is saving lives, not souls.

The more controversial aspect of Locke's account of the limits of toleration has to do with public necessity and the ban on certain practical, as opposed to speculative, opinions. In a familiar passage in the *Letter*, Locke argues that despite the general principle of state neutrality toward religion, there may be instances driven by public exigencies in which civil interference is justified. The example Locke provides is that of an individual or church that is normally allowed to slaughter calves as part of its worship but may be legally forbidden to do so in times of depletion of the cattle stock (42). While some commentators suggest that Locke hereby asserts an unqualified civil supremacy over religion,[73] we should be careful not to misunderstand this passage.

While Locke affirms that certain practices and even opinions may be proscribed because they are incompatible with contestable judgments about the public good, the justification for this intolerance is some notion of harm to civil order rather than claims to superior judgment about religious truth. Locke allows that the magistrate may make a plausible claim to superior knowledge about what constitutes harm, but he insists that the magistrate cannot assume the right to determine what is and what is not properly a matter of religious belief. Indeed he insists that the government in the animal sacrifice case remains neutral precisely because "the Law is not made about a Religious, but a Political Matter" (42) and thus applies equally across society. He shows concern not only for the "neutrality of justification" but also for the "neutrality of effects" of civil action as he cautions the magistrate "always to be very careful that he not misuse his Authority, to the oppression of any Church, under the pretence of public good" (42).[74]

---

[73] See, for example, Kessler, "Locke's Legacy," 485; Robert Kraynak, "John Locke: From Absolutism to Toleration" *American Political Science Review*, 74, 1 (March 1980): 53–69, esp. 66; and George Winstrup, "Freedom and Authority: The Ancient Faith of Locke's 'Letter on Toleration'" *The Review of Politics*, 44, 2 (April 1982): 242–265, esp. 254.

[74] See also McCabe, "Strict Separation," 243–245. More recent proof that this often involves a fine balancing act for which we cannot reasonably expect Locke to provide a uniform rule for application in these matters can be seen in the United States Supreme Court's judgment in the 1990 *Smith* decision. In this case, the Court had to deal with the question of whether a state law prohibiting the use of hallucinogenic drugs violated the First Amendment Free Exercise rights of the members of a Native American church who used hallucinogenic peyote as a sacrament. In *Smith*, the Court upheld the state law on the grounds that it was generally applicable and neutral with respect to religion. However, in doing so the Court modified and for all intents and purposes overturned an earlier Supreme Court decision in *Sherbert v. Verner* (1963) that held that even religion-neutral laws that incidentally burden a church significantly must meet a constitutional test of strict scrutiny. Locke also seems to want to balance the public good with strict

More importantly, however, Locke frames this issue as a matter of competing principles rather than a bare assertion of civil supremacy over the right of conscience.

Locke here presents a situation in which the creative tension produced by conflicting moral claims between distinct institutions with differing ends and sources of obligation provides the means for determining the bounds of minority dissent and legitimate state action. He distinguishes between a magistrate who interferes with the churches *ex tempore* for reasons of public emergency and a government that acts upon the mistaken assumption that it is entitled to legislate on religious matters. The latter Locke dismisses as an abuse of power "which neither was in the Constitution of the Government granted him, nor ever was in the power of the People to grant," and hints darkly that revolution is justified in this case (49).[75] With respect to the former situation, Locke admits much more latitude for governments operating strictly on the basis of dire public necessity. However, even in this case, he is concerned to allow conceptual space for dissent and contestation. While Locke does not directly link such controversies to an institutional debate within a juridical or legislative process, he does suggest an important deliberative element to the practical application of toleration insofar as government has the burden to justify publicly any interference in church matters, and the individual such as the aggrieved animal sacrificer may accept civil punishment rather than violate individual conscience: "He is to undergo the Punishment, which it is not unlawful for him to bear" (48). Given Locke's epistemology of belief, it is absurd to assume that individuals forbidden to practice a certain form of worship would simply concur with the civil judgment. Other religious groups not directly affected by the ban, may also see an interest in publicly challenging government interference with churches for the sake of defending the general principle of religious freedom. Locke thus offers public discourse, and potentially even civil disobedience, as perhaps the only way for individuals to satisfy both their civil and religious commitments in a dynamic, deliberative process in which both government and civil society can assess, adjust, and theoretically adjudicate rights claims of various groups and interests.

---

scrutiny toward legal interference with religious practices. See *Employment Division, Department of Human Resources of Oregon v. Smith*, 494 U.S. 872 (1990) and *Sherbert v. Verner*, 374 U.S. 398 (1963).

[75] The implication of this argument with respect to the persecution of nonconformists in England seems clear. For Locke, popular resistance by English dissenters would be morally justified, even if very unwise politically or militarily (see James Tully, *An Approach to Political Philosophy: Locke in Contexts* [Cambridge: Cambridge University Press, 1993], pp.60–61).

Whereas Locke's treatment of speculative opinions inclines toward wide latitude in the toleration of diverse beliefs and practices, his account of practical opinions presents a more constrained interpretation of the range of opinions permissible within society. According to Locke, practical opinions differ from speculative opinions primarily because the former directly influence the "Will and Manners" and thus can produce actions that manifestly affect the temporal goods for which political society is created (46). It is on the basis of their harmful social effects that Locke adduces a number of practical opinions that may be proscribed. While on its face this account hardly seems representative of a desire for a maximally inclusive form of politics, Locke's treatment of these proscribed opinions is more ambiguous, and indeed richer, than is generally assumed. Not only does Locke strengthen the presumption in favor of tolerating all other practical opinions by limiting his proscriptions to a select few, but he also frames this discussion within the context of a discursive, contestatory process with multiple deliberative opportunities. Lacking the metaphysical support provided by the kind of dogmatic moral philosophy explicitly rejected by Lockean epistemology, in Locke's account these proscriptions assume the status of hypothetical propositions deduced from the nature of political society, and thus subject to critical examination and debate rather than as self-evident demonstrable principles.

For instance, the first, and perhaps most infamous, proscribed opinion involves Locke's call for the exclusion of atheists from general toleration on the grounds that "the Bonds of Humane Society" such as oaths and covenants "have no hold upon an Atheist" who lacks assurance of divine judgment and eternal life (51). He asserts that the denial of the existence of God "even in thought" is not to be tolerated (51). While the exclusion of atheists is often seen as evidence of Locke's belief in the religious foundations of morality,[76] in some respects this account raises more questions than it answers. Even if we grant the dubious conclusion that notorious public atheism may be proscribed because of its supposed ill effects on morality in general, it is by no means obvious how atheist ideas, as opposed to public confessions or vicious acts, could be detected by government or what interest civil government would have in banning such "thoughts" if they did not demonstrably produce immoral and antisocial actions.

Furthermore, it is not at all clear what to make of Locke's claim that "All men know and acknowledge that God ought to be worshipped publickly"

---

[76] See, for instance, Waldron, *God, Locke, and Equality*, 223–228 and Forster, *Moral Consensus*, 176.

given his stigmatization of atheists (38). As an empirical matter, this statement is patently false inasmuch as the atheists Locke seeks to proscribe presumably do not "know" any such thing. As a normative statement, it also has problematic elements. Given Locke's account of the wide scope for error in human understanding, it is clearly possible for an individual to conclude, however mistakenly, in Locke's view, that there is no God or that the deity does not require public worship. By the logic of Locke's account of the epistemological basis of faith, the issue of atheism puts the natural law duty to publicly worship God in serious tension with the individual right to publicly recognize only such propositions as to which the mind freely assents.[77] Official persecution becomes even less intelligible if lack of belief in God is not connected to any demonstrable social harm. Despite the obvious rhetorical advantage of excluding atheism in order to demonstrate that toleration does not involve indifference to religion, the ambiguities in Locke's account of atheism seem to invite debate about the very limits of toleration he ostensibly seeks to establish.

Locke's second example of proscribed beliefs relates to "Opinions contrary to human society" (49). While Locke insists that examples of such opinions in any church "are rare," he is frustratingly vague about the content of such opinions.[78] A third and "more secret evil" are the practical opinions maintaining some peculiar prerogative whereby the normal rules of morality do not apply to a certain sect. Here Locke is flush with examples, including the belief that one has a duty to depose heretical rulers, the notion that "Dominion is founded in grace," and the conviction that one is not obliged to keep oaths and promises with heretics (49–50). To this claim of peculiar sectarian prerogatives, Locke adds a fourth, and potentially related, intolerable practical opinion, namely that one's membership in a certain church carries with it political loyalty and "service" to a foreign prince (50). The danger in these practical opinions is their perceived connection to civil disorder and treason.

This cluster of intolerable opinions is often interpreted as directed to proscribe Catholicism, which was largely seen as the *bete noire* of the seventeenth-century English political imagination.[79] However, it is perhaps

---

[77] John Locke, *Essays on the Law of Nature*, 2nd ed., W. von Leyden, ed. (Oxford: Clarendon Press, 1958), p. 195.

[78] Perhaps Locke's earlier example of human sacrifice would qualify as a religious opinion with obvious practical and moral implications "contrary to human society."

[79] See Clement Fatovic, "The Anti-Catholic Roots of Liberal and Republican Conceptions of Freedom in English Political Thought" *Journal of the History of Ideas*, 66, 1 (2005): 37–58; David Lorenzo, "Tradition and Prudence in Locke's Exceptions to Toleration" *American Journal of Political Science*, 47, 2 (April 2003): 248–258, esp. 252; Marshall, *Toleration*,

wise to follow Waldron's suggestion and not jump to this conclusion too quickly.[80] While these doctrines arguably parallel standard Counter-Reformation Catholic teaching, Locke never explicitly associates any of them with Catholicism and they are by no means uniquely Catholic. Indeed, the notion of dominion founded in divine grace was central to Anglican divine right champions such as Robert Filmer, much as the duty to depose heretics has resonance with the Puritan rebellion against Charles I. Even the suspicion of loyalty to a foreign prince Locke ascribes to the relation of Muslims to the "Mufti of Constantinople" rather than Catholics and the Pope (50). The reference to Muslims indicates that clearly Locke wished to make a general point about the implications of certain actions, not a specific point about Catholics.[81] More importantly, however, as we have seen elsewhere in the *Letter*, Locke clearly indicates that Catholic speculative theology and religious practices are tolerable (42, 46).[82] Thus Locke's account of proscribed practical opinions seems to have as much to do with his perceptions of the dangers of theological claims on government as it does with the problem of sectarianism generally. This discussion alerts liberal civil society to the need for continuous practical examination of the sources of political legitimacy and as such, these limits on toleration are perhaps best understood as a function of Locke's general concern about the problem of divine right political theology rather than a statement of the inflexible boundaries of civil and religious liberty.

The fifth, and theoretically most important, of Locke's intolerable practical opinions is the denial of toleration. He asserts that toleration does not extend to "those that will not own and teach the duty of tolerating all men in matters of meer Religion" (50). The logic of intolerance provides the unifying thread linking the other intolerable opinions Locke considers because they each reflect some version of the idea that the individual has no, or only a reduced, moral obligation to others in their society who are not of the same belief. Crucially Locke directs this antisectarian logic to government as well as churches. Only a government committed to toleration can truly uphold the moral obligation it has to protect the rights of all individuals in society. Church-sanctioned intolerance violates natural and civic equality by arbitrarily excluding certain religious and moral

365–366; and Ellis Sandoz, "The Civil Theology of Liberal Democracy: Locke and His Predecessors" *The Journal of Politics*, 34, 1 (February 1972): 2–36, esp. 35.

[80] Waldron, *God, Locke and Equality*, 222–223.
[81] For Locke's views on Islam generally, see Nabil Matar, "John Locke and the 'Turbanned Nations'" *Journal of Islamic Studies*, 2, 1 (1991): 67–77.
[82] See also, Locke, "Third Letter," 231–233.

opinions from the realm of legitimate discourse and debate. However, in the context of a tolerant church, the intolerable practical opinions relating to sectarian prerogatives are either unintelligible or take on the properties of speculative opinions, matters of contestable theoretical principle, or of purely individual soteriological concern rather than socially harmful action. Tolerant churches may even be obliged to promote the civil rights of atheists as part of the moral law of works requiring "Charity, Meekness, and Goodwill" towards "all Mankind" (23). Any church that embraces the principle of toleration and maintains the importance of moral obligation toward those in society of other beliefs and opinions is itself tolerable. The mutually reinforcing tendencies of tolerant governments and churches allow wide scope for practical opinions as discursive elements in society, even as Locke's probabilistic epistemology encourages constant reexamination and revision of prevailing opinions.[83] Governments that adhere to the policy of nondiscrimination and noninterference in religion, together with churches that advocate the religious duty of toleration, have the capacity to transform potentially destructive opinions in the best case into subjects of salutary political debate, and at worst into matters of political indifference. Thus Locke's remedy to the problem of dangerous practical opinions is toleration, not limits on toleration.

The legal separation of church and state in Locke's toleration argument should not blind us to his idea of the dynamic of discursive engagement between these distinct and potentially competing sources of moral authority. For Locke, religious toleration supports a certain kind of politics, one that features discursive elements establishing, but also challenging, the intrinsic limits of power while also encouraging a form of moral dissent vital for free society. Far from simply subsuming religion into a comprehensive political perspective, Locke sought to weave the debate over religious and moral questions into the very fabric of liberal society.[84] The fundamental diversity of opinions reflected in, but by no means exhausted by, the right of conscience is both natural and good. The variety of interpretations about what is required for salvation rendered permissible by toleration establishes and regularizes a conception of the relation of the churches to the state that Locke held out as a model for understanding the importance of civil liberties. The churches serve as a standing reminder that while civil government typically reserves to itself the power of legislation and coercion,

---

[83] Lorenzo, "Locke's Exceptions," 253.
[84] In this respect, my reading runs directly contrary to Kirstie McClure, "Difference, Diversity, and the Limits of Toleration" *Political Theory*, 18, 3 (August 1990): 361–391.

it does not have a monopoly over interpretation of the law of nature and morality: "Municipal Laws of Countries, are only so far right, as they are founded on the Law of Nature, by which they are to be regulated and interpreted" (II: 12). Locke's modernized, voluntary church is meant to assist the cause of freedom by serving as an independent source of moral authority to which the individual and larger community may refer on matters of conflicting principles.

The Lockean state provides churches and individuals with social stability and protection of property, and in return the churches provide the state with a consensual and voluntary means to incorporate the soteriological concerns of the individual into a moral debate with both a civil and religious dimension. In absence of the right of conscience, it is certainly possible to imagine a society directed to the Lockean goals of promoting industry and economic productivity that would allow such a massive system of coercion as to be unrecognizably liberal.[85] Far from heralding the triumph of the political perspective over all comers, Lockean churches enjoy status as the exclusive institutional expression of what he took to be one of the most spontaneous aspects of human freedom. Locke condemns all churches to a sectarian existence, but he views this discovery as one of the great achievements of religion in modernity.

Perhaps the most decisive impact of religious toleration on Lockean politics is the principle of moderation he believed it would both reflect and engender in society. Locke concludes that toleration encourages an ethos of fallibility with both a religious and political resonance that produces the kind of moderation with respect to claims to knowledge and truth that Locke sees as essential to liberal politics. His toleration argument has theoretical and practical ambitions that extend beyond a mere doctrine of noninterference and legal separation. For Locke, toleration in its fullest expression requires that the fallibilistic principles of rational religion penetrate deeply into practically every aspect of modern life. The critical stance toward truth claims inherent in the logic of toleration not only severs the historical connection between political control of religion and the lack of political freedom; toleration also helps establish new intellectual habits and a general societal norm and belief that no individual or group can plausibly claim possession of the whole truth, religious or political. From the argument that different religious beliefs are the product of differing understanding rather than malicious will or defective conscience naturally flows

---

[85] Marshall suggests that Locke did, in fact, entertain a more authoritarian vision of society
       later in his career in the 1690s (*Toleration*, 381–383).

a principle of civic moderation according to which one may reasonably assume that one's political opponents or those of a different religion are in error but not necessarily willfully vicious or morally corrupt. In the framework of Locke's toleration argument, political and religious differences are transformed from self-justifying moral absolutes into probabilistic claims and contestable premises amenable to discursive engagement among the multiplicity of groups and opinions in society.

It was on the basis of his assessment of the profoundly subjective cognitive elements of human understanding that Locke reasoned that diversity of opinions on religion, as on a host of other important matters, is natural: "It is unavoidable to the greatest part of Men, if not all, to have several opinions, without certain and indubitable Proofs of their Truths" (E 4.16.4.659). However, it was perhaps only by virtue of his reflections on the value of intellectual freedom for society and individual human flourishing that Locke could declare with confidence: "It would, methinks, become all Men to maintain Peace, and the common offices of *Humanity*, and *Friendship* in the diversity of opinions" (E 4.16.4.659; emphasis original). From a thinker not known for his encomiums to the sweeter things in life, Locke's call for his readers to consider diversity of opinions, and even serious intellectual disagreement on important religious and moral questions, as the foundation for a kind of friendship is particularly disarming. We suspect that contrary to the common view of him today, Locke did not conceive of toleration purely, or even primarily, as a negative principle based on noninterference. For Locke, legal toleration was rather only the political, and hence narrowest, expression of a deeper and richer moral teaching with the possibility to completely transform modernity's understanding of the social value of human freedom.

Locke's new conception of a voluntary church anchors his effort to replace the rigid polarities of traditional sectarian and political conflict with an appreciation of the powerful discursive elements available to a natural rights-based society. The fundamental diversity of opinions reflected in, but by no means exhausted by, the right of conscience is both natural and good. For Locke, toleration has a similar effect on the societal and noetic level as the separation of powers has on the constitutional. In both cases, sovereignty is difficult and even impossible to locate institutionally. Locke's account of the relation of the churches to each other and to the state serves as a model for diverse civil interests. In the process of discursive engagement between the churches and government, as well as among the churches themselves, Locke sees not indifference to truth, but rather the outlines of a liberal form of distributive justice according to which toleration principles embedded in society provide conceptual space for the articulation of various and competing interests, both civil and religious.

Given his assessment of the natural diversity of opinions produced by human understanding, it is unlikely that Locke would accept the criticism that his argument deprives religion of the very thing that makes it attractive to many, namely the subjective feeling of certainty. He seems to assume that concerns about salvation, no less than claims to political justice, do not lose vigor simply because they are capable of being defined as partial from the perspective of a broader social and epistemic context. But did Locke perhaps exaggerate the centrality of soteriological concerns, and thus fix his argument for toleration in a historical context with little relevance for today? The resurgence of religious conflict and debates about the role of religion in public life in recent times suggests Locke may be as relevant today as ever. Moreover, while the secularized form of the right of conscience embodied in modern civil liberties may lack the theological tenor of its early modern predecessor, Locke's toleration theory clearly reflects the intellectual root of modern ideas of discourse and dissent embodied in the institutions of civil society familiar to us including not only the churches, but also the free press, nongovernmental organizations, professional associations, and the academy. At the very least, Locke's toleration argument, with both its civil and religious dimensions, perhaps contains discursive possibilities that still reflect, however imperfectly, the complex nature of liberal society.

7

International Relations

From the dawn of the modern period in the seventeenth century through to contemporary times, the existence of the nation-state has been the central organizing principle of the international system. Arguably, modernity in its most concrete form is inseparable from the modern idea of the nation-state to which it gave birth. However, debate about the moral basis of international relations is as old as the system itself. Today, as in the past, the recurring questions animating the debate about the role of the state in international relations include: Is the international system as the political realists maintain essentially anarchic, marked by competition among independent states pursuing their national interest and power, or does international relations provide a context of norms by which nations may be said to form a society of states?[1] Does justice among nations rest on the

---

[1] For the classical realist statement of the international system, see Hans J. Morgenthau, *Politics among Nations*. 2nd ed. (New York: Alfred A. Knopf, 1954). The divided legacy of classical realism can be seen in the current debate between "American Realism" (e.g., Dale C. Copeland, "A Realist Critique of the English School" *Review of International Studies*, 29, 3 [July 2003]: 427–441; Michael C. Desch, "It Is Kind to Be Cruel: The Humanity of American Realism" *Review of International Studies*, 29, 3 [July 2003]: 415–426; and Charles L. Glaser, "Structural Realism in a More Complex World" *Review of International Studies*, 29, 3 [July 2003]: 403–414) and the "English School" (e.g., Hedley Bull, *The Anarchical Society: A Study of Order in World Politics* [New York: Columbia University Press, 1977]; Barry Buzan, "The English School: An Underexploited Resource in IR" *Review of International Studies*, 27, 3 [July 2001]: 471–488; and Richard Little, "The English School's Contribution to the Study of International Relations" *European Journal of International Relations*, 6, 3 [2000]: 395–422), who disagree as to whether to view the international system in societal rather than anarchical terms. For a good overview of this debate, see Richard Little, "The English School vs. American Realism: A Meeting of Minds or Divided by a Common Language?" *Review of International Studies*, 29, 3 (July) 2003): 443–460.

core principles of deference towards sovereignty and nonintervention, or is humanitarian intervention and the use of force to punish wrongdoing and protect the innocent justified by an overarching standard of international morality?[2] Given the continuing theoretical and ethical debates in the supposedly "postmodern" twenty-first century about the rights and responsibilities of sovereign states and the limits and possibilities of international law and institutions, there is no less urgency now than perhaps at any other time in the past to inquire: What, if anything, does it mean to speak of morality in international relations?

This chapter will consider this question by examining the intersection of political philosophy and international relations in the work of John Locke. At first glance international relations theory may not appear to be an aspect of modernity to which Locke made much of a contribution. International relations were not the primary focus of his work, and foreign affairs are treated less systematically by Locke than other modern political philosophers such as Machiavelli, Grotius, and Kant. However, Locke's significance as a seminal thinker in the liberal tradition of natural rights and constitutional government suggests that his relatively modest reflections on international relations merit more attention than they have historically received. Thankfully, a number of recent commentators have begun to reconsider Locke's importance as a thinker on international relations. Of course, renewed interest does not imply consensus. Some identify Locke's state of nature theory with the early modern realist school of international relations founded by Machiavelli and Hobbes, which was based on the twin principles of the international state of anarchy and the primacy of sovereignty.[3] In this view, Locke's assessment of the practical impotence of natural law and international morality left sovereignty, self-defence, and national interest as the only reliable normative standards for international relations.

Other commentators have discovered a rather different Locke: a proponent of a robust internationalism whose law of nature teaching provides a permissive rationale for the use of force in international relations including

---

[2] For good discussions about the various positions involved in the debate over intervention, see Alex J. Bellamy, "Humanitarian responsibilities and interventionist claims in international society" *Review of International Studies*, 29, 3 (July 2003): 321–340 and Terry Nardin, "The Moral Basis of Humanitarian Intervention" *Ethics & International Affairs*, 16, 1 (April 2002): 57–70.

[3] See, for instance, Richard Cox, *Locke on War and Peace* (Oxford: Oxford University Press, 1960) and Peter Ahrensdorf and Thomas Pangle, *Justice among Nations: On the Moral Basis of Power and Peace* (Lawrence: University Press of Kansas, 1999), pp. 153–157.

not only a right of intervention, but even a justification for punitive wars.[4] A number of recent works have taken this line of reasoning even further to argue that Locke's natural law theory was deliberately designed, at least in part, to legitimize seventeenth-century English colonial and mercantilist policies supporting military intervention against premonetarized, non-European societies.[5] Locke scholars, if not yet political theorists more generally, are beginning to take Locke seriously as an international relations thinker.

The argument in this chapter rests on the contention that Locke has important things to say about international relations. More specifically, Locke reflected more deeply upon the practical and theoretical challenges to received assumptions about justice among nations and peoples than is typically supposed. It is indeed striking the great extent to which Locke's account of the rights of individuals in the pre-civil state of nature and the prerogatives and capacities of communities vis-à-vis governments is saturated with the logical and semantic categories supplied by traditional moral and legal debates about just and unjust war. Far from marginalizing international relations as a theoretical concern, it can be argued that Locke's individualist moral and political philosophy consistently and in crucial matters blurred the distinction between the rights of individuals and the rights of nations. In a fundamental sense, for Locke, uncovering the moral basis of international relations was inseparable from the central theoretical imperatives of his political philosophy. This is not to suggest that Locke simply deduced international relations theory from the moral premises of his individualist philosophy. Rather Locke candidly addressed the considerable tension that often exists between individual rights claims and the legitimate actions of peoples and governments acting in their corporate capacities in the international sphere. Locke was well aware that the greatest, and from the humanitarian perspective the most urgent, tests of the efficacy of moral reasoning and the limits of natural justice arise in the context of conquest, war, and international aggression. Thus, on one level, our analysis of Locke's view of international relations builds upon important

---

4 See, for example, Martin Seliger, *The Liberal Politics of John Locke* (London: Allen & Unwin, 1969), pp. 114–118 and Richard Tuck, *The Rights of War and Peace: Political Thought and the International Order from Grotius to Kant* (Oxford: Oxford University Press, 1999), pp. 173–178.
5 See Barbara Arneil, *John Locke and America: the defence of English Colonialism* (Oxford: Clarendon Press, 1996), pp. 16–20; Anthony Pagden, "Human Rights, Natural Rights, and Europe's Imperial Legacy" *Political Theory*, 31, 2 (April) 2003): 171–199, esp. 183–184; and James Tully, *An Approach to Political Philosophy: Locke in Contexts* (Cambridge: Cambridge University Press, 1993), pp. 154–155.

aspects of his moral and political theory we have considered in previous chapters.

However, on another level, Locke's treatment of international relations also adds another dimension to his political philosophy that cannot be simply extracted from doctrines of individual rights and domestic constitutional government. Rather the profoundly modern character of Locke's international relations teaching also requires us to consider the opposite approach. That is to say, the democratic character of Locke's political philosophy invites us to draw parallels between his treatment of the moral basis of international relations and contemporary reflections upon the idea of international society. Perhaps understandably, Locke scholars have typically shown little desire to do this.[6] However, while paying due diligence not to transpose current debates onto an earlier thinker who functioned in a very different context, it is possible both to understand Locke more clearly by reflecting upon the assumptions contemporary liberal societies carry into the international sphere, as well as to show how Locke's treatment of sovereignty, natural law, and the international state of nature might elucidate our thinking about international relations. The aim is to refocus analysis of Locke's theory of international relations away from the familiar discourse of sovereignty and natural law, and toward a different discourse involving self-government and international society. These ideas with such strong contemporary resonances have a deep structural connection to Locke's thinking and flow naturally from his central premises. We will see that Locke's vision of the moral basis of international relations rested on an idea of international society that balanced interrelated, overlapping, and even competing moral claims about sovereignty and natural law in a general framework of international norms governing the relations among self-governing societies. In Locke's multidimensional conception of international society, norms deduced from the law of nature govern nations and societies even as independent societies and nations remain the chief executors of the law of nature in the international sphere.

This chapter approaches Locke's understanding of international relations by focusing on three main elements of his teaching. First, we consider Locke's seminal state of nature account in light of its important implications for his theory of international relations. It will be argued

---

[6] An exception is Dunn who discusses Locke in terms of contemporary international relations theory, but he does so only tangentially (John Dunn, "The Dilemma of Humanitarian Intervention: The Executive Power of the Law of Nature, after God" *The History of Political Theory and Other Essays* [Cambridge: Cambridge University Press, 1996], pp. 136–147, esp. 144–160.

that Locke's doctrine of the natural executive power of the law of nature, which as we saw in Chapter 2 rests on the fundamental moral principle of nonaggression, somewhat problematically establishes a permissive standard for the use of force in the international state of nature. The implication of the Lockean principle of nonaggression is a normative vision of international relations that combines both a deep respect for the idea of self-government, as well as morally compelling authorization for direct violations of the principle of sovereignty including military intervention, punitive war, and even lawful conquest and occupation. Locke advances the radical claim that self-governing commonwealths in the international sphere are no less subject to punishment for violating the natural law than are individuals in the state of nature. Nonaggression is not coterminus with nonintervention.

The second aspect of Locke's argument we will examine is his conception of the problematic nature of the principle of sovereignty. It will be shown that Locke's theory of just war, which endorses punishment of those responsible for aggression, represents a powerful critique of the traditional idea of national sovereignty. In Chapter 3, we saw how Locke's dissatisfaction with the traditional idea of political sovereignty as the institutional expression of supreme power led him to construct a new conception of constitutionalism that connected sovereignty with the community rather than institutions. In the context of foreign relations, Locke's effort to replace the discourse of sovereignty with the logic of legal supremacy signified not only his departure from regnant ideas about sovereignty, but also helped him establish a moral justification of "lawful conquest" based on principles of natural justice extrinsic and superior to the claims of political sovereignty deriving from the consent of the community.

The third element of Locke's argument, which flows directly out of this critique of sovereignty, is his conception of international society. It will be demonstrated that while Locke sees the state of nature as the permanent condition of international relations, he also envisions a rational basis for international norms derived from natural law and convention that regulates conflict and cooperation among independent societies in a broader international society. This vision of international society rests on Locke's crucial conceptual distinction between government and civil society. The constituent units of Locke's international society are distinct societies conceived in terms of their inherent right of self-government, rather than the principle of inviolable national sovereignty. It is in the context of Locke's argument for international society that we will reconsider the important question of Locke's relation to colonialism, and conclude by considering how Lockean reflections on international relations contribute to contemporary debates about sovereignty, the use of force, and the ethics of intervention.

THE INTERNATIONAL STATE OF NATURE
AND THE DOCTRINE OF NONAGGRESSION

In order to understand Locke's reflections on international relations, it is first necessary to reexamine the moral and political significance of the state of nature. According to Locke, the natural human condition is "a State of perfect Freedom" and "a State of Equality, wherein all Power and Jurisdiction is reciprocal, no one having more than another."[7] While the state of nature is in one sense profoundly individualistic – there is no government – Locke contends that there is a natural law derived from reason regulating the relations of individuals in the natural condition. The law of nature contains three distinct but interrelated commands. First, it enjoins "no one ought to harm another in his Life, Health, Liberty or Possessions" (II: 6). Second, every individual "is bound to preserve himself" (II: 6). Third, each person ought "when his own Preservation comes not in competition,... as much as he can, to preserve the rest of Mankind" (II: 6). Locke claims that the power to execute the natural law is "put into every Mans hands," whereby each individual has the right to punish anyone who violates the natural law by threatening one's self-preservation or harming another in their life, liberty, or possessions (II: 7). The law of nature would "be in vain, if there were no body that in the state of Nature, had a Power to execute that, and thereby preserve the innocent and restrain offenders" (II: 7).

Perhaps the most striking feature in Locke's account of the state of nature, a condition practically defined by the absence of civil law, is his emphasis on the logic and rhetoric of law enforcement. While Locke affirms that the scope of the self-defence right enjoyed by every individual in the state of nature must be proportionate to the goal of "Reparation and Restraint" (II: 8), he also reveals that this punishment right extends to "the power to kill" (II: 11) an aggressor. There are, however, two elements of Locke's natural executive power teaching that extend well beyond a self-defence right.[8] First, Locke argues that one may punish and even kill not

---

[7]   John Locke, *Two Treatises of Government*. Peter Laslett, ed. (Cambridge: Cambridge University Press, 1988 [1690]): *Second Treatise*, section 4 (hereafter treatise and section in notes and text).

[8]   For a good sense of the variety of interpretations about the political implications of Locke's natural punishing power, see Kirstie McClure, *Judging Rights: Lockean Politics and the Limits of Consent* (Ithaca: Cornell University Press, 1996), pp. 127–132; John Simmons, *The Edge of Anarchy* (Princeton: Princeton University Press, 1993), pp. 40–42;

only an actual physical aggressor, but anyone who has shown "an Enmity to his being" (II: 16). The state of war, which activates the natural executive power, therefore relates not only to the actual use of force, but may reasonably be deduced from the discovery of any "sedate settled design" upon one's life (II: 11). Second, Locke extends the punishment right beyond the direct victims of aggression by advancing the right of "every man" and "any other Person" (II: 8, 10) to intervene against an aggressor who endangers another. Not only is the natural executive power emphatically not restricted to a special victims right, Locke extends it, in principle at least, into a right of every individual to intervene in a conflict in order to punish wrongdoers and protect the innocent.

The law of nature is a mixed blessing as it provides the state of nature with both its moral foundation and its most fundamental problem. Auto-interpretation of the law of nature and its permissive stance toward the use of force for punishing wrongdoers and protecting the innocent practically ensures that "the Inconveniences" of the state of nature must be great "where Men may be Judges in their own Case" (II: 13). As we discussed in Chapter 3, civil government emerges as Locke's primary remedy to the "Inconveniences" of the state of nature. By surrendering their natural executive power of the law of nature to a common "Umpire" in the legislative and executive power of society, individuals consent to form a civil arrangement that promises to better secure their life and property (II: 87–88). The formerly discrete individuals of the natural condition now agree to form "One Body Politick" (II: 89) distinct from the rest of humankind by delegating their general right of executing the law of nature to a civil government empowered not only to punish injuries within the community, but also crucially any "Injuries from without" (II: 88, 3).

The law of nature supplies the conceptual and moral link between Lockean civil government and international relations. The primary evidence Locke provides to support the existence of the state of nature is notably that "since all Princes and Rulers of Independent Governments all through the World, are in a State of Nature, 'tis plain the World never was, nor ever will be without Numbers of Men in that State" (II: 14). For Locke, the definitive demonstration of the existence of the state of nature is the permanent condition of international relations. The significance of Locke's identification of an international state of nature is twofold. First, he indicates that

Tully, *Locke in Contexts*, 315–323; Lee Ward, *The Politics of Liberty in England and Revolutionary America* (Cambridge: Cambridge University Press, 2004), pp. 231–240; and Michael Zuckert, *Natural Rights and the New Republicanism* (Princeton: Princeton University Press, 1994), pp. 235–236.

the international state of nature exists despite the many leagues and compacts between the "Governours of Independent Communities" (II: 14).[9] Agreements and promises among independent communities do not form civil society in the proper sense of "One Body Politick" with a common legislative to which a group of individuals have transferred their natural executive power. The rulers of independent communities retain their natural freedom and equality regardless of leagues and compacts with other commonwealths. However, Locke also insists that treaties and compacts among nations possess genuine normative force, and are "binding to them, though they are perfectly in a State of Nature" (II: 14).[10] Even in absence of a common legislative power or "Umpire" among independent commonwealths, Locke suggests that some form of moral rule operates in the international state of nature.

Second, Locke maintains that the state of nature is the permanent feature of the international arena. Independent commonwealths subject to no higher secular authority are, and "ever will be," the primary actors in the international arena. By removing from the international state of nature the possibility of a common legislature among distinct bodies politic, Locke rejects the idea of global government or a return to the pristine "great and natural Community" of humankind before the division of peoples into separate societies (II: 128). He thus effectively precludes the sole reliable remedy for the "inconveniences" of the state of nature, which must be great when independent communities and rulers, no less than individuals "may be Judges in their own Case" (II: 13). Each independent commonwealth invests in its government the right to act in foreign relations with the degree of freedom and moral authority that "answers to the Power every Man naturally had before he entered into Society" (II: 145). Thus the personhood of each independent community flows from the natural law command about self-preservation, or in the case of independent commonwealths, the aggregate preservation right of each of its members.

The moral core of Locke's law of nature is the prohibition on aggression, which he defines broadly as the use of "Force without Right" (II: 19). This definition of aggression serves a double duty for Locke. First, it applies, by virtue of the "domestic analogy," inclusively to the international, domestic and even the individual context: no commonwealth, civil government

---

9   At II: 133 Locke employs the term "commonwealth" as a generic term for any "Independent Community," despite its controversial connotations with English civil war radicalism. I will use commonwealth and independent community interchangeably in this chapter.

10 John Dunn, *The Political Thought of John Locke* (Cambridge: Cambridge University Press, 1969), p. 163.

or individual may use "Force without Right" against others.[11] Second, it simultaneously defines the *rightful* use of force narrowly in terms of self-defence and punishment for aggression. In this respect Locke departs some-what from the older tradition of Christian natural law according to which commonwealths were authorized to enforce natural law provisions, but the crimes for whose punishment justifies punitive wars need not be restricted to aggression.[12] For example, traditional Christian natural law held that punitive war can be justified by the iniquity of the adversary, which may include punishment for practices perceived to be contrary to natural reason such as idolatry, cannibalism, human sacrifice, and even the violation of the rights of hospitality.[13] While the later form of Christian natural law thinking on just war, advanced most notably by Spanish scholastics such as Vitoria and de las Casas, tried to limit the justification for punitive war in order to check the bellicosity of Spanish imperialism and the maltreat-ment of native peoples, it still retained a strong connection to the idea of war as a way to enforce certain norms and punish certain practices.[14] In this older tradition of natural law, the claims of sovereignty and political independence had less normative status than the moral imperative to pun-ish wrongdoers and protect the innocent.

In contrast to the Christian natural law tradition, Locke's effort to define just war solely in terms of self-defence and punishment of aggression makes respect for the political independence of separate commonwealths a much more integral feature of international relations. Locke's interna-tional state of nature simply reinterprets the natural law teaching about equality of individuals in terms of independent public persons or common-wealths: Aggression is in either context fundamentally a violation of the principle of natural equality. However, the domestic analogy supporting

[11] For the use of the domestic analogy in early modern international relations theory, see Hedley Bull, "The Grotian Conception of International Society" *Diplomatic Investigations: Essays in the Theory of International Politics*. Herbert Butterfield and Martin Wight, eds. (London: George Allen & Unwin, 1966), pp. 51–73, esp. pp. 64–68 and Michael Walzer, *Just and Unjust Wars* (New York: Basic Books, 1977), p. 58.

[12] For good accounts of the Christian natural law tradition of just war theory, see Ahrensdorf and Pangle, *Justice Among Nations*, ch. 4; Nardin, "Moral Basis," 58–61; and Pagden, "Human Rights," 184–188.

[13] St. Thomas Aquinas, *On Law, Morality, and Politics*. William P. Baumgarth and Richard J. Regan trans. (Indianapolis: Hackett, 1988), p. 221 and St. Augustine, *City of God*. (New York: Penguin, 1972), pp. 861–862.

[14] See, for example, Bartholome de las Casas, *In Defence of the Indians*. Stafford Poole, trans. (DeKalb: Northern Illinois University Press, 1992 [1552]), p. 207) and Francisco de Vitoria, *Political Writings*. Anthony Pagden and Jeremy Lawrance, eds. (Cambridge: Cambridge University Press, 1991 [1528]), p. 30, 225–226, 288.

the doctrine of nonaggression is highly strained, especially with regard to the punitive dimension of the natural law. In the moral economy of Locke's law of nature, the punishment of aggression typically involves the forfeiting of rights by one party to another. With regard to the individual in the state of nature, the aggressor may forfeit his or her right of self-preservation to the victim, and indeed to every individual who is entitled to legitimately intervene in the conflict (II: 8, 10). Locke graphically illustrates that the range of legitimate punishment may extend from reparation and restraint (imprisonment), to capital punishment, and even a morally permissible form of slavery (II: 23–4). In the context of aggression among individuals in the state of nature, the forfeiture of rights is, in principle, absolute.

With respect to punishment of aggression in the international state of nature, the moral significance of the social reality that commonwealths instantiate necessarily makes the situation much more complex. In one sense, the domestic analogy between individual and commonwealth is relatively unambiguous. Just as the natural law authorizes the individual to punish an aggressor with a view to reparation and restraint, so too may a victim society and its allies reasonably compel an aggressor state to pay reparation for damages or agree to external restraints, perhaps in the form of arms limitation or a nonaggression treaty (II: 181). However, the natural law authorization of capital punishment and slavery strains the domestic analogy and the legal fiction of the public person of the commonwealth to its logical extreme. Does the forfeiture of rights involve the entire aggressor commonwealth or is it limited to specific parties in it? Are the aggressor's rights forfeited to the whole victim society, restricted to specific individuals in it, or even extended to the entirety of humankind?

The law of nature authorizes conquest as a legitimate punishment for aggression, but Locke is careful to place limits on the rights even of lawful conquerors. He admits the shaky basis of the domestic analogy when he establishes moral limits on the punitive conduct of governments that simply do not pertain to individuals in the state of nature.[15] His strategy is to narrow the scope of responsibility for aggression to those individuals "who have actually assisted, concurr'd, or consented to that unjust force" (II: 179). With respect to this group, "what Power a lawful Conqueror has over the Subdued...is purely Despotical" (II: 178). While the defeated aggressor may likely (and legitimately) feel the sword or the lash, Locke vehemently maintains that noncombatants in the defeated society, and particularly

---

[15] Patrick Coby, "The Law of Nature in Locke's Second Treatise: Is Locke a Hobbesian?" *Review of Politics*, 49, 1 (Winter 1987): 1–28, esp. 19.

women and children, must be exempt from this fate (II: 182–3). Moreover, lawful conquest – military action authorized by the natural law – brings the conqueror no title to the property of the defeated people apart from proportionate monetary reparation (II: 180, 184), and must in no sense be construed to be the basis for legitimate government without the free consent of the conquered (II: 186–7). In the international state of nature, lawful conquest is a mixture of self-defence and punishment, but it is in no circumstances the basis of legitimate government.

Although conquest may not in itself produce government without consent of the conquered, the meaningful political independence of the lawfully conquered people can hardly be taken for granted either. Locke recognizes the difficulty, if not practical impossibility, of harmonizing a natural law authorizing conquest, on the one hand, and the idea of inviolable sovereignty, on the other. The natural equality of independent commonwealths signifies simultaneously one of the guiding moral principles of Locke's international state of nature, as well as perhaps its most problematic feature.

THE PROBLEM OF SOVEREIGNTY

The defining characteristic of the international state of nature is, according to Locke, the natural freedom and equality of independent commonwealths. Thus, in one sense, some element of the idea of national sovereignty is woven into the very fabric of Lockean international relations, inasmuch as the international state of nature recognizes no higher legislative and political authority than independent civil governments with sole competence to make and execute law within a given body politic (II: 131). However, in a more fundamental sense, Locke's conception of political independence departs considerably from the traditional notion of sovereignty. For Locke, the idea of legal supremacy replaces sovereignty as the central organizing principle of legitimate government.[16] He is typically careful not to identify the highest legal authority in the commonwealth as sovereign, preferring rather to describe it as supreme in relation to the subordinate magistrates

---

[16] For a fuller treatment of this point, see Chapter 3 above. A thoughtful examination of Locke's effort to develop conceptual alternatives to the regnant theories of sovereignty in the seventeenth-century England is found in Julian Franklin, *John Locke and the Theory of Sovereignty* (Cambridge: Cambridge University Press, 1978). Franklin argues that in his effort to formulate a conception of popular sovereignty and dissolution of government that could provide theoretical grounding for the right of revolution, Locke followed the English Civil War-era thinker George Lawson who made the first crucial steps toward reconceptualizing political sovereignty by articulating the devolution of power from government to the community (*Theory of Sovereignty*, 71–81, 93–97).

and inferior offices. The "supreme" legislative power, whether held solely by the legislature or shared with the executive, represents the organic unity or "soul" of the society that "puts Men out of a State of Nature into that of a Commonwealth" (II: 89, 151, 212).

While the supreme power is a delegated authority given by society and held in trust (and thus cannot be sovereign in the traditional sense), the commonwealth as a distinct social and political entity is nonetheless quint-essentially independent in a way in which the individual in the state of nature can never be. Unlike the individual person, the supreme power of the independent commonwealth is incapable of surrendering its natural executive power, at least in any significant sense, to a higher institutional authority (II: 141).[17] Thus, Locke's concept of legal supremacy reveals the problem in trying to understand his notion of the international state of nature in terms of the discourse of sovereignty. On the one hand, the doctrine of non-aggression seems to endorse the idea of sovereignty by asserting the natural equality of self-governing communities. For Locke, independent common-wealths represent a moral good in themselves inasmuch as their purpose is to guarantee human welfare and security (II: 158).[18] On the other hand, legal supremacy, as Locke conceives of it, implicitly undermines the idea of sovereignty because it offers no theoretical or moral obstacle to natural law authorization for the defensive use of force broadly conceived to include not only repulsing aggression, but even permitting a form of conquest and occupation.

Locke's theory of lawful conquest undermines the moral primacy of sov-ereignty in three ways. The first can be seen in Locke's suggestion that it "seldom happens" that the conquered and conquerors fail to incorporate "into one People under the same Laws and Freedoms" (II: 178). Indeed, his prime example for this historical pattern is the foundation of modern English society in the gradual incorporation of Normans and Saxons fol-lowing the Conquest of 1066 (II: 177).[19] While Locke suggests that the

[17] Franklin, *Theory of Sovereignty*, 93–95.
[18] Ruth Grant, *John Locke's Liberalism* (Chicago: University of Chicago Press, 1987), p. 128.
[19] Locke's interpretation of the Norman Conquest in consensual terms had important rhe-torical value in his immediate political context in the English constitutional battles of the seventeenth century, which pitted constitutionalist Whigs like Locke against divine right monarchists such as Filmer and secular absolutists such as Hobbes who made arguments about the origins of the monarchy that were compatible with, or even logically depended on, conquest (see Robert Filmer, *Patriarcha and Other Writings*. Johann Somerville, ed. [Cambridge: Cambridge University Press, 1991], pp. 33–34, 53–54 and Thomas Hobbes, *Leviathan* [Indianapolis: Hackett, 1994 (1651)], ch. 20).

consent of the conquered is the moral precondition for this political union, it is nonetheless striking that the incorporation of two peoples does not, strictly speaking, originate in consent but rather in the *ex post facto* agreement to a situation produced by prior military intervention and conquest. Far from endorsing the inviolability of sovereignty, Locke suggests that the reasonable, and in some respects natural, course of events is for lawful conquest to eventuate in a new body politic.[20] The redemptive power of compact even extends to aggressors who have forfeited their lives and liberty, for "once Compact enter between" the lawful conqueror and captive, "the state of War and Slavery ceases, as long as the Compact endures" (II: 24). Thus, even the most absolute form of subjection contains the seeds of new civil association.

The second aspect of Locke's conquest theory with direct bearing on the status of sovereignty is his restriction of responsibility for aggression to those who "actually assisted, concurr'd, or consented" to the unjust use of force (II: 178). The obvious interpretive difficulty in this formulation of war guilt lies in determining what constitutes assistance, concurrence, or consent. Depending on the criteria employed, the category of individuals subject to despotic punishment may include not only the political and military leadership of the defeated community, but also a wide swath of enemy combatants and potentially even segments of the public supportive of the war.[21] Does Locke's argument for selective war guilt preserve the integrity of the defeated society? Selective responsibility is incompatible with full sovereignty insofar as, despite his tendency to eschew the discourse of sovereignty,[22] Locke's idea of supremacy retains one important connection to the more traditional idea of sovereignty, according to which "making War and Peace are marks of Sovereignty" solely reserved to the "Supream Power" in society (I: 131).[23] The group or individuals possessing this

20 See Peter Josephson, *The Great Art of Government: Locke's Use of Consent* (Lawrence: University Press of Kansas, 2002), pp. 191–196

21 Waldron's suggestion that Locke excludes conscripts from criminal responsibility is interesting, but unsupported in the text (Jeremy Waldron, *God, Locke and Equality* [Cambridge: Cambridge University Press, 2002], p. 148). More likely, Grant (*Locke's Liberalism*, 130) is correct that Locke sees, in principle at least, no natural law protections for prisoners of war at all. Locke would in this respect at least be following the conventional usages of the law of nations of the time (Bull, "Grotian Conception,"58; Steven Forde, "Hugo Grotius on Ehtics and War" *American Political Science Review*, 92, 3 [September] 1998: 639–648, esp. 645).

22 For Locke's departure from the traditional language and logic of sovereignty, see also John Scott, "The Sovereignless State and Locke's Language of Obligation" *American Political Science Review*, 94, 3 (September 2000): 547–561.

23 Geraint Parry, *John Locke* (London: Allen & Unwin, 1978), p. 134.

sovereign right of war and peace are logically the parties directly responsible for the actual prosecution of an unjust war. Thus, whether we interpret assistance, concurrence, and consent narrowly to signify command responsibility or more broadly to include a wide range of combatants and civilians, Locke's natural law authorization for punishment, for all intents and purposes, necessarily included the supreme legal power in the aggressor commonwealth.

Alternatively, however, Locke's rationale for selective responsibility does make an important concession to the principle of self-government by framing aggressive war as an abuse of power not delegated by the community to its governors. The legitimate war power of a government cannot justify aggression, because "the People [have] given to their Gouvernours no Power to do an unjust thing, such as is to make an unjust War" (II: 179). A government that launches an unjust war loses its claim to legitimacy. The aggressor government loses its public character by this abuse of power; it effectively relinquishes its claim to legal supremacy and becomes a collection of private individuals subject to natural law punishment by the conqueror.[24] Accordingly, to the extent that Locke retains any significant connection with the idea of sovereignty, this supreme power must be said to devolve to society when the community's governors forfeit their natural rights by an act of aggression. This argument, at least partially, serves Locke's moral aim of restricting war guilt and exempting whole societies from the despotic punishment of lawful conquest. Aggression cannot be justified in the name or interests of the people.

However, there are two serious difficulties in Locke's reasoning about delegated powers and aggression. First, the argument that an aggressor government loses its legitimacy does not clarify in what sense supremacy can be understood to devolve to the community. To argue that the government loses its public, and by implication its supreme character, does not automatically indicate who or what body may rightfully assume the public representation of that society to the other bodies politic in the international state of nature. Lawful conquest appears to leave a community in a form of legal and national limbo – neither fully subject, nor possessing an independent government of its own. The second problem relates to Locke's ambiguous use of the domestic analogy. On the one hand, he maintains that the people had no more "Power in themselves" to consent to an unjust war than they would to enslaving themselves or voluntarily submit to arbitrary rule (II: 179, 23, 135). Yet, on the other hand, Locke gives no evidence for the proposition that we must assume that the general public would never

---

[24] Grant, *Locke's Liberalism*, 129–130.

be so wicked or foolish as to consent to or support an unjust war. Indeed, even in his most restrictive formulation of war guilt, Locke included those individuals who "consented" to the unjust use of force (II: 179). He appears to accept the commonsense empirical observation that communities manifestly can, have in the past, and probably will in the future support aggressive, expansionist policies.

The unifying thread in Locke's analogy between external aggression and domestic arbitrary rule is the purportedly self-destructive character of each, inasmuch as both endanger the basic freedom instrumental to self-preservation.[25] Once again, however, the domestic analogy between civil and international relations is by no means obvious. Is consenting to or supporting aggression against a weaker neighbour as clearly self-destructive as enslaving oneself or submitting to an arbitrary government? Admittedly, the aggressor government subjects itself to the possibility of universal punishment by all other peace-loving peoples, but this punishment is hardly guaranteed in the international state of nature. The more fundamental moral imperative against international aggression must be that as a general principle aggression undermines the equal respect for political independence which, in theory at least, all commonwealths including the aggressor have a presumptive right to enjoy.

The third aspect of Locke's lawful conquest theory with a direct bearing on the issue of sovereignty is his treatment of the concept of total war. Locke considers the possibility that every adult male may be held responsible for aggression by virtue of their membership in a given political society: "Let us suppose that all Men of that Community being all Members of the same Body Politick, may be taken to have joyn'd in that unjust War, wherein they are subdued, and so their Lives are at the Mercy of the Conquerour" (II: 188). From this very expansive idea of war guilt, Locke nonetheless still manages to establish clear limits on lawful conquest that never extends to punishing "innocent" women and children or claiming the property originally held by the captive men (II: 180, 182–4). Even Locke's broadest construction of responsibility for aggression does not justify national enslavement or mass expropriation and annexation of territory. In this situation, the lawful conqueror is checked primarily by the natural right of children to inherit their parent's estate (II: 190).[26] The blameless legitimate

---

[25] See Gary D. Glenn, "Inalienable Rights and Locke's Argument for Limited Government: Political Implications of a Right to Suicide" *Journal of Politics*, 46, 1 (February 1984): 80–115, esp. 90–96 and Zuckert, *Natural Rights*, 240–246.

[26] See the excellent discussion of the political implications of Locke's account of inheritance in David P. Gauthier, "The Role of Inheritance in Locke's Political Theory" *Canadian Journal of Economics and Political Science*, 32, 1 (February 1966): 38–45, esp. 41–45.

inheritors of the national wealth retain an indefeasible right both to possess their family property and to establish their own government charged with securing it (II: 192). A conquered people cannot be ruled without their consent, and those who retain the right to inherit estates forfeited by their fathers have a complementary right to form or consent to a government directed to protecting their property.

The argument that self-government flows in some sense out of the structure of the right to property may explain why conquerors cannot rightfully claim permanent government over the conquered; however, the natural right of inheritance does not demonstrate that the political independence of a given society survives intact in any form but *in potentia* through the course of actual invasion and occupation.[27] This limit on conquest has perhaps as much to do with the natural law obligation on the conqueror to refrain from despoiling a conquered people as it has to do with conflicting rights claims arising from the presumptive independence of the vanquished.

Locke's theory of lawful conquest, then, is in considerable tension with the notion of inviolable sovereignty. Conquest does not produce a right to govern in absence of the consent of the governed. But while the conquered retain a moral right to choose their governors, or may be said never as a society to have wholly forfeited this right, the retention of an abstract right is a far cry from full sovereignty or meaningful independence. Whether we (or the conqueror) interpret Locke's conception of war guilt broadly or narrowly, we are left with the inescapable conclusion that a society's effective political independence can be lost or suspended due to actions punishable on the basis of principles of natural justice extrinsic to the consent of the community.

INTERNATIONAL SOCIETY

While Locke insists that independent communities operate in a context of fundamental norms superintending their relations, neither sovereignty nor natural law adequately articulates the moral basis of international relations, which he conceives as forming a society without government. Locke does not flinch from the harsh conclusion that lawful conquest potentially involves a severe diminution of political independence. However, he maintains that distinct societies retain an inherent right of self-government, even following lawful conquest. In the moral framework of mutually reinforcing limits, Locke's account of lawful conquest effectively nullifies the principle

---

27 See, for example, Locke's discussion of the Greeks' relation to their Turkish conquerors at II: 192.

of inviolable national sovereignty, while the normative claims of communal self-government strictly restrain the punitive measures allowed by the law of nature. In order to understand Locke's idea of international society and self-government, we need to reconsider the normative status of the bodies politic inhabiting the international state of nature.

The moral plane upon which independent peoples interact and conflict in international society has both a natural and a conventional or legitimist foundation. For Locke, the natural foundation of international society rests on the seminal distinction between government and society; two separate forms of association that like supremacy and self-government reflect distinct principles of construction and dissolution. Legal supremacy is a feature of civil government, a political phenomenon with a distinct institutional expression produced by the consent of the majority of society. According to the theoretical "original Compact" forming civil government, "every one of that Society" must submit "to the determination of the majority" with respect to the constitution of the legislative power (II: 97, 132). Locke indicates that the legislative power is "Supream" not only because its creation signifies "the first and fundamental positive Law of all Commonwealths" (II: 134), but also due to the quasi-natural law of "greater force" by which the majority may be held to act for the whole community in regards to matters of general societal concern (II: 96). Locke's endorsement of legislative supremacy means that only the legislature, or possibly a supreme executive with a share of the legislative power (II: 151–2), can be identified in any meaningful way as supreme. Civil government and the supreme power it possesses can only be dissolved by two means. First, the people have a natural right to revolt against oppressive or tyrannical rule, and thereby dissolve the government and reconstitute a new one as they see fit (II: 212–17). Second, the legislature may be destroyed and civil government *de facto* dissolved by the external force of conquest (II: 178–83). By this logic, civil governments are the primary victims of lawful conquest.

On one level, Locke's idea of civil society is simply the seedbed of civil government, a form of association produced "by the consent of every individual" in the community (II: 96). In theory, the unanimous consent grounding society informs and in essence authorizes the majority to act for the whole in determining the form of government for a community. Herein lies the radically democratic foundation of every "lawful government," whether the particular form of civil government established by the majority of society is democratic or most likely not (II: 99, 132).[28] However,

---

[28] Nathan Tarcov, "Locke's *Second Treatise* and the 'Best Fence against Rebellion'" *Review of Politics*, 43, 2 (April 1981): 198–217, esp. 205.

on a deeper level, society reflects the flesh-and-blood social reality of common life for which the cold abstractions of contractual legalism are always in some sense an impoverished metaphor.[29] In the normal course of events, civil government and society are practically inseparable. As independent commonwealths interact with others internationally and govern themselves by general standing laws domestically, the greater part represents the whole in a relatively seamless web of consensual connections. The dissolution of government by conquest or revolution exposes the fundamental distinction between these two interrelated but discrete modes of existence. Society reconstitutes governments. The implication for international relations is that it is not simply the establishment of a common legislative that separates one independent community from all others in the international state of nature. Rather the prior commitment to social union, to form one "Society," reflects the deeper moral and social reality that preexists and emphatically outlives the dissolution of any particular government a people may create. For Locke, society is where the people are.

Although society is not subject to the same logic of dissolution that affects government, it hardly needs to be said that Locke does not suggest that society is indestructible in the manner of Rousseau's general will.[30] He freely admits that societies may be dissolved consensually to form new ones through the act of incorporation (II: 177–8) or societies may be dissolved brutally by "Conquerors Swords," which "cut up Governments by the Roots, and mangle Societies to pieces" (II: 211). However, the distinction between consensual incorporation and brutal deracination may not be as clear as it initially appears. As a practical matter, Locke indicates that conquerors have historically been much less nice about the theoretical rights of conquered peoples than his eidetic treatment would suggest (II: 175, 180, 186). As a matter of natural history, dissolution of society by the "Conquerors Sword" can be seen as the prevalent historical practice to which Locke's entire conquest theory stands in opposition. The normative thrust of Locke's teaching on lawful conquest is to exempt and protect societies, as opposed to governments, from the full weight of natural law punishments. The humanizing tendency of Locke's limits on lawful conquerors, especially with regard to respecting property and civilian life, thus has a decidedly prescriptive character meant to reconceptualize notions of

---

[29] See Jeremy Rabkin, "Grotius, Vattel, and Locke: An Older View of Liberalism and Nationality" *Review of Politics*, 59, 2 (Spring 1997): 293–322, esp. 306–309 and Walzer, *Just Wars*, 53–54.

[30] Jean-Jacques Rousseau, *On the Social Contract*. Roger Masters, ed. (New York: St. Martin's Press, 1978 [1762]), pp. 108–109.

just war and natural law in moral terms compatible with a right of self-government inhering in the nature of society. The basic constituent elements of Locke's international order are societies.

Whereas Locke views the political independence associated with the idea of sovereignty as qualified or contingent on adherence to the natural law principle of nonaggression, he sees the inherent right of self-government as absolute. However, this right is absolute only in the negative sense that one society must not be governed arbitrarily or permanently by another without its consent. It is a right of nondomination rather than an absolute right in the positive sense of a right to have a particular form of government or rule by specific individuals.[31] The principle of nondomination involves the right of a people to choose any form of government consistent with natural law. The salutary consequences of lawful conquest may include the destruction and punishment of criminal leaders and even the elimination of aggressive regimes. In the harsh school of lawful conquest, societies may be instructed about the kinds of governments to which a people mindful of the natural law should consent.[32] In this sense, the inherent right of a society to govern itself is integrally linked to the framework of norms governing the international realm that may guide reasoned consent. Self-government as a right of nondomination contains the immanent causality of political independence, but it does not necessitate full sovereignty in the immediate sense.

There is also, however, a distinct conventional or legitimist dimension to Locke's conception of international society. As several commentators have observed, unlike his predecessor Hugo Grotius, Locke did not advance any substantive notion of the "law of nations" (*ius gentium*), an inductively established body of norms and general principles of law recognized in many different communities.[33] For Locke, the law of nature constitutes the only class of universally enforceable laws binding on all rational beings. This being granted, however, it is important to observe that much as Locke maintains that municipal laws strengthen the moral saliency of natural law principles by annexing "known penalties...to them, to enforce their

---

[31] Pettit's idea of freedom as "non-domination," as a condition free from arbitrary and exploitative measures but not from all forms of perhaps salutary interference, provides a good model for understanding Locke's idea of a society's inherent right of self-government (Philip Pettit, *Theory of Freedom: From the Psychology to the Politics of Agency* [Oxford: Oxford University Press, 2001], pp. 138–149).

[32] Josephson, *Art of Government*, 190–196.

[33] Hugo Grotius, *The Rights of War and Peace, 3 Vols.* (Indianapolis: Liberty Fund, 2005 [1625]), 162–164, 189. See also, Cox, *Locke on War*, 140–146; Forde, "Grotius," 643–645; Ahrensdorf and Pangle, *Justice among Nations*, 162–167; and Nardin, "Moral Basis," 58.

observation" (II: 135), so too do the various leagues, alliances, and compacts among nations signify a form of conventional glue binding the autonomous parts of international society (II: 14, 146). As Locke remarks, the various "Promises and Compacts" that individuals or communities make "are binding to them, though they are perfectly in a State of Nature, in reference to one another" (II: 14). The social character of the international state of nature derives in part from the capacity of these public persons to generate moral claims and obligations.

The kind of international agreement to which Locke attributes the greatest significance relates to the issue of territorial recognition. In the course of describing the manner in which "several Communities settled the Bounds of their distinct Territories," Locke makes reference to "the Leagues that have been made between several States and Kingdoms, either expressly or tacitly disowning all Claim and Right to the land in the others Possession" (II: 45). The legitimist aspect of international society involves both the explicit renunciation of territorial claims and an implicit recognition of the equality of the independent "States and Kingdoms" party to these reciprocal agreements. What is perhaps most striking about Locke's argument for the conventional legal basis of territorial recognition is his contention that this recognition may be explicit or tacit. We may understand this implicit recognition in several ways. First, Locke may mean no more than that any explicit agreement with another state regarding one matter includes implicit recognition of the territorial integrity of the various parties. For example, an agreement regarding trade or the establishment of diplomatic relations implies mutual recognition of borders. Alternatively, Locke may intend a more expansive construction of the meaning of implicit recognition such that any explicit assertion of territorial integrity by one state produces an implicit renunciation by that state of any territorial claim against any other state. Being a recognized member of international society would thus involve affirming, even if only tacitly, the independence and territorial integrity of the other members. Locke assumes that every society must have a territory of its own.

The argument for tacit territorial recognition suggests another international norm that limits conquest, in addition to the inheritance and self-rule rights of the "innocent" individuals in the defeated societies. Lawful conquerors are prohibited from annexing territory of the defeated society because of a moral obligation on the victor produced by the prior, often implicit, recognition of the territorial integrity of the other party. The recognition of distinct territorial units is, in essence, a validation of the right of self-government inhering in the society possessing and organizing that territory. But how does the legal principle of territoriality relate to the norm of nonaggression?

The various leagues and compacts establishing territorial boundaries provide legal or conventional markers for determining aggression in the international arena. By delimiting a recognizable threshold for measuring aggression, these international agreements establish a basis for self-defense and collective security arrangements allowing intervention and counter-intervention to assist allies and victims of aggression. However, this position begs the question as to whether annexation of territory is permissible not as reparation, but rather as a security guarantee to prevent future aggression.[34] In absence of a broadly accepted revision of the territorial settlement, such action would be inconsistent with international norms, inasmuch as the practice of violating treaties and implicit obligations threatens to unravel the moral fabric of international society. Nations are less likely to engage in diplomacy, and wars likely to be more bitterly fought, if permanent loss of territory is an acceptable outcome. Locke suggests that the broader security interest of every member of international society is served by refraining from strategic or punitive annexation. By similar reasoning, the international norms that permit preemptive war prohibit preventive war.[35] The natural law sanctions preemptive attack against an adversary showing an "Enmity to [ones] being" and a "sedate settled design" to harm (II: 16). However, preventive war lacking immediate threat of attack and intended to weaken a potential rival or future threat is itself a form of aggression and would be no more morally defensible than a war launched to preserve a nation's hegemony or restore a balance of power. Both annexation and preventive war involve violations of principles and norms, the universal renunciation of which would make international peace impossible.

LOCKE AND COLONIALISM

It is in light of the natural and legitimist basis of international morality that the question of Locke's relation to colonialism is clearly germane. While a full examination of the relation of liberalism and imperialism is well beyond the scope of the present study,[36] it may be fitting to consider briefly

---

34 Coby, "Is Locke a Hobbesian?" 21.

35 For the moral distinction between preemptive and preventive war, see Walzer, *Just War*, 74–85 and Malcolm Brailey, "Pre-emption and Prevention: An Ethical and Legal Critique of the Bush Doctrine and Anticipatory Use of Force in Defence of the State" *Institute of Strategic Studies Singapore* (November 2003): 1–22, esp. 1–9.

36 For good recent studies on this theme, see Uday Singh Mehta, *Liberalism and Empire: A Study of Nineteenth-Century British Liberal Thought* (Chicago: University of Chicago

the implications of Locke's international society argument for colonial-ism. Several recent commentators have offered studies associating Locke's permissive natural law justification of the use of force with the aggressive mercantilist and colonial policies of early modern England.[37] They gener-ally reach this conclusion by drawing together several pieces of evidence. First, there is Locke's admission that the prohibition on annexing territory does not extend to unoccupied land of which "anyone had liberty to make use of the waste" (II: 184). Second, the consequentialist logic of Locke's argument that the one who cultivates "the wild woods and uncultivated waste of America" does not by his industry deprive anyone else of their rights, but rather may be said to give the bounty of increased productiv-ity "to Mankind," is interpreted by some as a specious pseudohumanitar-ian rationalization for dispossessing native peoples of their land (II: 37). Finally, Locke's doctrine of nonaggression is sometimes viewed in the colo-nial context as little more than a transparent, self-serving justification for the destruction and enslavement of native peoples who have the temerity to resist their own dispossession. Together, these arguments form a serious indictment against Locke.

It may be helpful to analyze these charges in light of our findings regard-ing Locke's notion of self-government and international society. There are two central questions at issue. First, does Locke see non-European peoples as independent nations or distinct societies against whom the unprovoked use of force is simply aggression? Second, do these non-European peoples have property rights in the territory they inhabit?

When we consider the charges against Locke in terms of these questions, neither the punitive aspect of the law of nature nor the consequentialist jus-tification for private property necessarily serves the purposes alleged. It is important to observe that, in contrast to later liberal international lawyers such as Vattel, Locke does not refer to leaving land undeveloped as a viola-tion of the natural law that is in any way punishable by another party.[38]

Press, 1999); Sanka Muthu, *Enlightenment against Empire* (Princeton: Princeton University Press, 2003); and Jennifer Pitts, *A Turn to Empire: The Rise of Imperial Liberalism in Britain and France* (Princeton: Princeton University Press, 2005).

[37] For example, Arneil, *Locke and America*, 16–20; Pagden "Human Rights," 183–184; Tuck, *Rights of War*, 73–78; and Tully, *Locke in Contexts*, 154–155. For some critics, the punitive aspect of Locke's natural law served mainly as a rationalization for the dispos-session and enslavement of Africans and Native Americans by the European powers. For a good treatment of the literature dealing with Locke and slavery, see Wayne Glauser, "Three Approaches to Locke and the Slave Trade" *Journal of the History of Ideas*, 51, 2 (April 1990): 199–216.

[38] Emerich de Vattel, Emerich de, *Le Droit des Gens, et les devoirs des citoyes, ou principe de la loi naturelle. Vol I* (Nime 1793). Cf. Pagden, "Human Rights," 183.

While Locke is vague as to what constitutes insufficiently habited land, it is clear that he does not make the brutal argument that any nation that cannot protect private property cannot exclude foreign settlement.[39] Moreover, the consequentialist and utilitarian justification for private acquisition cannot on its own constitute an apology for colonialism, inasmuch as Locke in no way entertains this reasoning with respect to lawful conquest.[40] Why could a lawful conqueror not claim any land (not just "waste") on the grounds that they can make it more productive than its original owners? On the basis of the consequentialist argument alone, there is no reason why a lawful conqueror could not make such a claim, even though Locke denies any such permission to the conqueror. Clearly, any conflict between settler and native communities may be rationalized, even by the most tortured logic, as "force without right," and thus exploited by the moral hypocrisy of the colonial powers seeking to justify their territorial ambitions. However, would the natural law authorization for the use of lethal force and enslavement not apply at least as much, and with even more dramatic consequences for international society, to aggression among the settled peoples and kingdoms of Europe, who presumably are parties to the comprehensive territorial settlement, as it would to native peoples who may or may not be. The most radical thrust of Locke's punitive law of nature is perhaps directed against belligerent European autocrats such as Louis XIV, and much less suited to colonial apologetics.[41]

---

[39] Rabkin, "Older View of Liberalism," 313.

[40] It should be noted, however, that Locke's consequentialist argument for property rights would be more suited for justifying the displacement of native peoples if the standard for proprietary rights is cultivation rather than any specific claim to the enhanced productivity accruing from the institution of money. By this reasoning, the bare act of cultivation supplies a threshold for proprietary right that nomadic peoples presumably would have great difficulty meeting, at least to the satisfaction of the colonial powers. For accounts of the way in which this version of Locke's argument about agriculture was or could be used to justify the dispossession of native peoples, see Barbara Arneil, "Trade, Plantations, and Property: John Locke and the Economic Defense of Colonialism" *Journal of the History of Ideas*, 55, 4 (October 1994): 591–609, esp. 602–609; Matthew Kramer, *John Locke and the Origins of Private Property* (Cambridge: Cambridge University Press, 1997), pp. 114–119; Ralph Lerner, *The Thinking Revolutionary* (Ithaca: Cornell University Press, 1987), pp. 139–173; Mehta, *Liberalism and Empire*, 123–132; Muthu, *Enlightenment against Empire*, 187, 277; Pitts, *Turn to Empire*, 201 and Tully, *Locke in Contexts*, 139–151, 163–166.

[41] This is a line of argument pursued vigorously by Waldron, *God, Locke, and Equality*, 148–150. A similar interpretation is that of Ashcraft who maintains that Locke's teaching on conquest was meant to warn the tyrannical Stuarts that a foreign invasion to liberate England and punish its rulers would be entirely consistent with the law of nature (Richard Ashcraft, *Revolutionary Politics and Locke's Two Treatises of Government* [Princeton: Princeton University Press, 1986], p. 399).

Although Locke suggests that where there is "more Land, than the Inhabitants possess, and make use of, anyone has liberty to make use of the waste," he also displays a remarkable insouciance about this advantage claiming, "but there Conquerors take little care to possess themselves of the Lands of the Vanquished" (II: 184). Locke's underlying assumption here is that wasteland is unlikely anywhere money is widely used and available. This argument clearly leaves open the possibility for colonial powers to claim "waste" land that they might assert (reasonably or not) is not materially connected to the well-being of a people in a distinct territorial area. However, this argument serves as moral justification for colonial possession only with the crucial qualification that the land is not claimed by people "who have consented to the use of Money," a possibility increasingly foreclosed in Locke's view by the widespread use of money in his day (II: 45, 49, 184). Nonmonetarized native peoples would not, in this argument, constitute societies included in the implicit territorial settlement underlying Locke's international society, and thus are, or were, subject to colonial predations with respect to surplus land they could not "possess, and make use of" from which the monetarized societies of Europe were largely immune. However, Locke does suggest a version of the claim right to vacant or uncultivated land that holds potentially explosive populist implications even in Europe: "I have heard it affirmed that in Spain itself, a Man may be permitted to plough, sow, and reap, without being disturbed, upon Land he has no other Title to, but only his making use of it" (II: 36). With this statement, Locke takes a jab, if only in passing, at the premier colonial power of the age. In the final analysis, Locke's argument is perhaps best understood as a rights claim to vacant land that has colonial implications, but it is also historically contingent on the development of a global monetary system that would, by his own formulation, gradually make colonialism morally indefensible.

LOCKE AND THE ETHICS OF INTERVENTION

This chapter has tried to show that Locke's thoughts on international relations are better understood by shifting from the familiar discourse of natural law and sovereignty to a discourse of international society and self-government. The normative content of this international society rests on the recognition of distinct societies with an inherent right of self-government, a notion of just war as self-defense and law enforcement, and the identification of the source of international norms in a combination of natural law and conventional legitimist principles.

It may be helpful to conclude by briefly exploring Locke's vision of international society with a view to considering its application to the contemporary debate about sovereignty and intervention. This debate over the ethics of intervention raises fundamental questions about territorial integrity, political independence, and the right of nations to interfere in the internal affairs of other nations; and it typically involves two distinct conceptions of international society: the pluralist and solidarist models.[42] Pluralists derive the normative content of international society primarily from the mutual recognition of the component societal units' right to exist and promote their diverse national ends with minimal outside interference.[43] In the pluralist model of international society, as in international law generally, the emphasis is on the principle of nonintervention and the primacy of state sovereignty. The solidarist model, on the other hand, maintains that human solidarity assumes moral priority to state sovereignty since distinct national communities can reach broad agreement about substantive moral standards. According to solidarists, the use of force is legitimate when conceived as a form of law enforcement including not only self-defense and collective security, but also the possibility of intervening to uphold the shared moral purposes of international society.[44] The tension between the pluralist and solidarist view has, if anything, only intensified with recent developments such as the effort by the Canadian-inspired *International Commission on Intervention and State Sovereignty* to shift the terms of the debate from the "right of intervention" to the idea of the "responsibility to protect".[45] Proponents of the idea of international society, however conceived, feel the pressing need to establish clear criteria as to which kinds of situations constitute a legitimate exception to the general principle of state sovereignty and nonintervention underlying international law.

Locke offers a perspective on the contemporary debate about intervention that is neither wholly pluralist nor solidarist. With the pluralist model, Locke views the mutual recognition of the constituent units' right to exist

---

[42] For the origination of these two models, see Bull, "Grotian Conception," 52. For good overviews of the pluralist-solidarist debate, see Bellamy, "Humanitarian Responsibilities," 324–325 and Little, "The English School," 453.

[43] Robert Jackson, *The Global Covenant: Human Conduct in a World of States* (Oxford: Oxford University Press, 2000), pp. 155–184 and James Mayall, *World Politics: Progress and Its Limits* (Cambridge: Cambridge University Press, 2000), p. 14.

[44] Nicholas J. Wheeler, *Saving Strangers: Humanitarian Intervention in International Society* (Oxford: Oxford University Press, 2000) and Nardin, "Moral Basis," 64–70.

[45] See the International Commission on Intervention and State Sovereignty, *The Responsibility to Protect* (Ottawa: International Development Research Centre, 2001). Cf. Bellamy, "Humanitarian Responsibilities," 326

as self-governing entities as an important normative component of international society. Moreover, he shares the pluralists' enthusiasm for the diverse ends available to independent communities formed by the consent of their people and embodying the moral purpose of society in their distinctive fashion. Locke demonstrates no desire or confidence that international institutions will replace self-governing societies as the primary actors in the international state of nature. However, as we have seen, Locke departs from the pluralists insofar as he does not share their emphasis on the moral primacy of state sovereignty. Rather, more in keeping with the solidarist model, Locke's state of nature grounds an idea of human solidarity prior to the civil state that legitimizes the use of force broadly conceived as a form of law enforcement. While Locke does not deal systematically with the normative content of international morality, especially with regard to the status of individuals in international society, he does present a vision for the basis of international agreement about substantive moral standards in the generalities of the law of nature.

In order to develop a Lockean reading of the ethics of intervention, we must piece together various aspects of his argument about international society. The law of nature that grounds the right of each "to preserve himself" also commands "the preservation of Society" (II: 6, 134). The underlying tension between self-preservation and preservation of society only intensifies in international society wherein preservation of one society may conflict with the command to "preserve the rest of Mankind" (II: 6).[46] In the case of both the individual and society, Locke is adamant that the duty of universal preservation only assumes genuine moral saliency when it "comes not in competition" with communal or self-preservation. Whereas, as Dunn correctly observes, Locke sees the duty to preserve all humankind as "the most fundamental interpersonal claim of justice between human beings," he clearly also determines that the overarching moral purpose of each society is the security and welfare of its own people, and thus any moral duty on states to intervene can never be more than an imperfect duty qualified by the danger and difficulty involved.[47] On its face, this formulation of global responsibility appears to provide little guidance for the ethics of intervention. Does the natural law command to "preserve the rest of Mankind" authorize or even require states and international society to

---

[46] Grant, *Locke's Liberalism*, 128.
[47] Alex Tuckness, "Punishment, Property, and the Limits of Altruism: Locke's International Assymetry" *American Political Science Review*, 102, 4 (November 2008): 472–476. See also Dunn, "Dilemma of Humanitarian Intervention," 146, 137, and 144–145.

intervene in order, for example, to end humanitarian disasters or severe oppression when their own safety or prosperity is not in jeopardy?

Locke's discussion of the Turkish occupation of Greece may be significant in this regard. On one level, it is meant as an illustration of the natural right of revolution; a call for the Greeks to "cast off the Turkish yoke...whenever they have a power to do it" (II: 192). Locke clearly asserts the nondomination right of Greek society, or any distinct society that retains its inherent right of self-government despite the loss of political independence through conquest. What is not so clear, however, is whether Locke intended the Greek example to be simply an objective *observation* about the natural right of revolution, or if it can be construed as an *appeal* for intervention by sympathetic European states on behalf of the Greek people. As a theoretical question, Locke's general endorsement of the natural law principle of third-party intervention (II: 8) would be applicable to this situation if, as is likely, Locke and his European audience construed Greek society to be the victim of Turkish aggression. Admittedly, Locke does not explicitly identify a right of international society to intervene militarily on behalf of the oppressed Greeks. However, unlike John Stuart Mill, for instance, neither does he place strict terms and qualifications on the right of intervention, such as requiring a direct appeal for aid or a demonstration of actual military resistance by the oppressed party.[48] It is precisely the open-ended nature of Locke's appeal to the Greek cause that allows intervention to be, at least, a plausible interpretation of his broader intention.

While the Greek example may suggest Locke's openness to international support for, and even intervention in, wars of national liberation, contemporary analysts generally believe it is a much more questionable proposition to consider intervention in the purely internal affairs of a sovereign nation.[49] However, Locke's account of lawful conquest contains the core of an argument for even more direct intervention in the internal affairs of another nation than we saw in the Greek case. His theory of selective war

---

[48] John Stuart Mill, "A Few Words on Non-Intervention." *Dissertations and Discussions*, *Vol. III.* (New York: E.P. Dutton & Co, 1873 [1859]), pp. 238–263. Cf. Pitts, *Turn to Empire*, 142–143.

[49] See, for example, Walzer, *Just War*, 106; Stanley Hoffman, "Sovereignty and the Ethics of Intervention." *The Ethics and Politics of Humanitarian Intervention*. Ed. Stanley Hoffman. (Notre Dame: University of Notre Dame Press, 1996), pp. 12–37, esp. p. 19; and Martin Wight, "Western Values in International Relations." *Diplomatic Investigations: Essays in the Theory of International Politics* (London: George Allen & Unwin, 1966), pp. 89–131, esp. 112–113. But for a contrary view, see Fernando Teson, *Humanitarian Intervention: An Inquiry into Law and Morality* (Dobbs Ferry, NY: Transnational Publishers, 1988), pp. 15–16.

guilt proposed that the people of a given society are no more to be thought responsible for external aggression than they are "to be thought guilty of any Violence or Oppression their Gouvernours should use upon the People themselves, or any Part of their Fellow Subjects, they having impowered them no more to the one, than to the other" (II: 179). Locke employs the argument that aggressive war violates the *raison d'etre* of society and is thus inconceivable as a delegated power of legitimate government. One effect of Locke's moral parallel between external aggression and domestic oppression is to present every lawful conquest as a kind of foreign intervention to liberate an oppressed people who can no more be thought to authorize aggressive war by their government against others than against themselves. The theoretical distinction between government and society allows Locke to suggest that society is the party injured by an aggressive government.[50] The extension of this logic to aggression against "Part" of society forms the basis for a conception of sovereign responsibility that makes government oppression of minorities a justification not only of revolution, but also conceivably for intervention to aid oppressed groups.

External aggression and domestic oppression against a "Part of their Fellow Subjects" violates the same basic principle of natural justice. Insofar as a given society may no more be held responsible for one than the other, then, at least in principle, international society is no less restricted in its right to punish those responsible for either kind of aggression. Although Locke does not detail the precise forms of government action that would constitute such oppression of minorities, the logic of the Greek example, as a kind of minority within an empire, suggests the framework for establishing the normative content of international standards regarding the status of individuals that might include a prohibition against discriminatory treatment or the systematic violation of fundamental natural rights pertaining to physical security, ownership and inheritance of property, and freedom of religion. In lieu of concrete international agreement on the substantive normative content of the individual rights governments are charged to secure, Locke's theory arguably limns the outline of what form such an agreement might take.

Another topic that receives considerable attention in the contemporary debate over intervention is the idea of "supreme humanitarian emergencies."[51] Even strong proponents of the principle of nonintervention

---

[50] David Lowenthal, "Locke on Conquest." *Understanding the Political Spirit: Philosophical Investigations from Socrates to Nietzsche.* Catherine Zuckert, ed. (New Haven: Yale University Press, 1988), pp. 126–135, esp. 132.

[51] See Bellamy, "Humanitarian Responsibilities," 335–338; Nardin, "Moral Basis," 66–67; and Walzer, *Just Wars,* 251–254.

frequently admit that there are rare situations of extreme humanitarian crisis, such as genocide or natural disasters, that "shock the conscience of mankind" and may justify intervention. Locke's account of lawful conquest speaks to this issue indirectly. His insistence on the humane treatment of those conquered people not directly implicated in aggression provides a rather stringent moral framework regulating how states and militaries should conduct themselves when intervening. The law of nature "that willeth the preservation of all Mankind as much as is possible" (II: 182) requires lawful conquerors to respect the property rights of noncombatants and even to remit legitimate reparation if it threatens the survival of innocent people. With this argument, Locke indicates that a lawful conqueror assumes a considerable measure of moral responsibility for the security and well-being of the defeated people. Does this notion of responsibility extend globally into a justification for intervention in order, for example, to relieve a supreme humanitarian emergency?

Although Locke does not address this question directly, the general direction of his argument suggests two distinct lines of thought on the issue of humanitarian intervention. On the one hand, he indicates that the normal rules of justice such as those applying to reparation may be suspended by the greater humanitarian need of those "who are in danger to perish without" these resources (II: 183). By this reasoning, supplemented by the natural law imperative to preserve humankind, Locke could endorse temporary suspension of the nonintervention principle, at the very least, to relieve rare and severe cases of humanitarian crisis such as mass starvation.[52] On the other hand, there is an aspect of the domestic analogy with decidedly more radical implications for intervention. According to Locke, the federative power that conducts a commonwealth's foreign policy "answers to the Power every Man naturally had before he entered into Society" (II: 145). The natural executive power of the individual includes the general, or even universal, right to "joyn with" another that is injured and assist in the punishment of the offender (II: 10). One implication of Locke's argument would be that when individuals in the state of nature transfer this punishment right to their government it is thereby authorized by this third-party right to punish governments that abuse their own people, and even to prosecute violators of the law of nature who may escape punishment in their

---

[52] In a related context, Locke suggested that the normal laws of economics can be suspended in famine conditions (John Locke, "Venditio." *Political Essays.* Mark Goldie, ed. (Cambridge: Cambridge University Press, 1997 [1695]), pp. 339–343). For the humanitarian imperatives of the natural law, see also Alex Tuckness, *Locke and the Legislative Point of View* (Princeton: Princeton University Press, 2002), p. 81.

own country.[53] While the claim that borders may be crossed in order to punish wrongdoers does not necessarily translate into a similar permission with respect to protecting the innocent, the logic of punishment and protection are clearly interwoven in the moral framework of Locke's international society. Thus, the extraterritorial implications of such a punishment right could make humanitarian intervention a common feature of Lockean international relations.

While Locke's argument may be said to support the logic of humanitarian intervention, he offers little guidance with respect to the vital question regarding who, if anyone, would have an obligation to fight in humanitarian causes? There is a clear Lockean argument that a soldier's duty to fight in a just, primarily defensive, war follows from one's obligation to one's own society and the government's legitimate power to preserve the society (II: 139, 143). However, the moral duty to fight in wars of intervention on behalf of others is more ambiguous. Possibly these wars would have to be fought solely by volunteer armies. However, another potential source for the individual's obligation to fight in wars of humanitarian intervention is the obligation arising from the comprehension of the individual's natural executive power into the federative power of the government. By this reasoning, the individual would authorize the government to execute the natural law in the international sphere on the same moral basis that he or she is obliged to assist in the execution of the civil law internally. Of course, according to Locke, the individual would still have the natural right to decide whether the intervention by his or her government is justified, and thus would always retain the right of resistance and even revolution.

Locke's treatment of the moral basis of international relations outlines what he takes to be the promise and problems of international society. He exhibits promise regarding possible agreement about international norms pertaining to territorial integrity, the limits on conquest, and the mutual recognition of the right of self-government inhering in distinct societies. Locke even provides a rough sketch of the normative basis for a way of thinking about rights of individuals and minorities in the international context. There are also, however, definite limits to Locke's optimism about international cooperation. He shows little confidence that the natural law principles of morality can be effectively embodied in international institutions. Moreover, the latent possibility of anarchy is no less apparent where each society is its own judge of humanitarian justice, than it is for the

---

[53] John Simmons, *The Lockean Theory of Rights* (Princeton: Princeton University Press, 1992), pp. 129–130.

individual who judges in the state of nature. Indeed, Locke's deep episte-mological scepticism about the notion of innate moral sense, as well as his general pessimism with respect to the normative value of historical tradi-tion and the customary law of nations, point to what he must have seen as powerful social, cultural, and intellectual obstacles to the formaliza-tion and effective enforcement of international norms of behaviour (I: 58; II: 103, 175, 180, 186).[54] In the final analysis, however, Locke's account of the moral basis of international relations may speak more to his cautious hope for general moral and intellectual progress than to a radical transfor-mation in the international state of nature. The natural, if more distant, corollary to the creation of citizens who have developed the proper rational habits and conduct befitting rights bearing individuals in liberal society may be the global citizen who respects and secures rights at home and in international society. Perhaps the prescriptive thrust of Locke's theory of international society aimed toward the inculcation of liberal principles in areas and aspects hitherto scarcely observed.

[54] See also John Locke, *Essay Concerning Human Understanding*. Peter Nidditch, ed. (Oxford: Oxford University Press, 1975 [1700 4th Ed], pp. 65–84.

Conclusion

In an age in which the intellectual life of the West as expressed in its art, culture, spirituality, and philosophy identifies itself as incurably postmodern, it is perhaps wise to heed Charles Taylor's warning that "understanding modernity aright is an exercise in retrieval."[1] In order to cast our minds back to the seventeenth century when the modern period was born, the student of modernity must excavate through many layers of thought in the subsequent history of ideas; that is, dig through assumptions about the philosophical meaning of history, culture, and material forces that have long since hardened imperceptibly over time into fundamental ideological commitments. To rediscover modernity as it first appeared in the world brash and confident, it requires that in some respects we forget who we are, or perhaps whom we think we are.

This study constitutes a modest effort to contribute to the enormous task of retrieving modernity by recovering an authentic understanding of John Locke's important role in its creation. We have tried to restore a sense of Locke's work as he intended it to be read; that is, as philosophical reflections upon the fundamental questions of human existence. Our analysis of Locke's mature writings reveals a bold and original thinker whose probing examination of the workings of the human mind and the manifold interpersonal relations characterizing social reality leads us to question many of the prevailing assumptions about this complex figure. Over the course of this study, we have become reacquainted with a thinker whose depth and range of insights resists any serious attempt to confine him to the intellectual horizons of a long-past historical period or to the narrow intellectual

[1] Charles Taylor, *Sources of the Self: The Making of the Modern Identity* (Cambridge, MA: Harvard University Press, 1989), p. xi.

paradigms of the present. Reexamining Locke with fresh eyes allows us to engage with the spirit of inquiry in which modernity was born, and thus makes possible the daunting project of retrieval that will allow us to understand the genesis of modernity but also hopefully to recognize the great challenges and opportunities in the future direction of modern life.

Locke obviously lived in a world very different from our own. However, he also lived in a period of great change and thus was born into an England different from the one in which he died. Born in 1632, almost a decade before the political, constitutional, and religious tumults that tore England apart in civil war, Locke died in 1704, at the start of a new century. He lived to see the transformation of his homeland from the quasi-absolutist regime of the Stuarts into a parliamentary monarchy bearing the marks of the first recognizably modern state. Despite his self-effacing description of himself as a man "content with a modest lot,"[2] he also lived to experience the satisfaction of passing his last years as one of the recognized leading lights of the revolutionary intellectual movement that would come to be known as the Enlightenment. As a major figure of the seventeenth-century Enlightenment, Locke set his philosophical sights on nothing less than a critical examination of practically every important aspect of the *ancien régime* that had embodied European civilization for centuries. The *ancien régime* was animated by both a series of hierarchical assumptions characterizing the relations of rulers and ruled, men and women, and God and humankind, as well as a set of metaphysical and theological doctrines that weaved these relations together in a comprehensive account of human nature and cosmic order that had governed western life for a millennium. Locke's vision of modernity presupposed a thorough rejection of this majestic alliance of biblical revelation and classical philosophy.

The heart of Locke's contribution to the creation of modernity was his articulation of a philosophy of freedom that pervaded practically every dimension of human life. As we have seen, Locke's conception of modernity extended far beyond the alteration of political phenomena narrowly defined. Indeed, he recognized that the transformation of the meaning of what is political must be one of the central goals of modernity as he introduced a new understanding of freedom not only into analysis of government and international relations, but also into theorizing about the family, the churches, and educational practices. The intellectual core of Locke's

---

[2] This was how Locke described himself in the epitaph he wrote shortly before he died. See Roger Woolhouse, *Locke: A Biography* (Cambridge: Cambridge University Press, 2007), p. 1.

new, modern approach to political life was his discovery of the internal mechanics of the human mind. In the democratization of mind, Locke believed he had discovered a new mental continent, a hitherto unexamined realm of subjectivity and interiority, which surpassed in significance the discoveries of the age of explorations in the terrestrial realm. With characteristically modern confidence in the transformative power of the new philosophical methods, Locke set about mapping and charting the contours of human understanding as it stood shorn of the metaphysical certainties of the past – the individual alone, as it were, in the "vast ocean of being."[3] Locke's compact conception of philosophy and his assessment of its legitimate theoretical ambitions presented the classical quest for the basis of moral knowledge in a new and more complex form. While bounded firmly by cognitive fields of probability relating to religious faith and natural substance, Locke insisted that the faculties of the human mind contain "light enough" to determine our natural rights and moral duties by way of multiple modes of moral reasoning admitting of varying degrees of certainty and probability. The goal of incorporating the complexity of nature and fallible judgments into any meaningful speculation about the human good would be one of the characteristically Lockean contributions to the creation of modernity.

In addition to illuminating Locke's central role in establishing the modern break from pre-modern philosophy, another, and perhaps more fundamental, aim of this study has been to recover a sense of both the greatness and danger of the vision of modern life Locke presents. We have tried to show that beneath the superficial appearance of conservatism affecting some commentators lay Locke's more essential effort to transform inherited assumptions about the limits and possibilities confronting philosophy and politics in the modern period. In contrast to what he took to be the overly ambitious metaphysical tendencies of philosophy old and new, Locke sought to refocus modern philosophy toward rigorous examination of the connection, and indeed the tension, existing between the eidetic and genetic approaches to the understanding and intelligibility of being and becoming. But far from confining philosophy to the conservative function of simply legitimating things as they are or traditionally have been, Locke formulated a profoundly dynamic and progressive construction of the relation between the intellectual properties of mind and the instantiation of ideas in the world. Contrary to the suggestion of contemporary critics of Locke,

---

[3] John Locke, *An Essay Concerning Human Understanding*, Peter Nidditch, ed. (Oxford: Oxford University Press, 1975 [1700, 4th ed.]), bk. 1, ch. 1, sec. 7, p. 47.

who charge that his philosophy encourages individual disengagement from one's social and contextual reality, this study has tried to show that the great paradox underlying Locke's vision of modernity lies in the extent to which his philosophical discoveries relating to subjectivity and interiority were quite consciously directed toward the articulation of a distinctly modern conception of the "public" rooted in the flesh-and-blood relations composing Locke's reflections upon constitutional government, the family, the church, and international relations. Locke's philosophical idealism sought to embrace rather than transcend this paradox and thus proposed that the articulation of new principles of legitimacy for these evolving interpersonal relations would be the perpetually shifting goal rather than the unmoving foundation of modern politics and philosophy.

The considerable degree to which the questions and debates Locke examined are still alive to us today are a testament to the enduring impact of Locke's contribution to the formation of modernity. Despite the great challenges to the Lockean conception of political rationalism posed by the philosophical movements of the nineteenth and twentieth centuries that gave rise to revolutionary interpretations of history, culture, and material reality, the world at the dawn of the twenty-first century in many respects remains stubbornly modern. This is not to suggest that the triumph of modernity in the seventeenth and eighteenth centuries wholly effaced biblical piety or the classical conception of civic life as authentic alternatives to modern individualism with their own compelling claims to wisdom about the good and full human life. Indeed, the recent resurgence of religious fundamentalism and signs of a deep longing for a richer sense of community among significant segments of the public in several advanced liberal democracies indicates that certain aspects of pre-modern life still find many adherents today.

Moreover, the solipsistic tendencies of modernity present, but by no means simply dominant, in Locke became in their radicalized, postmodern form the impetus for fresh and powerful challenges to the regnant philosophy of modernity based on the moral sovereignty of the individual. Whether Locke's new conception of philosophy consigned to its "underlabourer" role as the theoretical handservant of the various sciences possessed the conceptual heft to support Enlightenment optimism about the inevitable progress of human understanding is, of course, a question beyond the scope of the present study. However, the relevance we have found in Locke's work as it relates to contemporary issues revolving around questions of executive power, gender equality, public education, religious pluralism, and humanitarian intervention at the very least suggests that Locke still speaks with probity and in a more than residual way on important matters of concern today.

It has been our hope that this reexamination of Locke will help us understand the genesis of modernity and by extension the basis of many of our fundamental moral and philosophical commitments. This study also sought to raise the possibility that Locke provides some of the theoretical resources that may illuminate the future direction of the many liberal democratic societies that are still fundamentally modern in their self-understanding. The conflicts between science and faith, freedom and equality, and rights and duties that increasingly characterize contemporary life are the current manifestations of distinctively modern tensions already present within Locke's thought. If the retrieval and rediscovery of Locke's role in the creation of modernity is to have more than just antiquarian significance, the ultimate test may be whether Locke's thought speaks in a palpable way to the most serious moral, political, and ethical issues confronting liberal society in the twenty-first century. Recent advances in biotechnology, our increasing sensitivity to the problems facing the environment, and the new pressures on traditional notions of civic life emerging in increasingly multicultural societies present powerful challenges to the adequacy of received ideas about democratic representation, the moral basis of human dignity, and the human relation to the physical world. In order to address these questions sufficiently, modern liberal democracies must first understand the meaning of what is being asked. Perhaps recovering Locke's seminal role in making the world we inhabit and inherited will help us achieve a degree of moral and intellectual clarity that makes this possible.

Bibliography

Aarsleff, Hans. "The State of Nature and the Nature of Man in Locke." In *John Locke: Problems and Perspectives*. John Yolton, ed. Cambridge: Cambridge University Press, 1969: 99–136.

Aaron, Richard I. *John Locke*, 2nd Ed. Oxford: Oxford University Press, 1955.

Ahrensdorf, Peter and Thomas Pangle. *Justice among Nations: On the Moral Basis of Power and Peace*. Lawrence: University Press of Kansas, 1999.

Aquinas, Thomas. *On Law, Morality and Politics*, 2nd ed. William P. Baumgarth and Richard J. Regan, eds. Indianapolis: Hackett Publishing, 2002.

   Political Writings, R.W. Dyson, ed. Cambridge: Cambridge University Press, [1274] 2002.

Aristotle. *Nicomachean Ethics*. Martin Oswald, trans. New York: MacMillan, 1962.

Arneil, Barbara. "Trade, Plantations, and Property: John Locke and the Economic Defense of Colonialism." *Journal of the History of Ideas*, vol. 55, no. 4 (October 1994): 591–609.

   John Locke and America: The Defence of English Colonialism. Oxford: Clarendon Press, 1996.

Arnhart, Larry. "The 'God-Like Prince': John Locke, Executive Prerogative, and the American Presidency." *Presidential Studies Quarterly*, vol. 9, no. 2 (Spring 1979): 121–30.

Ashcraft, Richard. "Locke's State of Nature: Historical Fact or Moral Fiction?" *American Political Science Review*, vol. 42, no. 3 (September 1968): 898–915.

   Revolutionary Politics & Locke's Two Treatises. Princeton: Princeton University Press, 1986.

   Locke's Two Treatises of Government. London: Allen & Unwin, 1987.

Augustine, St. *City of God*. New York: Penguin, 1972.

Ayers, Michael. *Locke: Epistemology & Ontology*, Vol. I & II. London: Routledge, 1993.

Balibar, Etienne. *Spinoza and Politics*. Peter Snowdon, trans. Verso: New York, 1998.

Becker, Ronald. "The Ideological Commitment of Locke: Freemen and Servants in the Two Treatises of Government." *History of Political Thought*, vol. 8, no. 4 (1992): 631–56.

Bellamy, Alex J. "Humanitarian Responsibilities and Interventionist Claims in International Society." *Review of International Studies*, vol. 29, no. 3 (July 2003): 321–40.

Blackstone, William. *Commentaries on the Laws of England*, Vol. I. London, 1791.

Bou-Habib, Paul. "Locke, Sincerity and the Rationality of Persecution." *Political Studies*, vol. 51, no. 4 (December 2003): 611–26.

Brady, Michelle. "The Nature of Virtue in a Politics of Consent: John Locke on Education." *International Philosophical Quarterly*, vol. 45, no. 2 (June 2005): 157–73.

Brailey, Malcolm. "Pre-emption and Prevention: An Ethical and Legal Critique of the Bush Doctrine and Anticipatory Use of Force in Defence of the State." *Institute of Strategic Studies Singapore* (November 2003): 1–22.

Brennan, Teresa and Carole Pateman. "'Mere Auxiliaries to the Commonwealth': Women and the Origins of Liberalism." *Political Studies*, vol. 27, no. 2 (1979): 183–220.

Bull, Hedley. "The Grotian Conception of International Society." *Diplomatic Investigations: Essays in the Theory of International Politics*. Herbert Butterfield and Martin Wight, eds. London: George Allen & Unwin, 1966: 51–73.

    The Anarchical Society: A Study of Order in World Politics. New York: Columbia University Press, 1977.

Butler, Melissa. "Early Liberal Roots of Feminism: John Locke and His Attack on Patriarchy." *American Political Science Review*, vol. 72, no. 1 (March 1978): 135–50.

Buzan, Barry. "The English School: An Underexploited Resource in IR." *Review of International Studies*, vol. 27, no. 3 (July 2001): 471–88.

Carr, Craig and Michael Seidler. "Pufendorf, Sociality and the Modern State." *History of Political Thought*, vol. 13, no. 3 (Autumn 1996): 352–78.

Carrig, Joseph. "Liberal Impediments to Liberal Education: The Assent to Locke." *Review of Politics*, vol. 63, no. 1 (Winter 2001): 41–76.

Casas de las, Bartholome. *In Defence of the Indians*. Stafford Poole, trans. DeKalb: Northern Illinois University Press, 1992 [1552].

Chappell, Vere. "Power in Locke's Essay." In *The Cambridge Companion to Locke's "Essay Concerning Human Understanding."* Lex Newman, ed. Cambridge: Cambridge University Press, 2007: 130–52.

Clark, Lorenne. "Women and Locke: Who Owns the Apples in the Garden of Eden?" In *The Sexism of Social and Political Theory*. Lorenne Clark and Lynda Lange, eds. Toronto: University of Toronto Press, 1979: 16–40.

Coby, Patrick J. "The Law of Nature in Locke's Second Treatise: Is Locke a Hobbesian?" *Review of Politics*, vol. 49, no. 1 (Winter 1987): 3–28.

Colman, John. *John Locke's Moral Philosophy*. Edinburgh: Edinburgh University Press, 1983.

Coole, Diana. *Women in Political Theory*. Boulder: Lynne Reinner, 1979.

Copeland, Dale C. "A Realist Critique of the English School." *Review of International Studies*, vol. 29, no. 3 (July 2003): 427–41.

Cottingham, John. "Cartesian Dualism: Theology, Metaphysics and Science." *The Cambridge Companion to Descartes*. John Cottingham, ed. Cambridge: Cambridge University Press, 1992: 236–57.

Cox, Richard. *Locke on War and Peace*. Oxford: Oxford University Press, 1960.

Creppell, Ingrid. "Locke on Toleration: The Transformation of Constraint." *Political Theory*, vol. 24, no. 2 (May 1996): 200–240.

Crittenden, P. J. "Thoughts about Locke's Thoughts about Education." *Journal of Philosophy of Education*, vol. 15, no. 2 (1981): 149–60.

Daly, James. *Sir Robert Filmer and English Political Thought*. Toronto: University of Toronto Press, 1979.

Dawson, Hannah. "Locke on Language in (Civil) Society." *History of Political Thought*, vol. 26, no. 3 (Autumn 2005): 397–425.

Descartes, René. *The Philosophical Writings of Descartes Vol. I & II*. John Cottingham, Robert Stoothoff, and Dugald Murdoch, eds. and trans. Cambridge: Cambridge University Press, 1984.

Desch, Michael. C. "It Is Kind to Be Cruel: the Humanity of American Realism." *Review of International Studies*, vol. 29, no. 3 (July 2003): 415–26.

Dickinson, H. T. *Liberty and Property*. London: Weidenfeld and Nicolson, 1977.

Dufour, Alfred. "Pufendorf." In *Cambridge History of Political Thought, 1450–1700*. J. H. Burns and Mark Goldie, eds. Cambridge: Cambridge University Press, 1991: 561–88.

Dunn, John. "Consent in the Political Theory of John Locke." *The Historical Journal*, vol. 10, no. 2 (1967): 153–82.

 The Political Thought of John Locke. Cambridge: Cambridge University Press, 1969.

 "What Is Living and What Is Dead in the Political Theory of John Locke?" In *Interpreting Political Responsibility: Essays 1981–89*. Princeton, NJ: Princeton University Press, 1990.

 "The dilemma of humanitarian intervention: the executive power of the Law of Nature, after God." In *The History of Political Theory and Other Essays*. Cambridge: Cambridge University Press, 1996: 136–47.

 "Measuring Locke's Shadow." In *Two Treatises and a Letter Concerning Toleration*. Ian Shapiro, ed. New Haven: Yale University Press, 2003: 257–85.

Eisenach, Eldon. *Two Worlds of Liberalism*. Chicago: University of Chicago Press, 1981.

Elshtain, Jean B. *Public Man, Private Woman*. Princeton: Princeton University Press, 1981.

Farr, James and Roberts, Clayton. "John Locke on the Glorious Revolution: A Rediscovered Document." *The Historical Journal*, vol. 28, no. 2 (June 1985): 385–98.

Fatovic, Clement. "Constitutionalism and Contingency: Locke's Theory of Prerogative." *History of Political Thought*, vol. 25, no. 2 (Summer 2004): 276–97.

 "The Anti-Catholic Roots of Liberal and Republican Conceptions of Freedom in English Political Thought." *Journal of the History of Ideas*, vol. 66, no. 1 (2005): 37–58.

Faulkner, Robert. *Richard Hooker and the Politics of a Christian England.* Berkeley: University of California Press, 1981.

"The First Liberal Democrat: Locke's Popular Government." *Review of Politics,* vol. 61, no. 3 (Fall 2001): 5–39.

Filmer, Robert. *Patriarcha and Other Writings.* Johann Somerville, ed. Cambridge: Cambridge University Press, 1991.

Fliegelman, Jay. *Prodigals and Pilgrims: The American Revolution against Patriarchal Authority 1750–1800.* Cambridge: Cambridge University Press, 1982.

Forde, Steven. "Hugo Grotius on Ehtics and War." *American Political Science Review,* vol. 92, no. 3 (September 1998): 639–48.

"Natural Law, Theology, and Morality in Locke." *American Journal of Political Science,* vol. 45, no. 2 (April 2001): 396–409.

"What Does Locke Expect Us to Know?" *Review of Politics,* vol. 68, no. 1 (2006): 232–58.

Forster, Greg. *John Locke's Politics of Moral Consensus.* Cambridge: Cambridge University Press, 2005.

Foster, David. "Taming the Father: John Locke's Critique of Patriarchal Fatherhood." *Review of Politics,* vol. 56, no. 3 (Fall 1994): 641–70.

Franklin, Julian. *Constitutionalism and Resistance in the Sixteenth Century.* New York: Pegasus, 1968.

John Locke and the Theory of Sovereignty. Cambridge: Cambridge University Press, 1978.

Gay, Peter. "Introduction." *John Locke on Education,* Peter Gay, ed. New York: Columbia University, 1964: 1–14.

Galeotti, Anna Elisabetta. *Toleration as Recognition.* Cambridge: Cambridge University Press, 2002.

Gauthier, David P. "The Role of Inheritance in Locke's Political Theory." *Canadian Journal of Economics and Political Science,* vol. 32, no. 1 (February 1966): 38–45.

Glaser, Charles L. "Structural Realism in a More Complex World." *Review of International Studies,* vol. 29, no. 3 (July 2003): 403–14.

Glauser, Wayne. "Three Approaches to Locke and the Slave Trade." *Journal of the History of Ideas,* vol. 51, no. 2 (April 1990): 199–216.

Glenn, Gary D. "Inalienable Rights and Locke's Argument for Limited Government: Political Implications of a Right to Suicide." *Journal of Politics,* vol. 46, no. 1 (February 1984): 80–115.

Goldie, Mark. "John Locke and Anglican Royalism." In *John Locke: Critical Assessments,* Vol. 1. Richard Ashcraft, ed. New York: Routledge, 1991: 152–75.

Gough, J. W. *John Locke's Political Philosophy.* Oxford: Clarendon Press, 1950.

Grant, Ruth. *John Locke's Liberalism.* Chicago: University of Chicago Press, 1987.

"John Locke on Women and the Family." In *Two Treatises of Government and a Letter Concerning Toleration.* Ian Shapiro, ed. New Haven: Yale University Press, 2003: 286–308.

Grotius, Hugo. *The Rights of War and Peace*, 3 Vols. Richard Tuck, ed. Indianapolis: Liberty Fund, 2005 [1625].

Harris, Ian. *The Mind of John Locke*. Cambridge: Cambridge University Press, 1994.

"Tolérance, église et état chez Locke," *Les fondements philosophiques de la tolérance en France et en Angleterre au xviie siècle*, 3 vols. Yves Charles Zarka, Franck Lessay, John Rogers, eds. Paris: Presses Universitaires de France, 2002. Vol. 1: 175–218.

Harrison, Ross. *Hobbes, Locke and Confusion's Masterpiece*. Cambridge: Cambridge University Press, 2003.

Harvey, Martin. "Grotius and Hobbes." *British Journal of the History of Philosophy*, vol. 14, no. 1 (February 2006): 27–50.

Herbert, Gary B. *Thomas Hobbes: The Unity of Scientific and Moral Wisdom*. Vancouver: University of British Columbia Press, 1979.

Hobbes, Thomas. *Leviathan*, Edwin Curley, ed. Indianapolis, Hackett, 1994.

Hoffman, Stanley. "Sovereignty and the Ethics of Intervention." In *The Ethics and Politics of Humanitarian Intervention*. Stanley Hoffman, ed. Notre Dame: University of Notre Dame Press, 1996: 12–37.

Hooker, Richard. *Of the Laws of Ecclesiastical Polity*. Arthur Stephen McGrade, ed. Cambridge: Cambridge University Press, 1989 [1593].

Hopfl, Harro and Martyn Thompson. "The History of Contract as a Motif in Political Thought." *American Historical Review*, vol. 84, no. 4 (October 1979): 919–44.

Horwitz, Robert. "John Locke and the Preservation of Liberty: A Perennial Problem of Civic Education." In *The Moral Foundations of the American Republic, Third Edition*. Robert H. Horwitz, ed. Charlottesville: University Press of Virginia, 1986: 136–64.

Hume, David. *A Treatise of Human Nature*. L. A. Selby-Bigge, ed. Oxford: Clarendon Press, 1967.

"Of the Original Contract." In *Essays Moral, Political and Literary*. Eugene Miller, ed. Indianapolis: Liberty Fund, 1985 [1748]: 465–87.

International Commission on Intervention and State Sovereignty. *The Responsibility to Protect*. Ottawa: International Development Research Centre, 2001.

Israel, Jonathan. *Radical Enlightenment: Philosophy and the Making of Modernity 1650–1750*. Oxford: Oxford University Press, 2001.

Enlightenment Contested: Philosophy, Modernity and the Emancipation of Man 1670–1752. Oxford: Oxford University Press, 2006.

Jackson, Robert. *The Global Covenant: Human Conduct in a World of States*. Oxford: Oxford University Press, 2000.

Jefferson, Thomas. *Notes on the State of Virginia*. New York: Palgrave, 2002 [1785].

Jeffreys, M. V. C. *John Locke: Prophet of Common Sense*. London: Methuen & Co, 1967.

Jesseph, Douglas. "Hobbes and the Method of Natural Science." In *The Cambridge Companion to Hobbes*. Tom Sorrel, ed. New York: Cambridge University Press, 1996: 86–107.

Jolley, Nicholas. "Locke on Faith and Reason." In *The Cambridge Companion to Locke's Essay Concerning Human Understanding*. Lex Newman, ed. Cambridge: Cambridge University Press, 2007: 436–55.

   "The Reception of Descartes' Philosophy." In *The Cambridge Companion to Descartes*. John Cottingham, ed. Cambridge: Cambridge University Press, 1992: 393–423.

Jones, Peter. "Toleration, Recognition and Identity." *The Journal of Political Philosophy*, vol. 14, no. 2 (2006): 123–43.

Josephson, Peter. *The Great Art of Government: Locke's Use of Consent*. Lawrence: University Press of Kansas, 2002.

Kendall, Willmoore. *John Locke and the Doctrine of Majority-Rule*. Urbana: University of Illinois Press, 1941.

Kessler, Sanford. "John Locke's Legacy of Religious Freedom." *Polity*, vol. 17, no. 3 (Spring 1985): 484–503.

Kingdon, Robert. "Calvinism and Resistance Theory, 1550–1580." In *Cambridge History of Political Thought, 1450–1700*. J. H. Burns and Mark Goldie, eds. Cambridge: Cambridge University Press, 1991: 194–218.

Kramer, Matthew. *John Locke and the Origins of Private Property*. Cambridge: Cambridge University Press, 1997.

Kraynak, Robert. "John Locke: From Absolutism to Toleration." *American Political Science Review*, vol. 74, no. 1 (March 1980): 53–69.

Kreiger, Leonard. *The Politics of Discretion: Pufendorf and the Acceptance of Natural Law*. Chicago: University of Chicago Press, 1965.

Laslett, Peter. "Introductory Essay." In *Two Treatises of Government*. John Locke. Cambridge: Cambridge University Press, 1988: 3–122.

Lerner, Ralph. *The Thinking Revolutionary*. Ithaca: Cornell University Press, 1987.

Leyden, Wolfgang von. "Locke's Strange Doctrine of Punishment." In *John Locke: Symposium Wolfenbuttel 1979*. Reinhard Brandt, ed. Berlin: Walter de Ruyter, 1981: 113–27.

Little, Richard. "The English School's Contribution to the Study of International Relations." *European Journal of International Relations*, vol. 6, no. 3 (2000): 395–422.

   "The English School vs. American Realism: A Meeting of Minds or Divided by a Common Language?" *Review of International Studies*, vol. 29, no. 3 (July 2003): 443–60.

Locke, John. *The Works of John Locke*, 10 Vols. London: Thomas Tegg, 1823 [1692].

   "A Third Letter Concerning Toleration," *The Works of John Locke*. 10 Vols. London: Thomas Tegg, 1823 [1692]. Vol. 6: 141–546.

   "Letter from a Person of Quality." *The Works of John Locke*. 10 Vols. London: W. Sharpe & Sons, 1823 [1676]. Vol. 10: 200–46.

   Essays on the Law of Nature. 2nd Ed. W. von Leyden, ed. Oxford: Clarendon Press, 1958 [1660].

   The Reasonableness of Christianity. I. T. Ramsey, ed. Stanford: Stanford University Press, 1958 [1695].

   The Two Tracts of Government. Philip Abrams, ed. Cambridge: Cambridge University Press, 1967 [1661].

"Letter to Mrs. Clarke, February 1685." *Locke's Educational Writings*. James Axtell, ed. New York: Cambridge University Press, 1968.

An Essay Concerning Human Understanding. Peter Nidditch, ed. Oxford: Oxford University Press, 1975 [1700, 4th ed.].

The Correspondence of John Locke, Vol. 5. E. S. de Beer, ed. Oxford: Clarendon Press, 1979.

The Correspondence of John Locke, Vol. 6. E. S. de Beer, ed. Oxford: Oxford University Press, 1981.

A Letter Concerning Toleration. James H. Tully, ed. Indianapolis: Hackett, 1983 [1689].

Two Treatises of Government. Peter Laslett, ed. Cambridge: Cambridge University Press, 1988 [1689].

Some Thoughts Concerning Education and Of the Conduct of the Understanding. Ruth Grant and Nathan Tarcov, eds. Indianapolis: Hackett, 1996.

"Some Thoughts Concerning Reading and Study for a Gentleman." In *Political Essays*. Mark Goldie, ed. Cambridge: Cambridge University Press, 1997: 348–55.

"An Essay on the Poor Law." In *Political Essays*. Mark Goldie, ed. Cambridge: Cambridge University Press, 1997: 182–98.

"Venditio." In *Political Essays*. Mark Goldie, ed. Cambridge: Cambridge University Press, 1997 [1695]: 393–43.

"The Fundamental Constitutions of Carolina." In *Political Essays*. Mark Goldie, ed. Cambridge: Cambridge University Press, 1997 [1669]: 160–81.

Lorenzo, David. "Tradition and Prudence in Locke's Exceptions to Toleration." *American Journal of Political Science*, vol. 47, no. 2 (April 2003): 248–58.

Lowenthal, David. "Locke on Conquest." In *Understanding the Political Spirit: Philosophical Investigations from Socrates to Nietzsche*. Catherine Zuckert, ed. New Haven: Yale University Press, 1988: 126–35.

Mabbott, J. D. *John Locke*. London: MacMillan, 1973.

MacPherson, C. B. *The Political Theory of Possessive Individualism*. Oxford: Oxford University Press, 1962.

Madison, James, Alexander Hamilton and John Jay. *The Federalist Papers*. Clinton Rossiter, ed. New York: New American Library, 1961 [1788].

Makus, Ingrid. *Women, Politics and Reproduction*. Toronto: University of Toronto Press, 1996.

Mansfield, Harvey. *Taming the Prince: The Ambivalence of Modern Executive Power*. New York: Free Press, 1989.

"On the Political Character of Property in Locke." In *Powers, Possessions, and Freedoms: Essays in Honour of C. B. MacPherson*. Alkis Kontos, ed. Toronto: University of Toronto Press, 1979: 23–38.

Marshall, John. *John Locke: Resistance, Religion, and Responsibility*. Cambridge: Cambridge University Press, 1994.

Martinich, A. P. *Hobbes*. New York: Routledge, 2005.

Matar, Nabil. "John Locke and the 'Turbanned Nations'." *Journal of Islamic Studies*, vol. 2, no. 1 (1991): 67–77.

Mayall, James. *World Politics: Progress and Its Limits*. Cambridge: Cambridge University Press, 2000.

McCabe, David. "John Locke and the Argument against Strict Separation." *The Review of Politics*, vol. 59, no. 2 (Spring 1997): 233–58.

McCann, Edwin. "Locke on Substance." In *The Cambridge Companion to Locke's "Essay Concerning Human Understanding"*. Lex Newman, ed. Cambridge: Cambridge University Press, 2007: 157–91.

McClure, Kirstie. "Difference, Diversity, and the Limits of Toleration." *Political Theory*, vol. 18, no. 3 (August 1990): 361–91.

  Judging Rights: Lockean Politics and the Limits of Consent. Ithaca: Cornell University Press, 1996.

Mehta, Uday Singh. *Liberalism and Empire: A Study of Nineteenth-Century British Liberal Thought*. Chicago: University of Chicago Press, 1999.

  The Anxiety of Freedom: Imagination and Individuality in Locke's Political Thought. Ithaca: Cornell University Press, 1992.

Mendle, Michael. *Henry Parker and the English Civil War*. Cambridge: Cambridge University Press, 1995.

Mill, J. S. "A Few Words on Non-Intervention." In *Dissertations and Discussions*, Vol. III. New York: E. P. Dutton & Co, 1873 [1859]: 238–63.

Mill, John Stuart. "On Liberty." In *The Basic Writings of John Stuart Mill*. New York: Modern Library, 2002 [1859]: 17–76.

Mitchell, Joshua. "John Locke and the Theological Foundations of Liberal Toleration: A Christian Dialectic of History." *The Review of Politics*, vol. 52, no. 1 (Winter 1990): 64–83.

Morgenthau, Hans J. *Politics among Nations*. 2nd ed. New York: Alfred A. Knopf, 1954.

Muthu, Sanka. *Enlightenment against Empire*. Princeton: Princeton University Press, 2003.

Myers, Peter C. *Our Only Star and Compass: Locke and the Struggle for Political Rationality*. Lanham: Rowman & Littlefield, 1998.

Nardin, Terry. "The Moral Basis of Humanitarian Intervention." *Ethics & International Affairs*, vol. 16, no. 1 (April 2002): 57–70.

Neill, Alex. "Locke on Habituation, Autonomy, and Education." *Journal of the History of Philosophy*, vol. 27, no. 2 (April 1989): 225–45.

Nidditch, Peter. "Foreword." In *An Essay Concerning Human Understanding*. John Locke. Oxford: Oxford University Press, 1975.

Okin, Susan Moller. *Justice, Gender and the Family*. New York: Basic Books, 1989.

Owen, Judd. *Religion and the Demise of Liberal Rationalism*. Chicago: University of Chicago Press, 2001.

Pagden, Anthony. "Human Rights, Natural Rights, and Europe's Imperial Legacy." *Political Theory*, vol. 31, no. 2 (April 2003): 171–99.

Pangle, Thomas. *The Spirit of Modern Republicanism: The Moral Vision of the American Founders and the Philosophy of Locke*. Chicago: University of Chicago Press, 1988.

Parry, Geraint. *John Locke*. London: Allen & Unwin, 1978.

Pasquino, Pasquale. "Locke on King's Prerogative." *Political Theory*, vol. 26, no. 2 (April 1998): 198–208.

Passmore, John. *The Perfectibility of Man*. New York: Charles Scribner's Sons, 1970.

Passmore, J. A. "Locke and the Ethics of Belief." In *Locke*. Vere Chappell, ed. Oxford: Oxford University Press, 1998: 279–99.

Pateman, Carole. *The Sexual Contract*. Stanford: Stanford University Press, 1988.
The Disorder of Women. Stanford: Stanford University Press, 1989.

Perkinson, Henry J. *Since Socrates: Studies in the History of Western Educational Thought*. New York: Longman, 1981.

Pettit, Phillip. *Theory of Freedom: From the Psychology to the Politics of Agency*. Oxford: Oxford University Press, 2001.

Pfeffer, Jacqueline. "The Family in Locke's Political Thought." *Polity*, vol. 33, no. 4 (Summer 2001): 593–618.

Pitts, Jennifer. *A Turn to Empire: The Rise of Imperial Liberalism in Britain and France*. Princeton: Princeton University Press, 2005.

Plato. *Republic*. Allan Bloom, trans. New York: Basic Books, 1991.

Plutarch. "The Life of Lycurgus." In *The Lives of Noble Grecians and Romans*. John Dryden, trans. New York: Everyman, 1952.

Pufendorf, Samuel. *De Jure Naturae et Gentium*. C. H. and W. A. Oldfather, trans. Oxford: Clarendon Press, 1934.
On the Duty of Man and Citizen According to Natural Law. James Tully, ed. Cambridge: Cambridge University Press, 1991.
Of the Nature and Qualification of Religion in Reference to Civil Society. Indianapolis: Liberty Fund, 2002.

Rabieh, Michael. "The Reasonableness of Locke, or the Questionableness of Christianity." *The Journal of Politics*, vol. 53, no. 4 (November 1991): 933–57.

Rabkin, Jeremy. "Grotius, Vattel, and Locke: An Older View of Liberalism and Nationality." *Review of Politics*, vol. 59, no. 2 (Spring 1997): 293–322.

Rahe, Paul. "John Locke's Philosophical Partisanship." *Political Science Reviewer*, vol. 20 (1991): 1–43.
Republics Ancient and Modern: Classical Republicanism and the American Revolution, 3 Vols. Chapel Hill: University of North Carolina Press, 1992.

Rawls, John. *A Theory of Justice*. Cambridge: Harvard University Press, 1971.
Political Liberalism, Expanded Edition. New York: Columbia University Press, 2005.

Rickless, Samuel C. "Locke's Polemic against Nativism." In *The Cambridge Companion to Locke's "Essay Concerning Human Understanding."* Lex Newman, ed. Cambridge: Cambridge University Press, 2007: 33–66.

Rogers, A. J. "The Intellectual Setting and Aims of the Essay." In *The Cambridge Companion to Locke's "Essay Concerning Human Understanding."* Lex Newman, ed. Cambridge: Cambridge University Press, 2007: 7–32.

Rosen, Stanley. "Benedict Spinoza." In *History of Political Philosophy*, 3rd ed. Leo Strauss and Joseph Cropsey, eds. Chicago: University of Chicago Press, 1987: 456–75.

Rousseau, Jean-Jacques. *On the Social Contract*. Roger Masters, ed. New York: St. Martin's Press, 1978 [1762].
Emile, or On Education. Allan Bloom, trans. New York: Basic Books, 1979.

Sandel, Michael J. *Democracy's Discontents: America in Search of a Public Philosophy*. Cambridge, MA: Harvard University Press, 1996.

Sandoz, Ellis. "The Civil Theology of Liberal Democracy: Locke and His Predecessors." *The Journal of Politics*, vol. 34, no. 1 (February 1972): 2–36.

Scheuerman, William. "Liberal Democracy and the Empire of Speed." *Polity*, Vol. 34, no. 1 (Fall 2001): 41–67.

Schochet, Gordon. *Patriarchalism in Political Thought*. Oxford: Oxford University Press, 1975.

"John Locke and Religious Toleration." In *The Revolution of 1688–89*. Lois Schwoerer, ed. Cambridge: Cambridge University Press, 1992: 147–64.

Schouls, Peter A. *Reasoned Freedom*. Ithaca: Cornell University Press, 1992.

Schuurman, Paul. "Locke's Way of Ideas as Context of His Theory of Education in Of the Conduct of the Understanding." *History of European Ideas*, 27 (2001): 45–59.

Scott, John. "The Sovereignless State and Locke's Language of Obligation." *American Political Science Review*, vol. 94, no. 3 (September 2000): 547–61.

Seliger, Martin. *The Liberal Politics of John Locke*. London: Allen & Unwin, 1969.

Shanley, Mary. "Marriage Contract and Social Contract in Seventeenth Century English Political Thought." *Western Political Quarterly*, vol. 32, no. 1 (March 1979): 79–91.

Shapiro, Ian. "John Locke's Democratic Theory." In *Two Treatises and a Letter Concerning Toleration*. Ian Shapiro, ed. New Haven: Yale University Press, 2003: 309–40.

Simmons, A. John. *The Lockean Theory of Rights*. Princeton: Princeton University Press, 1992.

The Edge of Anarchy. Princeton: Princeton University Press, 1993.

Skinner, Quentin. *The Foundations of Modern Political Thought*, Vol. 2. Cambridge: Cambridge University Press, 1978.

Smith, Steven B. *Spinoza, Liberalism and the Question of Jewish Identity*. New Haven: Yale University Press, 1997.

Spellman, W. M. *John Locke and the Problem of Depravity*. Oxford: Oxford University Press, 1988.

Spinoza, Benedict. *Ethics Including the Improvement of the Understanding*. Amherst: Prometheus Books, 1989.

A Theologico-Political Treatise and A Political Treatise. Mineola: Dover Publications, 2004.

Spragens, Thomas A. *The Politics of Motion: The World of Thomas Hobbes*. Lexington: University Press of Kansas, 1973.

Stanton, Timothy. "Locke and the Politics and Theology of Toleration." *Political Studies*, vol. 54, no. 1 (March 2006): 84–102.

Strauss, Leo. *Natural Right and History*. Chicago: University of Chicago Press, 1953.

Suarez, Francisco. *Selections from Three Works*. Glwadys Williams, trans. Oxford: Clarendon Press, 1944 [1612].

Tarcov, Nathan. "Locke's Second Treatise and the 'Best Fence against Rebellion'." *Review of Politics*, vol. 43, no. 2 (April 1981): 198–217.

Locke's Education for Liberty. Chicago: University of Chicago Press, 1984.

Taylor, Charles. *Sources of the Self: The Making of the Modern Identity*. Cambridge, MA: Harvard University Press, 1989.

Philosophy and the Human Sciences. Cambridge: Cambridge University Press, 1985.

"The Politics of Recognition." In *Multiculturalism and "The Politics of Recognition.*" Amy Gutmann, ed. Princeton: Princeton University Press, 1993: 25–73.

Teson, Fernando R. *Humanitarian Intervention: An Inquiry into Law and Morality*. Dobbs Ferry: Transnational Publishers, 1988.

Tuck, Richard. "Grotius and Selden." In *Cambridge History of Political Thought, 1450–1700*. J. H. Burns, ed. Cambridge: Cambridge University Press, 1991: 499–529.

The Rights of War and Peace: Political Thought and the International Order from Grotius to Kant. Oxford: Oxford University Press, 1999.

Natural Rights Theories. Cambridge: Cambridge University Press, 1979.

Tuckness, Alex. *Locke and the Legislative Point of View*. Princeton: Princeton University Press, 2002.

"Punishment, Property, and the Limits of Altruism: Locke's International Assymetry." *American Political Science Review*, vol. 102, no. 4 (November 2008): 467–79.

Tully, James. *A Discourse on Property: Locke and His Adversaries*. Cambridge: Cambridge University Press, 1980.

An Approach to Political Philosophy: Locke in Contexts. Cambridge: Cambridge University Press, 1993.

Vattel, Emerich de. *Le Droit des Gens, et les devoirs des citoyes, ou principe de la loi naturelle*. Nime, 1793.

Vernon, Richard. *The Career of Toleration: John Locke, Jonas Proast, and After*. Montreal: McGill-Queen's University Press, 1997.

Vile, J. M. *Constitutionalism and the Separation of Powers*, 2nd ed. Indianapolis: Liberty Fund, 1998.

Vitoria, Francisco de. *Political Writings*. Anthony Pagden and Jeremy Lawrance, eds. Cambridge: Cambridge University Press, 1991 [1528].

Waldron, Jeremy. "Locke: Toleration and the Rationality of Persecution." In *Justifying Toleration: Conceptual and Historical Perspectives*. Susan Mends, ed. Cambridge: Cambridge University Press, 1988:61–86.

"John Locke: Social Contract versus Political Anthropology." *Review of Politics*, vol. 51, no. 2 (Winter 1989): 3–28.

The Dignity of Legislation. Oxford: Oxford University Press, 1999.

God, Locke and Equality: Christian Foundations in Locke's Political Thought. Cambridge: Cambridge University Press, 2002.

"Locke, Adam, and Eve." In *Feminist Interpretations of John Locke*. Nancy J. Hirschmann and Kirstie M. McClure, eds. University Park: Pennsylvania State University Press, 2007: 247–67.

Walsh, Mary. "Locke and Feminism on Private and Public Realms of Activities." *Review of Politics*, 57 (Spring 1995): 251–77.

Walzer, Michael. *Just and Unjust Wars*. New York: Basic Books, 1977.

Toleration. New Haven: Yale University Press, 1997.

Ward, Lee. "The Problem of Courage in Aristotle's Nicomachean Ethics." *American Political Science Review*, vol. 95, no. 1 (March 2001): 71–83.

The Politics of Liberty in England and Revolutionary America. Cambridge: Cambridge University Press, 2004.

Weaver, David. "Leadership, Locke and the Federalist." *American Journal of Political Science*, vol. 41, no. 2 (April 1997): 421–46.

Weil, Rachel. "The Family in the Exclusion Crisis: Locke versus Filmer Revisited." In *A Nation Transformed: England after the Restoration*, Alan Houston and Steven Pincus, eds. Cambridge: Cambridge University Press, 2001: 100–24.

Wheeler, Nicholas J. *Saving Strangers: Humanitarian Intervention in International Society*. Oxford: Oxford University Press, 2000.

Wight, Martin. "Western Values in International Relations." In *Diplomatic Inverstigations: Essays in the Theory of International Politics*. London: George Allen & Unwin, 1966: 89–131.

Wilhelm, Anthony G. "Good Fences and Good Neighbors: John Locke's Positive Doctrine of Toleration." *Political Research Quarterly*, vol. 52, no. 1 (March 1999): 145–66.

Wilson, Catherine. "The Moral Epistemology of Locke's Essay." *The Cambridge Companion to Locke's "Essay Concerning Human Understanding."* Cambridge: Cambridge University Press, 2007: 381–405.

Winstrup, George. "Freedom and Authority: The Ancient Faith of Locke's 'Letter on Toleration'." *The Review of Politics*, vol. 44, no. 2 (April 1982): 242–65.

Wolfson, Adam. "Toleration and Relativism: The Locke-Proast Exchange." *The Review of Politics*, vol. 59, no. 2 (Spring 1997): 213–31.

Wolterstorff, Nicholas. *John Locke and the Ethics of Belief*. Cambridge: Cambridge University Press, 1996.

Woolhouse, Roger. *Locke: A Biography*. Cambridge: Cambridge University Press, 2007.

Wood, Ellen Meiskins. "Locke against Democracy: Consent, Representation and Suffrage in the Two Treatises." *History of Political Thought*, vol. 13, no. 4 (Winter 1992): 657–89.

Wood, Neal. *The Politics of Locke's Philosophy*. Berkeley: University of California Press, 1983.

Yaffe, Gideon. "Locke on Ideas of Identity and Diversity." In *The Cambridge Companion to Locke's "Essay Concerning Human Understanding."* Lex Newman, ed. Cambridge: Cambridge University Press, 2007: 192–230.

Yolton, John. *The Two Intellectual Worlds of John Locke*. Ithaca: Cornell University Press, 2004.

Zagorin, Perez. "Hobbes without Grotius." *History of Political Thought*, vol. 21, no. 1 (Spring 2000): 16–40.

Zarka, Yves Charles. "First Philosophy and the Foundations of Knowledge." In *The Cambridge Companion to Hobbes*. Tom Sorrel, ed. Cambridge: Cambridge University Press, 1996: 62–85.

Zuckert, Michael. "Fools and Knaves: Reflections on Locke's Theory of Philosophical Discourse." *Review of Politics*, vol. 36, no. 2 (1974): 544–64.

"Of Wary Physicians and Weary Readers: The Debate on Locke's Way of Writing." *Independent Journal of Philosophy*, 2 (1977): 55–66.

"An Introduction to Locke's First Treatise." *Interpretation*, 8 (January 1979): 58–74.

"John Locke and the Problem of Civil Religion." In *The Moral Foundations of the American Republic*. 3rd Ed. Robert H. Horwitz, ed. Charlottesville: University Press of Virginia, 1986: 181–203.

Natural Rights and the New Republicanism. Princeton: Princeton University Press, 1994.

Launching Liberalism: On Lockean Political Philosophy. Lawrence: University Press of Kansas, 2002.

"Locke – Religion – Equality." *Review of Politics*, vol. 67, no. 3 (Summer 2005): 419–31.

Index

Note: For John Locke's views on particular subjects, please refer to the individual subject headings (e.g. "natural rights"). Entries listed under "Locke, John" are limited to Locke's life and career. Locke's specific works are listed under their titles (e.g. "*Second Treatise of Government*").